Feminism in Practice

Communication Strategies for Making Change

Karen A. Foss
Sonja K. Foss
Alena Amato Ruggerio

Illustrated by Liza Faire

WAVELAND PRESS, INC.
Long Grove, Illinois

For information about this book, contact:
Waveland Press, Inc.
4180 IL Route 83, Suite 101
Long Grove, IL 60047-9580
(847) 634-0081
info@waveland.com
www.waveland.com

Artist website: https://www.lizafaire.com/

Copyright © 2022 by Waveland Press, Inc.

10-digit ISBN 1-4786-4758-2
13-digit ISBN 978-1-4786-4758-4

All rights reserved. No part of this book may be reproduced, stored in a retrieval system, or transmitted in any form or by any means without permission in writing from the publisher.

Printed in the United States of America

7 6 5 4 3 2 1

Contents

Acknowledgments xi

PART ONE
Feminism as a Blueprint for Change 1

CHAPTER
1   **Making Meanings: Defining Feminism**   7
    Feminism as a Perspective   8
    Feminism Multiplied   10
    Feminisms, not Feminism   17
    ■ REFLECTIONS 18
    ■ NOTES 18

CHAPTER
2   **Making Waves: A History of Feminism**   21
    First Wave Feminism   22
        Triggering Event   23
        Happening Places   23
        Key Ideas   24
    Second Wave Feminism   24
        Triggering Events   25
        Happening Places   26
        Key Ideas   28

Postfeminism   29
   Postfeminism = Feminism Is Dead   29
   Postfeminism = Feminism Revised   30
   Postfeminism = Third Wave Feminism   31

Third Wave Feminism   31
   Triggering Events   32
   Happening Places   33
   Key Ideas   34

Fourth Wave Feminism   36
   Triggering Events   36
   Happening Places   38
   Key Ideas   40

Feminism Continued   42

■ REFLECTIONS   42

■ NOTES   43

PART TWO
Proclaiming Identity   47

CHAPTER 3

Padma Lakshmi   53

Definition of Feminism   56

Change Strategies   57
   Reinterpreting Identity Markers   57
   Enacting Self-Determination   58
   Sharing Personal Challenges   58

■ REFLECTIONS   59

■ NOTES   60

CHAPTER 4

Kat Blaque   63

Definition of Feminism   65

Change Strategies   66
   Revealing Hidden Perspectives   67
   Controlling the Narrative   68
   Facilitating Further Conversation   69

■ REFLECTIONS   70

■ NOTES   71

Contents v

CHAPTER 5   **Vilissa Thompson**   **75**

Definition of Feminism   77

Change Strategies   78
- Centering Intersectionality   78
- Holding Others Accountable   79
- Educating Responsibly   80

■ REFLECTIONS   80

■ NOTES   81

CHAPTER 6   **Lizzo**   **83**

Definition of Feminism   85

Change Strategies   86
- Disrupting Norms   86
- Celebrating Every Body   87
- Representing Marginalized Others   89

■ REFLECTIONS   90

■ NOTES   90

PART THREE
Naming a Problem   93

CHAPTER 7   **Nadya Okamoto**   **99**

Definition of Feminism   101

Change Strategies   102
- Acknowledging a Taboo   102
- Destigmatizing the Taboo   103
- Facilitating Further Conversation   104

■ REFLECTIONS   105

■ NOTES   106

CHAPTER 8   **Jamie Margolin**   109
- Definition of Feminism   112
- Change Strategies   113
  - Continuing to Learn   113
  - Developing Personal Activist Skills   114
  - Showing Up   115
- ■ REFLECTIONS   117
- ■ NOTES   117

CHAPTER 9   **Margaret Cho**   119
- Definition of Feminism   122
- Change Strategies   123
  - Exaggerating Stereotypes   123
  - Valuing the Self   124
  - Enacting Self-Determination   125
- ■ REFLECTIONS   126
- ■ NOTES   126

CHAPTER 10   **Camille Paglia**   129
- Definition of Feminism   131
- Change Strategies   132
  - Attending to History   132
  - Encompassing Diversity   133
  - Assuming Responsibility   135
- ■ REFLECTIONS   136
- ■ NOTES   136

PART FOUR
Enriching a System 139

CHAPTER 11 **Shonda Rhimes** 145
  Definition of Feminism 148
  Change Strategies 149
    Normalizing Diversity 149
    Enacting Self-Determination 150
    Claiming Power 151
  ■ REFLECTIONS 152
  ■ NOTES 153

CHAPTER 12 **Jacinda Ardern** 157
  Definition of Feminism 159
  Change Strategies 161
    Normalizing Feminism 161
    Implementing an Ethic of Care 162
    Valuing Authenticity 162
  ■ REFLECTIONS 163
  ■ NOTES 164

CHAPTER 13 **Joana Vasconcelos** 167
  Definition of Feminism 169
  Change Strategies 170
    Recontextualizing 170
    Cultivating Ambiguity 171
    Celebrating the Positive 173
  ■ REFLECTIONS 174
  ■ NOTES 175

CHAPTER 14 **Malala Yousafzai** 177
  Definition of Feminism 180
  Change Strategies 181
    Holding Others Accountable 181
    Modeling Agency 182
    Empowering Others 183
  ■ REFLECTIONS 184
  ■ NOTES 184

PART FIVE
Changing a System 187

CHAPTER 15 **Carrie Goldberg** 193
  Definition of Feminism 197
  Change Strategies 197
    Learning a System 197
    Deploying the Resources of a System 197
    Transforming Trauma 199
  ■ REFLECTIONS 200
  ■ NOTES 200

CHAPTER 16 **Nadia Bolz-Weber** 203
  Definition of Feminism 205
  Change Strategies 206
    Normalizing Outsiders 207
    Nostalgizing the System 208
    Updating the System 209
  ■ REFLECTIONS 211
  ■ NOTES 211

CHAPTER 17 **Serena Williams** 215
  Definition of Feminism 217
  Change Strategies 218
    Making Boundaries Visible 218
    Transforming Limitations 220
    Modeling Agency 221
  ■ REFLECTIONS 222
  ■ NOTES 223

CHAPTER
18   **Amanda Gorman   225**

   Definition of Feminism   228

   Change Strategies   229
      Expanding Platforms for Change   229
      Enacting Change   231
      Conjuring Hope from Negativity   231

   ■ REFLECTIONS   233
   ■ NOTES   233

PART SIX
Creating an Alternative System   237

CHAPTER
19   **Sara Ahmed   243**

   Definition of Feminism   244

   Change Strategies   245
      Recognizing a Problem   246
      Becoming a Problem   247
      Enacting Willfulness   248

   ■ REFLECTIONS   249
   ■ NOTES   250

CHAPTER
20   **Leslie Kanes Weisman   253**

   Definition of Feminism   256

   Change Strategies   257
      Critiquing the System   257
      Fantasizing   258
      Exercising Agency   259

   ■ REFLECTIONS   260
   ■ NOTES   260

CHAPTER 21   **Jennifer Armbrust**   263

    Definition of Feminism   264

    Change Strategies   265
        Critiquing the System   266
        Enacting Self-Determination   267
        Learning Through Improvising   268

■ REFLECTIONS   269

■ NOTES   270

CHAPTER 22   **Alexandria Ocasio-Cortez**   273

    Definition of Feminism   276

    Change Strategies   277
        Critiquing the System   277
        Making Complexity Accessible   278
        Enacting Change   280

■ REFLECTIONS   282

■ NOTES   282

Questions for Reflection   285

Acknowledgments

We would like to begin with a special acknowledgment from Karen and Sonja to Alena: Thank you for "making" us write this book. Many years ago, we wrote a book with Cindy Griffin called *Feminist Rhetorical Theories*, in which we developed the rhetorical theories of nine feminists to show how feminist perspectives can transform the rhetorical tradition. When you contacted us to see if we had plans to update it, we initially said *no* because we didn't think we had more to say about feminism and change. But you persisted, suggesting that contemporary feminists in all different fields are embracing feminism and enacting it in various ways that we would probably appreciate. A weekend of brainstorming demonstrated that you were right, and the three of us went on to strategize what this book might look like. We're glad you convinced us because learning about these impressive and amazing women has been a joy. Furthermore, we would not have had access to their biographies, perspectives on feminism, and change strategies without your skill at navigating social media and finding internet resources that we certainly would not have found on our own. We are so glad to have had the opportunity to get to know you as a feminist coconspirator.

From Alena to Karen and Sonja: I remember the day I emailed you to ask if *Feminist Rhetorical Theories* would be updated someday. *Feminist Rhetorical Theories* had been creating magical moments in my Women Transforming Language course for many years but needed to be expanded with the current evolutions of feminism. When you replied that you had no plans for *Feminist Rhetorical Theories* to be published in a new edition, I wrote back—with my heart hammering in my throat—asking for your permission to attempt a second volume in the form of an edited collection. I wanted to use the same structure you used in the earlier book but featuring contemporary feminists. It's a wonder you did not hear all the way in Colorado and New Mexico the primal noise of shock and jubilation I made in Oregon when you wrote back that it should not be an edited collection but authored by the three of us together. The concept evolved creatively as we talked and resulted in this book. Your embodiment of the feminist principles of collaboration, graciousness in shaping my role to maximize my strengths, and drawing on your power to create a professional opportunity for another woman is something for which I will be forever grateful.

Our next thank you goes to the twenty women in this book. We appreciate all you do to live feminist principles, for letting us get to know you, and for expanding our toolbox of feminist change strategies. So watch out, world!

A big thanks to Liza Faire whose line drawings of the twenty feminists featured in the book truly bring the women to life. We so appreciate your willingness to solve problems creatively as they arose and to keep making changes until we were satisfied. You were fun to work with and always ahead of schedule. Thanks, too, to Barbara Walkosz for directing us to Liza.

As always, our thanks to Carol Rowe and Neil Rowe at Waveland Press for trusting our vision for this book and for not only producing professional products but also for always being so much fun.

Finally, we thank our husbands—Stephen Littlejohn, Anthony Radich, and Bradley Ruggerio—feminists all, who can always be counted on to offer love and support, affirmation that what we are doing is important, and a good laugh when we need it.

PART ONE

FEMINISM AS A BLUEPRINT FOR CHANGE

Multiple times during a day, you have experiences where you want things to be different. Perhaps you are trying to convince a friend to join you in a Black Lives Matter protest. Maybe you would like your city to install more bike lanes or would like a particular candidate to win in the upcoming election. You might want your partner to share in the cooking, or you are trying to stop smoking. In all of these situations, there is some kind of imperfection, defect, or obstacle that you want to remove. How do you go about doing this? You use communication. Any change that happens is the result of communication, whether it takes place in conversations, social media, music, sculpture, dress, speeches, books, films, or another medium.

When you want to make changes in your life and world, you consciously or unconsciously make use of strategies. *Strategies* are tools, actions, or mechanisms you use to bring a new state or condition into being. Sometimes, you employ change strategies within institutions or organizations, as when you lobby legislators to encourage passage of a bill or join a group to address a safety issue on campus. At other times, you use change strategies as part of social movements, such as when you boycott a particular company, march in a protest, sign a petition, or create a GoFundMe site to collect money for a cause. You also can engage in change strategies at an individual or interpersonal level. Creating a YouTube video that expresses your opinion on an issue, speaking up and objecting to racist and sexist jokes, or choosing to act to improve your own life—by exercising regularly, for example—are more personal approaches to changing a condition.

This book is designed to introduce you to a variety of change strategies, some of which will be familiar to you and others that are likely to be new. We would like this book to be a handbook or inventory of options that you can use to create change in your life when you notice something that isn't the way you would like it to be. By expanding your toolbox of change strategies, you can be an even more effective change agent as you work to create a better world.

What's Feminism Got to Do with It?

You might have been wondering why *feminism* is in the title of this book when it's about change strategies. We are going to use feminism and feminist strategies as a blueprint for exploring change strategies generally. We will offer a much more elaborate definition—in fact, many definitions—of the term *feminism* in chapters 1 and 2. For now, we can say that feminism is the effort to reorganize society to eliminate oppression and injustice.

Why did we choose to focus on feminism to inventory various strategies for change? The most important reason is that feminism has been a resounding success, which means that many of its strategies have been effective. Certainly, inequalities of all kinds still exist, but there have been major strides in US society since the 1960s: women can choose whether to marry, and their marriage partner can be another woman; women can choose whether and when to have children; women can work in almost any occupation; women have legal recourse if they are sexually harassed; and girls are allowed to wear pants to school, to name just a few of the changes that can be attributed to feminism. In addition, feminism has made men's lives better, too. Men don't have to adhere to restrictive norms of masculinity—they are able to be stay-at-home fathers, for example, and they don't have to be solely responsible for supporting their families. As feminist writer and activist Natasha Walter suggests, the story of feminist movement[1] is "a great story, a happy, triumphant story." Feminism is a "movement that has transformed women's lives, that has brought about the greatest and most peaceful social revolution that has ever been seen."[2] Because of its success, feminism offers an excellent model for how to generate change.

Feminism is also an appropriate movement for studying change strategies because it has been around for a long time, so feminists have used many different kinds of strategies over the course of the movement. Feminism formally started in the United States in 1848, when the first women's rights convention was held in Seneca Falls, New York, and it has progressed through four different periods or waves since then. As you will see from our description of the waves in chapter 2, it is still very much alive and well. Because of its long history, the strategies used by feminists have evolved to meet new challenges as the social, political, and cultural landscape has changed. What this means is that the practice of feminism demonstrates considerable depth and variety in terms of strategies designed to effect change.

A third reason why we are using feminism as a source for change strategies is that, as you can tell from the list of achievements we noted earlier, feminism affects almost all areas of life. Feminism's fingers have reached into all cracks and crannies of US culture, leaving virtually nothing untouched in the arenas of business, education, sports, the arts, medicine, and politics. Feminist values such as equality, access, fairness, and self-determination are prominent considerations in issues such as access to health care, gun violence, hunger, poverty, affordable housing, early childhood education, the cost of a college education, and economic security. Because many issues are feminist issues, the change strategies involved in feminist movement are broad in scope. Feminism's reach, then, is another reason why we are using feminism as a blueprint or framework for identifying change strategies.

As we explore feminist change strategies, our focus will be on feminist practice—how feminists apply or exercise their feminist commitments in a regular and ongoing way. This is the kind of practice that soccer teams do to prepare for games or what public speakers do when they rehearse a speech before delivering it. Just as athletes or public speakers use practice to try to improve their skills, feminists keep working out ways to enact their feminisms—experimenting, refining, and innovating in order to deploy the best strategies they can to address a particular issue or problem.

You might be thinking that you have no interest in studying feminist change strategies because of the derogatory stereotypes circulating about feminism and feminists—stereotypes that are so strong, in fact, that some people consider the term *feminist* to be an insult. You can probably name these negative stereotypes easily: Feminists are bra burners, lesbians, kooks, bitches, man haters, and feminazis. They are also depicted as ugly, angry, uptight, militant, strident, selfish, loud, extreme, irritating, and whiny. This is quite a list! We certainly understand why, given these stereotypes, you might not want to call yourself a *feminist*. Feminism is about choice, and you are welcome to embrace it, to consider it, or to disregard it altogether. We hope, however, that you will find the strategies used by feminists useful for thinking about how change happens because many of these strategies are not unique to feminism. They can be and are used by individuals who want to create changes unrelated to feminism.

What's Ahead?

Because we know that many of you may not be all that familiar with feminism, the two chapters in part 1 are designed to provide some context for the movement. Chapter 1 offers definitions of feminism and summaries of many different kinds of feminism. In chapter 2, we provide a brief history of feminism as it has progressed through its four waves, beginning with the women's suffrage movement in the late nineteenth century and culminating with the kinds of feminism being practiced today. Part 2 consists of twenty chapters that feature individual feminists and the change strategies they employ. For each of the women featured, we offer a brief biography, her definition of feminism, and her major change strategies.

The twenty women are organized in five sections according to the major objectives they are hoping to accomplish with their change strategies. "Proclaiming Identity," the first section, involves asserting one or more marginalized identities as the basis for social change. The second category, "Naming a Problem," features change strategies in which the objective is to identify a problem that needs to be solved—one that involves some kind of inequity or discrimination. "Enriching a System" highlights feminists whose strategies are designed to make adjustments to an existing system in order to incorporate a greater array of voices and perspectives in that system. The fourth section includes feminists who focus on "Changing a System." These feminists believe some aspects of a current system are dysfunctional and defective and call for changes to address those defects. The last section, "Creating an Alternative System," spotlights feminists whose objective is the creation of an entirely new system because they believe the system itself is the problem.

In each of the five sections, we summarize the key assumptions that inform that objective. For each assumption, we define it, briefly explain its theoretical underpinnings, and give an example to show it at work in the world. We use examples from all kinds of change efforts to provide concrete illustrations of the assumptions in practice and to suggest the value of these strategies across various contexts.

Choosing the women to include in the twenty chapters was not an easy task. There were so many women we could have chosen (and we contemplated including men, too, because many men are feminists). We couldn't include them all, of course, which means that your favorites might have been left out—just as many of our favorites were. We used three primary criteria to choose the women we included. The first criterion was that all of the women define themselves as feminists—they proudly claim the label and conceptualize what they are doing as feminist practice. The second was that all the women are influencers in their fields—they have been recognized for the work they do in their specific fields, whether these are formal occupations or a commitment to some kind of activism. The third criterion we used to select the women is that they represent diversity of various kinds—in occupation, race and ethnicity, age, national affiliation, type of feminism to which they adhere, objectives for their feminist work, and the strategies they use to generate change. All of these different variables serve as resources for the women to create their particular brands of feminism. Taken together, these women offer a wide range of change strategies from which you can choose to create change in your life and your world.

We hope the chapters in the book will leave you wanting more—that you will want to find out more about these and other feminists who are working to contribute to the unfinished business of feminism. We also hope you'll do more than simply read about the strategies. After you see what feminists are doing, we encourage you to try out their strategies as you work to expand your own repertoire of tools for challenging and improving conditions around you. Experiment with the strategies described here, play with them, see how they work, and develop ones of your own. We predict that the results will be surprisingly effective, and we look forward to seeing how the changes you make create a better future for us all.

■ Notes

[1] Inspired by bell hooks's use of the phrase, we are using "feminist movement" rather than "the feminist movement" in this book. "The feminist movement" suggests that there is one type of feminism characterized by a singular definition of feminism and a shared set of objectives, and that is certainly not the case.

[2] Natasha Walter, *The New Feminism* (London, UK: Little, Brown/Virago, 1998), 50.

CHAPTER
ONE

Making Meanings
Defining Feminism

Part 1 offered a very brief definition of the term *feminism*, but the word and the movement are much more complicated than we suggested there. In this chapter, we explore what *feminism* means so that you have a more comprehensive and accurate picture of it. As we suggested earlier, a typical definition of feminism is a belief in equal rights for women and men, and this is not a bad place to start in defining feminism because the term certainly involves a commitment to equality.

There are, however, some problems with defining feminism as the effort to achieve equality between women and men. One is that it assumes that "*all* men have more power, wealth, freedom, and status than *all* women,"[1] and, of course, that's not the case. Men who are poor, who aren't white, or who don't fit dominant definitions of masculinity, for example, do not have greater power than all women. In addition, some women enjoy greater opportunities than other women, depending on such factors as class, race, education, occupation, physical appearance, religion, and sexual orientation. When feminism is defined as the effort to secure equal rights for women with men, that raises the question: "Which men do women want to be equal to?"[2]

There is a second problem when feminism is defined as the effort to gain equality for women with men. Even if the men to whom women should be equal could be identified, the definition suggests that the "point of feminism is to get women to measure up to what (at least some) men already are." From this perspective, "men remain the point of reference; their lives are the lives women would naturally want to live."[3] This perspective is called *androcentrism*, which means "male centered," and it is the view that men are the standard for what is seen as normal for human beings. If the first problem with the equality definition is equal to *which* men?, the second problem is why equal to *any* men?[4] Reforming a system in which men are the point of reference "forces women to focus on men and address men's conceptions of women rather than creating and developing women's values about themselves."[5]

There is a third problem with a definition of feminism as the effort to gain equal rights for women with men: determining who is considered to be a woman and who is considered to be a man is not always easy. Some people with XY chromosomes, for example, do not have penises. Other people have ambiguous genitals or internal reproductive structures that don't correspond to their external genitalia. There are also those whose bodies do not match up with their felt gendered identities—people who identify as gender nonconforming. How should they be classified if we are talking about achieving equality between women and men?

Feminism as a Perspective

Because of the problems with a definition of feminism as the effort to achieve equality between women and men, we are going to go in a different direction. We are choosing to define feminism as a perspective or a way to approach the world in which individuals try to understand, critique, and transform practices of domination, especially those that involve gender. Feminism is a way of approaching experiences that involves three processes—understanding, critique, and transformation.[6]

What feminists want to *understand* is how gender operates in the world. Although many people have been discriminated against and oppressed throughout human history, feminists focus on gender oppression, which deals with how femininity and masculinity construct inequalities. Instead of taking the gender system for granted, as people usually do, feminism encourages people to understand the gender system in which they live and to scrutinize their beliefs and assumptions about it. The effort to understand how gender functions usually begins when individuals encounter a practice or policy involving gender that seems odd, where they "sense that something is wrong or . . . things don't seem right."[7] They reflect on that experience and keep coming back to it because it doesn't make sense. As a result, they begin to think consciously about gender and start to link that experience to other experiences they've had, noticing patterns that give them clues about how gender works and how it could work differently.[8]

A feminist perspective not only helps individuals understand how gender is functioning, but it also involves a *critique* of the conception of gender. Feminists critique gender in two primary ways. The first is by challenging the restrictions imposed by the gender binary. Most Western countries, including the United States, organize gender according to a male-female binary. Two realms—feminine and masculine—are set up as opposites, and every person is supposed to fit into one of the two categories. The deciding factor is your body. If you have a penis and testicles, you are assumed to be male and thus masculine; if you have a vagina and a uterus, you are assumed to be female and thus feminine. Although gender restrictions are loosening up—there is increasing acceptance of those who identify as gender nonconforming—the binary system still exerts a significant amount of pressure on individuals. It generally dictates certain ways of thinking and behaving, a particular set of values, a prescribed physical appearance, and life roles. Feminism challenges the gender restrictions that limit people's lives and suggests that such restrictions don't have to remain in place.

Feminists critique not only the gender binary but also the subordinate position that women typically occupy in society and the systematic injustices they experience simply because they are women. This asymmetry has been given many names, including *sexism*, *misogyny*, *kyriarchy*, and *phallocracy*, but it is most commonly known as *patriarchy*—a social system in which men are superior to women and have privileges that women don't have. In this system, men's activities and ideas are accorded higher status than women's, men hold more leadership positions than women, men own or control more economic resources than women, and men often have authority over women in the family.[9] At the same time, feminists recognize that gender as a social system not only distributes power unequally between women and men, but it interacts with other identity markers such as class, race, age, education, religion, sexual orientation, and physical ability to distribute power unevenly within the categories of women and men.

Feminists not only want to understand and critique gender relations in all of their iterations, but they also want to *transform* or change them. But if feminists want to change women's position in society, what kind of changes are they after? After all, antifeminist groups also want to change women's position in society, so we need to clarify what it is that feminists want to change.[10] In the future that feminists envision, all genders are liberated from the constraints of the gender binary—individuals are free to be themselves without being disciplined or punished because they do not conform to a certain idea of masculinity or femininity. They are able to live their lives in ways that suit their desires, preferences, and abilities unconstrained by the dictates of the gender binary.

Feminists' efforts to transform society also include eradicating the ideology of domination that permeates Western and many other cultures. Feminist theorist bell hooks[11] explains that the ideology of domination is marked by "the belief in a notion of superior and inferior, and its concomitant ideology—that the superior should rule over the inferior."[12] This ideology is so pervasive, she says, that "most citizens of the United States believe in their heart of hearts that it is natural for a group or an individual to dominate over others."[13] Feminism addresses this ideology of domination by seeking to "undermine and destroy the entire system of power-over other human beings."[14] As communication theorists Natalie Fixmer-Oraiz and Julia Wood explain: "We don't think oppression and domination foster healthy lives for individuals or societies as a whole. We believe there are better, more humane and enriching ways to live."[15] From this perspective, feminism is a commitment to eliminate oppression and domination in general, whether of women, African Americans or other racial groups, old people, lesbians, gay men, trans people, people with disabilities, coworkers, friends, or family members.

Once individuals begin to challenge and think critically about gender, questioning what once seemed natural and normal, they are not likely to stop with gender. Feminists challenge the "unmarked, presumably universal reality"[16] that appears to be inevitable but really is not. In its broadest sense, this kind of feminism is a way of thinking outside of established categories and boundaries; it involves a "radical skepticism"[17] toward the status quo, and it seeks to generate "ideas which stand in direct opposition to accepted 'knowledge.'"[18] As feminists challenge fundamental assumptions, they might begin to explore and think critically about issues such as power, the distribution of resources, globalization, human rights, and the environment. Because feminism generates alternative assumptions about society and produces alternative ways of seeing, it is a "theory of emancipation"[19] that is designed to "disrupt, transgress, and invent possibilities."[20] As feminist theorist Sonia Johnson explains, feminism is "a way of looking at all the issues," a "totally different human possibility, a . . . way of being in the world. It is about a new universal habit, a new mind."[21]

Feminism Multiplied

Although we have offered a definition of the term *feminism* that works for the three of us, it is not how all feminists define the term. As you will soon see, feminism is not a unitary category. It has always come in many varieties, and it has mobilized feminists in different places, at different times, and in different ways in their efforts to understand, critique, and transform gender relations. In this section, we provide a description of some of the most common types of feminism. Most of them emerged from and can be identified with particular historical periods, so not all of them are equally popular today. They all, however, continue to be espoused by some feminists. Maybe you'll find yourself gravitating toward one or more of them or perhaps you won't—remember that we don't require that you be a feminist to learn about feminist change strategies. Our list, arranged alphabetically, begins with cosmopolitan feminism.

Cosmopolitan Feminism. The philosophy of cosmopolitanism aligns in many ways with key principles of feminist movement. Both cosmopolitanism and feminism are based on the notion that people worldwide share certain characteristics as humans, that all people are entitled to human rights, and that differences among individuals need to be acknowledged.[22] Both involve "a commitment to treating all human beings with equal concern within a global frame."[23] But cosmopolitan feminists break with the general cosmopolitan philosophy because they do not believe it sufficiently accounts for the gendered power dynamics that characterize globalization. Discussions about human rights often privilege civil and political rights that men see as most important—rights such as "denials of freedom of expression, arbitrary arrest, torture in detention, and the death penalty."²⁴ Cosmopolitan feminists, in contrast, ask that abuses that primarily affect women also be taken seriously as human rights issues—abuses such as domestic violence, sex trafficking, forced pregnancy, poverty, economic exploitation, and involuntary immigration.

Cultural Feminism. Cultural feminists believe that women and men are different psychologically because of processes of socialization. Gender socialization encourages women to develop behaviors and ways of approaching the world that differ from the approaches of men. As a result, women are more nurturing, supportive, self-aware, empathic, cooperative, peaceful, nonviolent, caring, and altruistic than men. Men, on the other hand, are socialized to be aggressive, confident, self-centered, and domineering. Cultural feminists are likely to see differences in leadership skills between women and men—differences such as resilience, integrity, honesty, and teamwork—as due to differences in their cultural socialization.²⁵

Digital Feminism. Digital or cyberfeminism focuses on two connections between cyberspace and feminism. Some digital feminists critique gender inequality in digital technology, analyzing how women and men differ in their approaches to technology, the ways in which women are marginalized by it, and how educational settings and industries hinder women's advancement in the technology arena. A second project of cyberfeminism is the use of technology to further feminist objectives. Digital feminists use tools of technology such as social media to challenge gender stereotypes and sexism.²⁶ The Twitter hashtag #effyourbeautystandards is an example; it was created by plus-size model Tess Holliday to challenge conventional standards for feminine beauty.

Ecofeminism. Ecofeminism—or what is sometimes called *ecological feminism*—approaches environmental issues through the lens of gender. Ecofeminists link women's oppression to the destruction of the environment and claim that the oppression, domination, exploitation, and colonization of women and other marginalized groups have caused irreversible environmental damage. Ecofeminists note, for example, the parallels between the oppression of women and the destruction of the environment: both women and nature are viewed as property, and there are similarities between how men dominate women and how humans dominate nature. There is, in other words, a "social mentality that leads to the domination and oppression of women [that] is directly connected to the social mentality that leads to the abuse of the environment."²⁷ Ecofeminists' analysis of the effects of climate change on women is an example of the application of a lens of gender to environmental problems. When they address rising temperatures and deforestation rates, for example, they are concerned with how women trying to support their families are affected by these problems.

Essentialist Feminism. Essentialist feminists attribute some of the behavioral differences between women and men to fixed, innate biological qualities. Essentialist feminists claim that because of women's reproductive functions, some traits come naturally to women—nurturing, caregiving, empathy, cooperation, and a tendency toward peace and nonviolence, for example. In contrast, men are more likely to engage in violence, destruction, and warfare because of their levels of testosterone and how it functions in their bodies. They believe that women will achieve equality once a culture comes to value the special contributions women make to society as a result of their biological traits. Essentialist feminists cite menstruation as an example of a biological difference between women and men that leads women to behave in certain ways. Because most women menstruate monthly, they must keep track of their cycles, so they are more attentive to details in general. They must pay attention to their bodies and care for them, so they develop caregiving skills. They must keep menstrual supplies on hand, so they develop an ability to plan ahead, and they also must learn how to deal with surprises effectively and calmly such as when a period arrives unexpectedly.

Girlie Feminism. Also called *lipstick feminism* or *cupcake feminism*, girlie feminism exists at the intersection of feminism and traditional feminine culture. Girlie feminism embraces both feminist politics and traditionally feminine interests, desires, and activities and reclaims them as psychologically, socially, and politically empowering. Girlie feminists celebrate popular modes of femininity such as Barbie dolls, fashion magazines, Brazilian bikini waxes, pedicures, makeup, stilettos, low-cut tops, and thong underwear. They also may celebrate traditionally feminine skills like knitting, baking, and quilting. Rather than seeing themselves as deceived, swindled, or trapped by the patriarchy because of their embrace of these modes of femininity, girlie feminists see these activities as sexy, campy, ironic, or simply a means of self-expression. Not only should traditional female skills be valued by society, girlie feminists believe, but also conventionally masculine spaces would benefit by having feminine activities and interests incorporated into them.[28]

Hegemonic Feminism. *Hegemony* is the social, cultural, ideological, and economic influence exerted by one dominant social group over others. Hegemonic feminism, sometimes called *white, mainstream, Western, Anglo-American,* or *dominant feminism*, is a derogatory term applied to a kind of feminism that is concerned exclusively with the experiences of white, middle-class, heterosexual women. It is used to describe a type of feminism that assumes a unified female subject and ignores the differences among women's experiences. Those who offer this kind of critique argue that mainstream feminist theory does not speak to the intersectionality of oppression experienced by women of color or working-class women.

Hood Feminism. Hood feminism is most associated with Mikki Kendall and her book, *Hood Feminism: Notes from the Women that a Movement Forgot*. Kendall defines hood feminism as "lived feminism," which is "about survival and sustainability for the long-term—for your community and yourself." It is "the feminism of the working class who live in inner cities and rural communities and who struggle to get basic needs met."[29] Feminist movement typically has focused not on the women who must address these needs on a daily basis but on "those who already have most of their needs met."[30] For Kendall, "everything that affects women is a feminist issue"[31]—food insecurity, clean water, quality education, a living wage, safe neighborhoods, gun violence, and access to transportation. Kendall asks white women to begin to focus on the concerns of marginalized women and to show up for them, to say something to support them, and to use their privilege to "make sure things are better for a community."[32]

Indigenous Feminism. Indigenous feminism involves the integration of the knowledge and perspectives of Indigenous people into feminism. It acknowledges the devastating consequences of colonization and is concerned primarily with decolonization—the dismantling of the oppressive systems introduced as a result of colonization. The objective of this type of feminism is to validate Indigenous women—such as Native American women in North America, First Nations women in Canada, and Aboriginal women in Australia—in the context of their own cultures rather than from the perspective of mainstream, white, patriarchal values and priorities.[33] Indigenous feminists are concerned with restoring relationships among people, land, water, and other animals; the abduction of children into the child-welfare system; the disproportionate sexual victimization of Indigenous women; and the epidemic of missing and murdered Indigenous women.

Lesbian Feminism. Lesbian feminists encourage women to become woman identified, changing the focus of their attention, efforts, energies, activities, and relationships from men to women as a way to resist patriarchal oppression. Lesbian feminists see heterosexuality as an institution that supports male supremacy and female subordination. As feminist theorist Sarah Lucia Hoagland explains, "Heterosexualism is a way of living . . . that normalizes the dominance of one person in a relationship and the subordination of another."[34] Lesbian feminists encourage various kinds of identifications among women—such relationships do not have to include a sexual attraction to women. Adrienne Rich proposed a "lesbian continuum," employing the term to include "many more forms of primary intensity between and among women, including the sharing of a rich inner life, the bonding against male tyranny, the giving and receiving of practical and political support."[35] Lesbian feminists see lesbians and their relationships as presenting a major challenge to the social and economic order because lesbians actually demonstrate the independence that feminists believe all women should enact.

Liberal Feminism. Liberal feminists are satisfied with the systems currently in place but want women to have equality within those systems. They work to achieve political and legal reform without substantially altering the structure of society. Liberal feminists don't want to destroy existing institutions and practices such as the law, the family, the workplace, or marriage; they simply want to eradicate the injustices inherent in them. If a system is conceptualized as a pie, liberal feminists want women to have a larger piece of that pie. The Lilly Ledbetter Fair Pay Act of 2009 is an example of the kinds of legislation liberal feminists support. The act amended Title VII of the Civil Rights Act of 1964, which included a 180-day statute of limitations for filing an equal-pay lawsuit regarding pay discrimination. The Lilly Ledbetter Act eliminated the filing period for pay discrimination claims, so the statute of limitations for presenting an equal-pay lawsuit now resets with each new paycheck or post-retirement benefits check, even if the allegedly discriminatory pay occurred years before.

Neoliberal Feminism. Neoliberal feminism, which is sometimes also called *choice feminism*, is rooted in the philosophy of neoliberalism. Neoliberalism espouses policies designed to reduce state influence on the economy, including deregulating markets, lowering trade barriers, and eliminating price controls. As part of their interest in reducing government control and influence, neoliberal feminists believe that addressing inequalities is the responsibility of individuals, not the government. In other words, collective liberation dictated by government is rejected in favor of individualism and personal transformation.[36] In effect, neoliberal feminism transforms the feminist slogan "the personal is political" into "the political as *only* personal."[37] If a woman discovers she earns less than a man who is doing the same job, the remedy is not government legislation, according to neoliberal feminists, but her individual pursuit of equity in the organization in which she works.

Postcolonial Feminism. Colonialism occurs when a country establishes settlements and governmental structures on another country's land, displacing its "traditional homesteads, earning activities, and governance organizations" in the process.[38] Postcolonial analyses highlight the persistence of colonialism after the end of formal decolonization, which has less to do with geographic territories and politics and more to do with cultural and economic factors and influences. Postcolonial feminists seek to address processes such as double colonization, which refers to the ways in which women are oppressed by both patriarchy and the ongoing processes of colonization that reproduce and maintain the colonial experience.

Poststructural Feminism. Poststructural feminism is also sometimes called *postmodern feminism*, and it focuses on how language works and serves some interests over others. Poststructuralists do not believe that language represents or reflects reality; rather, language is productive and creates the world and how individuals understand it. Poststructural feminists use the idea that language creates reality to argue that gender and the gender binary are constructed through language and are neither natural nor innate. Feminist poststructuralists "work to expose power relations and oppressions associated with gender, race, class, able-bodied-ness, and sexual orientation" by "paying attention to our language/practices and making discourses visible."[39]

Power Feminism. Power feminism is a type of feminism most often associated with Naomi Wolf and her book *Fire with Fire: The New Female Power and How It Will Change the 21st Century*. She argues that although women now have many new opportunities that did not exist before the advent of feminism, women "lack a psychology of female power to match their new opportunities."[40] She asserts that feminism often encourages the adoption of a victim stance in which women seek "power through an identity of powerlessness" or helplessness,[41] flaunting their lack, their suffering, and how pitiful their resources are in the face of the opposition.[42] Wolf coined the term *power feminism* to advocate for a different kind of feminism in which women choose an identity rooted in responsible power rather than in victimage. Power feminists recognize that women's choices can change the world, and they encourage women to acquire money to achieve their own dreams and to facilitate social change.[43] An example of power feminism is Emily's List, a political action committee that aims to help elect Democratic women candidates who favor abortion rights. The group's name is an acronym for "Early Money is Like Yeast," and the organization focuses on raising millions of dollars in early money for women candidates.

Profeminism. *Profeminism* is a term sometimes used to describe men who are feminists; other terms for these men are *feminist allies, antisexist activists, meninists, men of conscience,* or simply *feminists.*[44] You might think that the words *feminist* and *man* don't go together, but we hope you now understand that feminism doesn't require a certain kind of body; instead, it is a perspective or a way of thinking. Profeminists realize that men as a group benefit from patriarchy, but they also see that those benefits come at a cost. Both women and men are harmed by traditional gender roles, so both women and men benefit from feminism. Among their many efforts, profeminists work to prevent violence against women, engage in anti-rape activism, and campaign against pornography.

Radical Feminism. Radical feminism is based on the idea that current systems of domination are too badly flawed to be transformed, so revolution is the only viable option for change. They do not want women to have a bigger slice of the pie; they want a different pie. Isabel Allende explains the radical feminist perspective: "In my youth I fought for equality. I wanted to participate in the men's game. But in my mature years I've come to realize that the game is a folly; it is destroying the planet and the moral fiber of humanity."[45] Radical feminists want "to completely dismantle current social structures"[46] and construct alternatives that are more equitable and just. They argue, for example, that the entire traditional family system is oppressive, with men expected to work outside the home and women expected to care for children and the home. Consequently, the traditional family structure should be rejected, and new ways of doing family should be explored.

Separatist Feminism. Separatist feminism is based on the idea that women's oppression will never be eradicated as long as women live with and among men, so they encourage women to separate or withdraw—"to cease attending to the existing system."[47] Feminist theorist Sarah Lucia Hoagland explains how separatism functions: "When we separate, when we withdraw from someone's game plan, the game becomes meaningless, at least to some extent, ceasing to exist for lack of acknowledgment."[48] Feminist separation or withdrawal assumes many forms. Some separatist feminists see it as a temporary withdrawal or a break from men—excluding men from certain gatherings, for example, refusing to listen to music with sexist lyrics, or choosing to attend a women's college.[49] Others consider separatism to be a lifelong practice, building lives that involve minimal interaction with men, as is the case with many lesbian separatist communities.

Socialist Feminism. Socialist feminists focus on analyses of economic systems, with a particular focus on capitalism. They believe that capitalism is the root cause of women's oppression and focus on the ways capitalism and gender intersect to the detriment of women. Socialist feminists highlight the gendered division of labor and women's exclusion from the public sphere as the source of women's economic dependence on men and advocate instead for a socialist reformation of the economy. Other major concerns are the lack of acknowledgment of women's free caregiving and household labor, which allows the state to save money on public services, and the lack of equal pay for women when they do the same jobs as men.

Transfeminism. Transgender individuals—those whose physical sex does not match their inner sense of their gender—"move away from the gender they were assigned at birth and cross over (*trans-*) the boundaries constructed by their culture to define and contain that gender."[50] Transfeminists seek to unsettle and denaturalize normative gender and to confront social and political institutions that inhibit or narrow gender choices. Although feminists of the 1960s and 1970s popularized the idea that gender is distinct from biological sex and is socially and culturally constructed, they did not question the idea that there is such a thing as true biological sex. In contrast, transfeminism "holds that both sex and gender are socially constructed," and biological sex, for trans people, "is felt to be more artificial and changeable than their inner sense" of their gender.[51] Transfeminists believe that individuals should construct their "own gender identities based on what feels genuine, comfortable, and sincere," and they challenge institutions that limit the range of choices available to them.[52]

Transnational Feminism. Transnational feminism focuses on how global capitalism has created relations of inequality for people across nations, races, genders, classes, and sexualities. The objective of transnational feminism is "to create organizations, networks, and movements that acknowledge the multiple power differentials that exist among women while still allowing for concerted political action."[53] This type of feminism highlights how people in different locations and circumstances are affected by and have the capacity to resist capitalism's relations of exploitation and inequality, even as their experiences of these phenomena are not the same.

The wearing of burkas by Muslim women provides an example of how transnational feminists address such issues. The burka is considered by many in the West to be a symbol of women's oppression and victimage. Transnational feminists, however, offer more complex explanations for the wearing of the burka grounded in the experiences and explanations of Muslim women themselves. The burka can serve, for example, as a form of resistance to Western colonization, a form of freedom from the male gaze, and even a way to conceal items seen as inappropriate for use by women.

Womanism. The term *womanist* was created by writer Alice Walker to refer to a Black feminist or a feminist of color.[54] This type of feminism makes Black women and other women of color central to feminist movement and focuses on how such women "experience power, oppression, and status within the social hierarchy."[55] Womanism originated out of Black feminists' critique of hegemonic feminism, which treated sexism as the ultimate oppression with little consideration for the ways in which class and race intersect with gender. Because Black women traditionally have played a strong role in their families, womanism also takes into account the well-being of men, children, and community. "When black women talk about women's movements and liberation, they're always talking about more than themselves," notes historian Paula Giddings. "They're always talking about the community at large."[56]

Feminisms, not Feminism

There are, of course, many other feminisms besides those we have identified here, but we hope we have provided enough examples to support the idea that feminists are "multifaceted and diverse."[57] Because of the diversity among feminists, the term *feminisms* in the plural is probably a more accurate description than the singular *feminism*.[58] At the same time, the various types of feminism have some things in common. What unites all of the types of feminism is that they embody a set of feminist values on which most feminists would agree—equality, immanent value, and self-determination.

Equality (and some people prefer the term *equity*) is a commitment to the elimination of the notions of superiority and inferiority that characterize many human relationships. Both equality and equity suggest that everyone is seen as deserving of the same respect and the same opportunities for self-expression. The term *equality* has to do with giving everyone the exact same resources, while *equity* involves distributing resources based on the needs of the recipients.[59] Regardless of approach, feminists seek a world that "is less unfair" and where people's needs and prospects "are unrelated to their gender, sexual orientation, class of origin, skin color, age, ethnicity, ablebodiedness, or any other circumstance beyond their control."[60]

Immanent value is a second principle that characterizes most feminisms, and it derives from the principle that "your life is worth something. . . . You need only be what you are."[61] Worth cannot be determined by positioning individuals on a hierarchy, ranking and comparing them, or attending to emblems of external achievement because worth cannot be "earned, acquired, or proven."[62] Immanent value means that all participants in an interaction are seen as having experiences and holding perspectives that are valuable and legitimate.

A third feminist value, *self-determination*, suggests that all individuals should be allowed to make their own decisions about how they wish to live their lives: "The fulfillment of feminism ensures, in a word, dignity centering on the right of each human being to live the life she chooses for herself as long as her choices do not injure other people or curtail their choices."[63] This principle involves a trust that others are doing the best they can at the moment and simply need "to be unconditionally accepted as the experts on their own lives."[64]

So what is feminism? If you are asked to give an elevator speech about what feminism is, we hope you take into account some of the ideas we have introduced here. It would be fine to say that feminism generally involves equality for everyone, just as long as you make a mental note to yourself that it's more complicated than that—and you could add something about immanent value and self-determination. If your elevator ride is a bit longer, you could say that feminism is a way to approach the world in which individuals try to understand, critique, and transform practices of domination, especially those that involve gender. You could also add information about some of the types of feminism you just reviewed. We hope, at a minimum, that you and those with you in the elevator no longer view *feminism* as the *f*-word it often is considered to be and agree that it is deserving of more exploration. That is exactly what is going to happen in the next chapter, where we introduce key ideas of feminism and explain how they have evolved throughout its history.

■ REFLECTIONS

1. Did you grow up with positive or negative views of feminism? What were the main sources of your views of feminism?
2. Do you agree or disagree with the authors' critique of feminism defined as the effort to achieve equality between women and men?
3. Compare and contrast the various terms for the systematic oppression of women: *patriarchy, sexism, misogyny, kyriarchy,* and *phallocracy*. Which term do you prefer and why?
4. The authors argue that feminism is a process of understanding, critiquing, and transforming structures of domination. Can change result from just one of these? If so, which do you see as the most important? How realistic is it to attempt all three of these processes in order to achieve feminist change?
5. Do you agree with the assertion that we should talk about *feminisms* rather than *feminism*? Why or why not? What difference does this distinction make?
6. Pick two or three of the types of feminism described in chapter 1 that you especially like. What do they have in common? What do these types of feminism tell you about your own perspective on feminism?
7. Pick two or three of the types of feminism described in chapter 1 with which you disagree. What do they have in common? What do these types of feminism tell you about your own approach to feminism?
8. Write an elevator speech in which you provide your own definition of feminism. Can you imagine sharing this "speech" with others?

■ NOTES

[1] Deborah Cameron, *Fem-i-nism: A Brief Introduction to the Ideas, Debates and Politics of the Movement* (Chicago, IL: University of Chicago Press, 2019), 16.
[2] bell hooks, *Feminist Theory: From Margin to Center*, 3rd ed. (New York: Routledge, 2015), 18.
[3] Hilde Lindemann, *An Invitation to Feminist Ethics*, 2nd ed. (New York: Oxford University Press, 2019), 8.
[4] Lindemann, *An Invitation to Feminist Ethics*, 8.
[5] Sarah Lucia Hoagland, *Lesbian Ethics: Toward New Value* (Palo Alto, CA: Institute of Lesbian Studies, 1988), 57.

6 Lindemann, *An Invitation to Feminist Ethics*.
7 Sara Ahmed, *Living a Feminist Life* (Durham, NC: Duke University Press, 2017), 22.
8 Ahmed, *Living a Feminist Life*, 21, 27.
9 Cameron, *Fem-i-nism*, 15–16.
10 Cameron, *Fem-i-nism*, 8.
11 Hooks does not capitalize the first letters of her name because she wants people to focus on her ideas rather than on her.
12 bell hooks, *Talking Back: Thinking Feminist, Thinking Black,* 2nd ed. (New York: Routledge, 2015), 19.
13 bell hooks, *Outlaw Culture: Resisting Representations* (New York: Routledge, 1994), 200.
14 Sally Gearhart, "She Who Hath Ears," in *Women and the Word: Toward a Whole Theology*, ed. Jean Crosby and Jude Michaels (Berkeley, CA: Office of Women's Affairs of the Graduate Theological Union, 1972), 77.
15 Natalie Fixmer-Oraiz and Julia T. Wood, *Gendered Lives: Communication, Gender and Culture*, 13th ed. (Boston, MA: Cengage, 2019), 4.
16 Mary F. Rogers and C. D. Garrett, *Who's Afraid of Women's Studies? Feminisms in Everyday Life* (Walnut Creek, CA: Altamira/Rowman & Littlefield, 2002), x.
17 Myra Jehlen, "Archimedes and the Paradox of Feminist Criticism," *Signs* 6 (1981): 575.
18 Dawn Currie and Hamida Kazi, "Academic Feminism and the Process of De-radicalization: Re-examining the Issues," *Feminist Review* 25 (1987): 77.
19 John Hoffman, "Blind Alley: Defining Feminism," *Politics* 21(2001): 197.
20 Dawn M. Shinew, "'Disrupt, Transgress, and Invent Possibilities': Feminists' Interpretations of Educating for Democratic Citizenship," *Theory & Research in Social Education* 29 (2001): 488.
21 Sonia Johnson, *Going Out of Our Minds: The Metaphysics of Liberation* (Freedom, CA: Crossing, 1987), 237.
22 Diana Elena Neaga, "Feminism and Cosmopolitanism: Some Inevitable Connections," *Lex ET Scientia International Journal* 18 (2011), 323–24.
23 Niamh Reilly, "Cosmopolitan Feminism and Human Rights," *Hypatia* 22 (2007): 182.
24 Reilly, "Cosmopolitan Feminism and Human Rights," 185.
25 Jack Zenger and Joseph Folkman, "Research: Women Score Higher Than Men in Most Leadership Skills," *Harvard Business Review*, June 25, 2019, https://hbr.org/2019/06/research-women-score-higher-than-men-in-most-/
26 Menoukha Robin Case and Allison V. Craig, *Introduction to Feminist Thought and Action: #WTF and How Did We Get Here? #WhosThatFeminist #WhatsThatFeminism* (New York: Routledge, 2020), 167–69.
27 Alyssa Adamovich, "News Update," West Michigan Environmental Action Council (WMEAC), February 9, 2015, https://wmeac.org/ecofeminism-environmental-justice-gender-intersectional-lens/2015/
28 Jennifer Baumgardner and Amy Richards, *Manifesta: Young Women, Feminism, and the Future*, 10th anniversary ed. (New York: Farrar, Straus and Giroux, 2010), 126–66.
29 Mikki Kendall, "'There Have Been Points in my Life When I have Felt Like Feminism Was Not for Me,'" interview by Megan DiTrolio, *Marie Claire*, July 1, 2020, https://www.marieclaire.com/politics/a32936025/mikki-kendall-hood-feminism-interview/
30 Mikki Kendall, *Hood Feminism: Notes from the Women that a Movement Forgot* (New York: Viking, 2020), xv.
31 Kendall, *Hood Feminism*, 3.
32 Kendall, "'There Have Been Points.'"
33 For more on Indigenous feminism, see Katherine Fisher, "A Bibliography Research Plan: Indigenous Feminism," December 16, 2015, http://www2.hawaii.edu/~irvinv/students/finalfisherf15.pdf/
34 Hoagland, *Lesbian Ethics*, 29.
35 Adrienne Rich, "Compulsory Heterosexuality and Lesbian Existence," *Signs* 5 (1980): 648–49.
36 Prudence Chamberlain, *The Feminist Fourth Wave: Affective Temporality* (Cham, Switzerland: Palgrave Macmillan, 2017), 128.

37 Erica Burman, "Childhood, Neo-Liberalism and the Feminization of Education," *Gender and Education* 17 (2005): 357.
38 Case and Craig, *Introduction to Feminist Thought and Action*, 81.
39 M. J. Barrett, "Making [Some] Sense of Feminist Poststructuralism in Environmental Education Research and Practice," *Canadian Journal of Environmental Education* 10 (2005): 88.
40 Naomi Wolf, *Fire with Fire: The New Female Power and How It Will Change the 21st Century* (London, UK: Chatto & Windus, 1993), xvi.
41 Wolf, *Fire with Fire*, 147.
42 Wolf, *Fire with Fire*, 165.
43 Wolf, *Fire with Fire*, 149–50.
44 Shira Tarrant, "This is What a Feminist Looks Like," in *Gender and Women's Studies: Critical Terrain*, 2nd ed., ed. Margaret Hobbs and Carla Rice (Toronto, Canada: Women's Press, 2018), 52.
45 Isabel Allende, *The Soul of a Woman: On Impatient Love, Long Life, and Good Witches* (New York: Ballantine, 2021), 12.
46 Case and Craig, *Introduction to Feminist Thought and Action*, 12.
47 Hoagland, *Lesbian Ethics*, 63.
48 Hoagland, *Lesbian Ethics*, 55.
49 Marilyn Frye, "Some Reflections on Separatism and Power," in *Feminist Social Thought: A Reader*, ed. Diana Tietjens Meyers (New York: Routledge, 1997), 408.
50 Susan Stryker, *Transgender History: The Roots of Today's Revolution*, 2nd ed. (New York: Seal, 2017), 1.
51 Emi Koyama, "The Transfeminist Manifesto," in *Catching a Wave: Reclaiming Feminism for the 21st Century*, ed. Rory Dicker and Alison Piepmeier (Boston, MA: Northeastern University Press, 2003), 249.
52 Koyama, "The Transfeminist Manifesto," 251, 247.
53 Asha Nadkarni, "Transnational Feminism," Oxford Bibliographies, July 26, 2017, https://www.oxfordbibliographies.com/view/document/obo-9780190221911/obo-9780190221911-0006.xml/
54 Alice Walker, *In Search of Our Mothers' Gardens* (San Diego, CA: Harcourt Brace, 1983), xi–xii.
55 Tarrant, "This is What a Feminist Looks Like," 55.
56 Paula Giddings, quoted in Mabinty Quarshie, "#BlackWomenAtWork Shows Why Some Women Identify as Womanists, not Feminists," *USA Today*, March 30, 2017, https://www.usatoday.com/story/news/2017/03/30/black-women-womanism-feminism/99514484/
57 Cameron, *Fem-i-nism*, 7.
58 We have chosen to use the terms *feminism* or *feminist movement* because they are the terms most often used, but we intend these terms to cover the range and diversity of feminisms.
59 An example of three people of different heights trying to look over a fence illustrates the difference between the terms *equality* and *equity*. An equal distribution of resources would involve giving all three individuals identical boxes to stand on. But this approach does not take into account the fact that the tallest person does not need a box to see over the fence, while the shortest person needs a bigger box than the one she was given. An equitable distribution of resources would give the tallest person no box, the middle person a medium-sized box, and the shortest person a large box.
60 Rogers and Garrett, *Who's Afraid of Women's Studies?*, 134.
61 Starhawk, *Truth or Dare: Encounters with Power, Authority, and Mystery* (San Francisco, CA: Harper and Row, 1987), 115–16.
62 Starhawk, *Truth or Dare*, 21.
63 Rogers and Garrett, *Who's Afraid of Women's Studies?*, 134.
64 Sonia Johnson, *The Ship that Sailed into the Living Room: Sex and Intimacy Reconsidered* (Estancia, NM: Wildfire, 1991), 162.

CHAPTER
TWO

Making Waves
A History of Feminism

Many of you reading this book were born into a world in which a large number of feminist objectives have been realized and are now a normal part of culture. As we noted in part 1, feminist movement has been a phenomenal success and has changed many aspects of society in significant ways. Our goal in this chapter is to provide a brief history of feminism and some context for the twenty feminists and their change strategies you will encounter in the chapters that follow.

When we study the history of something, we usually study it in some kind of segments such as stages, periods, or eras. When the history of feminism in the United States is discussed, it is often conceptualized as a series of waves—chronological groupings marked by different objectives and gains. The first wave began in the mid-1800s and ended when the Nineteenth Amendment was passed that gave women the right to vote.[1] The second wave began in the 1960s and focused on legal and social equality for women in areas such as work, education, and language. The third started in the early 1990s; it focused on activism at the individual level and emphasized differences among women's experiences. Many feminists believe we are now in the fourth wave, which began sometime in the first two decades of this century and emphasizes intersectionality, individuality, and policing behavior.

Not all feminists believe that structuring the history of feminism through a metaphor of waves is the best way to present this history. Among the problems with the wave metaphor is that individuals are encouraged to overlook the diversity, dynamism, and complexity of feminist movement and to see each wave as monolithic, starkly separated from the other waves. For example, the wave metaphor would place the effort to pass the Equal Rights Amendment in one wave, while the effort to be more inclusive of all women's experiences would belong in another. A second problem with the wave metaphor is that it suggests that all feminists born in a particular time period belong in the same wave and share the same concerns and goals for feminism.[2] According to this view, baby boomers would be part of the second wave, and millennials would be part of the third or fourth waves.

We believe, however, that the wave metaphor can recognize the multiplicity and diversity of feminist movement. When they occur in nature, waves are not homogeneous, predictable, uniform, or monolithic. They are, as scientist Rachel Carson explains, "a mixture of countless different wave trains, intermingling, overtaking, passing, or sometimes engulfing one another; each group differing from the others in the place and manner of its origin, in its speed, its direction of movement."[3] Like the overlapping nature of waves in the ocean, the waves of feminist movement allow for a highlighting of the diverse experiences, contributions, practices, and objectives of feminism. Indeed, vast differences have existed in every wave and among women of every generation, and today, you can find feminists who represent the key thinking of all four of the waves. In addition, there are many overlaps among waves in terms of issues. The Equal Rights Amendment, a proposed amendment to the US Constitution that would prohibit discrimination on the basis of sex, was introduced during the first wave, became an issue of focus in the second wave, and may actually pass in the fourth wave. Similarly, some feminist organizations that remain active today had their roots in the first wave, including Planned Parenthood, founded in 1916, and the League of Women Voters, founded in 1920.

Although we acknowledge problems with the wave metaphor, we are going to use it here not only because it has staying power but also because it actually does provide an apt description of some key features of feminism. If you conceptualize a wave as "an energy-carrying disturbance,"[4] you can see each wave of feminism as a kind of surge that "creates a passage through patriarchal society,"[5] offering "an alternative to the norm."[6] Each wave or surge emerged to meet the challenges of a changing sociopolitical culture in which different issues attracted attention and interest. A wave, then, can be seen as a moment in time when particular feminist goals came to the forefront of the culture and received attention not just from feminists but from the larger public.

We turn now to the specific waves to give you a sense of what feminist movement, in all of its diversity, is about. For each wave, we will discuss the events that triggered that wave, the places where the most important activism of that wave occurred, and the key ideas that distinguished the wave. We hope you will take away from this short history an idea of how feminist practices and ideas have evolved and also the extent to which feminism has been a significant force in shaping American culture.

First Wave Feminism

The first wave of feminism is the only wave that has a starting and an ending date on which just about everyone agrees. The women's rights convention in Seneca Falls, New York, in 1848 is considered the beginning of the first wave, which ended with the passage of the Nineteenth Amendment that gave (primarily white) women the right to vote in 1920. There was considerable feminist activity, however, before the first wave. In every historical period, women have questioned basic assumptions about the nature of the sexes, challenged the limitations placed on women by male-dominated social institutions, and argued for greater participation in all spheres of life. Whether calling for the vote, equal access to education, dress reform, or a rethinking of the institution of marriage, women have recognized that they can marshal considerable energy, creativity, and commitment on behalf of feminist causes. Not until the late nineteenth century, however, did the efforts for women's equality coalesce into a clearly identifiable and self-conscious movement that is considered the first wave of feminism.

Triggering Event

The event that precipitated the first wave of feminism was the World Anti-Slavery Convention, held in London in 1840. Although they were leading abolitionists in the United States, Lucretia Mott and Elizabeth Cady Stanton were prohibited from participating in the convention because they were women. They carried that rejection with them for eight years until, in July 1848, they decided to do something about it. With Martha Wright, Mary Ann McClintock, and Jane Hunt, they organized a two-day women's rights convention in Seneca Falls. Although they planned the convention with just five days' notice and publicized it with only a small advertisement in their local newspaper, 200 women and men attended. Stanton drafted a document, "Declaration of Sentiments," modeled on the US Declaration of Independence, that began with the statement, "We hold these truths to be self-evident: that all men and women are created equal." The document provided a list of facts to support its claim that "the history of mankind is a history of repeated injuries and usurpations on the part of man toward woman" and addressed discriminatory laws concerning marriage and divorce, property ownership, education, and suffrage. The Seneca Falls convention was followed by women's rights conventions in other states that addressed a similarly wide range of issues. Although feminists originally focused on a variety of demands, after the Civil War ended in 1865, feminist movement focused on a single issue—obtaining the vote for women.

Happening Places

Various women's suffrage organizations led the campaign for the vote. Two organizations were founded in 1869—the National Woman Suffrage Association, started by Susan B. Anthony and Elizabeth Cady Stanton, and the American Woman Suffrage Association, founded by Lucy Stone and Antoinette Brown Blackwell. The two organizations differed primarily in whether they supported the Fifteenth Amendment to the Constitution, which gave men of color (but neither Black nor white women) the right to vote. The

National Woman Suffrage Association opposed the amendment and argued that white women deserved the vote over men of color, many of whom were immigrants, while members of the American Woman Suffrage Association argued that the extension of the vote to any group of disenfranchised individuals should be supported. Twenty years after the Fifteenth Amendment passed in 1870, the two groups reconciled their differences, merging into the National American Woman Suffrage Association in 1890.

Because Black women faced additional challenges and discrimination that white women did not, they formed separate suffrage organizations to focus on issues of both race and gender. Josephine St. Pierre Ruffin and Charlotte Forten Grimké founded the National Association of Colored Women in Boston, Massachusetts, in 1896. Although suffrage was an important goal for the organization, its members also advocated for a wide range of reforms designed to improve life for African Americans generally. In 1913, Ida B. Wells founded another Black suffrage organization, the Alpha Suffrage Club of Chicago. Women in Chicago had been granted the right to vote in 1910, and the club was formed to ensure that all women, regardless of race, would be able to vote. The Alpha Club also sought to educate Black women about and encourage their involvement in civic concerns. The Alpha Club helped register Black voters, trained Black women to be precinct judges, and campaigned for candidates—both Black and white—who would work on behalf of African American interests in Chicago.

Yet another feminist organization—the National Women's Party—was founded in 1916 by Alice Paul, who brought radical tactics from the British suffrage campaign to the United States. Following World War I, the National Women's Party took the lead in the campaign to secure the vote for women, staging hunger strikes, picketing the White House, and organizing dramatic parades. Building on the activities of other suffrage organizations, the National Women's Party brought greater visibility and urgency to the suffrage cause.

Key Ideas

Although first wave feminists initially addressed a variety of issues concerning women's rights, they eventually focused only on securing the right to vote for women. Suffragists[7] argued that if women won the right to vote, they would be able to secure all other rights through the ballot box. After more than seventy years of effort, women won the right to vote on August 18, 1920; the passage of the Nineteenth Amendment to the Constitution marked the end of the first wave of feminism in the United States.

Second Wave Feminism

Without the unifying goal of suffrage, feminist movement in the United States petered out and essentially stopped with World War II. The war benefited the feminist cause, however, in that many women who had not worked outside the home before began to work in factories and shipyards to support the war effort. Their employment made visible feminists' claims that occupations did not have to be gendered and that women could effectively do what previously had been considered men's work. When the war ended, government-sponsored messages urged these women back into the home, and their jobs were given to returning veterans. The resulting cult of domesticity saw women marrying younger and having more children than they had in the previous decade, and they were expected to be happy with lives devoted almost exclusively to homemaking and motherhood.

Triggering Events

Several events initiated the second wave of feminism. Two books appeared on the scene that influenced thinking about women's lives in dramatically new ways. One was feminist writer Simone de Beauvoir's *The Second Sex*, published in France in 1949 and in the United States in 1953. Her idea that "one is not born, but rather becomes, a woman" was a revolutionary idea at the time.[8] She detailed various factors, including history, mythology, and socialization, that make women different from men. The second book was *The Feminine Mystique*, published in 1963 by journalist Betty Friedan, in which she identified "the problem that has no name"—the systematic sexism that taught women that they should aspire to a life of motherhood and homemaking. She described the problem in this way: "It was a strange stirring, a sense of dissatisfaction, a yearning that women suffered in the middle of the twentieth century in the US. Each suburban wife struggled with it alone. As she made the beds, shopped for groceries, matched slipcover material, ate peanut butter sandwiches with her children, chauffeured Cub Scouts and Brownies, lay beside her husband at night—she was afraid to ask even of herself the silent question—'Is this all?'"[9] Friedan's answer was that of course women were unhappy because they were not allowed to fully exercise their creative and intellectual faculties.

In addition to the books by de Beauvoir and Friedan, other events served as catalysts for feminist movement. Women participating in the civil rights and antiwar movements of the 1960s discovered that male colleagues did not apply the movements' objectives of freedom and equality to their female coworkers. Women were doing much of the basic work, but they were not allowed to formulate policy, to draft papers and manifestos, or to speak at public events. They also were seen by many of their male coworkers primarily as sex objects. As a result of these experiences, some women decided to organize feminist groups and to campaign on behalf of their own rights and their own liberation.

A protest at the Miss America pageant in Atlantic City, New Jersey, on September 7, 1968, often is credited with making the second wave of feminism visible to the public. It was organized by the New York Radical Women and was attended by hundreds of women from around the country. The pageant was selected as the target for the protest because it was taken very seriously by the public at the time. As protest organizer Robin Morgan explained, "It taught young girls that the important thing in life, even though you might pretend you had a talent, was to get a man, to be sexy, to be superficial." At the protest, a sheep was crowned Miss America "to represent how the contestants had to obey as they were being paraded around." A huge "Freedom Trashcan" on the boardwalk invited women to throw away symbols of their oppression—into the trashcan went stiletto heels, girdles, false eyelashes, diapers, cleaning tools, magazines such as *Ladies' Home Journal* and *Playboy*, and bras.[10] This event led to the myth that feminists are "bra burners," although no bras were actually burned that day.[11]

Happening Places

Feminist activity during the second wave took place primarily in a number of formal organizations. Betty Friedan, Shirley Chisholm, Pauli Murray, and Muriel Fox founded the National Organization for Women (NOW) in 1966. The organization's goals were to achieve and protect the equal rights of women and girls in social, political, and economic arenas. Two other feminist organizations were spin-offs from NOW. The Women's Equity Action League, founded in 1968 by Elizabeth Boyer, was a more conservative organization that focused on securing equal opportunities for women—often through litigation—in education, economics, and employment. Its members supported the proposed Equal Rights Amendment to the Constitution but did not support NOW's efforts to legalize abortion. A radical group called *The Feminists*, led by Ti-Grace Atkinson, also split off from NOW in 1968 because its members objected to NOW's hierarchical structure; they proposed that all offices in NOW be eliminated and replaced with committees. When the NOW leadership declined to make these changes, The Feminists created its own organization to challenge various social norms, including the hierarchical nature of society, the normativity of heterosexual sex, and the institution of marriage.

Other organizations with more specific aims followed. In 1969, the National Association for the Repeal of Abortion Laws was created to engage in lobbying, political action, and advocacy efforts to expand access to abortion. This organization later became *NARAL Pro-Choice America* and now is known simply as *NARAL*. The National Women's Political Caucus, founded in 1971 by, among others, Gloria Steinem, Shirley Chisholm, Bella Abzug, Dorothy Height, Jill Ruckelshaus, and LaDonna Harris, was dedicated to increasing women's participation in all areas of political and public life, including as elected and appointed officials, campaign organizers, judges, and lobbyists.

Two organizations were formed during the second wave to address the unique issues faced by Black women in the United States. The founding members of the National Black Feminist Organization (NBFO) included Florynce Kennedy, Michele Wallace, Faith Ringgold, Doris Wright, and Margaret Sloan-Hunter. They had participated in various civil rights and feminist groups but did not feel completely accepted. White women dominated feminist movement and were typically not attuned to Black women's concerns; the civil rights movement tended to ignore Black women and their contributions. A second organization for Black women was the Combahee River Collective, a Black feminist lesbian organization active in Boston between 1974 and 1980 that broke away from the NBFO to address the specific needs of Black lesbians. Named after a military campaign led by Harriet Tubman at the Combahee River in South Carolina in 1863, the Collective is best known for the "Combahee River Collective Statement." This document is credited with early theorizing of the interlocking oppressions of gender, race, and class.

Two mechanisms were responsible for the spread of feminism in the second wave. One was *Ms.* magazine, founded by Gloria Steinem, Dorothy Pitman Hughes, Patricia Carbine, and others. The preview issue dealt with welfare as a feminist issue, desexing the English language, and the "click" of feminist awakening; it also included a list of women who admitted they had had abortions. Published in December 1971, the issue sold out its 300,000 copies in three days and generated 16,000 subscriptions within the next few weeks. Because it was a slick, glossy magazine that was sold on newsstands, the magazine helped to mainstream the feminist message.

Consciousness-raising groups also helped spread feminism across the larger culture by introducing many women to feminist movement. These groups enacted the slogan that became synonymous with the second wave, "the personal is political." Consciousness-raising groups encouraged women to see problems they previously considered petty and unique as examples of systemic gender inequality. Group members engaged in self-revelation, active listening, and discussion to link their individual problems with larger social forces and issues.

Language was another arena in which second wave feminists sought to create equality between women and men. They argued that language privileged the experiences of men and often excluded women or depicted them in negative ways. By changing the language to make it more equitable, feminists hoped that perceptions of women would change. As feminist theorist Sarah Lucia Hoagland suggests, "Our judgment, our perception, is directed by the values embedded in the language we use, setting limits to what we might imagine."[12] Feminists protested the use of language that supposedly included women and men but was gendered male such as *policeman, fireman, mankind,* and *guys.* They worked to equalize descriptors for women and for men for the same state or condition. *Bachelor,* for example, suggests a carefree, attractive, desirable single man, while *spinster,* the common equivalent for a woman, suggests that she is unattractive, undesirable, and an "old maid." Feminists challenged the titles used for men and women—*Mr.* for men and *Miss* or *Mrs.* for women. They noted that such titles made marital status the most important thing to know about a woman, while such knowledge was deemed unimportant for men. Second wavers also challenged the convention that women were expected to change their surnames to those of their husbands when they married, a practice that suggested that marriage is a woman's greatest achievement and that she is her husband's possession.[13]

Key Ideas

Second wave feminism proposed widespread changes to US society, so collapsing its ideology into a few key concerns is difficult. Three major ideas, however, stand out: construction of women as an oppressed class, social equality for women, and passage of the Equal Rights Amendment. The starting point for second wave feminists was that women were members of an oppressed class. They sought social equality for the members of that class, and they saw the proposed Equal Rights Amendment to the Constitution as a major remedy that would address the injustices done to this class.

Women as an Oppressed Class. Second wave feminists assumed that women share common features that make them an oppressed class. Some feminists argued that these features are biological characteristics related to sex, such as wombs, breasts, the process of menstruation, and the capacity to bear children. Others argued that what women share are gender characteristics such as the experience of oppression, women's special responsibility for domestic or nurturing labor, and women's construction as sex objects. In their efforts to identify characteristics that women share—whether biological or socially constructed—second wave feminists tended to treat women as a homogenous group.

Social Equality. When second wave feminists began their efforts to achieve social equality, women and men were treated very differently in almost every area of life. In response, feminists tackled social change in numerous arenas. They campaigned to have newspapers drop the practice of listing job openings in the classified section as exclusively for men or for women. They worked to overturn protective labor laws that restricted what women could do on the job—how much they could lift, for example—that kept them out of many occupations. They worked to open up professions to women from which they had been excluded, allowing women to become construction workers, pilots, and engineers. They gave a label to sexual harassment and worked to make it illegal, they enabled women to secure credit in their own names, and they campaigned for equal pay for equal work.

Second wave feminists also were active in the field of education. They promoted Title IX, which gave women the right to educational equality, guaranteeing equal participation in any educational program or activity that receives federal funding. They worked to change the curricula of high schools and universities to include women's ideas and contributions. They critiqued movies, TV programs, and advertisements for their portrayal of women, pointing out both the limited and stereotypical roles women were given and how often they were absent from entertainment venues. They began to do research on gender and women's issues; created women's studies departments; and implemented academic majors, minors, and graduate degrees in women's studies, feminist studies, and gender and sexuality studies.

Second wave feminists worked to facilitate changes in the area of reproductive freedom as well. The birth-control pill gained widespread use during the second wave, and in 1973 the Supreme Court's decision in *Roe v. Wade* established the right to abortion in the first trimester of pregnancy. Feminists also tackled issues relating to rape and violence against women, creating organizations and promoting legislation for the protection of battered women, working to outlaw marital rape, opening rape crisis centers, and organizing Take Back the Night rallies.

Equal Rights Amendment. Although second wave feminists worked on many issues, one received much of their attention and energy—the Equal Rights Amendment (ERA). The proposed Twenty-Eighth Amendment to the US Constitution reads: "Equality of rights under the law shall not be denied or abridged by the United States or by any state on account of sex." Conceived by Alice Paul in 1923, the ERA was introduced into every subsequent congressional session until it passed both houses of Congress in 1972. It was sent to the states for ratification; thirty-eight states were required to ratify it within seven years in order for it to become law. In 1978, with three states still needed for ratification, Congress extended the ratification deadline to June 30, 1982. Because no additional states ratified the ERA within the required time period, the amendment died.

Postfeminism

We interrupt our discussion of the four waves of feminism here with a discussion of postfeminism, which many believe followed the second wave. *Postfeminism* has three major and quite different definitions. One is that feminism is dead, so postfeminism is a period when feminism was no longer needed or wanted. Another is that feminism needs to be revised to correct some of its earlier inadequacies. A third definition is that it is simply the period that followed the second wave. Let's begin with the first definition of postfeminism—that the need for feminism had disappeared.

Postfeminism = Feminism Is Dead

A common definition of the term *postfeminism* is that feminism was dead after the second wave. *Post* means *after*, so this meaning of *postfeminism* suggests that the United States was "past" feminism. The first mainstream use of this meaning of the term occurred in a *New York Times* article in 1981 titled "Voices from the Post-Feminist Generation," in which author Susan Bolotin found that young, middle-class women were actively retreating from feminism.[14] The media continued to perpetuate the idea that feminism was dead in a number of other articles. The *New York Times Magazine* ran an article in 1988 called "When Feminism Failed,"[15] a cover of *Time* magazine in 1988 featured the question "Is Feminism Dead?,"[16] and a *Newsweek* column in 1990 was titled "The Failure of Feminism."[17]

Two very different reasons were given for why some people believed feminism was not only dead but no longer necessary. One was that gender equality had been achieved: feminism as a movement had been successful and had accomplished its primary objectives. Journalist Claudia Wallis, writing in *Time* magazine in December 1989, cited this reason for the death of feminism: "In many ways, feminism is a victim of its own resounding achievements. Its triumphs—getting women into the workplace, in elevating their status in society and in shattering the 'feminine mystique' that defined female success only in terms of being a wife and a mother—have rendered it obsolete, at least in its original form and rhetoric."[18]

Antifeminist backlash is another reason given for the end of feminism and the emergence of a postfeminist era. From this perspective, feminism was dead because women had discovered that it was harmful to them and detrimental to society. Feminism was seen to be "responsible for nearly every woe besetting women"[19]—high divorce rates, children's failure in school, economic recession, burnout among professional women, and an increase in crime rates among women.[20] In other words, women were seen to be unhappy precisely because they were free.[21] The considerable backlash against second wave feminism also saw gender-neutral language attacked as political correctness, with feminists characterized as feminazis. Many women no longer called themselves *feminists* "although they often voiced feminist sentiments."[22]

Postfeminism = Feminism Revised

Challenges to feminism by feminists themselves created the second definition of *postfeminism*. In this iteration of the term, an older version of feminism was considered past or dead, and a new version was proposed—feminism was reworked and reconceptualized to address the limitations of earlier approaches. One of the challenges was to dominant, hegemonic feminism with its focus on white, middle-class women. Books began to be written that addressed both gender and race, including Cherríe Moraga and Gloria Anzaldúa's *This Bridge Called My Back* (1981/1983); Angela Davis's *Women, Race and Class* (1981); and bell hooks's *Ain't I a Woman: Black Women and Feminism* (1981). Other similarly influential works were Gloria T. Hull, Patricia Bell Scott, and Barbara Smith's *All the Women are White, All the Blacks are Men, But Some of Us Are Brave* (1982); Paula Giddings's *When and Where I Enter: The Impact of Black Women on Race and Sex in America* (1984); and Audre Lorde's *Sister Outsider: Essays and Speeches* (1984). These books served as foundational texts for a new kind of multicultural feminism that explained how race and class intersect to inform and influence women's lives and offered a more expansive and inclusive form of feminism.

Another group of feminists who challenged second wave principles rejected what they called the *victim feminism* of the second wave and introduced a new type of feminism as a corrective. For these feminists, the biggest obstacle standing in the way of women's liberation was feminism itself because it encouraged women to see themselves as victims. They believed that the view of women as oppressed was "unnecessary and even harmful, serving to constrain women rather than inspire them to action."[23] In its place, they embraced power feminism, encouraging women to take full advantage of the opportunities available to them. Naomi Wolf's *Fire with Fire: The New Female Power and How to Use it* (1994); Katie Roiphe's *The Morning After: Sex, Fear and Feminism* (1993); and Christina Hoff Sommers's *Who Stole Feminism?* (1994) all involved this kind of "critical interrogation of the foundations of feminism."[24]

Postfeminism = Third Wave Feminism

A third definition of *postfeminism* fits most neatly into the feminist waves—postfeminism as a period that followed second wave feminism. Because some people thought feminism ended with the second wave, they called the next period *postfeminist*. Because another wave of feminism did in fact follow the second wave, however, some feminists see postfeminism as really just the third wave of feminism. We have chosen to conceptualize postfeminism as essentially overlapping with the third wave, which is where we turn next.

Third Wave Feminism

The waves of feminism became more blurred and overlapping as they progressed, so there is not a clear consensus on when the third wave of feminism began. Some say it refers to feminists who were born in the 1960s and 1970s,[25] some say it emerged during the middle 1990s,[26] and some say it occurred during the late 1990s and early 2000s.[27] To assign third wave feminism to a specific historical period is difficult in part because there is no single piece of legislation or major social change that belongs to the third wave the way the Nineteenth Amendment belonged to the first wave and the ERA belonged to the second. To pinpoint what third wave feminism was and when it happened is also difficult because, for third wavers, "the presence of feminism . . . is taken for granted." As activists and writers Jennifer Baumgardner and Amy Richards explain, "For our generation, feminism is like fluoride. We scarcely notice that we have it—it's simply in the water."[28]

The first documented mention of the term *third wave* can be traced back to an anthology by M. Jacqui Alexander, Lisa Albrecht, and Mab Segrest entitled *The Third Wave: Feminist Perspectives on Racism*, never published because the publishing house closed. The next reference to the third wave occurred in 1991 in Chela Sandoval's article on US third world feminism published in the journal *Genders*.[29] An article in *Ms.* magazine by Rebecca Walker, daughter of second wave feminist and author Alice Walker, included a more public and dramatic reference to the third wave: "I am ready to decide, as my mother decided before me, to devote much of my energy to the history, health, and healing of women. . . . I am not a postfeminism feminist. I am the Third Wave."[30]

Triggering Events

Several events were responsible for precipitating the third wave of feminist movement. All of them made feminists realize that they could not take the gains of the second wave for granted. One such event was lawyer Anita Hill's challenge to the nomination of Clarence Thomas to the US Supreme Court in 1991. She accused him of sexual harassment when they had worked together at the US Department of Education and the Equal Employment Opportunity Commission. Many feminists were outraged by the hearings, in which "Hill was subjected to harsh and dismissive questioning," and her "accusations of sexual harassment were belittled and dismissed by both Thomas and the white male senators conducting the hearings."[31] In response, feminists wore buttons that read "We believe her." Although Thomas was confirmed, the hearings led to a national conversation about sexual harassment, the lack of credence given to women, and the overrepresentation of men in national leadership roles.

Two events related to women's bodies functioned as triggering events for the third wave as well. One was the 1991 rape trial of William Kennedy Smith, a nephew of President John F. Kennedy. Although a rape-kit examination showed his accuser had been raped and three women were willing to testify that Smith had sexually assaulted them previously, their testimony was excluded from the trial, and he was acquitted. A Supreme Court ruling concerning abortion also led to concerns about women's control over their bodies. *Planned Parenthood v. Casey*, decided in 1992, upheld the constitutional right to have an abortion but also broadened states' authority to regulate abortion, opening the door to a multitude of new restrictive abortion laws. All of these events brought new urgency to ongoing issues that affect young women—sexual harassment, rape, and reproductive health—and demonstrated that the world continued to be shaped by inequalities.[32]

Something else that helped initiate the third wave was the emergence of the riot grrrl underground feminist punk subculture in Olympia, Washington, in the early 1990s. Bands associated with the movement included Bikini Kill, Bratmobile, Heavens to Betsy, Excuse 17, Huggy Bear, Skinned Teen, Emily's Sassy Lime, Sleater-Kinney, Team Cresch, and The Third Sex. Riot grrrl music addressed issues such as rape, domestic abuse, sexuality, and female empowerment. Band members also offered new—and sometimes contradictory—models of femininity with their "disheveled vintage dresses, short dyed hair, luminescent red lipstick and heavy combat boots."[33] The riot grrrl movement quickly spread beyond its musical roots to create a vibrant zine culture consisting of self-published magazines and pamphlets dealing with feminist issues. One example was the zine *Riot Grrrl*, started by Allison Wolfe, Molly Neuman, Kathleen Hanna, and Tobi Vail, which embodied the belief that "girls constitute a revolutionary soul force that can, and will change the world for real."[34]

Happening Places

Third wave feminism took place in four major arenas—everyday interactions, cyberspace, popular culture, and language. For the most part, these offered sites of activism that were different from the locations in which second wave feminism occurred. Third wavers' happening places were less likely to be formal organizations; instead, the sites intersected naturally and easily with everyday lives.

In part because they saw that laws and policies implemented during the second wave did not completely eradicate sexism, racism, ableism, and heterosexism,[35] third wave feminists made everyday interaction in their personal worlds a key site for their efforts. If change wasn't happening at institutional or societal levels, their efforts were better applied, they believed, to the everyday arenas over which they had more control. Adhering to the notion that "everyday interactions are political in and of themselves, and are pivotal to social change,"[36] they worked to enact feminism at the microlevels of daily interaction,[37] embedding feminism in their "perspectives, personalities, interactions, language, relationships, understanding of their own privilege, beauty norms, and consumption habits."[38] They spoke out "when others violated their feminist sensibilities in school, at work, and in social settings."[39] They were acute observers of power dynamics and challenged organizations that excluded minority voices or kept members of marginalized communities from assuming leadership roles. They complained when professors "devoted more time to the subject and research of White men in contrast to women or communities of color."[40]

Increased technological capacity also is associated with the third wave, and much third wave feminism happened online. Zines, blogs, webrings, newsletters, organizational websites, online bulletin boards, Facebook feeds, hashtags, and tweeting were among the technological tools third wave feminists used for their activism. These technologies allowed them to learn about feminism and its history; to contribute, curate, and circulate feminist information; and to engage in feminist critiques of current events and pending legislation. The technologies also allowed them to reflect on the process of being a feminist and to learn about individual feminists and feminist organizations.

Although third wavers were sometimes accused of slacktivism—engaging in the easy actions enabled by technology rather than in more demanding forms of activism such as lobbying legislators or organizing protests—online activism offered a number of advantages to third wave feminists. It provided accessible information about feminism, was cost effective, and democratized feminist activity by allowing individuals of diverse identities "to share their experiences and thoughts about feminism."[41] It also allowed activists in more isolated locations, where being outwardly feminist is not always popular, to find welcoming communities.

Third wave feminism also took place in popular culture. Third wavers inherited a number of institutions created by second wavers, including women's studies programs at universities, long-standing feminist organizations, and well-established publishing outlets such as *Ms.* magazine and academic journals. These outlets, however, became a less important part of the culture of the third wave than they had been for the second wave because so much of its feminism was embedded in popular culture. Music, television, lifestyle magazines, and advertising emerged as sites for activism. Singers such as Madonna, Queen Latifah, and Mary J. Blige provided images of powerful women during the third wave. Television series such as *Buffy the Vampire Slayer* (1997–2003), *Sex & the City* (1998–2004), and *Dora the Explorer* (1999–2019) depicted girls and women as capable and independent. Feminist magazines for young women—*Sassy,* founded by Jane Pratt in 1988; *HUES* (Hear Us Emerging Sisters), founded by Taji Edut, Ophira Edut, and Dyann Logwood in 1992; and *Bust,* founded by Debbie Stoller, Marcelle Karp, and Laurie Henzel in 1993—provided a counterpoint to traditional magazines for girls and women such as *Seventeen*. Advertisements celebrated women's equality, and products touted feminist sensibilities, including Stila Cosmetics, which included quotes from Elizabeth Cady Stanton on its packaging.[42] Popular culture made it seem "cool, vibrant, sexy to be a feminist."[43]

Third wave feminism also happened in language as third wavers coopted and appropriated sexist, racist, and classist symbols "to subvert sexist culture and deprive it of verbal weapons."[44] They reclaimed words like *girl, bitch, slut,* and *pussy* that traditionally had been seen as derogatory and turned them into empowering words to describe women. Inga Muscio's book *Cunt: A Declaration of Independence* (2004) is an example. It rendered a derogatory word impotent, insignificant, and ineffective and transformed it into a defiant label for feminist commitment rather than an insult to women.

Key Ideas

Three key themes stand out in the ideology of feminism's third wave: emphasizing individualism, foregrounding difference, and celebrating femininity. Third wavers emphasized individual responsibility over collective action for addressing inequalities. Their commitment to individualism was concomitant with their honoring of differences among individuals. They also celebrated conventional modes of performing femininity, deliberately breaking with the efforts of second wave feminists to disrupt conventional prescriptions for femininity.

Individualism. The third wave of feminism was guided by a commitment to individualism, with women seen as "responsible to and for themselves."[45] In this wave, women were encouraged "to pursue their individual freedoms at the expense of a collective female identity."[46] The problems that young women encountered in achieving their goals "were constructed as individual challenges, rather than political problems that are best faced collectively."[47] When they experienced racism, homophobia, or domestic violence, they framed those experiences "in exclusively personal terms in a way that turns the idea of the personal-as-political on its head."[48] Third wavers tended to take a first-person, confessional approach to solving problems they encountered, with "various individuals piping up to reveal their frustration with a specific situation and how they resolved it."[49]

Difference. Foregrounding difference was a major concept embraced by feminists of the third wave. Third wavers challenged the second wave's essentialist definitions of woman, which overemphasized the experiences of middle-class, heterosexual, white women. The commonality once thought to constitute women's experience was replaced in the third wave by an understanding that the category is not nearly as homogenous as previously believed. Although gender as a category of analysis is useful, third wavers believed, "it is incomplete without understanding that other categories of identity (race, sexuality, class, age, etc.) are equally as important in gaining accurate knowledge about people's lives and experiences."[50] In stressing "the necessity of knowing, acknowledging and understanding" women's multiple identities,[51] third wave feminists welcomed the different perspectives and contributions of feminists of various races and sexualities, especially bisexual and trans identities.

Femininity. Many third wave feminists criticized second wave feminists for their rejection of femininity. Rather than seeing femininity as at odds with feminism, third wavers embraced femininity as a response to the negative stereotypes of feminists as "shrill, hairy, and unfeminine and that no man would ever want them."[52] Second wave feminists worked hard to be called *women* instead of *girls*; they believed *girl* to be an infantilizing term and proclaimed that they were fully grown adults, not children. But third wavers often conceptualized and called themselves *girls* and embraced the connotations of youth and traditional femininity that accompany the label.

Third wavers engaged with traditional femininity in various ways—having a sexy body; expressing sexual desire; and embracing the beauty products, paraphernalia, and rituals of femininity. For many third wavers, femininity was at the center "of an ideology of agency, confidence, and resistance."[53] They wore lipstick and stiletto heels, proudly displayed their cleavage, were attuned to fashion trends, wore makeup, and subjected themselves to Brazilian waxes to remove their pubic hair. Such practices were perceived as expressing individuality rather than capitulating to beauty imperatives—something done to please women themselves and to make them feel good rather than to attract or please a man. Third wave feminists argued that this stance shifted the way power operates from an external, male gaze to an inner gaze that they themselves controlled.[54]

Fourth Wave Feminism

Fourth wave feminism is not always classified as separate from the third wave because the two waves share many similarities. But as early as 2008, some activists and journalists began to label a surge in feminist activity as the *fourth wave* when Facebook, Twitter, and YouTube were firmly entrenched in the cultural fabric, and feminist blogs like *Jezebel* and *Feministing* were spreading across the web.[55] Some journalists say the fourth wave began in 2013, when they noticed an uptick in feminist activity, not just in social media but in other arenas as well,[56] and yet others see it originating somewhere in between.

Triggering Events

A number of events are credited with launching feminism's fourth wave. A key trigger was the Slut Walk movement, which began in Toronto, Canada, on January 24, 2011. A Toronto police officer, Michael Sanguinetti, spoke at York University and suggested that if women did not want to be raped, "they should not dress like sluts," ignoring the fact that "the majority of rapes are committed by people that the victim knows, in spite of what they might be wearing."[57] In response, Sonya Barnett and other feminists organized a Slut Walk on April 3, 2011, reclaiming a pejorative word that is often used against women. More than 3,000 people attended the Toronto protest, and the movement spread to over forty countries in its first year.

On June 25, 2013, Texas state senator Wendy Russell Davis initiated a feminist action that captured the attention of the media and the public and spurred a surge in feminist activity. Davis filibustered in an effort to block a bill that would have banned abortions after twenty weeks of pregnancy, required abortion clinics to meet the same standards that hospital-style surgical centers do, and mandated that doctors who perform abortions have admitting privileges at nearby hospitals. She attempted to hold the floor until midnight, when the senate's special session ended, after which a vote could no longer be held on the measure. She was not allowed to eat, drink, use the restroom, sit down, or even lean against her desk during the eleven-hour filibuster. Davis's filibuster ended three hours short of midnight when Lieutenant Governor David Dewhurts ruled that she had gone off topic, forcing a vote on whether the filibuster could continue. Because of noise in the gallery and various parliamentary maneuvers, the outcome of the vote was unclear, and thus the abortion bill died. It passed, however, when Governor Rick Perry called a special session of the legislature the following month.

Several events concerning sexual harassment and sexual assault also contributed to increased feminist activity. Although sexual harassment and sexual assault are crimes, they are not always prosecuted or their penalties enforced; several cases on university campuses brought attention to these issues. At Stanford University, for example, student and star swimmer Brock Turner was arrested and convicted of the felony sexual assault of Chanel Miller. In January 2015, he was sentenced to six months in jail and three years of probation—a sentence that outraged the community. His release from jail after only three months added to the outrage. *The Hunting Ground*, a documentary film about sexual assault on US campuses, also developed the theme that perpetrators of sexual assault often go unpunished. Released in 2015, the film featured multiple students who were sexually assaulted on their college campuses and who claimed that college administrators either ignored them or required that they navigate complex bureaucracies to have their cases addressed.

The election of Donald Trump as president of the United States in 2016 also reinvigorated a fourth wave of feminist activity. Women's marches were held around the world on January 21, 2017, the day after Trump's inauguration. Although marchers were protesting his inauguration for many reasons, a major one was that he was able to engage in sexual harassment and even sexual violence without consequences. In a video released in October 2016, Trump explained that famous men can sexually assault women with impunity: "And when you're a star, they let you do it. You can do anything. Grab them by the pussy. You can do anything."[58]

Trump's election was followed by two movements—Me Too and Time's Up—that also targeted sexual assault and the lack of punishment for offenders, especially if they are famous or wealthy. After publication of an article by Ronan Farrow in *The New Yorker* in October 2017 about the "open secret" of movie producer Harvey Weinstein's sexual behavior, actor Alyssa Milano tweeted, "If you've been sexually harassed or assaulted, write 'me too' as a reply to this tweet."[59] By the next day, over 55,000 people had replied. The Me Too movement actually started in 1997, when Tarana Burke created the organization Just Be Inc. and called her movement *Me Too*. Just Be Inc. was designed to help survivors of sexual violence heal, particularly girls and women of color from low-income communities. The Me Too movement helped uncover sexual harassment and abuse in arenas such as the music industry, the sciences, sports, medicine, politics, and academia and spawned hashtags such as #ChurchToo, #MeTooMilitary, and #MeTooSTEM.

The Time's Up movement brought high-profile sexual assault cases into the spotlight as well. "The clock has run out on sexual assault, harassment, and inequality in the workplace. It's time to do something about it," the organization's website reads. Time's Up was founded by Hollywood celebrities in response to the Weinstein case and the #MeToo movement, with Lisa Borders serving as its first president and CEO. Well-known men such as FOX News chair and CEO Roger Ailes, television news anchor Matt Lauer, and journalist and television host Bill O'Reilly were exposed for their acts of sexual harassment and sexual assault. Although the objective of Time's Up was to address sexual harassment and assault in all industries, its focus is on the movie industry. In 2019, the organization launched the 4-percent challenge, referencing the fact that only 4 percent of the top 1,200 studio films made between 2007 and 2018 were directed by women. The challenge asked production companies to show their commitment to working with a female director on a feature production in the next eighteen months.

Happening Places

Although the third wave of feminism also happened online, technological possibilities continued to grow exponentially, so digital space is also a critical place for fourth wave feminism. Fourth wave feminists consider the internet to be part of public space, and "to draw a line between what happens online and offline" is increasingly difficult.[60] As one fourth wave feminist, Stephanie Herold, explains, "Whether we tweet feminism or blog about it, young feminists use the Internet to expand and explore what it means to be involved in the feminist movement. We usually do it in addition to other feminist work, using the Internet to launch campaigns, reach new audiences with our message, and create a sense of feminist community."[61]

The pervasiveness of technology is creating new ways in which individuals can access feminist writing, engage in dialogue, and protest. Protests can be organized through a series of clicks, online petitions can circulate quickly, and money can be raised by nonprofit organizations through their own websites or on GoFundMe sites. Digital technology also allows people to participate who might otherwise be marginalized "by disability, distance, or caring responsibilities"[62] or who are at greater risk in physical protests, such as people of color because they are more likely to be criminalized.

A few examples suggest the ways in which fourth wave feminists are using internet technology for activism. Many activists take on concerns that have affected them or that move them personally, developing campaigns "powered by a strong, personal story, bringing the feminist slogan, 'the personal is political,' into the present day."[63] One such campaign, initiated by Laura Bates, Soraya Chemaly, and Jacklyn Friedman, concerned misogynist material on Facebook. They noticed that some major companies had ads on misogynist pages and, in response, they created a campaign on social media that caused several companies to remove their ads from Facebook. Facebook then updated its guidelines "to address misogynist hate speech, and train their moderators accordingly."[64]

Another form of online feminist activism involves the creation and circulation of Twitter hashtags. #SolidarityIsForWhiteWomen, for example, was created by Mikki Kendall as a way to critique the tendency of some white feminists to exclude issues relevant to women of color in their conceptions of feminism. The hashtag #StandWithWendy was implemented when Texas state senator Wendy Davis filibustered the bill designed to limit access to abortion, while Janet Mock's #GirlsLikeUs focuses on trans women. #NotYourAsianSidekick was founded by Suey Park to examine Asian American feminism, calling out issues such as patriarchy, white supremacy, and the stigma against mental illness in Asian American communities. After US representative Alexandria Ocasio-Cortez called out sexist culture on the floor of the House in 2020, women flooded Instagram with black-and-white images of themselves and nominated other women to do the same, using the hashtags #challengeaccepted and #womensupportingwomen.

In addition to internet activism, there is ongoing engagement with language in the fourth wave. Language is being used differently, however, from how second and third wave feminists used it. Instead of creating gender-neutral language, as second wavers did, or appropriating and reclaiming derogatory terms, as third wavers did, fourth wavers are being influenced by the internet, a commitment to intersectionality, and a desire to shield individuals from distress.

Feminists in the fourth wave have created a number of new terms to use in digital technologies such as *WoC* (woman of color), *cis* (individuals whose gender and sexual identities map cleanly onto one another), and *TERF* (trans-exclusionary radical feminist). These terms respond to the 140-character limit originally imposed by Twitter and lend themselves to the practice of hashtagging. They also speak to fourth wavers' commitment to intersectionality and are designed to ensure that all individuals are included and not carelessly stereotyped.

Fourth wave feminists' popularization of the term *kyriarchy* in place of *patriarchy* demonstrates their commitment to intersectionality and their acknowledgment of difference. Although coined much earlier by Elisabeth Schussler Fiorenza, the term has been popularized by fourth wave feminists as a replacement for the term *patriarchy*. Fourth wave feminists do not see *patriarchy* as a useful way of framing gender inequality when ethnicity, class, education, and gender intersect to oppress women and men alike. *Kyriarchy*, in contrast, is defined as a social system or set of connecting social systems built around domination, oppression, and submission. It encompasses sexism, racism, ableism, homophobia, transphobia, classism, xenophobia, economic injustice, the prison-industrial complex, colonialism, militarism, ethnocentrism, and other forms of dominating hierarchies in which the subordination of one person or group to another is internalized and institutionalized.

Fourth wave feminists also embrace language designed to protect individuals from disturbing ideas or experiences. An emphasis on the term *consent*—agreement between participants to engage in sexual activity—is one such example. Similarly, there is an emphasis on trigger and content warnings designed to alert audiences that an article, film, or topic may contain potentially distressing material. Fourth wavers also emphasize safe spaces on university campuses or in workplaces to provide individuals who feel marginalized to come together in places free of threatening actions, ideas, or conversations.

Celebrity culture is another arena in which feminism is playing out in the fourth wave. Although some see celebrity feminism as devaluing "pure or true feminism,"[65] others note that celebrity culture has helped make feminism more appealing to a larger public audience. Beyoncé, for example, included a sample of Nigerian writer Chimamanda Ngozi Adichie's TED Talk, "We Should All Be Feminists," in her song "Flawless" in 2013, and in 2014, at the MTV Video Music Awards, she performed in front of the word *FEMINIST*, spelled out in neon lights.

Actors involved in fourth wave feminist movement include Emma Watson, who spoke on gender equality at the United Nations in 2014 after being named a Goodwill Ambassador for United Nations Women and launching her HeForShe campaign. Reese Witherspoon, accepting a Cinematheque award in 2015, exhorted the audience, "Women make up 50 percent of the population, and we should be playing 50 percent of the roles on the screen"; she was called "a true, modern-day feminist" for her remarks. Frances McDormand, in her acceptance speech for best actress at the Academy Awards in 2018, asked every female nominee in the theatre to stand with her in solidarity and implored industry big shots to pay attention to female talent.

Key Ideas

Three key ideas animate the fourth wave of feminism: intersectionality, individuality, and documentation of transgressions. Two of these key ideas of the fourth wave carry over from third wave feminism—fourth wavers are committed to the incorporation of intersectionality into feminist analyses and activism, and they focus on achieving feminist goals at the level of individual, interpersonal interactions. A third key idea, however, is new—an emphasis on documenting transgressions and the expression of outrage at those transgressions.

Intersectionality. Fourth wavers continue third wavers' commitment to intersectionality, "the idea that different axes of oppression intersect, producing complex and often contradictory results."[66] Although some feminists in all of the waves have attended to the intersection of race and gender, feminism in the fourth wave is increasingly committed to intersectionality and to incorporating and supporting marginalized and overlooked identities. Because of their commitment to intersectionality, fourth wave feminists do not see feminism as "a 'natural' political destination for all women" but "as a *limited* political home."[67] They reject a "politics of inclusion (which is always ultimately based on a notion of commonality and community)" in favor of diversity among feminists, which for them is a key strength of feminism.

Individuality. Fourth wavers not only continue the third wave focus on intersectionality but also its emphasis on individuality. They shift "the responsibility for women's success from the collective to the individual."[68] Instead of challenging the sexism of an external system, they pursue individual solutions, placing the responsibility for change "firmly with the individual."[69] Consequently, individuals are expected to be "rational, calculating and self-motivating" and are encouraged to make sense of their lives "in terms of discourses of freedom, autonomy, and choice."[70]

Documentation of Transgressions. Fourth wave feminists add to their agenda an item not found in the third wave. They are committed to documenting the transgressions of individuals and organizations for sexist, racist, and classist statements and acts. The purpose of such documentation is to hold others accountable by publicly pointing out instances or patterns of oppressive behavior. It is designed to educate others on their misbehavior and to "wake up" the transgressing individuals, forcing them "to recognize their subconscious biases and internalized bigotry."[71] Such documentation is not typically designed to initiate dialogue among individuals or to actually address transgressions or indiscretions. Rather, its primary purpose is policing—to point out where others have spoken or acted incorrectly. Anyone may be attacked "for not being enlightened, for not boycotting a certain celebrity, for not aligning with an ideal progressive identity paradigm."[72] Those doing the documenting typically take the "moral high ground, with a lot of righteous indignation," inviting "others to participate in a public shaming exercise"[73] that not everyone sees as productive. Some see this online shaming as the active seeking of offense and suffering,[74] with everyone watching "everyone else for a fatal slip-up."[75]

The documentation of transgressions can take a variety of forms in online platforms. It may involve "calling out" others using insulting language, sarcasm, mockery, and character assassination.[76] Online feminists may identify instances of "mansplaining," for instance, in which a man speaks condescendingly to a woman as though he knows more than she does. Exhortations to "check your privilege" are also common, reminding others that the body and life into which they are born come with specific privileges that individuals need to acknowledge.[77] Charges of "tone-policing" are made against those who criticize the manner in which an idea is expressed rather than the idea itself. Documenting transgressions also may assume the form of "canceling," in which participants agree not to amplify or give money or attention to a person, an event, or an organization. The backlash in response to an inaccurate definition of bisexuality in the Netflix series *Big Mouth* provides an example of documenting transgressions in practice. When the show misrepresented bisexuals as not being attracted to trans individuals, members of the queer community voiced their anger, and producer Andrew Goldberg responded with an apology and a pledge to do better in the future.

Sometimes, the documentation of transgressions involves the creation of websites that invite individuals to share their experiences of sexism and to call out offenders either implicitly or explicitly. The website Hollaback!, for example, was created in 2005 by seven residents of New York City to address street harassment. Individuals who experience street harassment are encouraged to tell their personal stories through the website and, if they choose, to take and post photographs of their harassers. Another such website, Everyday Sexism, was created by Laura Bates in 2012. Bates realized that women become "so accustomed to regular incidents of sexism that they no longer register,"[78] so she wanted a space where anyone can record such incidents.

After only a year, almost 50,000 experiences of sexism had been shared, and the project had almost 100,000 Twitter followers.[79]

As you can tell from this brief journey through the four waves, feminism has had a long and colorful history, with feminist surges characterized by various triggering events, sites of activism, and key ideas. All versions of feminism, however, challenged and continue to challenge the perceived normalcy and naturalness of systems of domination. Like literal waves, they insert themselves into and around such systems, disrupting them and calling for something new. Isabel Allende aptly describes how feminist waves contrast with the systems they hope to disrupt: "Patriarchy is stony. Feminism, like the ocean, is fluid, powerful, deep, and encompasses the infinite complexity of life; it moves in waves, currents, tides, and sometimes in storms. Like the ocean, feminism never stays quiet."[80]

Feminism Continued

Feminism is still very much alive—thriving, growing, and evolving—as you will see from the women who are featured in the remaining twenty chapters in this book. What is now the fourth wave is certainly not likely to be the last because feminists continue to envision new possibilities for more just and equitable futures. You will have the opportunity in the chapters that follow to see feminists from the second, third, and fourth waves who embody diverse definitions of feminism, align with various types of feminism, and use strategies of all kinds to achieve their objectives to generate change at the individual, community, and societal levels.

■ REFLECTIONS

1. Investigate the current status of the Equal Rights Amendment. Do you believe it still should become a part of the US Constitution? Why or why not?
2. Read the "Declaration of Sentiments" written by Elizabeth Cady Stanton for the Seneca Falls women's rights convention. What do the demands in the document tell you about how women were viewed in the mid-nineteenth century in the United States? Do any of their demands still need to be addressed today?
3. A major dispute among feminists in the first wave was whether to support the vote for Black men or to insist that white women deserved the vote before men of color. What were the major arguments made on behalf of each of these positions? Can you see reasons for both positions, or are you in favor of one or the other?
4. Suffragists in the first wave ultimately decided to focus on the vote because they believed that if women were allowed to vote, they would be

able to secure all their other rights. How accurate was this assessment? Does substantial change happen today through the ballot box? Have feminists been able to achieve their objectives in this way?

5. Interview your parents or other family members about their experiences with feminism. Do they call themselves *feminists*? What feminist waves did they live through, and what impact did feminism have on their lives?
6. Read Simone de Beauvoir's *The Second Sex* or Betty Friedan's *The Feminine Mystique*. Try to imagine what it would have been like to read it when it was first published. What did you find most revealing when reading it today?
7. The issue of language has been important in all of the feminist waves. How important is changing language to you? Which approach to language seems most effective?
8. Some have argued that we are currently in a state of postfeminism. Do you believe feminism is dead? Why or why not?
9. Read a current issue of *Ms.* magazine. What does the issue say about what feminism is and the issues that feminists are trying to address now?
10. Technology has substantially changed feminist movement. What do you see as the advantages and disadvantages of the use of technology for furthering feminism?
11. Documenting transgressions is a feminist issue specific to the fourth wave. Is there value to this practice? Are there any ways in which it might be detrimental to feminist movement?
12. Do you believe we are currently in a fourth wave of feminism? Why or why not?
13. Which of the four feminist waves resonates with you the most?

■ NOTES

[1] The Nineteenth Amendment reads: "The right of citizens of the United States to vote shall not be denied or abridged by the United States or by any State on account of sex. Congress shall have power to enforce this article by appropriate legislation." While seeming to guarantee the vote to all women, in practice, most women of color were excluded by tactics including literacy tests, complex registration forms, poll taxes, and violence directed at those who attempted to exercise their right to vote.

[2] Lise Shapiro Sanders, "'Feminists Love a Utopia': Collaboration, Conflict and the Futures of Feminism," in *Third Wave Feminism: A Critical Exploration*, ed. Stacy Gillis, Gillian Howie, and Rebecca Munford (New York: Palgrave Macmillan, 2007), 8–9.

[3] Rachel Carson, *The Sea Around Us* (New York: Oxford University Press, 2018), 112.

[4] Gillian Howie and Ashley Tauchert, "Feminist Dissonance: The Logic of Late Feminism," in *Third Wave Feminism: A Critical Exploration*, ed. Stacy Gillis, Gillian Howie, and Rebecca Munford (New York: Palgrave Macmillan, 2007), 47.

[5] Prudence Chamberlain, *The Feminist Fourth Wave: Affective Temporality* (Cham, Switzerland: Palgrave Macmillan, 2017), 91.

[6] Chamberlain, *The Feminist Fourth Wave*, 27.

7. Feminists who worked to secure the right to vote for women called themselves *suffragists*, not *suffragettes*. *Suffragette* was a term used by the opposition to denounce the suffragists. The *ette* ending means small and diminutive, and thus the term was seen as offensive by suffragists.
8. Simone de Beauvoir, *The Second Sex*, trans. H. M. Parshley (New York: Vintage/Random House, 1974), 301.
9. Betty Friedan, *The Feminine Mystique* (New York: Dell, 1963), 11.
10. Robin Morgan, "I Was There: The 1968 Miss America Pageant Protest," History Stories, October 19, 2018, http://www.history.com/news/miss-america-protests-1968/
11. Lindsy Van Gelder, "How We Got Here: The Truth About Bra-Burners," *Ms.*, September-October 1992, 80–81.
12. Sarah Lucia Hoagland, *Lesbian Ethics: Toward New Value* (Palo Alto, CA: Institute of Lesbian Studies, 1988), 15.
13. Dale Spender, *Man Made Language* (Boston, MA: Routledge & Kegan Paul, 1980); Una Stannard, *Mrs Man* (San Francisco, CA: Germainbooks, 1977).
14. Susan Bolotin, "Voices From the Post-Feminist Generation," *New York Times*, October 17, 1982, p. 29.
15. Mary Anne Dolan, "When Feminism Failed," *New York Times Magazine*, June 26, 1988, sec. 6, p. 20.
16. "Is Feminism Dead?," cover, *Time*, June 29, 1998, http://content.time.com/time/covers/0,16641,19980629,00.html/
17. "The Failure of Feminism," *Newsweek*, November 18, 1990, https://www.newsweek.com/failure-feminism-205870/
18. Claudia Wallis, "Living: Onward, Women!," *Time*, December 4, 1989, http://content.time.com/time/subscriber/article/0,33009,959163-3,00.html/
19. Susan Faludi, *Backlash: The Undeclared War Against American Women* (New York: Three Rivers/Random House, 1991), 3.
20. Virginia L. Bromley, "What's Feminism Done (For Me) Lately?," in *Gender and Women's Studies: Critical Terrain*, 2nd ed., ed. Margaret Hobbs and Carla Rice (Toronto, Canada: Women's Press, 2018), 31; Faludi, *Backlash*, 1–4.
21. Faludi, *Backlash*, 2.
22. Valerie R. Renegar and Stacey K. Sowards, "Liberal Irony, Rhetoric, and Feminist Thought: A Unifying Third Wave Feminist Theory," *Philosophy and Rhetoric* 36 (2003): 333.
23. Helene A. Shugart, "Isn't It Ironic?: The Intersection of Third-Wave Feminism and Generation X," *Women's Studies in Communication* 24 (2001): 133.
24. Shelley Budgeon, *Choosing a Self: Young Women and the Individualization of Identity* (Westport, CT: Praeger, 2003), 162. For an updated version of power feminism, see Sonja K. Foss and Karen A. Foss, "Our Journey to Repowered Feminism: Expanding the Feminist Toolbox," *Women's Studies in Communication* 32 (2009), 36–62.
25. Renegar and Sowards, "Liberal Irony, Rhetoric, and Feminist Thought," 330.
26. Laura Brunell and Elinor Burkett, "Feminism," *Encyclopedia Britannica*, https://www.britannica.com/topic/feminism/
27. Alison Dahl Crossley, *Finding Feminism: Millennial Activists and the Unfinished Gender Revolution* (New York: New York University Press, 2017), 159.
28. Jennifer Baumgardner and Amy Richards, *Manifesta: Young Women, Feminism, and the Future*, 10th anniversary ed. (New York: Farrar, Straus and Giroux, 2010), 17.
29. Chela Sandoval, "U. S. Third World Feminism: The Theory and Method of Oppositional Consciousness in the Postmodern World," *Genders* 10 (1991): 4.
30. Rebecca Walker, "Becoming the Third Wave," *Ms.*, January/February 1992, 41.
31. Christie Launius and Holly Hassel, *Threshold Concepts in Women's and Gender Studies: Ways of Seeing, Thinking, and Knowing*, 2nd ed. (New York: Routledge, 2018), 15–16.
32. Crossley, *Finding Feminism*, 57, 164.
33. Stacy Gillis and Rebecca Munford, "Genealogies and Generations: The Politics and Praxis of Third Wave Feminism," *Women's History Review* 13 (2004): 171.

34 "Riot Grrrl Manifesto," History is a Weapon, https://www.historyisaweapon.com/defcon1/riotgrrrlmanifesto.html/
35 Kate Lockwood Harris, "Feminist Dilemmatic Theorizing: New Materialism in Communication Studies," *Communication Theory* 26 (2016): 159.
36 Crossley, *Finding Feminism*, 146.
37 Harris, "Feminist Dilemmatic Theorizing," 159–60.
38 Crossley, *Finding Feminism*, 154.
39 Crossley, *Finding Feminism*, 154.
40 Crossley, *Finding Feminism*, 155.
41 Crossley, *Finding Feminism*, 158.
42 Andi Zeisler, *We Were Feminists Once: From Riot Grrrl to CoverGirl®, the Buying and Selling of a Political Movement* (New York: Public Affairs/Perseus, 2016), 160.
43 Amy Annette, Martha Mosse, and Alice Stride, "Introduction," in *I Call Myself a Feminist*, ed. Victoria Pepe, Rachel Holmes, Amy Annette, Martha Mosse, and Alice Stride (London, UK: Virago, 2015), xiii.
44 Martha Rampton, "Four Waves of Feminism," Pacific University, October 25, 2015, https://www.pacificu.edu/magazine/four-waves-feminism/
45 Shugart, "Isn't It Ironic?," 133.
46 Shelley Budgeon, "Emergent Feminist(?) Identities: Young Women and the Practice of Micropolitics," *European Journal of Women's Studies* 8 (2001): 13.
47 Budgeon, *Choosing a Self*, 161.
48 Rosalind Gill, "Postfeminist Media Culture: Elements of a Sensibility," in *Gender and Women's Studies: Critical Terrain*, 2nd ed., ed. Margaret Hobbs and Carla Rice (Toronto, Canada: Women's Press, 2018), 393.
49 Stacy Gillis, Gillian Howie, and Rebecca Munford, "Introduction," in *Third Wave Feminism: A Critical Exploration*, ed. Stacy Gillis, Gillian Howie, and Rebecca Munford (New York: Palgrave Macmillan, 2007), xxviii.
50 Launius and Hassel, *Threshold Concepts in Women's and Gender Studies*, 145.
51 Diana Elena Neaga, "Feminism and Cosmopolitanism: Some Inevitable Connections," *Lex ET Scientia International Journal* 18 (2011): 330.
52 Constance Grady, "The Waves of Feminism, and Why People Keep Fighting Over Them, Explained," Vox, July 20, 2018, https://www.vox.com/2018/3/20/16955588/feminism-waves-explained-first-second-third-fourth/
53 Gillis and Munford, "Genealogies and Generations," 171.
54 Gill, "Postfeminist Media Culture," 390–400.
55 Nicola Rivers, *Postfeminism(s) and the Arrival of the Fourth Wave: Turning Tides* (Cheltenham, UK: Palgrave/Macmillan, 2017), 22.
56 Kira Cochrane, "The Fourth Wave of Feminism: Meet the Rebel Women," *The Guardian*, December 10, 2013, https://www.theguardian.com/world/2013/dec/10/fourth-wave-feminism-rebel-women/
57 Chamberlain, *The Feminist Fourth Wave*, 111.
58 "Transcript: Donald Trump's Taped Comments About Women," *New York Times*, October 8, 2016, https://www.nytimes.com/2016/10/08/us/donald-trump-tape-transcript.html/
59 Mary Pflum, "A Year Ago, Alyssa Milano Started a Conversation about #MeToo. These Women Replied," NBC News, October 15, 2018, https://www.nbcnews.com/news/us-news/year-ago-alyssa-milano-started-conversation-about-metoo-these-women-n920246/
60 Kira Cochrane, *All the Rebel Women: The Rise of the Fourth Wave of Feminism* (London, UK: Guardian, 2013), chap. 4.
61 Stephanie Herold, "Young Feminists to Older Feminists: If You Can't find Us, It's Because We're Online," Young Feminist Wire, July 19, 2010, http://yfa.awid.org/2010/07/young-feminists-to-older-feminists-if-you-cant-find-us-its-because-were-online/
62 Cochrane, *All the Rebel Women*, chap. 4.
63 Cochrane, *All the Rebel Women*, chap. 4.
64 Cochrane, *All the Rebel Women*, chap. 4.

65 Rivers, *Postfeminism(s) and the Arrival of the Fourth Wave*, 73.
66 Ealasaid Munro, "Feminism: A Fourth Wave?," *Political Insight* 4 (2013): 24, https://journals.sagepub.com/doi/10.1111/2041-9066.12021
67 Ien Ang, "I'm a Feminist but . . . 'Other' Women and Postnational Feminism," in *Transitions: New Australian Feminisms*, ed. Barbara Caine and Rosemary Pringle (New York: St. Martin's Press, 1995), 57–58.
68 Rivers, *Postfeminism(s) and the Arrival of the Fourth Wave*, 20.
69 Rivers, *Postfeminism(s) and the Arrival of the Fourth Wave*, 63.
70 Rosalind Gill and Christina Scharff, "Introduction," in *New Femininities: Postfeminism, Neoliberalism and Subjectivity*, ed. Rosalind Gill and Christina Scharff (New York: Palgrave Macmillan, 2011), 6.
71 Rachel Wayne, "The Problem with Call-Out Culture," Medium, January 12, 2019, https://medium.com/@rachelwayne/the-problem-with-call-out-culture-4edecb31e192/
72 Wayne, "The Problem with Call-Out Culture."
73 Adrienne Matei, "Call-Out Culture: How to Get it Right (and Wrong)," *The Guardian*, November 1, 2019, https://www.theguardian.com/lifeandstyle/2019/nov/01/call-out-culture-obama-social-media/
74 Rivers, *Postfeminism(s) and the Arrival of the Fourth Wave*, 48.
75 Shaun Scott, "In Defense of Call-Out Culture," City Arts, February 1, 2018, https://www.cityartsmagazine.com/defense-call-culture/
76 Sarah Sobieraj and Jeffrey M. Berry, "From Incivility to Outrage: Political Discourse in Blogs, Talk Radio, and Cable News," *Political Communication* 28 (2011): 19–41.
77 Munro, "Feminism," 25. The concept of a social privilege checklist was popularized by Peggy McIntosh, "White Privilege: Unpacking the Invisible Knapsack," in *Understanding Prejudice and Discrimination*, ed. Scott Plous (New York: McGraw Hill, 2003), 191–96.
78 Chamberlain, *The Feminist Fourth Wave*, 121.
79 Cochrane, *All the Rebel Women*, chap. 4.
80 Isabel Allende, *The Soul of a Woman: On Impatient Love, Long Life, and Good Witches* (New York: Ballantine, 2021), 13.

PART
TWO

PROCLAIMING IDENTITY

With this section, we begin our journey through five major change objectives—proclaiming identity, naming a problem, enriching a system, changing a system, and creating an alternative system. Although the chapters that follow show how twenty feminists are guided by these objectives, we see these different objectives as applicable to all kinds of change efforts, not just to feminism. Many change agents use strategies that address several or all of the objectives, depending on issues, conditions, and circumstances. Others find a focus that they are particularly passionate about and devote their energies to that one objective.

Proclaiming identity, the first objective for change that we identify and discuss, is grounded in the assertion that the "personal is political." When the assertion of identity is an organizing frame for change, identity markers such as gender, race, class, age, and ability are highlighted in a belief that "the most profound and potentially most radical politics come directly out of our own identity."[1] When marginalized individuals join with others to work to gain rights and recognition in society on the basis of shared identity attributes,[2] they are engaging in identity politics. Those who focus on identity in their change efforts demand respect for "the universal human potential in every person" and for the "intrinsic value of the different cultural forms in and through which individuals actualize their humanity and express their unique personalities."[3]

In the following four chapters, the strategies of Padma Lakshmi, Kat Blaque, Vilissa Thompson, and Lizzo rely on three assumptions that ground identity politics: (1) the intersectionality of identity categories influences how individuals see the world and how others respond to them, (2) marginalized individuals—dismissed and denigrated by the dominant culture—reclaim, value, and celebrate their identities, and (3) the process of proclaiming identity can result in both self-change and societal change. These assumptions reveal how marginalized groups that often are dismissed within a dominant culture find ways to reclaim, revalue, and assert those identities in order to instigate change.

Assumption 1: The intersectionality of identity categories influences how individuals see the world and how others respond to them.

A primary assumption for those who proclaim identity in their change efforts is that identity is composed of various intersectional and interactive characteristics. The identity markers that describe an individual—gender, race, class, age, religion, for example—are experienced simultaneously. All of these markers are integrated in a person's lived experience; they can't be separated.[4] For example, a woman is never perceived only as female because gender is always affected by factors such as race and class. Furthermore, because certain identity attributes have social capital and others function as social deficits, the interlocking of identity characteristics necessarily has social consequences in the world.

The notion of intersectionality first was theorized by several Black feminist scholars who understood the need to account for the multiple identities that influence the experience of oppression. In a document released in 1977, the Combahee River Collective laid the groundwork for the notion of intersectionality by explaining how all women of color face "manifold and simultaneous oppressions."[5] In 1982, Audre Lorde anticipated intersectionality with her statement that "there is no such thing as a single-issue struggle because we do not live single-issue lives."[6] The work of Patricia Hill Collins also was important to the development of the theory of intersectionality. She describes how the distinctive perspectives and experiences of Black women are shaped by the material and historical conditions of both race and gender.[7] Kimberlé Williams Crenshaw is credited with coining the term *intersectionality* in 1989 in an essay in which she used the analogy of individuals stacked in a basement to convey the impact of multidimensional marginalized identities.[8]

> Imagine a basement which contains all people who are disadvantaged on the basis of race, sex, class, sexual preference, age and/or physical ability. These people are stacked—feet standing on shoulders—with those on the bottom being disadvantaged by the full array of factors, up to the very top, where the heads of all those disadvantaged by a singular factor brush up against the ceiling. Their ceiling is actually the floor above which only those who are *not* disadvantaged in any way reside.... A hatch is developed through which those placed immediately below can crawl.... Those who are multiply-burdened are generally left below unless they can somehow pull themselves into the groups that are permitted to squeeze through the hatch.[9]

Together, these Black feminists articulated the distinctive position Black women occupy and laid the foundation for the application of intersectionality to all identity categories.

An encounter in New York City in May 2020 offers an example of how intersectionality affects social interactions. Amy Cooper, a white woman, had her dog off leash in Central Park in clear violation of posted policies. When Christian Cooper, a Black bird watcher, asked her to leash her dog, she refused. At that point, Christian started filming with his phone, knowing from past experience the importance of documenting such encounters. Amy responded by calling the police and telling them that a Black man was threatening her. By anticipating a positive and immediate response from police, she was relying on centuries of history in which white women have falsely and successfully accused Black men of various forms of assault.[10] She assumed, in other words, that she could use the intersection of her sex, race, and class to her advantage in racially targeting a Black man.[11]

Assumption 2: Marginalized individuals—dismissed and denigrated by the dominant culture—reclaim, value, and celebrate their identities.

Those who are assigned marginalized identities by the dominant culture are considered to be "strangers" or "bodies out of place"[12] and are likely to be treated as "not being entitled to be here."[13] Consequently, members of marginalized groups must manage the stereotypical, demeaning, and often degrading images of themselves that pervade mainstream culture, embodied in labels such as *dirty drunken Indians*, *bitches* and *dumb blondes*, and *perverts* and *faggots*, for example. Presented with such negative and contemptible stereotypes,[14] marginalized group members have two choices. They can adopt the negative self-image in a kind of internalized oppression, accepting the inferiority and invisibility bestowed upon them by the dominant culture,[15] or they can do as feminist theorist bell hooks suggests and "talk back."[16]

Talking back involves defying the norms of the dominant culture—norms that insist that a marginalized individual or group accept and stay contained within the labels provided by that culture. It is the first step in the process of decolonization, the "disruption of the colonized/colonizer mindset."[17] The term *decolonization* originally referred to the literal process by which colonies gained political independence from their colonizers, but now it is used more broadly to refer to any process by which members of a traditionally subordinated group reject the oppressive notions of identity provided by the dominant culture. According to hooks, decolonization occurs by means of rigorous critique—a critical gaze that is "fiercely confronting, challenging, interrogating."[18] Critique must be followed by a process of imagining, envisioning, and creating "new habits of being, different ways to live in the world"[19] in order to generate an alternative to the oppressive attitudes that govern the mindsets of both colonizer and colonized.

The emergence of queer identity is an example of the reversal and celebration of what once was a disparaged and colonized identity. As a negative epithet used to mark gay, lesbian, and bisexual individuals as social deviants and outcasts, the term *queer* began to be reclaimed in the 1980s as an umbrella term for anyone who was nonconforming because of "sexual and/or gender presentation and expression."[20] The organization Queer Nation was one of the first to publicly adopt the term, making use of it in chants such as "We're here! We're queer! Get used to it!"[21] As a result of the process of decolonization, many who do not conform to binary gender norms now use the term proudly to assert rather than hide their queer identities.

Assumption 3: The process of proclaiming identity can result in both self-change and societal change.

When marginalized individuals begin to take control of the ways their identities are seen, there can be positive personal and social consequences. In the process of "establishing, defining, and affirming" their selfhood,[22] such individuals shift from object to subject—from being objectified by others to becoming the subject of their own lives. In the process of extricating themselves from the definitions given them by others, marginalized group members engage in "psychological refurbishing and affirmation"[23] and come to experience a newfound sense of authenticity, authority, and agency.

Experiences of self-transformation among marginalized identities also can lead to change in the larger world. In his book *The Tipping Point*, writer Malcom Gladwell explains how self-change generates social change. Gladwell analyzed several dramatic social changes in the United States, such as the sudden drop in crime in New York City in the 1990s, to understand the moment of critical mass that tips an idea over the edge and causes what appears to be sudden social change. He discovered that a "small number of people" in a "small number of situations" start "behaving very differently," and that behavior spreads to others.[24] This phenomenon, sometimes called the *butterfly effect*, suggests that a "nearly imperceptible change . . . will produce a qualitative change in the system's behavior."[25] The butterfly effect was discovered by meteorologist Edward Lorenz, who found that incremental changes in weather in South America can generate changes in weather conditions in the United States the following month. Changes to self-definition on the part of marginalized individuals can similarly cause substantial changes to the larger systems of which they are a part.

Sit-ins at lunch counters in the South in 1960 to protest racial segregation provide an example of the larger social transformations that can accompany changes in self-definition. The first sit-in was held at a Woolworth's store in Greensboro, North Carolina, on February 1, 1960. Four Black students from North Carolina Agricultural and Technical College—Ezell Blair Jr., David Richmond, Franklin McCain, and Joseph McNeil—sat down at the lunch counter where only white people were allowed to eat and, as expected, they were denied service.[26] When the students refused to give up their seats, the police were called, but because the students did not provoke them in any way, the police did nothing, and the four students came back the next day. Within several days, 300 students had joined the protest, and heavy television coverage sparked sit-ins in other stores, restaurants, libraries, hotels, and beaches across the South. In their refusal to acquiesce to the system of racial segregation, the students chose to claim the "respect and dignity that segregation systematically denied them" and experienced "freedom as an inside job."[27] As the students themselves changed, society changed around them. Across the country that summer, many facilities were integrated, including the Woolworth's where the original sit-in of the Greensboro Four occurred.[28] Both self-change and larger social changes were accomplished as the Black student activists asserted and enacted their rights and their dignity.

■ NOTES

[1] Combahee River Collective, "The Combahee River Collective Statement," [1977], https://combaheerivercollective.weebly.com/about.html/

[2] Daphna Oyserman, Kristen Elmore, and George Smith, "Self, Self-Concept, and Identity," in *Handbook of Self and Identity*, 2nd ed., ed. Mark R. Leary and June Price Tangney (New York: Guilford, 2012), 93.

[3] Steven C. Rockefeller, "Comment," in *Multiculturalism and "The Politics of Recognition*," by Charles Taylor with commentary by Amy Gutmann, Steven C. Rockefeller, Michael Waltzer, and Susan Wolf (Princeton, NJ: Princeton University Press, 1992), 87.

[4] Jane Ward, *Respectfully Queer: Diversity Culture in LGBT Activist Organizations* (Nashville, TN: Vanderbilt University Press, 2008), 34.

[5] Combahee River Collective, "The Combahee River Collective Statement."

[6] Audre Lorde, "Learning From the 60s," BlackPast, August 12, 2012, https://www.blackpast.org/african-american-history/1982-audre-lorde-learning-60s/

[7] Patricia Hill Collins, *Black Feminist Thought: Knowledge, Consciousness, and the Politics of Empowerment*, 2nd ed. (New York: Routledge, 2000).

[8] Kimberlé Crenshaw, "Demarginalizing the Intersection of Race and Sex: A Black Feminist Critique of Antidiscrimination Doctrine, Feminist Theory and Antiracist Politics," *University of Chicago Legal Forum* (1989): 139–67.

[9] Crenshaw, "Demarginalizing the Intersection of Race and Sex," 151–52.

[10] Joan Walsh, "Birding While Black: Just the Latest Bad Reason for White People to Call Police," *The Nation*, May 26, 2020, https://www.thenation.com/article/society/amy-cooper-birding-police/

[11] Amy Cooper later apologized and acknowledged her privileges in a statement to the media: "When I think about the police, I'm such a blessed person. I've come to realize especially today that I think of [the police] as a protection agency, and unfortunately, this has caused me to realize that there are so many people in this country that don't have that luxury." See Walsh, "Birding While Black."

[12] Sara Ahmed, *Living a Feminist Life* (Durham, NC: Duke University Press, 2017), 143.

[13] Ahmed, *Living a Feminist Life*, 117.

[14] Charles Taylor, "The Politics of Recognition," in *Multiculturalism and "The Politics of Recognition*," by Charles Taylor with commentary by Amy Gutmann, Steven C. Rockefeller, Michael Waltzer, and Susan Wolf (Princeton, NJ: Princeton University Press, 1992), 25.

[15] bell hooks, *Killing Rage: Ending Racism* (New York: Henry Holt, 1995), 142–45.

[16] bell hooks, *Talking Back: Thinking Feminist, Thinking Black*, 2nd ed. (New York: Routledge, 2015), 5.

[17] bell hooks, *Outlaw Culture: Resisting Representations* (New York: Routledge, 1994), 5.

[18] hooks, *Outlaw Culture*, 156.

[19] bell hooks, *Race, Gender, and Cultural Politics*, 2nd ed. (New York: Routledge, 2015), 218.

20. Gust A. Yep, "Queer Theory," in *Encyclopedia of Communication Theory*, vol. 2, ed. Stephen W. Littlejohn and Karen A. Foss (Thousand Oaks, CA: Sage, 2009), 818.
21. "Queer Nation NY History," Queer Nation, https://queernationny.org/history/
22. Richard B. Gregg, "The Ego-Function of the Rhetoric of Protest," *Philosophy & Rhetoric* 4 (1971): 74.
23. Gregg, "Ego-Function," 74.
24. Malcolm Gladwell, *The Tipping Point: How Little Things Can Make a Big Difference* (New York: Little, Brown, 2000), 8.
25. Gladwell, *The Tipping Point*, 69.
26. "Greensboro Sit-In," History, February 4, 2010, https://www.history.com/topics/black-history/the-greensboro-sit-in/
27. Wesley C. Hogan, *Many Minds, One Heart: SNCC's Dream for a New America* (Chapel Hill, NC: University of North Carolina Press, 2007), 255.
28. In July 1960, the Woolworth's in Greensboro quietly integrated its lunch counter, and four Black employees of the store were the first to be served. See "Greensboro Sit-In."

CHAPTER
THREE

Padma Lakshmi

The two things I remember about every important day or evening of my life are what I wore and what I ate. In fact, I can say with great conviction that food has played a central role not only in my professional but also in my emotional life, in all of my dealings with loved ones and most of all in my relationship to myself and my body. I am what feeds me. And how I feed myself at any given moment says a lot about what I'm going through or what I need.[1]

Padma Parvati Lakshmi Vaidynathan is a model, actress, author, and host of the television cooking show *Top Chef*. She has transformed negative identity markers into positive attributes and hopes her journey will inspire others to do the same. Born in 1970 in Madras [now Chennai], India, Lakshmi's mother was a nurse and her father an executive with the pharmaceutical company Pfizer. When Padma was two years old, her parents divorced, and her mother moved to the United States "where she wouldn't be a pariah because of her marital status."[2] At the age of four, Lakshmi joined her mother, and one of her strongest memories from the long trip was the flight attendants, who offered her a vision of the life she wanted to live: "They were so glamorous. They wore these beautiful saris. They had these big bouffant hairdos and little Samsonite beauty cases. They got to travel the world and were independent and . . . didn't answer to anybody. They knew what was important in their lives, and they had the opportunity to see the world and do what they wanted."[3]

In the third grade, Padma was molested by a relative of her stepfather, and her mother sent her back to India to live with her grandparents. After her mother divorced her stepfather, she brought Lakshmi back to the United States, and the two of them moved to La Puente in Southern California to be near some of her mother's relatives. Padma was bullied by her high-school classmates—called *Black Giraffe* for being too tall and *Dictionary* for her extensive vocabulary and academic ambitions. In addition, her classmates made fun of her because she had brown skin but did not speak Spanish.[4] To try to fit in, Lakshmi changed her name—first to *Angie* and then to *Angelique*. Adding to the trauma and self-consciousness of her high school years, Padma's right hip and upper arm were shattered in a car accident when she was fourteen years old, leaving her with a seven-inch scar between her elbow and shoulder.

Lakshmi attended Clark University in Worcester, Massachusetts, graduating in 1992 with a BA with honors in theater arts and a minor in American literature. Padma's modeling career began during her senior year when she was studying abroad in Madrid, Spain. A friend who worked as a booker for a modeling agency encouraged her to audition with the agency, and her first assignment was as a fitting model for *Elle* magazine. When Lakshmi returned to the United States, she was hired by the Nina Blanchard Agency in Los Angeles to model for designers such as Emanuel Ungaro, Giorgio Armani, Gianni Versace, and Alberta Ferretti. She appeared on the covers of *Redbook, Vogue India, Cosmopolitan, L'Officiel India, Asian Woman, Avenue, Industry Magazine, Harper's Bazaar, Town & Country,* and *Newsweek* and was "the first Indian model to have a career in Paris, Milan, and New York."[5]

Despite her modeling success, Padma was insecure about her looks. Not until photographer Helmut Newton wanted to take her picture because of the scar on her arm did she begin to see her brown skin and scar as commercial assets. Lakshmi also worried that she was not taken seriously because she was relying on her looks and not using her brains. Eventually, however, Padma recognized the practical value of modeling: "Get over yourself. You're lucky to be doing what most people would kill to do. Just [sock] your money away and be thankful."[6] Lakshmi, in fact, used the money she made from modeling to pay off her student loans.

Padma has also pursued an acting career, which allows her to use her theatre degree and to do more than just "shut up and look pretty."[7] Lakshmi's first roles were in Italian pirate movies—*The Son of Sandokan* and *Caraibi*—roles she was given in part because her dark skin meant she could pass as Italian. She played Sylk, a pop diva, in *Glitter*; the alien princess Kaitaama in the TV series *Star Trek: Enterprise*; Sheila Bardez in the Bollywood film *Boom*; Geeta in *The Mistress of Spices*; and Princess Bithia in the TV series *The Ten Commandments*.

Padma's cookbook-writing career began in 1998 when she met Harvey Weinstein, movie producer and cofounder of Miramax Books, at a movie premiere. Lakshmi told him she "always had a fantasy to write a cookbook, because everyone wants to know what a model eats," and Weinstein agreed to publish it.[8] In *Easy Exotic: Low-Fat Recipes From Around the World*, published in 1999, Padma shares recipes that can be prepared in thirty minutes or less. The cookbook was selected as best first book at the Gourmand World Cookbook awards in Versailles, France. Her second cookbook, *Tangy, Tart, Hot and Sweet*, which features elegant international cuisine that is still easy to prepare, was released in 2007. *Love, Loss, and What We Ate*, a memoir about food, love, and family, appeared in 2016, and she published *The Encyclopedia of Spices and Herbs*, a culinary reference book, that same year. In addition to her cookbooks, Lakshmi has written essays for various newspapers and magazines, including the *New York Times*, *Vogue*, and *Harper's Bazaar*.

Padma's television-hosting career developed parallel to her writing career. In 1997, she was asked to host *Domenica In*, Italy's version of the *Today* show. In 2001, she joined the Food Network with a program called *Padma's Passport*, where she cooked recipes from around the world. She also hosted cooking specials for the British culinary tourism show *Planet Food*. Interested in continuing to host food programs, Lakshmi proposed a show to the television network Bravo that would feature conversations with interesting people around a dinner table, similar to what Padma does in her own home. Bravo, however, was already developing a show to be called *Top Chef* and asked her to host. Because Lakshmi was acting in a British mini-series when *Top Chef* began production, she joined as host for the second season, which began in 2006, and she became an executive producer for the show in 2013. *Top Chef* has been nominated for seven Emmys for "outstanding competition program," and in 2009, Padma received an Emmy nomination for "outstanding host for a reality or competition program."[9] In 2020, Lakshmi premiered a ten-episode series on Hulu called *Taste the Nation*, in which she traveled around the country spotlighting "the diverse and abundant cuisines found in communities around our nation."[10]

Padma has continued to expand on her brand by launching various collections related to food and fashion. Introduced in 2013, the Padma Collection is a line of dinnerware consisting of Moroccan ceramics and Turkish glass, and Easy Exotic is a more casual line of dishware that also includes specialty spices and teas. Lakshmi also premiered a jewelry line in 2013 called *PL*, inspired in large part by her Indian heritage. In 2015, she brought out a line of organic frozen foods called *Padma's Easy Exotic* that includes paella, rices, and lentils.

Padma has used her public platform to bring attention to issues that are important to her. She cofounded the Endometriosis Foundation of America, a nonprofit organization devoted to increasing awareness, education, and research about endometriosis, a disease in which the tissue that normally lines the uterus migrates to other parts of the body. Although she suffered from it her entire life, Lakshmi was not diagnosed with endometriosis until the age of thirty-six, when she had several surgeries to address the condition. She was told she would not be able to get pregnant because of the disease, but Padma gave birth to a daughter in 2010. She has been instrumental in advocating for more research on all aspects of endometriosis and its consequences. In 2009, she helped found and gave the keynote address at the opening of the Center for Gynepathology at the Massachusetts Institute of Technology. Appointed a visiting scholar at the center in 2018, she continues to give presentations to organizations, companies, and universities about endometriosis and its impact on those who suffer from it.

Since the rise of the #MeToo movement, Lakshmi has also been vocal about her experiences with sexual abuse, assault, and harassment. In an opinion piece she wrote for the *New York Times*, she described how, after telling her mother and stepfather that a relative had touched her inappropriately, she was sent away: "The lesson was: If you speak up, you will be cast out."[11] Padma also disclosed that she had been raped by an older boyfriend when she was sixteen.[12] As publisher of her first two cookbooks, Lakshmi is often asked about her experiences with film producer Harvey Weinstein, accused of multiple counts of sexual assault.[13] Padma explained that her experiences with Weinstein were not as "bad" as what many recounted: "I knew enough to keep somewhat of a distance, but I wasn't spared."[14]

In addition to speaking out about endometriosis and issues related to sexual assault and harassment, Lakshmi has served as a global ambassador for Keep a Child Alive, an organization that provides comprehensive HIV and AIDS treatment for children and families around the world. She has worked as well with the Center for Reproductive Rights, a legal advocacy organization whose mission is to advance reproductive rights. Padma also supports the Albert Kennedy Trust, which supports LGBTQIA+ and homeless youth in crisis, and the Somaly Mam Foundation, a charity dedicated to ending sex slavery.

Definition of Feminism

Lakshmi is "shocked some women hesitate to call themselves feminists. I don't know any woman who wants less compensation for the same work."[15] She acknowledges that "there was a trend among young women in the public eye to say: 'Oh no, I believe in equal rights but I wouldn't call myself a feminist.' . . . Feminism as a term got misaligned." For Padma, "feminism just means: you believe in equal rights for everybody. It has nothing to do with body politics." She continues, "I am a proud, flag-bearing feminist. You would have to be unhinged not to call yourself a feminist."[16] In fact, she believes most people are feminists because they believe in the goal of gender equality: "I think more people are feminists than they let on."[17]

Lakshmi doesn't limit feminism to women—everyone can and should be active in feminist movement. To achieve equality, both sexes must commit to addressing gender bias in whatever form it appears: "We all have bias. Women and men. In our personal and professional relationships and in our policies, we should acknowledge this bias and look for remedies."[18] Padma also emphasizes the intersection of gender and race in her approach to feminism. Because she is an immigrant and a "brown woman living in a man's world,"[19] she sees feminism as encompassing "equal rights, equal pay, immigration, health care. . . . Feminism is not just about feminine issues."[20] Feminism for her is a movement that is concerned with all issues that intersect with gender, and consequently, it is a movement that should be of concern to everyone.

Padma acknowledges several family members who are responsible for her strong sense of feminism. She first credits the strong women in her family: "I would say that I come from a long line of feminists. Maybe my grandmother wouldn't call herself one—just because she didn't know to—but if she started describing her philosophies, they would be in line with the notion that men and women are equal."[21] She calls her grandfather a "closet feminist" who supported her mother's divorce and move to the United States for the equal opportunities it offered.[22]

Change Strategies

Lakshmi's feminist strategies center on creating a positive self-definition from identity markers typically seen as unfavorable. They suggest that personal evolution is part of a feminist journey and that reflecting on life experiences and learning from them enhances and facilitates self-understanding. Her strategies—(1) reinterpreting identity markers, (2) enacting self-determination, and (3) sharing personal challenges—have been important to her own sense of identity and self-acceptance and serve as models she hopes will be useful for others.

Reinterpreting Identity Markers

Padma has transformed aspects of her identity that she initially saw as limiting into positive and empowering features. The first of these was her outsider status. Moving frequently between India and the United States made her feel like an outsider in both cultures: "I would never be fully at home in India again or fully at home in America."[23] Yet, she ultimately realized that these circumstances were responsible for her career: "Who would I have become if my mother and I had never immigrated to the States? My work in food, fashion, and jewelry was definitely a result of all my travels, of the comingling of cultural influences I got to experience because I'd always had one foot in the East and one foot in the West."[24]

Having absorbed Western ideals of beauty, Lakshmi's brown skin was also a source of dissatisfaction: "What I truly disliked . . . was my skin color *itself*."[25] She wished she could be a "more salable color, a better commodity, a toothpaste-commercial-worthy girl."[26] Ultimately, however, her "dark features"[27] were responsible for Padma's first major acting job in Italy, and she came to value her skin color as part of what gave her a distinctive appearance, although "it took years" for the "internalized self-loathing to fade."[28] Similarly, she initially resisted a modeling career because it meant she was not using her mind, and she felt guilty about the amount of money she was making. But she eventually accepted and appreciated what her appearance and the subsequent modeling career gave her: "It has allowed me to travel, allowed me to see the world. I did feel guilty about it. You know, I made in one day what it took my mother, for example, as a nurse to make in a month."[29]

The long scar on her arm was another impediment that Lakshmi at first viewed negatively. She called it a "stain"[30] for which she apologized at every modeling audition early in her career, saying things like, "before we begin, let me show you my hideous scar."[31] Those aspects about which Padma used to be self-conscious, such as her scar, have become "badges of honor" as her attitudes about her body have "grown and changed and morphed and evolved."[32] The scar has become a trademark—a "talisman" that she would not remove "even if a doctor could wave a magic wand and erase it from my arm."[33] What she initially considered impediments to her career, she explains, are "what sets me apart and makes me me."[34]

Enacting Self-Determination

Enacting self-determination is another strategy that characterizes Lakshmi's approach to identity. Just as she had defined several identity markers as impediments, so Padma initially had a limited sense of the extent to which she could determine the nature of her career: "I had mostly waited for the phone to ring, for someone to give me an assignment, whether it was modeling, writing, acting, or hosting.... I had chased every lead because those were the only opportunities I could see."[35]

The first instance in which Lakshmi realized that she could create her own opportunities was with cooking. She had always loved cooking but viewed it as nothing more than a personal fascination: "I was just a good cook with a bottomless curiosity about food. I had never in my life entertained the idea of a career in the culinary arts in any form."[36] Even after writing two cookbooks and hosting three cooking shows, she still questioned whether she could in fact call herself a *cooking expert*. Once Padma realized she could be deliberate about defining the trajectory of her career, she began to take her culinary hobby seriously and went from "hoping things would work out to seeing that they were working out." She continues, "maybe I'm not just flying by the seat of my pants,"[37] and she began to claim the identity that she realized she had had a major role in creating.

Lakshmi then began to imagine and design opportunities—to "think proactively about shaping my career" and "what I wanted it to look like."[38] She began to live "intentionally, with agency" and to do what she "really loved,"[39] actions that impacted both her career trajectory and her self-image. Her move from food to fashion is one example of this newfound sense of self-determination. More deliberate about all areas of her life, Padma embraces her identity as one that includes modeling, acting, cooking, fashion, and writing.

Sharing Personal Challenges

Lakshmi's transition from reacting to events to creating opportunities for herself was accompanied by a third strategy—sharing personal challenges. By sharing her insecurities about the various aspects of her career, Padma hopes to install confidence in other women to trust their capabilities and accomplishments, a process that was not easy for her. As host of *Top Chef*, for example, she felt she needed to prove she was more than just "a five-foot-niner plucked at random from the catwalk. . . . I had more than a touch of imposter syndrome."[40] Padma discloses her insecurities so that other women need not go through them. She wants women to claim their expertise and accomplishments—something that was hard for her to do at first.

Although difficult, Lakshmi has also become comfortable speaking about her personal experiences with both endometriosis and sexual assault. In discussing her experiences with endometriosis, she explains that "it was not my wish to get up in front of a room and talk about my vagina. . . . But I had to step up. I just want young women to know they're not alone."[41] Choosing to focus on "the greater goal," Padma speaks out so her experiences can be of value to other women: "What's more important—my privacy, or the lives of women? I chose the latter."[42] Lakshmi's decision to speak about her experience with sexual assault was similarly motivated by the desire to ensure that other girls and women be spared similar trauma: "Now, 32 years after my rape, I am stating publicly what happened. I have nothing to gain by talking about this. . . . I am speaking now because I want us all to fight so that our daughters never know this fear and shame and our sons know that girls' bodies do not exist for their pleasure and that abuse has grave consequences."[43] In acknowledging and sharing the most vulnerable aspects of herself, Padma hopes that she can help other women as they navigate similar challenges in their own lives.

Lakshmi is distinguished by several identity attributes that have shaped her life and career. Her feminist strategies—reinterpreting identity markers, enacting self-determination, and sharing personal challenges—highlight features of her identity and show how they changed over time as her own interpretation of them changed. In choosing to make salient dimensions of identity that she has both resisted and celebrated, she hopes to serve as a model for other women to do the same. In celebrating all aspects of her identity, Padma urges all women to similarly claim and assert who they are. Women, she says, no longer "have to turn the volume on ourselves down, diminish our personality and the force of our arguments." Instead, women should do just the opposite: "Summon all your strength, stack it upon itself and get taller. . . . Because if we women don't start sticking up for ourselves, . . . we bear even heavier consequences."[44]

■ REFLECTIONS

1. Lakshmi feels like an outsider in both the United States and India. Is there anything from your own life that makes you feel like an outsider in two cultures or systems? What have you done to try to resolve this discomfort?
2. Lakshmi first considered the scar on her arm a "stain," but it is now a trademark for her. Do you have something in your life that you once considered to be negative but that you now think of as a positive? What caused the transformation in your thinking?

3. Lakshmi has had several careers, including modeling, acting, writing, and hosting cooking shows, but she has only recently deliberately chosen to direct the trajectory of her professional life. How deliberate have you been about choosing your own career path?
4. Watch several episodes of *Top Chef* or another show that Padma Lakshmi hosts. What evidence do you see of her feminism in the show?
5. One of Lakshmi's change strategies is sharing personal challenges, and she talks openly about her experiences with endometriosis and sexual assault. Have you had an experience that you were able to navigate more easily because someone else spoke out about it?
6. How closely do Lakshmi's change strategies align with the assumptions outlined in the introduction to part 2? Are there any assumptions that you don't believe pertain to her approach to change?
7. In which feminist wave would you place Lakshmi and why?

■ Notes

[1] Padma Lakshmi, *Love, Loss, and What We Ate: A Memoir* (New York: HarperCollins/Ecco, 2016), 273.
[2] Lakshmi, *Love, Loss, and What We Ate*, 51.
[3] Padma Lakshmi, "20 Questions: Padma Lakshmi," interview by David Hochman, *Playboy*, November 15, 2012, https://web.archive.org/web/20180328050250/http://www.playboy.com/articles/20-questions-padma-lakshmi/
[4] Lakshmi now speaks English, Spanish, Italian, Tamil, and Hindi.
[5] Annabel Rivkin, "Salman's Siren," *Evening Standard*, April 7, 2006, https://web.archive.org/web/20060516160152/http://www.lakshmifilms.com/padma_lakshmi_press43.htm/
[6] E. Alex Jung, "Padma Lakshmi, Scars and All," *Vulture*, January 3, 2019, https://www.vulture.com/2019/01/padma-lakshmi-top-chef-profile.html/
[7] Lakshmi, *Love, Loss, and What We Ate*, 170.
[8] Nancy Jo Sales, "A Taste of Fame," *Vanity Fair*, December 2007, https://www.vanityfair.com/news/2007/12/lakshmi 200712/
[9] "Padma Lakshmi: Awards and Nominations," Television Academy, n.d., https://www.emmys.com/bios/padma-lakshmi/
[10] "Padma Lakshmi Is Getting Her Own Hulu Series," Grub Street, July 26, 2019, https://www.grubstreet.com/2019/07/padma-lakshmi-hulu-series.html/
[11] Padma Lakshmi, "I Was Raped at 16 and I Kept Silent," *New York Times*, September 26, 2018, sec. A, p. 27, https://www.nytimes.com/2018/09/25/opinion/padma-lakshmi-sexual-assault-rape.html/
[12] Lakshmi, "I Was Raped."
[13] Over eighty allegations of sexual abuse were leveled against Harvey Weinstein in 2017; he was arrested on May 25, 2018, convicted of two of five felonies on February 24, 2020, and sentenced to twenty-three years in prison. See "Harvey Weinstein Sentenced to 23 Years in Prison. Finally," Project When, March 11, 2020, https://projectwhen.org/our-insights/harvey-weinstein-sentenced-to-23-years-in-prison-finally/?gclid=CjwKCAjw5p_8BRBUEiwAPpJO69LMbD0BTh5In3o8VkM30PJakHhcYbq-8-5_gRnWOAl2UiH2MIqwAhoC7H8QAvD_BwE/
[14] Jung, "Padma Lakshmi."
[15] Padma Lakshmi, "Padma Lakshmi: 'I'm Shocked Women Hesitate to Call Themselves Feminists,'" interview by Claire Stern, *InStyle*, March 9, 2016, https://www.instyle.com/news/padma-lakshmi-shocked-women-hesitate-call-feminists/

[16] Donna Freydkin, "Padma Lakshmi on Taking Her Daughter to the Women's March," Yahoo!Life, February 2, 2017, https://www.yahoo.com/lifestyle/proud-flag-bearing-feminist-padma-lakshmi-on-taking-her-daughter-to-the-womens-march-152857487.html

[17] Allison P. Davis, "Let Padma Lakshmi Give You Some Great Dating Advice," The Cut, March 17, 2016, https://thecut.com/2016/03/padma-lakshmi-dating-feminist.html/

[18] Padma Lakshmi, "90% of People are Biased Against Women. That's the Challenge We Face," CNN Opinion, March 8, 2020, https://www.cnn.com/2020/03/08/opinions/women-gender-bias-padma-lakshmi/index.html

[19] Padma Lakshmi, "The Padma Lakshmi Interview: On Rushdie, Being a Feminist and Trump," interview by Raghav Bahl, The Quint, YouTube, February 8, 2017, 14:09, https://www.youtube.com/watch?v=sPJS5zIiPM0/

[20] Freydkin, "Padma Lakshmi on Taking Her Daughter to the Women's March."

[21] Davis, "Let Padma Lakshmi."

[22] Lakshmi, *Love, Loss, and What We Ate*, 51.

[23] Lakshmi, *Love, Loss, and What We Ate*, 183–84.

[24] Lakshmi, *Love, Loss, and What We Ate*, 223.

[25] Lakshmi, *Love, Loss, and What We Ate*, 103.

[26] Lakshmi, *Love, Loss, and What We Ate*, 124.

[27] Lakshmi, *Love, Loss, and What We Ate*, 140.

[28] Lakshmi, *Love, Loss, and What We Ate*, 124.

[29] Padma Lakshmi, "Brief But Spectacular," interview by Gwen Ifill, *PBS News Hour*, March 31, 2016, https://www.pbs.org/newshour/brief/177044/padma-lakshmi/

[30] Lakshmi, *Love, Loss, and What We Ate*, 167.

[31] Lakshmi, *Love, Loss, and What We Ate*, 159.

[32] Sales, "A Taste of Fame."

[33] Lakshmi, *Love, Loss, and What We Ate*, 167.

[34] Amy Marturana Winderl, "Why Padma Lakshmi Isn't Afraid to Show Her Scars Anymore," Self, September 19, 2016, https://www.self.com/story/why-padma-lakshmi-isnt-afraid-to-show-her-scars-anymore/

[35] Lakshmi, *Love, Loss, and What We Ate*, 175–76.

[36] Lakshmi, *Love, Loss, and What We Ate*, 22.

[37] Lakshmi, *Love, Loss, and What We Ate*, 175–76.

[38] Lakshmi, *Love, Loss, and What We Ate*, 176.

[39] Lakshmi, *Love, Loss, and What We Ate*, 176.

[40] Lakshmi, *Love, Loss, and What We Ate*, 70.

[41] Kara Mayer Robinson, "Padma Lakshmi Sheds Light on Endometriosis," WebMD, n.d., https://www.webmd.com/a-to-z-guides/features/padma-lakshmi-endometriosis#1

[42] Ros Krasny, "Top Chef's Lakshmi Details Struggle with Illness," Reuters, December 7, 2009, https://www.reuters.com/article/us-lakshmi/top-chefs-lakshmi-details-struggle-with-illness-idUSTRE5B63LU20091207/

[43] Lakshmi, "I Was Raped."

[44] Padma Lakshmi, "Padma Lakshmi Has a Call to Action for Women," *Teen Vogue*, July 21, 2020, https://www.teenvogue.com/story/padma-lakshmi-has-a-call-to-action-for-women/

CHAPTER
FOUR

Kat Blaque

Hi, I'm Kathryn. . . . I'm a transgender woman living in Los Angeles, California. I'm polyamorous, kinky, pro sex, pro feminism, lots of pro things. Oh, and I'm an atheist, too.[1]

Vlogger Kat Blaque proudly proclaims herself to be an "intersectionality salad"[2] composed of multiple identities important to her. Ascribed male at birth, Blaque was born in Lynwood, California, in 1990, and was adopted, along with a brother, by Black Christian parents. She was an androgynous child, a perception heightened when she developed breasts in her teenage years. Her father resisted her androgynous gender presentation and tried to make her conform to conventional masculinity. One of Kat's earliest memories is dancing like a ballerina on her birthday and her father telling her that boys do not dance like that. "I always wonder what my life would be like," she reflects, "if instead of telling me to dance more like a man, he saw that that's how I liked to dance and allowed me to just enjoy being myself."[3] Blaque muses, "My parents tried so hard to get me to be their son, but they didn't really understand that I was really their daughter."[4]

Kat began to identify as genderqueer in middle school. She came out to her parents as gay because, at the time, she did not know that being trans was an option. At the age of fifteen, she began to dress as a woman and to sew her own clothes—mostly turning T-shirts into dresses—because she was nervous about buying clothes in the women's section of department stores. She also began to research transitioning, and when she was eighteen, she decided to pursue hormone therapy. Because her father did not agree with her lifestyle, he announced that he would no longer support her, so she did sex work to secure the money for the hormones. At the end of her freshman year in college, she went full time as a trans woman and in her senior year changed her name to *Kathryn Wilkins*.

Blaque attended the California Institute of the Arts in Valencia, a university founded by Walt Disney and others for students in the visual and performing arts. She had learned about the school in the fifth grade and worked hard to be accepted into its character animation program. After graduating in 2012 with a BFA, Kat was offered an internship at Fox Animation Studios in Hollywood. She worked at the studio for three months before she realized that the animation industry was not for her: "I had worked so hard to get to a place where I thought I wanted to be, only to realize that I didn't want to be there. I remember going home on the subway, crying and wondering what I was going to do."[5]

Blaque decided to devote herself to vlogging, and because she was no longer working at the animation studio, she had the time and energy to put into *Kat Blaque*, the YouTube channel she has had since she was fifteen years old.[6] Vlogging was the perfect career for her, she decided, because it allowed her to use her animation degree, her own experiences, her knowledge, and her passion for educating about social issues: "I found a clear path, one that I probably wouldn't have found had I not had the experience of failing at something I had worked so hard to achieve. I think that was the pivotal moment of my life."[7] Kat's first videos were autobiographical videos about her transition, but then she began to make videos about feminism, racism, transness, intersectional identity, and the other issues that affect her. When Blaque did a video for BuzzFeed in 2015 about pronouns and why they matter for trans people, her online popularity soared.[8] The pronoun video had another impact as well: it outed her to many people who did not know she was trans. She discovered that "being visible wasn't as terrifying as she'd imagined" it would be.[9]

Kat is now a full-time vlogger who sees social media as a "powerful force for change and awareness."[10] She has several video series on her YouTube channel, including *Art Bitch*, where she shares videos related to makeup, art, and sewing. Another is *JSYK with Kat Blaque*, where she interviews guests whose lives have not been "represented in an honest and transparent way" such as "Jewish people of color, Indigenous folks, Trans people who have families post transition."[11] Blaque is most known for her series *True Tea*, where she educates viewers on issues of identity by addressing relevant current events, answers viewers' questions, and reflects on her own personal experiences.

Kat dramatically decreased the number of videos she posted in 2018 in part because she was lecturing extensively on college campuses. Because she had less time to create videos, interest in her *True Tea* series decreased, and she used the hiatus to rebrand her channel. She had grown tired of making "take-down" or reaction videos in which she responded to events or addressed issues that surfaced in the news around transness, racism, and sexism. Blaque also realized that she sometimes had been "trying to cultivate a respectable image" so that "people would take what she had to say seriously."[12] She is no longer trying to be "this pure goody two shoes"[13] and has committed to talking about issues "the way we're supposed to talk about them," rather than . . . trying to "pretty" them up.[14] Kat also wants to focus her primary channel on education: "Occasionally, I will talk about a popular issue, but ultimately I'm going to do what best serves my community. My heart is teachers and people who are looking for resources to teach their classes. That's my heart, and that's not always going to be the most popular thing. It's not always the trending thing, but it's going to be most useful for my community."[15]

Blaque is involved in a number of other media projects as well. She is active on Facebook, Twitter, and Tumblr and has appeared on online media outlets such as Everyday Feminism, BuzzFeed, Pride.com, and Upworthy. She has animated several short films, including *Sometimes You're a Caterpillar*, and has illustrated children's books, including *My Best Friend is a Monster*.

Kat's definition of herself is complicated and has evolved over the course of her many projects. One label that Blaque does not claim is *queer*. Although she did identify as queer when she first began exploring her gender identity as a young teenager, when she went to college, she realized that her self-identification was not as someone who is genderqueer. Instead, Kat discovered, she was "a very binary, straight trans woman."[16] Consequently, she has never really participated in a queer community, and she does not "really find a big safe haven in the LGBT community. I kind of just transitioned and started fading away from that crowd."[17] She continues to acknowledge the importance of queer spaces, but she does not feel the need to be personally connected to such spaces.

Blaque now performs a "very typical feminine gender expression" and conforms to society's image of how "a woman is supposed to look."[18] Because of how she presents, she is able to pass as a woman: "I leave the house tomorrow, and I am taken and accepted and embraced as a woman without challenge or question."[19] She recognizes that "the ability to pass is a privilege that not all trans people have or want,"[20] but because she is able to, she doesn't experience much discrimination in her life as a result of her transness. Kat recognizes that her "life would be so dramatically different" if she could not pass.[21]

Blaque added another identity to her intersectional mix when she acknowledged that she is kinky and engages in the practice of polyamory. She was in a monogamous relationship for five years but broke up with her partner when she realized that she was polyamorous: "I recognized that I needed certain things that he wasn't comfortable or interested in giving me."[22] Kat is quick to point out that she is "not polyamorous to have a lot of sex,"[23] which is how many people conceptualize the practice. Instead, she believes that "we have the capacity to maintain more than one relationship that is meaningful and committed."[24] She now has five such relationships but is "solo poly," meaning that none of these relationships is primary for her: "All these relationships fulfill me in a different way, and I feel very, very happy for now."[25]

Definition of Feminism

Blaque "used to be very much an anti-feminist"[26] until she came to understand that her work was actually feminist, and she now proudly claims the label. She does not believe, however, that individuals who advocate feminist objectives need to apply the label to themselves and their work; she "would rather somebody care about the issues than wear a badge that says 'feminism' on it."[27] Kat is baffled by those who reap the benefits of feminism and then question why feminism is needed: "I have a really hard time understanding how women can live in a society and not understand that sexism is a thing."[28]

Feminism, for Blaque, is "liberation from gendered oppression."[29] She explains that society views gender as a binary—male or female, man or woman—and then restricts individuals to certain roles and activities according to their gender assignments. She does not believe that gender should function this way and wants society to abandon binary gender roles and the limitations that accompany them: "Gender is fluid. . . . 'Masculine' and 'feminine' are a set of actions and expressions that anyone regardless of their biological makeup can perform."[30] Kat sees in history evidence that gender doesn't have to be the way it is constructed today: "What gender has meant to us as a society has changed over time. It was once seen as extremely masculine to wear makeup, high heels and dresses. Today these things are regarded as feminine."[31]

Although Blaque proudly embraces the feminist label, she differentiates between white feminism and womanism and identifies largely with the latter. She defines white feminism as "a form of feminism that focuses on the struggles of white women while failing to address distinct forms of oppression faced by ethnic minority women and women lacking other privileges."[32] She also notes that many white feminists are unconcerned about "supporting and empowering Black men, who are often an integral part of a Black woman's life and family."[33] In contrast, Kat aligns with Alice Walker's view of a womanist as "a woman who loves other women sexually or nonsexually and sometimes individual men sexually or nonsexually. She is committed to the survival and wholeness of ALL people, male and female. . . . She loves struggle, her people, and most of all, she loves herself."[34]

Another label Blaque gives to the perspective she takes on feminism is *intersectionality*, which is a response to a feminism that "largely focuses on white women's experiences."[35] Intersectionality is "the interconnected nature of social categorizations such as race, class and gender as they apply to a given individual or group, regarded as creating overlapping and interdependent systems of discrimination or disadvantage." It "is the belief that oppressions are interlocked and cannot be solved alone."[36] Thus, she explains, "people experience oppression differently because of their different identities. I am a black person; I am a woman; I am a trans woman, and these all impact the way power structures interact with me."[37]

Change Strategies

The various aspects of Kat's identity—her Blackness, her femaleness, her transness, and her nonnormative sexual behavior—serve as a vehicle for generating change. Although often seen as negative and used as the basis to marginalize and oppress, she proudly proclaims these identities as positive. Blaque seeks to correct the misconceptions around them and to encourage individuals to change how they think about and act toward those who claim such identities. She employs three major strategies that she hopes will lead to change: (1) revealing hidden perspectives, (2) controlling the narrative, and (3) facilitating further conversation.

Revealing Hidden Perspectives

Sharing her perspective on issues originating in her own experiences is a primary function of Kat's YouTube videos: "So much of what I do here is talk about the personal things I've experienced—the personal understandings and growth that I've had."[38] She expresses what is true to her because she believes "it's important that we do not dance around issues and that we speak with conviction about the things that impact us deeply."[39] Blaque promises her viewers that she will "share raw, unedited feelings"[40] in her videos as she responds to the questions and issues viewers raise in their emails and comments to her. Even if her stories are "embarrassing" and sometimes "scary" to tell, she wants to present an honest perspective rooted in her personal experiences.[41]

Kat shares her perspectives on myriad issues that affect her as a Black, trans, kinky woman. On the issue of race, for example, she discusses topics such as her rejection by the Black community and how Black women, in particular, do not accept her.[42] Blaque also discusses how her views on racism are often not trusted or given credence—she lacks "objectivity" because she is Black.[43] Another topic she covers is how white people who claim to be antiracist do not protest when white people say racist things to them.[44]

Kat often shares how she is treated as a trans woman as well. She discusses, for example, how cis women treat her[45] and refutes the myth that trans women transition primarily to engage in intimate relationships with straight men. She addresses the myth bluntly: "Straight men are not a prize. They're really not."[46] Blaque also discusses a common experience she has in her interactions with men: "I met a man who got along with me, who was attracted to me, who liked my personality, was impressed by my job . . . and was into me—genuinely into me—but that ended when they found out that I was transgender."[47]

Another common topic for Kat's videos and blogs is her experiences and practices around sex. She has revealed that she is a survivor of sexual violence, admitting that she has "been raped and assaulted several times" in her life.[48] Her sex-toy collection is another subject of frequent and frank discussion. She explains, for example, that her collection of silicone dildos was destroyed because she kept them "with her lube in my nightstand, and it spilled everywhere. And then my dildos melted."[49]

Blaque also freely discusses the BDSM community and the acts of bondage, discipline, dominance and submission, and sadomasochism involved in its sexual role-playing. She explains the reasons she loves BDSM practice, one of which is that it requires her to push herself physically. Kat's forthright description is typical of the honest insights she provides into experiences that are likely to be unfamiliar to many viewers.

> I kind of compare it to working out. . . . Sometimes when you're getting a workout in and you're trying to push your body a little bit more and more and more and more and more and then if you work out a lot, you get really kind of almost addicted to that feeling of pushing yourselves more and more and more and what it feels like after you've done that and you survived. For me, that's my personal high. I really enjoy being in a scene and taking on more than I initially think I could take and then being relaxed after I did that.[50]

Blaque has several aims for sharing her perspectives on such personal issues through her videos. She believes that her experiences and perspectives aren't represented accurately elsewhere, so she hopes to give people the opportunity to hear and learn from a different vantage point. Kat also wants to explain concepts that may be confusing to those who don't share these experiences and to encourage them to "critically apply" what they learn from her to things they themselves do.[51]

Controlling the Narrative

Because she is a representative of a number of identity groups, Blaque chooses to stay on YouTube "to just be there, be a face" and to allow people to look at her and say, "'I see myself in her.'"[52] In other words, she explains, "I became the representation that I desperately needed when I was a child."[53] As pleased as she is to be able to provide a public face for others who share her identities, she doesn't want to be defined exclusively by such characteristics: "I am generally the kind of person who doesn't like to organize around an identity or a moniker that could be projected onto me."[54] Clearly, the fact that she is Black and a woman is evident to anyone who meets her, but Kat's transness and her polyamorousness are not obvious. Although there was a time in her life when acknowledging her transness was important to her and she "could not have a conversation without acknowledging" it, she now says "it feels like a silly thing to bring up."[55] She does not believe individuals must always announce themselves in terms of where "they fall on the spectrum of sexuality or gender."[56] As Blaque explains, "Being trans is a footnote, you know, in my life—it's not the headline."[57] Her identities inform who she is "as a person, but they are not the beginning and ending of those things."[58]

Kat refuses to accept the inaccurate and erroneous narratives about her identities that others project on her. As she explains, "people have a narrative"[59] about who she is and believe they have the authority to define her. The narrative that typically is told about individuals with marginalized identities is that they live tragic and sad lives and have "been through so much."[60] Blaque resents such stories because they rob her of her "own agency" and of her own ability to interpret her experiences as she chooses—to say, in essence, "Hey, you know, actually, no, this is what my thing is."[61]

Kat is clear about how she wants to frame her experiences to construct an agentic and accurate narrative about her life. Although Blaque acknowledges that she has "been through a lot of shit," she notes that she has a choice about how to interpret her experiences, and she explains that she "would not be able to get to where I am now if I allowed myself to sit there and dwell" on them.[62] "I'm not someone who is immobilized by my past experiences that weren't so great," she explains. "I'm not someone who allows racism, sexism, transphobia, whatever stop me. That's not who I am."[63]

Facilitating Further Conversation

Kat understands that the experiences she has had as a Black trans kinky woman provide her with particular perspectives—and she recognizes that others have their own perspectives born from their own experiences. She thus encourages her viewers to share their perspectives with her so she can learn "things that I never ever considered."[64] Blaque wants to cultivate conversations in which she and others have the opportunity to consider "multiple perspectives"[65] because she recognizes that issues and perspectives are not "black or white" but exist "in various sorts of undulating shades of gray."[66] "I want to show that I don't know everything," she explains, "and I also want to show that not only am I open to sharing other perspectives but I'm also open to listening to other perspectives."[67]

One of the primary ways in which Kat encourages others to share their perspectives is by acknowledging that she is not always right. She often admits, "I might be wrong. I probably am wrong."[68] Blaque emphasizes her desire to be challenged by admitting that she often disagrees with herself, asserting that "I always say I'm of two minds on most things."[69] She also sees disagreement among individuals as normal: "I don't know. Maybe I'm just being weird here. I feel like it's normal for you to disagree with someone who is not you."[70] Kat believes "that it's really important to have your thoughts and opinions challenged . . . so I just guess I'm saying ultimately that I don't have a problem with people disagreeing with me."[71] In fact, she would like more disagreement than her videos usually prompt: "I wish more people would . . . disagree with me, challenge me, think about the ways in which our ideologies don't align. I just want people to be critical. I don't want for you to watch my channel and just blindly agree with everything I say."[72]

Sharing perspectives also means that Blaque does not criticize or condemn those who sharply disagree with her views. She realizes that individuals may choose not to accept her invitation to conversation, and she sees that choice as a perfectly appropriate one: "You might click on my shit and find out that you disagree with me so much that you don't even want to fucking watch me, and that's fine."[73] She has no desire, however, to interact with people who aren't really interested in listening to others' perspectives: "I'm not going to give space to people who are here just to be assholes . . . and I'm not going to engage with people who are here not to listen to what I'm actually saying. . . . If you're clicking on a video of mine and you're not interested in hearing what I'm saying, I really don't know why you're here."[74] Kat proclaims, "Learning, sharing, and growing is something I've been aspiring to do for the rest of my life. . . . I want to die . . . still trying to learn, share, and grow."[75] To continue to learn and grow, she invites those who are genuinely interested in doing the same to listen to her perspectives and to share their own with her.

Blaque openly embraces those aspects of her identity that are often judged to be negative, inappropriate, and deserving of scorn and oppression—her Blackness, femaleness, transness, and kinky sexual practices. By sharing her experiences, she provides insights into those identities that others may not have had the opportunity to contemplate. She recognizes that her perspectives aren't the only legitimate ones, however, and encourages others to share their diverse opinions, derived from their own experiences, so that everyone in the community has the chance to consider multiple perspectives. These change strategies enable Kat to be the agent of her own life, controlling representations rather than letting others decide who she is. She wants "people to see her as a functioning, vibrant . . . trans person."[76]

■ Reflections

1. Kat Blaque defines herself as an *intersectionality salad*. What key identities go into making you an intersectionality salad?
2. Blaque makes a distinction between feminism and womanism. If you are white, talk to a feminist who is a women of color about her experiences with these terms. If you are a woman of color, talk to a feminist who is white about her experiences with these terms. Do these conversations provide you with more context for and understanding of the distinction between the terms?
3. At times, her transness seems very important to Blaque; at other times, she calls it just a footnote. Is there something in your life that is sometimes all consuming and at other times is something you don't think about at all? What makes the difference in whether that event is at the foreground or in the background of your life?
4. Blaque wants to control the narrative that defines who and what she is. How important is it to control the stories others tell about you? If you are concerned about the alternative stories others tell about you, why? Is it not enough to simply tell your own story?
5. Blaque wants to facilitate conversations about experiences and perspectives with which many people are not familiar. How does this kind of sharing facilitate change, and what kind of change is achieved?

6. How closely do Blaque's change strategies align with the assumptions outlined in the introduction to part 2? Are there any assumptions that you don't believe pertain to her approach to change?
7. In which feminist wave would you place Blaque and why?

■ NOTES

[1] Kat Blaque, "Do I Even Belong in the Black Community?," YouTube, June 2, 2020, 5:57, https://www.youtube.com/watch?v=dM4dP-S2SWM/.
[2] Kat Blaque, "Sometimes I feel like I have to remind people that I am a boring straight girl," Facebook, December 13, 2015, https://www.facebook.com/kat.blaque.5/posts/954179834656837/.
[3] Kat Blaque, "I remember when I was a kid I used to love Power Rangers," Facebook, October 9, 2014, https://www.facebook.com/kat.blaque.5/posts/i-remember-when-i-was-a-kid-and-i-used-to-love-power-rangers-for-halloween-one-y/728861747188648/.
[4] Blaque, "I remember when I was a kid."
[5] Kat Blaque, "YouTube Celebrity Kat Blaque Discusses Her Life, Intersectionality and Technology," interview by Bill Reeve, Accelerate with Google, https://accelerate.withgoogle.com/stories/youtube-celebrity-kat-blaque-discusses-her-life-intersectionality-and-technology/
[6] The name she gave herself and her channel came from two sources: *Kat* is a derivative of *Kitty*, a name she often used when she was in the process of transitioning, and her last name comes from the fact that she is Black.
[7] Blaque, "YouTube Celebrity."
[8] Kat Blaque, "Why Pronouns are Important to Trans People," YouTube, May 28, 2015, https://www.youtube.com/watch?v=WXWmv1-4xFg&t=8s/
[9] Desirée Guerrero, "After Being Outed, Kat Blaque Became a Role Model for Trans Youth," *The Advocate*, May 1, 2017, https://www.advocate.com/advocate50/2017/5/01/blaque-out/
[10] "Kat Blaque," AAE Speakers Bureau, https://www.aaespeakers.com/speakers/kat-blaque/
[11] Kat Blaque, "Live for Yourself: An Interview with Kat Blaque," interview by Mandy Grathwohl, *Matador Review*, Summer 2019, http://www.matadorreview.com/kat-blaque/
[12] Sandra Song, "Kat Blaque Doesn't Give a Fuck," Paper, July 24, 2019, https://www.papermag.com/kat-blaque-youtube-2639319887.html?rebelltitem=1#rebelltitem1/
[13] Kat Blaque, "Why I'm Rebranding My Channel," YouTube, February 19, 2019, 29:48, https://www.youtube.com/watch?v=NZZ5CGJD2qk/
[14] Song, "Kat Blaque."
[15] Blaque, "YouTube Celebrity."
[16] Guerrero, "After Being Outed."
[17] Kat Blaque, "YouTuber Kat Blaque on Pride, Identity, and What It Means to Go Viral," interview by Nandita Raghuram, Mashable, June 6, 2019, https://mashable.com/article/kat-blaque-youtube/
[18] Kat Blaque, "Why Trans People Will Never Be Accepted," YouTube, January 14, 2020, 7:28, https://www.youtube.com/watch?v=zyiSCY0ij7Y/
[19] Kat Blaque, "Do I Belong in Black Cis Female Spaces?," YouTube, July 28, 2020, 32:47, https://www.youtube.com/watch?v=qwImsFis7KQ/
[20] Kat Blaque, "Defecating While Trans," *HuffPost*, March 30, 2016, https://www.huffpost.com/entry/defecating-while-trans_b_9560736/
[21] Blaque, "Do I Belong in Black Cis Female Spaces?," 34:23.
[22] Kat Blaque, "What Quarantine Taught Me About Interracial Relationships," YouTube, May 12, 2020, 21:17, https://www.youtube.com/watch?v=AiBlHcgEI5U/
[23] Kat Blaque, "Is Polyamory All About Sex?," YouTube, April 14, 2020, 3:43, https://www.youtube.com/watch?v=FV7AqNHtu0w/
[24] Blaque, "Is Polyamory All About Sex?," 6:23.
[25] Kat Blaque, "Why I Don't Want Marriage, and Love Polyamory," YouTube, June 30, 2020, 9:55, https://www.youtube.com/watch?v=DbT2WDTanDw/

26. Kat Blaque, "Women Against Feminism," YouTube, 2:45, https://www.youtube.com/watch?v=SgyHw9_MP5A/
27. Blaque, "Women Against Feminism," 3:14.
28. Blaque, "Women Against Feminism," 7:32.
29. Kat Blaque, "Why Feminists Never Disagree with Each Other," YouTube, April 12, 2017, 2:09, https://www.youtube.com/watch?v=_tFCHG5STcA/
30. Kat Blaque, "Cis people are literally so simple," Facebook, July 1, 2015, https://www.facebook.com/kat.blaque.5/posts/cis-people-are-literally-so-simple-i-dont-even-like-explaining-things-to-them-be/868128129928675/
31. Blaque, "Cis people are literally so simple."
32. Kat Blaque, "What Is: Womanism," YouTube, January 23, 2019, 1:24, https://www.youtube.com/watch?v=xWgOpOkSCOI/
33. Blaque, "What Is: Womanism," 2:25.
34. Blaque, "What Is: Womanism," 1:48.
35. Kat Blaque, "What Is: Intersectionality," Facebook, January 17, 2019, 3:06, https://www.facebook.com/watch/?v=289286648567884/
36. Blaque, "What Is Intersectionality and Why is It Important?," 3:04.
37. Blaque, "YouTube Celebrity."
38. Kat Blaque, "Why I've Been Quiet," YouTube, June 11, 2020, 3:55, https://www.youtube.com/watch?v=S4Mq6OU5ekY/
39. Kat Blaque, "Let me make something very clear," Facebook, September 7, 2014, https://www.facebook.com/kat.blaque.5/posts/let-me-make-something-very-cleari-am-turning-24-next-week-i-may-be-young-and-i-m/713823802025776/
40. Blaque, "I'm Trans, but I'm Not 'Queer,'" 0:35.
41. Kat Blaque, "Why I Hate Being a Youtuber," YouTube, July 7, 2020, 6:13, https://www.youtube.com/watch?v=dDaviz3aYAU/
42. Blaque, "Do I Belong in Black Cis Female Spaces?"
43. Song, "Kat Blaque."
44. Kat Blaque, "Friending and Forgiving Racists," YouTube, July 18, 2020, https://www.youtube.com/watch?v=s3-z6G2p80A/
45. Blaque, "Do I Belong in Black Cis Female Spaces?"
46. Kat Blaque, "Did I Transition to Date Heterosexual Men?," YouTube, June 23, 2020, 9:37, https://www.youtube.com/watch?v=AbX7jr2NvCU/
47. Kat Blaque, "Am I Jealous of Cis Women?," YouTube, August 25, 2020, 16:21, https://www.youtube.com/watch?v=fC-HrgpwUmY/
48. Kat Blaque, "My Experience with Ron Jeremy," YouTube, June 24, 2020, 0:09, https://www.youtube.com/watch?v=zetAhyagbV4/
49. Kat Blaque, "Am I Too Sex Positive?," YouTube, June 9, 2020, 14:32, https://www.youtube.com/watch?v=Lem6_4j81Uc/
50. Kat Blaque, "Why I Love the BDSM Community," YouTube, September 1, 2020, 19:59, https://www.youtube.com/watch?v=9kumSGuAI4Y/
51. Kat Blaque, "So You Disagree with Me, Huh?," YouTube, August 11, 2020, 15:37, https://www.youtube.com/watch?v=wREEVfGhKnM/
52. Blaque, "I'm Trans, but I'm Not 'Queer,'" 22:36.
53. Kat Blaque, "The Power of Words," YouTube, December 2, 2020, 10:00, https://www.youtube.com/watch?v=HMKPLI90haI/
54. Blaque, "I'm Trans, but I'm Not 'Queer,'" 4:41.
55. Blaque, "I'm Trans, but I'm Not 'Queer,'" 18:33.
56. Kat Blaque, "My 'Problem' with Coming Out," YouTube, July 2, 2019, 30:59, https://www.youtube.com/watch?v=MOYAPidGap0/
57. Blaque, "I'm Trans, but I'm Not 'Queer,'" 15:20.
58. Blaque, "What Quarantine Taught Me," 10:29.
59. Kat Blaque, "Am I a Victim or a Survivor?," YouTube, June 16, 2020, 5:16, https://www.youtube.com/watch?v=A_x-uQojpcM/

60 Blaque, "Am I a Victim or a Survivor?," 5:38, 4:25.
61 Blaque, "Am I a Victim or a Survivor?," 5:00.
62 Blaque, "Why I'm Rebranding My Channel," 27:22.
63 Blaque, "Why I'm Rebranding My Channel," 28:56.
64 Blaque, "Why I'm Rebranding My Channel," 25:27.
65 Blaque, "Do I Belong in Black Cis Female Spaces?," 6:04.
66 Kat Blaque, "Jeffree Star and Performative Activism," YouTube, July 24, 2020, 5:13, https://www.youtube.com/watch?v=_8PbzhrIU1A/.
67 Blaque, "Why I'm Rebranding My Channel," 24:00.
68 Blaque, "Why I'm Rebranding My Channel," 24:30.
69 Blaque, "So You Disagree with Me," 0:06.
70 Blaque, "So You Disagree with Me," 4:19.
71 Blaque, "So You Disagree with Me," 7:30.
72 Blaque, "So You Disagree with Me," 15:20.
73 Blaque, "So You Disagree with Me," 14:50.
74 Blaque, "Do I Belong in Black Cis Female Spaces?," 5:14.
75 Blaque, "Why I'm Rebranding My Channel," 22:58.
76 Blaque, "I'm Trans, but I'm Not 'Queer,'" 15:47.

CHAPTER FIVE

Vilissa Thompson

I am disabled. I was disabled in the womb, and was born disabled. Being disabled is an important part of my identity and human experience as being Black, a woman, American, heterosexual, and cisgender.... I cannot transcend disability; instead I can transcend from the ableism, discrimination, and stereotypes that are associated with being disabled.[1]

A writer, consultant, activist, and influencer working at the intersection of critical race theory and disability theory, Vilissa Thompson is a hard-of-hearing Black little woman (she is under four feet tall), born with osteogenesis imperfecta or brittle-bone disease. She wants to use her identity to educate others about issues of disability, especially as they affect women of color. Thompson was born in 1985 in Winnsboro, South Carolina. She was given six to eight years to live, so her mother wanted to place her in a children's home, anticipating the "hardships of raising a child with such a potentially short life span."[2] Instead, Vilissa's grandmother raised her as her own daughter, refusing to let Thompson feel out of place because of her disabilities.

Vilissa attended Winthrop University in Rock Hill, South Carolina, graduating in 2008 with a major in psychology. In 2012, she earned an MA degree in social work, also from Winthrop University. As part of her program, she interned at an HIV/AIDS organization and a kidney-dialysis center, and her capstone project focused on the experiences of homeless female veterans.[3] Thompson now chooses to concentrate what she calls her *social work perspective* on macro rather than micro concerns—on communities and systems—rather than on the single issues she examined in her master's program. At the core of her concerns is creating awareness around disability: "Shifting our mindset from a pity framework to one that sees disability as part of the diverse human experience is a priority for me. I am not a tragedy because I am in a wheelchair, nor am I an inspiration because I am living my life. Calling out how toxic views of disability can damage disabled members means that ignorance can no longer be the excuse—if you read my writings and the stories of disabled Black people, you can no longer proclaim that we do not exist."[4]

Vilissa considers herself a social media maven, and she works to identify significant and trending content around women and disabilities to share with her online community. Thompson started Ramp Your Voice! in 2013, a website focused on promoting empowerment and self-advocacy among people with disabilities. Her stated mission is to educate, inform, and empower—"a way of sharing an [intersectional] perspective as a disabled person—combining my social work, psychology, and African American studies educational backgrounds with my lived experiences as a Black disabled woman. I wanted to share my thoughts and views about topics such as sexuality, dating, politics, education, and others because I didn't see many women who looked like me writing about these issues."[5] At the same time, Thompson wants to give other disabled women "the space to tell their stories [because] that's the work we need people to be able to do to be empowered.... Just giving them the space to tell their stories without judgment."[6]

In 2016, Vilissa created a syllabus of resources that addresses and contextualizes the experiences of Black disabled women: "I decided that as someone who views herself as an 'educator'..., it would be fitting to create a compilation of books, essays/articles, speeches, music, and other bodies of work that accurately explains the diverse forms of Blackness that exist for Black women."[7] The syllabus, which Thompson sees as a living document to be updated as new materials become available, contains resources on Black feminism and womanism, identity and the Black disabled body, and Blackness in America. For many of the entries, Vilissa writes reviews and commentaries, and she encourages those who visit her website to do the same and to suggest additions to the syllabus.

In May 2016, after reading an article in which only white women with disabilities were discussed, Thompson originated the hashtag #DisabilityTooWhite to point out how disabled people of color are often left out of representations of and conversations about disability: "The hashtag forced me, and others, to discuss the elephant in the room—the racism, invisibility, erasure, lack of representation, and othering of disabled people of color."[8] The hashtag went viral, generating 13,000 tweets in a twenty-four-hour period,[9] and Vilissa appreciates how the hashtag continues to resonate with the disabled community: "I find great joy in learning how fellow advocates have mentioned the hashtag in their work, and introduce others to the meaning attached to it." She hopes the dialogues that occurred because of the hashtag will continue until "we will no longer need the hashtag."[10] Thompson remains committed to the ends for which #DisabilityTooWhite was created: "So for me the hashtag really speaks to all of those things that we have failed to do as a community—to be inclusive and accepting, and to have those conversations about disability and what it means to be of color and disabled, and some of the disparities surrounding that."[11]

In 2017, Vilissa began cohosting, with Neal Carter, a podcast called *Wheelin' & Dealin'*, which dissects politics from an intersectional lens. In 2019, Thompson became a senior fellow at the Center for American Progress, a think tank devoted to a progressive agenda for the United States, where she writes articles and develops discussion guides around reproductive and disability issues. She is also working on a children's book that she hopes will increase the visibility of disabilities in children's literature and call attention to disabled Black authors.

Vilissa's blogging and writing are supplemented by speaking and consulting about disability issues with helping professionals, organizations, educators, and activists. In 2018, Thompson joined CCMNT Speakers, a firm that features speakers at the intersection of activism and academia. Vilissa's presentations focus on disabled Black women and women of color as well as issues of intersectionality, racism, white supremacy, education, politics, and gender. She helped with Elizabeth Warren's "Protecting the Rights and Equality of People with Disabilities" plan in 2020 when Warren was seeking the Democratic nomination for president of the United States and also began working with Movement for Black Lives (M4BL), serving as an accessibility consultant for its events.

Thompson's accomplishments were acknowledged in 2018 when she was featured in the list of "Woke 100 Women" compiled by *Essence* magazine. Vilissa hopes to continue to contribute to disability studies by eventually teaching in a social work program; she feels social work is "very behind when it comes to understanding disability and really having disabled practitioners in the classroom."[12] She wants to help social workers address issues of intersectionality and disability in their programs and practices so that they can more fully and competently address the needs of their clients. Thompson is committed to doing whatever she can to bring about changes to the field of social work and society at large: "For me basically, I like to call myself a rightful troublemaker, because I don't feel that you're really doing good work, particularly if you're doing social justice, you know, if you're not shaking the table, if you're not ticking off somebody."[13]

Definition of Feminism

Vilissa identifies as a womanist rather than a feminist because she believes the *womanist* label better encompasses her three primary identities—woman, disabled, and Black. Womanism, rooted in the racial and gendered histories, experiences, and oppression of Black women, is a social theory that recognizes, respects, and accepts all of Thompson's identities: "I have my issues with feminism in relation to its history of ignoring and/or muffling the voices of disabled and Black women within the movement."[14] That terms such as *womanism* and *misogynair* (anti-Black sexism faced by Black women, often at the hands of Black men)[15] are not widely known offers additional evidence of the exclusion of women of color from feminist movement. If feminism continues to privilege the "experiences of white, able-bodied, neurotypical women,"[16] Vilissa is not interested in claiming the label.

At the same time, however, Thompson acknowledges that she supports the principles of feminism[17] and that most people would describe how her grandmother raised her as *feminist*: "I do not think my grandmother would have considered herself a feminist but some of the things she taught me about being true to your values and challenging leadership, leads into a lot of that."[18] Her grandmother, for instance, stressed the importance of women having their own money and doing more than just following a man around. Vilissa also learned "to be fearless, to do what is right, and not what is convenient. I do not have to follow the crowd, and I can be different, and that is just fine."[19] She elaborates: "I think it is so easy to become self-conscious when you are shaking and rocking the boat and realizing that people will not like you because of it. . . . I am going to use my head when I want to map out a plan and my heart to keep the fire burning when it wants to go dim. It means staying true to what brought you into this work and staying true to it until the end."[20]

Change Strategies

Thompson's change strategies emerge from her identity as a Black disabled woman and social worker. Vilissa wants to empower those with disabilities to share their stories and to help dispel the "myths surrounding disabilities and erroneous associations of disability with weakness."[21] By speaking out, more accurate information about disabled people becomes available, and services, policies, and education around disability issues can become more nuanced as well. Her strategies—(1) centering intersectionality, (2) holding others accountable, and (3) educating responsibly—function to encourage not only the disability community but all communities to understand and "'get woke'" on race, disability, and other intersectional identity categories.[22]

Centering Intersectionality

Centering intersectionality—demanding that diverse disabled experiences be represented in discourses of all kinds—is a primary strategy that characterizes Thompson's change efforts.[23] In her assertion that she is "boldly disabled" and "unapologetically and fiercely black,"[24] Vilissa models the intersectionality she highlights. She sees her mission as "making good trouble to shake up the status quo,"[25] and her writing, blogging, and speaking help produce the outcome that she wants to see—a world with "more diverse disabled voices."[26] For Thompson, if any identity issue is excluded from political, social, and policy discussions, those discussions will "always be incomplete."[27]

Vilissa believes everyone can become aware of the need to look at issues through an intersectional lens. Also crucial are discussions about the impact of intersectionality on particular policies: "So I think that's the thing that I really hold myself accountable is to dig deeper and to understand who are on the fringes of certain issues when certain policies are enacted. Or if certain policies are enacted, who would be most disadvantaged at the end of the day?"[28] Thompson wants discussions around intersectionality to take into account the real consequences of intersectionality on people's lives.

Holding Others Accountable

Vilissa's strategy of centering intersectionality is reinforced by holding others accountable for how they approach issues of disability and intersectionality. Although she appreciates the opportunity to work with groups in the Black community—what she calls "the black spaces that get it" and who are "willing to do the work"[29]—she recognizes that the real work is with those who do not get it. Thus, she calls out individuals, professionals, organizations, educators, and activists and asks them to be conscious of their biases and to take responsibility for "any type of erasure or harm or exclusion or coopting or tokenism that transpires" in regard to disabilities.[30]

Thompson fully acknowledges that most people are ignorant about issues around disability, but this ignorance should not be used to exempt any group from educating themselves. Vilissa is equally hard on people of color, disabled people, and white people in terms of their failure to attend to disability, intersectionality, and discrimination. Her critique begins with people of color who, although accustomed to dealing with various forms of oppression, often fail to think about disability, even though "everybody knows somebody with a disability."[31] Thompson similarly faults the disabled community for its lack of attention to intersectionality: "The disabled community is very uneducated on experiences that go beyond disability; meaning that anything that discusses differences outside of disability meets great resistance."[32] She also calls out white people with disabilities for thinking only about how they experience oppression and ignoring all other kinds: "I always say that your disability does not nullify your white privilege."[33] For Vilissa, then, every individual and group needs to be accountable for what they know and do not know about how disabilities intersect with other identity categories.

Thompson employs a direct style that complements how she holds others accountable. She insists on being honest and forthcoming because only then are dialogue, discussion, and learning possible: "I really want to continue to be that space to where you get your realism" or what she describes as "the in-your-face truth that I think sometimes isn't always there."[34] She wants the messages she offers to be fully authentic, by which she means they are "more empowering, more real, and more self-identifying."[35] According to Vilissa, when individuals are able to acknowledge the limits of their worldviews and have access to information that is accurate and truthful, change becomes possible.

Educating Responsibly

The role of educator is a large part of Thompson's identity as a Black female disabled activist, and "educate" is first on the list of services on Ramp Your Voice! Her approach to education can be seen in the syllabus of resources on Black disabled women that she developed for those who ask her how to deal with issues around disability. Rather than simply giving them the information—which would amount to her doing the work for them—Vilissa created the syllabus as a means of self-education: "Here's a starting point for you to educate yourself" about why "the black disabled experience as a whole matters and why you need to be more conscious of the way that you talk about disability, the way that you bring about disability topics in conferences and panels."[36]

Thompson's sense of responsibility means she takes a compassionate approach to education. As a social worker, Vilissa understands that education around issues of disability needs to take into account where each individual is: "We have to realize that some people have to find their way, and you have to give people space to do that. I think for me, that's the social worker in me. . . . Everybody's on a journey." She acknowledges that she herself did not "self-identify as disabled" until she started "doing activism. And I've been physically disabled my whole life. So in a way, who am I to judge?"[37] Not only does Thompson want to respect where each person is in terms of thinking about disability, but she also wants to be attentive to how she presents her ideas: "We have to kind of check ourselves and also check our approaches and how we're attracting people."[38] As an educator, she sees herself as a vehicle through which others are empowered to come to their own understanding of issues and to incorporate those insights into "their own work, within their own lives."[39]

Thompson's change strategies, designed to proclaim identity, function by educating those with whom she interacts about intersectional identities, especially as they impact disabled people of color. She wants her audiences to become aware of and accountable for the attitudes they hold about intersectionality and disability, and she is willing to help facilitate their understanding of these issues. Above all, Vilissa wants those with whom she works to see that disability is not a cause for pity or despair but something to be celebrated as a real and meaningful dimension of identity. She herself models this approach in her self-description: "I use a wheelchair, have brittle bones, am little/short, and hard of hearing—what a beautiful combination to be."[40]

■ Reflections

1. In the quote that opens the chapter on Thompson, she makes a distinction between her disabilities and the ability to transcend those. Is there something similar in your life that you transcend?
2. Thompson calls out those who are ignorant of disability issues. Are you ignorant about an identity that may be very important to others? What might you do to learn about and address this identity?

3. One of Thompson's primary change strategies is to center intersectionality. Take an issue of concern to feminists. Compare and contrast how it was addressed before intersectionality was highlighted and how it is being addressed through an intersectional lens. What difference does intersectionality make?
4. Thompson wants people to educate themselves about Black disabled women. Choose a topic that particularly interests you from Thompson's syllabus (http://www.rampyourvoice.com/black-disabled-woman-syllabus-compilation/) and read several of the resources she recommends. What did you learn that especially surprised you?
5. Thompson wants to educate people about Black disabled women, and she believes in starting from a compassionate place to take into account where individuals are in the learning process. At the same time, she is often very blunt about individuals' ignorance of issues because she believes they have a responsibility to be aware. How can these two stances be reconciled?
6. How closely do Thompson's change strategies align with the assumptions outlined in the introduction to part 2? Are there any assumptions that you don't believe pertain to her approach to change?
7. In which feminist wave would you place Thompson and why?

■ NOTES

[1] Vilissa Thompson, "There Is No Such Thing as Transcending Disability," Ramp Your Voice!, August 24, 2016, http://www.rampyourvoice.com/?paged=5/
[2] Clarkisha Kent, "Black History Now: Vilissa Thompson—Activist, Writer, Licensed Social Worker and Disability-Rights Advocate," *Essence*, February 11, 2019, https://www.essence.com/black-history-month-2019/black-history-now-vilissa-thompson/
[3] Vilissa Thompson, email message to Karen A. Foss, April 4, 2020.
[4] Vilissa Thompson, "Ramp Your Voice: An Interview with Vilissa Thompson," interview by Trimiko Melancon, Black Perspectives, African American Intellectual History Society, March 18, 2017, https://www.aaihs.org/ramp-your-voice-an-interview-with-vilissa-thompson/
[5] Vilissa Thompson, "RYV! Services," Ramp Your Voice!, http://www.rampyourvoice.com/?page_id=105
[6] Vilissa Thompson, "Supporting Black Women with #Disabilities with Vilissa Thompson," interview by Day Al-Mohamed, Day In Washington, July 23, 2018, 19:16, http://dayinwashington.com/supporting-black-women-with-disabilities-with-vilissa-thompson/
[7] Vilissa Thompson, "Black Disabled Woman Syllabus: A Compilation," Ramp Your Voice!, May 5, 2016, http://www.rampyourvoice.com/?p=2421/
[8] Vilissa Thompson, "The Hashtagversary of #DisabilityTooWhite," Ramp Your Voice!, May 18, 2017, http://www.rampyourvoice.com/?p=2998/
[9] Vilissa Thompson, "Revisiting #DisabilityTooWhite One Year Later (Hint: There's Still A Problem)," interview by Denarii Grace, The Establishment, May 18, 2017, https://medium.com/the-establishment/revisiting-disabilitytoowhite-one-year-later-hint-theres-still-a-problem-229aadcfl852/
[10] Thompson, "The Hashtagversary of #DisabilityTooWhite."
[11] Vilissa Thompson, "Confronting the Whitewashing of Disability: Interview with #DisabilityTooWhite Creator Vilissa Thompson," interview by Sarah Blahovec, *HuffPost*, June 28, 2016, https://www.huffpost.com/entry/confronting-the-whitewash_b_10574994/
[12] Thompson, "Supporting Black Women with #Disabilities," 34:22.

13. Zachary Nunn and Adesola Adesina, "58: Disabled While Other (w/Vilissa Thompson)," *Living Corporate*, March 15, 2019, 17:00, https:art19.com/shows/living-corporate/episodesf9b68f62-4c9a-4917-95c5-a35f03c9b611/
14. Kate Hart, "Badass Ladies You Should Know: Vilissa Thompson," Kate Hart, May 2, 2016, https://www.katehart.net/blog//2016/05/badass-ladies-you-should-know-vilissa.html/
15. The term *womanist* is defined by Alice Walker in *In Search of Our Mothers' Gardens: Womanist Prose* (New York: Harcourt Brace Jovanovic, 1983), xi–xii. The term *misogynair* is discussed in "Episode 8: Contra *Hashtag with Moya Bailey and Vilissa Thompson," interview by Aimi Hamraie, Mapping Access, May 6, 2019, https://www.mapping-access.com/podcast/2019/1/14/episode-8-contrahashtag-with-moya-bailey-and-vilissa-thompson/
16. Hart, "Badass Ladies You Should Know."
17. Hart, "Badass Ladies You Should Know."
18. Vilissa Thompson, "Get Right or Get Left: Dismantling Ableism, Racism, and on the Radical Imaginations of Transnational Black Disabled Feminist Solidarities," interview by Jaimee A. Swift, Black Women Radicals, December 2019, https://www.blackwomenradicals.com/blog-feed/get-right-or-get-left-dismantling-ableism-racism-and-on-the-radical-imaginations-of-transnational-black-disabled-feminist-solidarities/
19. Thompson, "Get Right or Get Left."
20. Thompson, "Get Right or Get Left."
21. Kent, "Black History Now."
22. Vilissa Thompson and Alice Wong, "#GetWokeADA26: Disabled People of Color Speak Out, Part 1," Ramp Your Voice!, July 26, 2016, http://www.rampyourvoice.com/?p=2578/
23. For an analysis of Thompson's approach to intersectionality, see Danielle C. Biss, "Getting 'Woke' on Intersectionality: Illuminating the Rhetorical Significance of Disability Discourse in Feminist Activist Spaces," *Kaleidoscope* 18 (2019): 41–59.
24. Vilissa Thompson, "DisabilityTooWhite: Disability Community and Its Diversity Problem," Disability Intersectionality Summit, Boston, MA, November 5, 2016, 2:29, https://www.youtube.com/watch?v=P3AukZg-U0c
25. Vilissa Thompson, CCMNT Speakers, https://ccmntspeakers.com/speaker-profiles/vilissa-thompson/
26. Thompson, "Supporting Black Women with #Disabilities," 2:05.
27. Thompson, "Supporting Black Women with #Disabilities," 5:29.
28. Thompson, "Supporting Black Women with #Disabilities," 27:26.
29. Thompson, "Supporting Black Women with #Disabilities," 32:13.
30. Thompson, "RYV! Services."
31. Thompson, "Supporting Black Women with #Disabilities," 6:05.
32. Vilissa Thompson, "DisabilityTooWhite: Making the 'Good Trouble' in Advocacy," Ramp Your Voice!, May 26, 2016, http://www.rampyourvoice.com/?p=2466#more-2466/
33. Thompson, "Supporting Black Women with #Disabilities," 4:20.
34. Vilissa Thompson, "Bookworms, Womanism, and Sundance with Curtiss Cook," interview by Jamie Broadnax, Black Girl Nerds, #103, https://soundcloud.com/blackgirlnerds/black-girl-nerds-bgn-103/, 1:01:34.
35. Thompson, "Supporting Black Women with #Disabilities," 20:34.
36. Thompson, "Supporting Black Women with #Disabilities," 2:59.
37. Thompson, "Supporting Black Women with #Disabilities," 18:20.
38. Thompson, "Supporting Black Women with #Disabilities," 20:34.
39. Samantha Harrington, "This Founder Creates Conversations on Disability and Intersectionality," *Forbes*, March 19, 2018, https://www.forbes.com/sites/samanthaharrington/2018/03/19/how-ramp-your-voice-founder-creates-conversations-on-disability-and-intersectionality/#5448105c73b4/
40. Vilissa Thompson, "Learning to Embrace My 'Secondary' Disabilities," Ramp Your Voice!, September 2, 2016, http://www.rampyourvoice.com/?paged=5/

CHAPTER SIX

Lizzo

> *Your body is perfectly yours, even if it ain't perfect to anybody else. If you only knew the complexities your body possesses, you would be so proud of it. I'm so proud of you for making it this far in a society that gives us a head start into self-loathing, that hands us a dysmorphic mirror and leaves us desperate to catch up with who we think we should be.*[1]

A Black, fat woman who proudly proclaims these aspects of her identity, Lizzo performs a message of body positivity by rapping, singing, dancing, playing classical flute, and acting. Melissa Viviane Jefferson, the youngest of three children, was born in Detroit, Michigan, in 1988. Her chosen name *Lizzo* is a combination of an early nickname, *Lissa*, and Jay-Z's song "Izzo."

Gospel music was a large part of Lizzo's childhood because her family belonged to the Church of God in Christ, which considered secular music to be the work of the devil. But her father loved the music of Queen and Elton John and her mother that of Stevie Wonder, so Lizzo encountered some secular music at home. Lizzo sang in the church choir, where she learned how to perform in front of an audience; when she was nine years old, she started a singing group with her two best friends. Called *Peace, Love and Joy*, the group sang songs Lizzo had written. In junior high and high school, she continued to form various rap groups with friends. For her, rap music wasn't that different from the spoken tongues she grew up witnessing in her church: "I really think that it's all kind of divine and comes from the same place."[2]

Her family moved to Houston, Texas, when Lizzo was ten years old, and there her musical focus turned to the flute. She started playing the instrument in the fifth grade, and when she was a junior in high school, she began studying with the principal flutist of the Houston Opera. Her teacher, who was also a professor at the University of Houston, helped Lizzo receive a scholarship to study at the university in the hopes that she would later be able to study flute at the Paris Conservatory. For a time, Lizzo set her sights on a career in classical music: "I was going to . . . wait in line for that first chair. I saw a life of concert black and Boston Pops and traveling the world."[3] But Lizzo was continuing to rap and decided she had to choose between a career in rap and a career in classical music. "You're about to be who you're going to be forever," she thought. "And now who is that?" She chose rap when she realized that she "was in college for a music performance degree, but I was already performing. . . . What do I need a music performance degree for? And I just stopped."[4] The choice was not as irrevocable as it seemed at the time, however, because Lizzo continues to play the flute and often features her flute playing in her songs and videos.

Lizzo moved to Minneapolis, Minnesota, in 2011 because of its reputation as a hub for hip-hop music. She formed a rap group, the Chalice, with two women friends, and the group was included in a PBS documentary in 2014 on up-and-coming musicians in Minneapolis. Prince was also featured in the documentary, and he invited Lizzo and her friend Sophia Eris to sing on the song "Boyfriends" on his album *Plectrumelectrum*. Lizzo and her group began performing at parties at Prince's house, and he regularly talked about her and her music in interviews. Despite her early successes in Minnesota, she was making very little money, and life was not easy. Lizzo slept on friends' floors, in her car, and in the studio while concentrating on pursuing her music. "It sucked," she acknowledges. "It was very lonely. It was very hard."[5]

Lizzo released her first album, *Lizzobangers*, in 2013, followed by a second, *Big GRRRL Smart World*, in 2015. She then moved to Los Angeles, California, to further her musical career. Her EP *Coconut Oil* was released in 2016, and her song "Truth Hurts" came out in 2017. Although she thought it was the best song she had written, it attracted little attention, and she seriously considered quitting the music business. Then the song was featured in the 2018 Netflix movie *Someone Great*, with actors Gina Rodriguez and DeWanda Wise dancing and singing along to the song. It went to the top of the Billboard Hot 100 two years after it was released and was rereleased on Lizzo's third studio album, *Cuz I Love You*, in 2019.

Lizzo's music has been recognized with a number of awards. *Time* magazine named her "Entertainer of the Year" in 2019. In 2020, she was nominated in eight categories for the Grammy awards and won in the categories of best pop solo performance for "Truth Hurts," best urban contemporary album for *'Cuz I Love You*, and best traditional R&B album performance for "Jerome." In 2020, she received eleven nominations at the Billboard Music Awards, winning in the category for top song sales artist.

Lizzo is not only involved in music but also in other aspects of the entertainment business. She cohosted a weekly live music and comedy show, *Wonderland*, in 2016. She served as a voice performer in the animated film *UglyDolls* and appeared in the film *Hustlers*. She has made guest appearances on shows such as *The Late Show with David Letterman*, *The Late Show with Ste-*

phen Colbert, *Full Frontal with Samantha Bee*, *RuPaul's Drag Race*, and *The Ellen DeGeneres Show*. She also has become the face of various product campaigns for companies such as Absolut, Urban Decay, Quay, and Weight Watchers. For Weight Watchers, she and Oprah Winfrey collaborated to bring about changes to the program so that it focuses less on calorie counting and more on staying active and prioritizing self-care.[6]

Definition of Feminism

Lizzo was initially reluctant to claim the label of *feminist* for several reasons. Most important, she didn't know much about feminism and had not yet decided if she was a feminist. As a Black woman, she felt excluded from feminism because "it was taboo to be a black feminist. It was almost unheard of."[7] She also resisted aligning herself with feminist movement because of the refusal of some feminists to see certain issues as feminist—the killing of Black men by police officers, for example: "How can you not care about a woman who lost her son, if it was a police officer that killed him? How can you not care about these women who are crying out for help? She's a woman, she's one of you."[8]

Once her feminist friends began to educate Lizzo about feminism, she embraced a feminist identity: "The more I started to realize that I was a feminist and what I was doing was feminism, and I got more attention from feminist publications and people, the more I grew in it, my journey has come to a point where I have embraced the F word and included myself in the conversation."[9] She continues, "Now I wear it proudly and I speak on it proudly."[10] She asserts, "At this point, I feel like I'm doing what a feminist does. I'm living how a feminist lives. And I believe what feminism is about; therefore I am."[11] She explains the benefits that have come to her as a result of her embrace of feminism: "You receive a different type of energy once you've claimed it and it's just been wonderful."[12]

Lizzo defines feminism as "what's fair between men and women and what's going to make all of us better."[13] As she explains: "I think what's fair is equal pay. What's fair is getting rid of rape culture and misogyny."[14] For her, fairness also includes allowing women to do what men do without being criticized: "If it's okay for a man to be on stage, shaking his butt with a bunch of scantily clad booty dancers, wearing all these chains or whatever, then it's okay for a woman to do the same without being slut-shamed."[15]

Lizzo situates her brand of feminism within the fourth wave of feminism and explains that one key difference between the fourth and earlier waves is its celebration of female sexuality. Earlier waves of feminism dismissed female sexuality because women's bodies were often used to sell products and to exist for the pleasure of male viewers. In contrast, Lizzo sees the expression of female sexuality as a primary aspect of both the fourth wave and of her type of feminism: "So where there was a wave of feminism where we were burning bras, now I'm like, my bra is in your face. You know what I'm saying? . . . And I think that the wave of feminism right now that's overtly sexual and in your face, I think, is just the response to where we were."[16] Lizzo rejects the notion that she cannot be a feminist because she frequently appears nude in photographs, performs in lingerie costumes, and engages in sexually provocative acts in her videos and performances. She sees her expression of sexuality as "an act of her fully defining herself, rather than an act of her selling herself with it."[17]

Lizzo's feminism is rooted in her belief that women should be valued because they create life: "Every person who is born in America was born from a woman. A woman has led your life for most of your life, or at least created you. Why does that not cross over into anything else? Why does that not cross over into the American culture or the infrastructure? We're the givers of life." A major objective of feminism, according to Lizzo, is to stop the management and control of women's bodies: "We have the f*cking universe between our thighs and somehow everything on our body is regulated and I think that that's the problem."[18]

Change Strategies

Lizzo's feminism is focused on proclaiming her identity as a means to generate change for marginalized individuals. Once individuals change how they see themselves, she hopes the larger world will change as well to become more accepting of difference. Lizzo employs three major strategies to accomplish this objective: (1) disrupting norms, (2) celebrating every body, and (3) representing marginalized others.

Disrupting Norms

Lizzo breaks a number of norms around appropriate femininity, including society's unrealistic and narrow standards of feminine beauty. As she explains, "No matter what you look like, as women we get this hard when [it] comes to beauty norms and norms in general. We all experience misogyny and hate, even if you fit into conventional ideas of beauty."[19] She encourages women to "look at our bodies as vehicles for success, and not a signifier of who you are, how good your pussy is, if dudes like you or not, or if you can fit certain clothes . . . that's not what your body's for."[20] Lizzo knows that because she is fat, her body doesn't conform to conventional beauty norms and, in response, she "asserts her own glowing image of herself" as someone who "doesn't ask for permission or find ways to make herself palatable to body standards."[21] Instead of covering her body up with clothing or starving herself to meet conventional beauty standards, she embraces her body as its own ideal. She never asks herself, "'Do I look like this model or this actress?'" Instead, she explains, "I have to hold myself to my own standards."[22] Lizzo's commitment to eschewing traditional beauty standards is reinforced in her song "Juice," where she sings, "I gotta be my own type."[23]

Lizzo also disrupts norms about appropriate sexual expression for women. Historically, women were seen either as sexually passive or as exclusively sexual beings for the use and pleasure of men. Fat women in particular are typically dismissed as sexual beings and are not considered sexy. Lizzo rejects the norms around female sexuality for fat women by engaging in the same kind of actions that women who conform to conventional presentations of sexuality do, such as wearing see-through apparel, twerking, and thrusting her butt and/or breasts into the viewer's face. But she engages in these actions on her own terms. She often shouts "bitch" in between these moves "as if to say, 'I'm doing this for my pleasure. Not yours.'"[24]

Lizzo also challenges norms around female sexuality by espousing various forms of sexuality. She explains, "When it comes to sexuality or gender, I personally don't ascribe to just one thing.... That's why the colors for LBGTQ+ are a rainbow! Because there's a spectrum and right now we try to keep it black and white. That's just not working for me."[25] Lizzo has long celebrated the queer community and has a strong LGBTQIA+ following (she has dubbed her fans *Lizzbians*).

A third way in which Lizzo disrupts norms is by proclaiming women's independence from men. She asserts that a woman's worth should not be defined by men and advocates for total female independence, financially and emotionally, reassuring women that they can be fulfilled without a partner. "I put the sing in single," she asserts in her song "Truth Hurts." The lyrics continue: "Ain't worried 'bout a ring on my finger."[26] In "Soulmate," she reiterates the message: "It's a 'me, myself' kind of attitude. 'Cause I'm my own soulmate. I know how to love me."[27] In that same song, she announces, "I'm 'a marry me one day,'"[28] and, in fact, she is shown marrying herself in the video for "Truth Hurts."

Celebrating Every Body

Lizzo has a number of physical attributes that society typically conceptualizes as negative. She is Black, a woman, and fat, all of which tend to be used by society to marginalize, denigrate, or devalue her and others like her. Lizzo transforms these physical characteristics into positive attributes that she loves and celebrates. She creates a positive image for herself in place of the negative one that typically would be ascribed to her, and she exuberantly and defiantly celebrates her identity as a fat, Black woman. She believes that women "should be celebrating ourselves more"[29] and wants all women to "just be yourself and love who you are."[30]

Lizzo did not always feel positively about her body. As she was growing up, she was taught to be ashamed of it: "I was being told every day that my face was great, but my body needs work. And I was being shamed in little ways that people didn't even realize they were shaming me. It was so ingrained. And I started to shame myself and actually believed what they were saying to me."[31] One of the incidents that pushed her to feel more positive about her body occurred when an interviewer asked her what her favorite thing was about herself. When she replied that it was her personality, the interviewer pushed her, asking, "OK, but physically, what's your favorite thing about yourself?" She realized she did not have an answer until she looked down at her skin and realized, "Oh, my God, my skin. That is my favorite thing about myself. . . . And that was the first time I'd ever discovered my body love."[32] She acknowledges that for her to love her Black skin so much might seem strange because that is "the thing that's held against [her] the most in the society."[33] But she has reframed her skin to be something positive, as reflected in her song "My Skin": "I woke up in this, I woke up in this / In my skin / I can't wash it away, so you can't take it from me / My brown skin."[34]

Lizzo moved from seeing her skin as positive to seeing other aspects of her body that way as well: "And I think about 10 years ago, I made the decision that I just wanted to be happy with my body, and I just wanted to be happy with who I am and that I would wake up every day in the same body, and it wasn't going to change." She encourages others to follow the same path: "You got to find out one thing you really like about yourself and then it just opens up the gates to all of these wonderful things."[35] Lizzo admits that she "had to work for many, many years to get to this point,"[36] and she is not completely there yet: "I've spent my hardest days trying to love me."[37]

Lizzo's message of body positivity "is about acknowledging the inherent worth of all human beings no matter their size."[38] She encourages her fans to enact their body positivity when they see themselves in a mirror: "Every time u walk by a mirror I want u to hear this: Who told you you could be so cute? Who?"[39] In another Instagram post, she is dressed in a net bodysuit with her butt in the viewer's face, and she gazes at herself in a mirror. "Just when you thought I couldn't love myself any more," she sings before kissing her lips in the mirror.[40] She also counters the common idea that the body positivity movement promotes poor health and fitness habits. Lizzo posts stories on Instagram of her workouts that show her running on a treadmill, jumping rope, doing calisthenics, and riding a stationary bike, and she has written a workout anthem called "Fitness."[41]

Lizzo now prefers to use the term *body normativity* instead of *body positivity*, although she continues to use both terms to describe her philosophy. She argues that body positivity "has been commercialized and appropriated to the point where it's simply cool, even complacent, which is not a space that promotes transformation."[42] She explains her rationale for the new term: "I think it's lazy for me to just say I'm body positive at this point. It's easy. I would like to be body-normative. I want to normalize my body. And not just be like, 'Ooh, look at this cool movement. Being fat is body positive.' No, being fat is normal. I think now, I owe it to the people who started this to not just stop here. We have to make people uncomfortable again, so that we can continue to change."[43] One of the reasons Lizzo posts naked pictures of herself is to further the normalizing of fat bodies: "We eventually get used to everything. . . . So people just gon' have to get used to my ass."[44]

Representing Marginalized Others

When she was growing up, Lizzo lacked role models who looked like her and that she could imagine becoming someday. She "grew up watching pop stars that were blonde, super skinny, that looked perfect in every way,"[45] so watching TV and music videos meant looking into a world in which she either did not exist or where she was depicted negatively. This lack of visible positive representation affected her self-esteem: "When you don't see yourself, you start to think something's wrong with you."[46]

Lizzo is determined to serve as a role model for all women like her who have been invisible. "I guess I am a body-positive role model. I'm pretty positive about my body. And I have rolls. And I model," Lizzo proclaims.[47] "I think it's important that I take full responsibility for the way the world perceives me because that is the way they're gonna perceive someone who looks like me in the future," she explains. "Maybe, hopefully, that would give some young girl someone to look up to and take away the opportunity for someone to weaponize her uniqueness against her."[48] As Lizzo sings in "Like a Girl,"

> If you fight like a girl,
> Cry like a girl,
> Do your own thing, run the whole damn world. If you feel like a girl, then you real like a girl.
> Do your own thing, run the whole damn world.[49]

As she "steps into the spotlight she is leaving a path for other" women to follow,[50] showing them that they are not invisible. "The space I'm occupying isn't just for me," she asserts. "It's for all the big black girls in the future who just want to be seen."[51]

Lizzo represents women of all kinds. She does not see her public identity as fitting into just one category: "I do feel a responsibility as a woman of color to make music that represents them. I also feel a responsibility to do other things. I'm a feminist. I'm a fat person. So, I need to be representing those people too."[52] She also represents women whose sexual orientation does not fit the gender binary and "successful, talented, and bold" women as well.[53] The women she represents have been described in this way: "They were seen by Lizzo and were taking her lead to love themselves a little bit harder."[54]

Lizzo boldly and confidently claims all aspects of her identity. She challenges and dismisses the norms that say she is imperfect or inappropriate, including norms around feminine beauty, the expression of women's sexuality, and women's presumed dependence on men. She celebrates the characteristics of her identity that society denigrates, working to make her body be considered normal. Lizzo then moves beyond a self-focus to represent others whose identities are also marked by difference: "Now being different makes you stand out. Now, being different makes you a star. And I think that I had to embrace those differences to become the person that I am . . . the star that I am. Or else I would have just been homogenized like everybody else."[55]

■ Reflections

1. Lizzo defines feminism as "what's fair between men and women and what's going to make all of us better." What do you consider to be "fair" between men and women, and what do you believe is going to make all of us "better"? Do you believe that Lizzo herself engages in actions that are going to make all of us better?
2. Lizzo believes that a celebration of sexuality differentiates the fourth wave of feminism from earlier ones. How important do you believe a celebration of sexuality is to feminism?
3. Listen to one of Lizzo's albums. Identify elements that make the songs feminist. Are there any elements in the music or lyrics that seem contradictory to feminism?
4. One of Lizzo's primary change strategies is disrupting norms, and she disrupts norms around feminine beauty, female sexuality, and women's independence from men. Are these the most important norms that feminists need to disrupt? Can you think of other norms that feminists might want to disrupt in order to achieve a feminist future?
5. Lizzo distinguishes between the terms *body positivity* and *body normativity*. Is this an important distinction to make? Which term do you prefer and why?
6. How closely do Lizzo's change strategies align with the assumptions outlined in the introduction to part 2? Are there any assumptions that you don't believe pertain to her approach to change?
7. Lizzo places herself in the fourth wave of feminism. Do you agree with her? Why or why not?

■ Notes

[1] Lizzo, "Your body is perfectly yours, even if it ain't perfect to anybody else," Instagram, December 15, 2020, https://www.instagram.com/p/CI1FvuFBap4/
[2] Lizzo, "Lizzo: Coconut Oil Rules," interview by Roxine Plummer, *Urbanology*, January 15, 2017, https://urbanologymag.com/lizzo-coconut-oil-rules/
[3] Lizzo, "Lizzo on Feminism, Self-Love and Bringing 'Hallelujah Moments' to Stage," interview by Terry Gross, "Fresh Air," *National Public Radio*, July 4, 2019, https://www.npr.org/programs/fresh-air/2019/05/23/725805264/fresh-air-for-may-23-2019-lizzo/
[4] Lizzo, "Lizzo on Feminism."
[5] Lizzo, "Lizzo on Feminism."
[6] Lakita Wilson, *Lizzo: Breakout Artist* (Minneapolis, MN: Lerner, 2020), 35.
[7] Lizzo, "The Feministing Five: Lizzo," interview by Senti Sojwal, Feministing, September 30, 2016, http://feministing.com/2016/09/30/the-feministing-five-lizzo/

8. Lizzo, "The Feministing Five."
9. Lizzo, "The Feministing Five."
10. Hannah Frank, "Lizzo Breaks the New 'F-Word' Taboo with Proud, Talented Rhymes," Madison.com, September 14, 2015, https://madison.com/daily-cardinal/lizzo-breaks-the-new-f-word-taboo-with-proud-talented-rhymes/article_9fcaa04c-5b61-11e5-9bee-3fd79de53623.html
11. Jessica McKinney, "Lizzo Is Here to Lead the New Wave of Girl Power," Vibe, August 18, 2016, https://www.vibe.com/2016/08/next-lizzo-interview/
12. Frank, "Lizzo Breaks."
13. McKinney, "Lizzo Is Here."
14. McKinney, "Lizzo Is Here."
15. Mike Diver, "Lizzo on Feminism, Blondie and Miley Cyrus," *Clash*, June 3, 2014, https://www.clashmusic.com/news/lizzo-on-feminism-blondie-and-miley-cyrus/
16. Lizzo, "Lizzo on Feminism."
17. Cristina Burack, "All Sizes, All Colors: Lizzo Celebrates Bodies," DW, November 14, 2019, https://www.dw.com/en/all-sizes-all-colors-lizzo-celebrates-bodies/a-51215686/
18. Lizzo, "Lizzo."
19. Lizzo, "The Feministing Five."
20. Phillip Picardi, "Lizzo is the Sex-Positive, Twerking, Gospel-Singing Artist the World Needs," *Teen Vogue*, June 15, 2018, https://www.teenvogue.com/story/lizzo-music-issue/
21. Ropafadzo Mugadzo, "Lizzo is Bringing Sexy Back," *Boshemia*, April 20, 2019, https://www.boshemiamagazine.com/blog/lizzo-sexy/
22. Lizzo, "Self-love isn't being delusional," Instagram, December 11, 2019, https://www.instagram.com/p/B58TZK8ha4v/?igshid=wkr80zaxddch/
23. Lizzo, "Juice," *Cuz I Love You*, Nice Life/Atlantic, 2019.
24. Linda Freund, "Lizzo is the Queen of Body Positivity on Social," Tubular Insights, January 16, 2020, https://tubularlabs.com/blog/lizzo-social-video/
25. Picardi, "Lizzo is the Sex-Positive."
26. Lizzo, "Truth Hurts," *Cuz I Love You*, Nice Life/Atlantic, 2019.
27. Lizzo, "Soulmate," *Cuz I Love You*, Nice Life/Atlantic, 2019.
28. Lizzo, "Soulmate."
29. Lizzo, "Lizzo Talks Diversity, Self-Confidence and Femininity," interview by Berenice Bautista, PBS News Hour, February 14, 2020, https://www.pbs.org/newshour/arts/lizzo-talks-diversity-self-confidence-and-femininity/
30. Sarah Hill, "What Lizzo's Success Means for Feminism," *The Crier*, March 16, 2020, https://www.sunycccthecrier.com/spring-2020/what-lizzos-success-means-for-feminism/
31. Lizzo, "Lizzo on Feminism."
32. Lizzo, "Lizzo on Feminism."
33. Lizzo, "Lizzo on Feminism."
34. Lizzo, "My Skin," *Big GRRRL Small World*, BGSW, 2015.
35. Lizzo, "Lizzo."
36. Lizzo, "Lizzo on Feminism."
37. Rania Aniftos, "Lizzo's 9 Best Body Positivity Messages of 2020," Billboard, December 29, 2020, https://www.billboard.com/index.php/articles/news/9504096/lizzo-best-body-positivity-messages-2020/
38. Rebecca Haddad, "How Lizzo Empowers Women to Feel 'Good as Hell,'" Her Campus at UWindsor, November 26, 2019, https://www.hercampus.com/school/uwindsor/how-lizzo-empowers-women-feel-good-hell/
39. Lizzo, "Every time u walk by a mirror I want u to hear this," Instagram, May 5, 2020, https://www.instagram.com/p/B_1HBXvh7BD/?hl=en/
40. Lizzo, "Just when you thought I couldn't love myself any more," Instagram, October 1, 2020, https://www.instagram.com/p/CF0RzsEB0Zb/?hl=en/
41. See, for example, the following Instagram posts: Lizzo, "I'm a bad bitch," Instagram, February 26, 2020 (https://www.instagram.com/p/B9C768uBlRO/); Lizzo, "Since this is goin

around the internet," Instagram, June 11, 2020 (https://www.instagram.com/p/CBUUvXKAQ-S/); and Lizzo, "Me & @mileycyrus training for the stadiums," Instagram, February 4, 2021 (https://www.instagram.com/reel/CK4up3qFMX8/).

[42] Calin Van Paris, "Lizzo Wants to Redefine the Body-Positivity Movement," *Vogue*, September 24, 2020, https://www.vogue.com/article/lizzo-october-cover-story-body-positivity-inclusivity/

[43] Claudia Rankine, "Lizzo on Hope, Justice, and the Election," *Vogue*, September 24, 2020, https://www.vogue.com/article/lizzo-cover-october-2020/

[44] Lizzo, "We eventually get used to everything," Instagram, January 22, 2020, https://www.instagram.com/p/B7oPh1KhRlP/?hl=en/

[45] Lizzo, "Lizzo Talks Diversity."

[46] Burack, "All Sizes."

[47] Freund, "Lizzo is the Queen."

[48] Rankine, "Lizzo on Hope."

[49] Lizzo, "Like a Girl," in *Lizzo: Cuz I Love You* (Milwaukee, WI: Hal Leonard, 2019).

[50] Mugadzo, "Lizzo is Bringing Sexy Back."

[51] Raisa Bruner, "'The Space I'm Occupying Isn't Just for Me.' Lizzo Fulfills Her Own Self-Love Prophecy," *Time*, April 11, 2019, https://time.com/5568320/lizzo-music-album-review/

[52] Burack, "All Sizes."

[53] Hill, "What Lizzo's Success Means."

[54] Rankine, "Lizzo on Hope."

[55] Lizzo, "Lizzo on Feminism."

PART
THREE

NAMING A PROBLEM

Change agents who choose to focus on *naming a problem* are interested in what needs to be addressed, resolved, or changed to achieve a different future. Language is at the heart of any act of naming and offers an infinite number of ways to talk about something—a speaker can always choose another word or phrase. At the same time, language is also a potential source of misrepresentation and misunderstanding. Two individuals might choose identical words to describe something and thus believe they understand it in the same way when, in fact, they are bringing vastly different meanings, interpretations, and cultural preferences to those words. In addition, language does not serve all speakers equally, and members of marginalized groups have a different relationship to language than do members of dominant cultural groups. Individuals who choose naming a problem as a change strategy understand that issues of naming are necessarily political.[1]

Nadya Okamoto, Jamie Margolin, Margaret Cho, and Camille Paglia make use of a range of strategies to approach and label the problems they believe should be addressed, all of which involve some kinds of discrimination, oppression, or injustice. Their strategies are informed by three assumptions: (1) a problem cannot be addressed unless it is named, (2) the language used to name something determines how it is perceived, and (3) naming a problem can be compounded by issues of privilege. These assumptions suggest that although naming is a vital aspect of any change movement, it is not a simple process.

Assumption 1: A problem cannot be addressed unless it is named.

When they seek social change, individuals must give a name to the problem or injustice they are hoping to ameliorate. This task is made more difficult if words are not available in a language to adequately describe that problem. Something can just feel off—vaguely wrong or uncomfortable—but if it cannot easily be talked about because there are no words to describe the experience, an individual might begin to doubt its veracity: "If this experience is real, why isn't there a word for it? Maybe it's not real, maybe it's not really a problem, maybe it's just me." Those whose perceptions and experiences are left out of a language often find they need to talk indirectly or "tell it slant"[2] because the language is inadequate for expressing their thoughts. Naming a problem, then, often involves having to negotiate a language that does not provide its speakers with the tools they need to accurately account for their experiences.

The theory of muted groups, developed by Edwin Ardener and Shirley Ardener and elaborated on by Cheris Kramarae, provides an explanation for why women and other marginalized groups often feel inarticulate in or disadvantaged by a language.[3] According to Kramarae, when the dominant language "is not a good 'fit' for women's expression of their experiences,"[4] women's voices are "muted," and their understandings of the world cannot easily be expressed in the dominant language. To show the degree to which women's experiences are left out of language, Kramarae, Paula Treichler, and Ann Russo compiled *A Feminist Dictionary*, which differs considerably from traditional dictionaries in which the agreed-upon meanings of a dominant culture are encoded.[5] *A Feminist Dictionary* includes entries with special meanings for women and feminists, such as *embedded rabbit*, which refers to discrimination that exists but has not yet reached the level of conscious awareness. The term derives from drawings in children's books in which a rabbit (or other animal or object) is hidden in the landscape. At first, the rabbit is difficult to see—just as discrimination often is—but once the rabbit has been located, to look at the drawing and not see the rabbit is impossible.[6] When language expands to encompass and express the perceptions and experiences of marginalized group members, they have more possibilities available for naming their experiences.

The term *sexual harassment* illustrates how a problem cannot be talked about until words are invented to describe it. Although the phrase *sexual harassment* is an accepted and widely used phrase today, the problem of sexual harassment could not be adequately acknowledged and addressed until there was a label for it. Lin Farley is credited with coining the term after teaching a class, Women and Work, at Cornell University. In class discussions, she noticed a pattern among her women students—they had either quit or been fired from a job because they were made uncomfortable by and/or had refused men's sexual advances.[7] In 1975, Farley was asked to testify before the New York City Human Rights Commission Hearings on Women and Work. As part of her testimony, she used the term *sexual harassment* to describe "unwanted sexual advances against women employees by male supervisors, bosses, foremen or managers."[8] A reporter heard Farley's remarks and incorporated the term into an article published in the *New York Times*, which then put the phrase into national circulation.[9] Today, *sexual harassment* is standard language in the antidiscriminatory policies of corporations, government agencies, and educational institutions. Until there was a label for the problem, however, sexual harassment was a phenomenon that was generally not seen, not discussed, and consequently not addressed.

Assumption 2: The language used to name something determines how it is perceived.

The choice of terms to describe a problem matters. Depending on the term chosen, change agents perceive, define, and approach the problems they encounter differently. The notion of linguistic relativity, or what is often called the *Sapir-Whorf hypothesis*, helps explain how the act of naming dictates or at least affects how something is viewed. According to this hypothesis, the language available to a speaker influences how that individual perceives, experiences, and names the world.

Kenneth Burke extends the notion that language is a filter through which reality is perceived. He suggests that language provides particular frames of reference or ways of looking that he calls *terministic screens*.[10] In other words, the terms chosen to describe something focus attention in one direction rather than another. Richard Weaver describes all language as sermonic because it encourages us "to look at the world, or some small part of it," in a particular way.[11] Since humans cannot not use terministic screens, what appear to be observations about reality are actually "the spinning out of possibilities implicit in our particular choice of terms."[12]

The labels *girl* and *boy* when used to refer to adult women and men illustrate the way language influences perceptions and behavior. In the second wave of feminism in the 1960s and 1970s, feminists challenged the almost universal use of the term *girl* to apply to women, no matter their ages.[13] They argued that because women were called *girls* across virtually all contexts, they were seen as childlike, frivolous, immature, and inconsequential. In contrast, *boy* is not used to describe grown men except on those occasions when they are misbehaving, fooling around, or having a boys' night out—in other words, when they are acting like boys. The use of *boy* by whites to address Black men is another instance of this phenomenon; in this case, the label *boy* functions to keep Blacks in their place by positioning them as not fully adult human beings. Feminists urged that language be reformed as a step toward seeing women and other marginalized groups as fully contributing members of society.

Assumption 3: Naming a problem can be compounded by issues of privilege.

Issues of privilege can potentially interfere in the naming of a problem and the ways it can be addressed. Privileges are advantages or benefits that are ascribed rather than earned, such as being white, heterosexual, and middle or upper class. In the process of tackling a problem, privileged individuals can unwittingly become part of or complicit with the problem they are seeking to solve if they are unaware of the benefits assigned to them. They may not realize, for example, that others are affected by a problem differently and may not have the same resources they do for solving it because of privilege.

Peggy McIntosh's essay on white privilege is considered a foundational piece that theorizes how privilege functions. She was aware that many men have difficulty recognizing their male privilege, but she had not recognized the extent to which her white privilege was similarly difficult for her to see. As part of her unpacking of her white privilege, McIntosh made a list of all of the racial privileges she enjoys because she is white, ranging from "I can go shopping alone most of the time, pretty well assured that I will not be followed or harassed" to "I can choose blemish cover or bandages in 'flesh' color and have them more or less match my skin" to "I can be pretty sure that if I ask to talk to the 'person in charge,' I will be facing a person of my race."[14] Although McIntosh's essay specifically described privileges related to race, her theory has been extended to illustrate how certain assumptions and practices go unquestioned with virtually all identity categories because of privilege.

Many Christians are unaware of the extent to which Christian privilege operates in the United States. Christians can assume that those around them will have a reasonable understanding of their beliefs and that their religion will be portrayed fairly in books and movies and on television. If they wish, Christian parents can find a school to which to send their children that is grounded in the Christian faith. Without special effort, children raised as Christians will have many friends who share that faith. Holiday breaks for US schools and government offices correspond to Christian holidays rather than to Muslim, Jewish, or Hindu ones, for example. When swearing an oath, Christians know that the book they swear on will be the Bible, the book sacred to their faith.[15] That the privileges of Christianity are taken for granted demonstrates how thoroughly assumptions and expectations associated with a dominant identity are embedded in a culture and how easily the accompanying privileges can go unquestioned and unchallenged.

■ NOTES

[1] Cheris Kramarae, *Women and Men Speaking: Frameworks for Analysis* (Rowley, MA: Newbury, 1981).

[2] The phrase "tell it slant" is taken from a poem by Emily Dickinson. See Emily Dickinson, "Tell All the Truth But Tell it Slant," *The Pocket Emily Dickinson*, ed. Brenda Hillman (Boston, MA: Shambala, 2009), 137.

[3] Shirley Ardener, *Perceiving Women* (London, UK: Malaby, 1975); Kramarae, *Women and Men Speaking*.

[4] Kramarae, *Women and Men Speaking*, 2.

[5] Cheris Kramarae and Paula A. Treichler with Ann Russo, *A Feminist Dictionary* (Boston, MA: Pandora, 1985).

[6] Kramarae and Treichler with Russo, *A Feminist Dictionary*, 136.

[7] Sarah Mearhoff, "#MeToo: Fight Against Workplace Sexual Harassment Began at Cornell in 1975," *Ithaca Journal*, February 21, 2018, https://www.ithacajournal.com/story/news/local/2018/02/21/metoo-fight-against-workplace-sexual-harassment-began-cornell-1975/347388002/; Lin Farley, *Sexual Shakedown: The Sexual Harassment of Women on the Job* (New York: McGraw-Hill, 1978).

[8] Mearhoff, "#MeToo."
[9] Enid Nemy, "Women Begin to Speak Out Against Sexual Harassment at Work," *New York Times*, August 19, 1975, p. 38.
[10] Kenneth Burke, *Language as Symbolic Action: Essays on Life, Literature, and Method* (Berkeley, CA: University of California Press, 1966), 44–52.
[11] Richard M. Weaver, *Language is Sermonic: Richard Weaver on the Nature of Rhetoric*, ed. Richard L. Johannesen, Rennard Strickland, and Ralph T. Eubanks (Baton Rouge, LA: Louisiana State University Press, 1970), 224.
[12] Burke, *Language as Symbolic Action*, 46.
[13] Mary Ritchie Key, *Male/Female Language* (Metuchen, NJ: Scarecrow, 1975), 39–44.
[14] Peggy McIntosh, "White Privilege: Unpacking the Invisible Knapsack," in *Understanding Prejudice and Discrimination*, ed. Scott Plous (New York: McGraw Hill, 2003), 191–96.
[15] Sam Killerman, "Christian Privilege Checklist," Project Humanities, Arizona State University, https://projecthumanities.asu.edu/content/christian-privilege-checklist/

CHAPTER
SEVEN

Nadya Okamoto

> *Let's get one thing straight—period shaming and the stigma in general are straight up misogyny (prejudice against, dislike of, or contempt for women). So, thinking that something like menstruation, a natural process that is inherently associated with the female body, should be considered dirty and worthy of shame is misogynistic. Period.*[1]

Nadya Okamoto is a passionate "period warrior"—"someone ready to fight the stigma around periods and to start conversations about menstruation"[2]—because the taboo around menstruation is a problem that affects everyone. A Japanese and Taiwanese American, Okamoto was born in New York City in 1998. When her parents divorced, her mother moved her and her two younger sisters to Portland, Oregon.

When Nadya's mother lost her job and could no longer afford their home, the family moved in with friends, and what had been a ten-minute commute to high school became a bus ride of over two hours for Okamoto. She had to change buses near a homeless shelter and because she could relate to not having "a place to call my own,"[3] Nadya began to talk with the women there. A question she frequently asked them was what they found "most challenging about their living situation,"[4] and she was surprised by the answer: menstrual hygiene. Okamoto had never considered how homeless women deal with their periods while living on the streets, and she began to collect stories of "using stolen pillowcases, toilet paper, and most commonly brown paper grocery bags found on the street" to deal with menstrual flow.[5]

Nadya "felt a sense of duty to these women and their stories,"[6] so in her sophomore year in high school, she founded, with her mother and classmate Vincent Forand, a nonprofit organization named *Camions of Care*. Later rebranded *PERIOD*,[7] the organization was established to distribute period products to those who do not have access to them. Unfamiliar with how to set up a nonprofit organization, Okamoto and Forand met at a Starbucks on a Saturday and literally Googled all of the questions they had concerning nonprofits, including "what's a 501 (c) (3)?," "what's a board of directors?," and "what's the IRS?"[8] With several grants as starting capital, they bought out all the menstrual supplies at local Dollar and Walmart stores and, with the help of friends, put together packs of period products that they distributed to homeless shelters.

The mission of PERIOD evolved from a singular focus on providing period products to those who need them to also addressing issues of education and policy around menstruation.[9] The educational mission of PERIOD is to erase the stigma attached to menstruation by encouraging open talk about periods. In addition, PERIOD targets laws and policies that affect those who menstruate, and Nadya concentrates in particular on reforming the tampon tax, which taxes menstrual products as luxuries.[10] In contrast, products for men such as Rogaine and Viagra are not considered luxuries and thus are not subject to the same tax. Upon learning about this disparity, Okamoto responded: "Are you &@%*$&# kidding me?! Old-man hair growth and erections are more of a necessity than feeling clean on your period? How?"[11]

PERIOD continues to provide information and outreach on all aspects of menstruation. The organization provides millions of free menstrual products to menstruators in homeless shelters, schools, prisons, and other settings nationally and globally each year and has chapters and partners in forty-nine US states and fifty countries.[12] PERIOD launched #NationalPeriodDay, first celebrated on October 19, 2019, with rallies in all fifty states, to demand access to period products, an end to the tampon tax, and education about period poverty—a lack of funds to purchase menstrual products.[13] In addition, PERIOD partners with various corporations such as Mahina, Always, Motrin, and Tampax that help fund PERIOD's activities.

After high school, Nadya enrolled in Harvard University, her mother's alma mater, where she majored in social studies and continued to run PERIOD. During her freshman year, she became aware of various issues affecting the city of Cambridge, including gentrification, housing and income inequality, climate change, and the arts, and she wanted to become more involved in city policy. She had no intention of running for office until she started to hear comments such as, "If you have so many ideas, why don't you just run yourself?"[14] She Googled the requirements for election to the Cambridge City Council, discovered that the minimum age was eighteen, and announced: "I'm more than qualified because I'm 19!"[15] In the 2017 election, Okamoto came in fifteenth out of twenty-six candidates. Although she didn't win a council seat, she found the experience invaluable: "It was amazing to be able to hear those messages that we were making a difference regardless of whether or not we won."[16]

Following her run for office, Nadya wrote *Period Power: A Manifesto for the Menstrual Movement* as "a tangible way of declaring that the menstrual movement is a real thing, that we're actually seeing this global movement for equitable access to period products and changing the way that people talk and think about periods."[17] The book made the *Kirkus Reviews* list of Best Young Adult Nonfiction for 2018.[18] Okamoto took a leave of absence from Harvard University that same year to promote her book and to continue her work with menstrual activism.

Nadya returned to school in the fall of 2019, when she also stepped down as executive director of PERIOD.[19] She wanted to continue speaking and touring on behalf of the menstrual movement and to devote more time to managing media and corporate partnerships.[20] Okamoto serves as chief brand officer for JUV Consulting, a marketing agency based in New York City that employs teenagers to serve as consultants to corporate executives who are attempting to target Gen-Z.[21] In addition, Nadya is the subject of a series of videos called *Nadya Talks* and is featured in a documentary, *Period Girl*, released in 2018. She has been recognized with a number of awards, including the President's Volunteer Service Award, 22 Under 22: Most Inspiring College Women, and Three Dot Dash: Global Teen Leader. When asked when she will be satisfied that she has done enough as a period warrior, her response is straightforward: When "something so natural as periods does not hinder any menstruator's experience" of reaching their full potential. She elaborates: "When there is no opportunity for me to speak out against a menstrual taboo, because it no longer exists—that is when I will be done."[22]

Definition of Feminism

At Harvard University, the Arthur and Elizabeth Schlesinger Library on the History of Women in America provided inspiration for Okamoto's feminist commitments. She came to appreciate what the women's movement had accomplished for someone like her—a woman of color and a period advocate: "There is something empowering about being surrounded by books and other documents written by feminist leaders who fought for my right, as a young woman of color, to attend an institution like Harvard—and also fought for my right to advocate for periods so publicly."[23]

Nadya does not shy away from the label *feminist*: "Feminism is literally a synonym for gender equality.... Regardless of gender, regardless of sexual identity, we are all equal."[24] Not only does Okamoto assert equality as key to her definition of feminism but she also sees menstruation as contributing to that equality because periods are a common denominator among all people. "Periods truly are a great equalizer because we all either menstruate or know someone who does—and it's (literally) a regular part of our lives that we need to bring out into the open."[25] Nadya connects the menstrual movement to intersectionality because of its centrality to human life: "Menstruation is such a central and natural part of human life that it crosses many industries, topics, identities, cultures, and movements. I find that the Menstrual Movement is the embodiment of *intersectional feminism*."[26]

Okamoto makes a special point of including transgender individuals in her advocacy of period equality. She recounts that "when I started my work as a menstrual activist, I hadn't thought about the fact that there are people who menstruate and do not identify as women.... If you think periods are stigmatized for women, imagine the taboo around periods for people who are not women but still menstruate."[27] Nadya now uses phrases such as *people with periods*, *people who menstruate*, and *menstruators* instead of *women* when discussing menstruation, and she refers to menstrual supplies as *period products* and *menstrual health products* instead of *feminine hygiene products*. Okamoto's feminism, then, includes everyone: "Our goal is gender equality, and fighting for the Menstrual Movement is one of the ways to reach that goal, and thus we need all gender identities to participate."[28]

Change Strategies

Nadya's change strategies are designed to make visible and address the taboo around periods. Taken together, her strategies equalize all genders by making menstruation an issue that everyone needs to consider. Her strategies consist of a set of steps that move from recognizing the problem with the menstrual taboo to overcoming it: (1) acknowledging a taboo, (2) destigmatizing the taboo, and (3) facilitating further conversation.

Acknowledging a Taboo

The taboo around menstruation is the impetus for Okamoto's primary change strategy. Although menstruation is central to human life, periods typically are not discussed: "Whether people like it or not, life is made possible because menstruation exists—it is literally the reason why pregnancy is possible and why we are all here."[29] Yet, the taboo has significant consequences for girls and their aspirations. Nadya explains that when boys reach puberty, "society pats them on the back for becoming men," and they are encouraged to "proclaim their power."[30] When girls begin menstruating, however, rather than celebrating their entrance into adulthood, women are faced with something shameful and something to keep hidden. Okamoto believes that acknowledging the existence of the taboo is a first step toward the global empowerment of women and girls.[31]

Recognizing the taboo around menstruation has larger societal implications than its impact on girls and women. Nadya notes: "As taboos about periods break down, it seems that the obstacles to period product innovation also shatter. But there is so much more that we can be doing to break down persisting stigmas to maximize the potential of our menstrual experience, like what periods can tell us about our health, how menstrual blood might be able to have other functions, and how we can make periods less disruptive for all menstruators."[32] When periods can be discussed openly and accurately, menstruators can be better informed about their bodies, and society can better address the needs and issues surrounding menstruation.

Okamoto acknowledges that the taboo around periods is not nearly as strong as it once was, and the media have played a major role in facilitating this shift. Television shows, advertising, and movies traditionally featured women as emotional and less rational when on their periods, and because these episodes provided the only information available to many men about periods, they contributed to the perpetuation of menstrual stereotypes. Recently, however, various media have begun to discuss periods more openly. The television series *Orange is the New Black*, for instance, directly addressed issues around menstruation and period products in prison.[33] Even advertising for period products is becoming more realistic, although not until 2017 was there an ad in which menstrual blood was depicted as red rather than blue.[34]

Destigmatizing the Taboo

Nadya not only names the taboo that surrounds menstruation but also seeks to destigmatize it by sharing her own stories around the taboo. She opens her book *Period Power* by telling about getting her first period. She grew up in a family that talked openly about body parts and periods, but she thought she was dying when she got her first period—bleeding from the inside out. "No matter how mentally prepared you are, it is rare to be *emotionally* prepared for that moment. You can know the details of menstruation and have period products ready to go," but "when I finally got my first period, there was still so much I didn't know—so much I didn't even know that I didn't know."[35] Okamoto was surprised, for instance, that there was so much blood, and she admits that during her first period, she used many more period products than necessary, worrying about leakage and toxic shock syndrome from tampons. She recounted being very frustrated with "how quickly I'd filled our bathroom trash can with those colorful wrappers from the many pads and tampons I had used."[36] Her mother then introduced her to the menstrual cup, which she admits she didn't take out for days because "it hurt very badly every time I tried to pull it out."[37] These experiences with learning to navigate her period resonate with those members of her audiences who menstruate and help destigmatize the experiences around the start of periods.

Nadya also shares another personal example about when she actually took advantage of the stigma around periods. In middle school, Okamoto and her friends would "get out of gym class every day" by telling their older male teacher that they were menstruating: "He never questioned the idea that we were on our periods 24/7 (all of us, at the same time, all the time). He just accepted that it made us unable to participate in physical activity."[38] By sharing how she herself took advantage of the stigma around menstruation, Nadya encourages her audiences to think about experiences they may have had with periods as a step toward destigmatizing the period taboo.

Okamoto admits, too, that when she began to work as a menstrual activist, she herself was apprehensive about talking about periods, so she also has experienced the strength of the taboo firsthand: "I realized that I had never thought about how nervous I myself felt when talking about periods openly. I had been so conditioned to accept that menstruation wasn't an appropriate conversation topic."[39] By discussing her own hesitancies, she makes it easier for others to learn to talk about the topic.

Facilitating Further Conversation

Nadya believes that the way to solve the problem of the menstrual taboo is to talk about it. Talking is critical because most people don't think about periods and certainly don't talk about them.

> If the combination of the taboo and stigma tells us that periods are something menstruators should keep quiet and feel ashamed about, then to reverse the taboo and the stigma, we need to do the exact opposite. . . . We will talk about periods openly and proudly—we will organize and talk about cycles and period products and menstrual health through megaphones on stages, and advocate for the Menstrual Movement to rooms full of initially uncomfortable listeners, who can then go on to do the same thing. Break the silence.[40]

Traditionally, talking about menstruation has been confined to those who menstruate: "If we do talk about periods, we usually do so only with other people who get their period," which "perpetuates the idea that only those who menstruate need to be responsible for learning about and discussing periods."[41]

Okamoto, however, believes everyone, including men, should talk about periods. She recalls that when she and Forand first started PERIOD, she had to explain to him what a period was. He grew up without sisters, and because sex education is typically sex segregated, menstruation is usually not discussed with boys.[42] Nadya makes a point, then, to address the men in her audiences specifically: "To the gentlemen out there—husbands, brothers, boyfriends, uncles—I'm talking to you and you. Don't avoid the topic, don't make derogatory comments if the lady in your life is on her period. Be accepting, be loving, be supportive. I'm not saying go out to the nearest grocery [store] or gas station and buy the amount of feminine hygiene products—although that would be a really beautiful gesture, I'm not expecting that. But be compassionate about it. . . . Start a conversation, talk to someone and discuss why are we so afraid to talk about something so natural."[43]

Okamoto sees facilitating conversations about menstruation as a responsibility: "I felt like I had something new to offer the world and a duty to speak up."[44] Nadya extends this sense of obligation to everyone: Those who have "the freedom and the platform (social media or otherwise) to ask questions, challenge systems, and speak out, we have a responsibility to do so—because so many in this world, including in our own communities . . . may still feel silenced."[45] Furthermore, if those who are able to speak up do not do so, they are contributing to the perpetuation of the taboo around periods: "Whether we like it or not, as members of society we participate in carrying the taboo forward. It's up to us to break it."[46] Okamoto encourages those in her audiences to do whatever they are comfortable doing to contribute to open conversations about menstruation: "If any of this has inspired or empowered you to act, do it. Whether it be simply starting a conversation or hosting something larger to collect period products to be donated to people who need them, just go for it."[47]

By naming and addressing the taboo around menstruation, Nadya makes the problem tangible, accessible, and solvable. She models how she progressed from not thinking about the issues surrounding menstruation to acknowledging the taboo, destigmatizing it, and speaking up about it. She enjoys the challenge of making people think and talk about periods, and every convert is "worth each uncomfortable conversation. If anything, when someone is adamantly against you, that just makes your job of convincing them that much more exciting—and makes the success of recruiting them into the Menstrual Movement that much more rewarding."[48] Okamoto does not see what she has accomplished as unusual in any way—it is just what needs to be done: "We have simply pursued a mission that we truly care about. Not for the money or for the recognition but to fight for every person's right to feel confident, capable, and dignified while menstruating."[49]

■ REFLECTIONS

1. If you menstruate or have menstruated, think back to when you got your first period. What aspects of the period taboo defined that experience? If you have never menstruated, what and how did you learn about periods, and what does your experience say about the period taboo?
2. Okamoto claims the period taboo keeps women from contributing fully to society. To what extent do you believe this is true? What difference would ending the period taboo make?
3. Examine advertising about menstruation products on television or in magazines. Are there ways in which the period taboo is still reflected in such advertising?
4. One of Okamoto's primary change strategies is destigmatizing the taboo that surrounds menstruation. She largely does this by talking openly about menstruation. Are there other ways in which she might destigmatize periods?
5. Start a conversation with a friend or family member about periods and the period taboo. How comfortable were you talking about periods? What does your conversation tell you about the period taboo?
6. How closely do Okamoto's change strategies align with the assumptions outlined in the introduction to part 3? Are there any assumptions that you don't believe pertain to her approach to change?
7. In which feminist wave would you place Okamoto and why?

■ Notes

1. Nadya Okamoto, *Period Power: A Manifesto for the Menstrual Movement* (New York: Simon and Schuster, 2018), 48.
2. Okamoto, *Period Power*, 12.
3. Nadya Okamoto, "The Menstrual Movement," TED Talk, Portland, OR, May 21, 2016, 2:24, https://www.youtube.com/watch?v=ncg2bw9s30M/
4. Okamoto, "The Menstrual Movement," 2:40.
5. Okamoto, "The Menstrual Movement," 2:51.
6. Okamoto, *Period Power*, 7.
7. *Camion* means *truck* in Spanish, and Okamoto chose this name to reference the way her organization was bringing period products to those who need them. She found herself constantly having to explain the name, however, and rebranded the organization *PERIOD*. See Okamoto, *Period Power*, 54.
8. Nadya Okamoto and Vincent Forand, "Let's Talk Periods," The 2019 Makers Conference, Dana Point, CA, February 8, 2019, 4:30, https://www.yahoo.com/lifestyle/clean-version-nadya-okamota-vincent-221923063.html/
9. Carly Stern, "'Period Shaming is Straight Up Misogyny': Meet the 20-Year-Old Harvard Dropout Who Is Changing the Way People Talk About Menstruation," *Daily Mail*, October 18, 2018, https://www.dailymail.co.uk/femail/article-6279541/Nadya-Okamoto-changing-people-talk-periods-nonprofit.html/
10. As of May 2021, thirty states still have laws that classify menstrual hygiene products as luxuries rather than necessities.
11. Okamoto, *Period Power*, 9.
12. Nadya Okamoto, email message to Karen A. Foss, October 26, 2019.
13. "About," Period. The Menstrual Movement, n.d., https://www.period.org/nadya/
14. Nadya Okamoto, "Period," *Teen Vogue* Summit, New York, NY, June 19, 2018, 7:51, https://www.youtube.com/watch?v=ZuNYBOiR56E/
15. Okamoto, "Period," 8:18.
16. Anika Mittu, "It Starts With Nadya," *Ms.*, March 20, 2018, https://msmagazine.com/2018/03/20/it-starts-with-nadya/
17. Julie Mazziotta, "This Harvard Student Started a Non-Profit at 16 that Gives Period Products to Homeless Women," *People*, October 16, 2018, https://people.com/health/college-student-non-profit-period-products-homeless-women/
18. "Best YA Nonfiction of 2018," *Kirkus Reviews*, December 3, 2018, https://www.cbcbooks.org/2018/12/03/best-young-adult-books-of-2018-from-kirkus-reviews/
19. Nadya Okamoto, email message to Karen A. Foss, October 26, 2019. By 2020, Vincent Forand had moved on to other endeavors, and PERIOD "separated from Nadya Okamoto, and grew in staff capacity and Board governance, hiring a new Executive Director and senior leadership." A youth advisory council was added to organizational leadership to ensure that youth activists remained central to programming. See "The PERIOD Mission," Period.org, https://period.org/who-we-are
20. Okamoto, *Period Power*, 183.
21. Mary Kate Fotch, "Women Who F*ck Sh*t Up: Nadya Okamoto," Betches, April 5, 2019, https://betches.com/women-who-fck-sht-up-nadya-okamoto/
22. Okamoto, *Period Power*, 264.
23. Okamoto, *Period Power*, 100.
24. Nadya Okamoto, "Ad for Adidas," Instagram, n.d., https://www.instagram.com/p/B2XjDFfH4lB/
25. Okamoto, *Period Power*, 254.
26. Okamoto, *Period Power*, 227.
27. Okamoto, *Period Power*, 232.
28. Okamoto, *Period Power*, 48.

[29] Okamoto, *Period Power*, 263.
[30] Okamoto, *Period Power*, 188.
[31] Okamoto, *Period Power*, 189.
[32] Okamoto, *Period Power*, 97.
[33] Okamoto, *Period Power*, 200.
[34] Okamoto, *Period Power*, 204–05.
[35] Okamoto, *Period Power*, 5.
[36] Okamoto, *Period Power*, 73–74.
[37] Okamoto, *Period Power*, 75.
[38] Okamoto, *Period Power*, 197.
[39] Okamoto, *Period Power*, 55.
[40] Okamoto, *Period Power*, 52–53.
[41] Okamoto, *Period Power*, 47.
[42] Okamoto and Forand, "Let's Talk Periods."
[43] Okamoto, "The Menstrual Movement," 12:16.
[44] Okamoto, *Period Power*, 10.
[45] Okamoto, *Period Power*, 149.
[46] Okamoto, *Period Power*, 58.
[47] Okamoto, *Period Power*, 288–89.
[48] Okamoto, *Period Power*, 56–57.
[49] Okamoto, *Period Power*, 282–83.

CHAPTER EIGHT

Jamie Margolin

The truth is, no changemaker ever, no youth activist ever, has fully known what they were doing. They just learned the best they could, did the best they could with the best intentions, and made the most change they could with what tools they had available to them. So what are you waiting for? The world is yours.[1]

Jamie Saraí Margolin is a Latina Jewish lesbian vegan feminist climate activist who wants to educate the world about the severity of the climate crisis. Not content to name the problem, she is committed to doing everything she can to ensure the survivability of the planet. Margolin was born in 2001 in Seattle, Washington. Her mother came to the United States from Colombia, where she worked as an office and sales manager in Bogotá; she now is an operations assistant at a Seattle food bank. Jamie's father, an Ashkenazi Jew, is an engineer.

Between the ages of eleven and fifteen, Margolin was a competitive rhythmic gymnast, a sport that combines gymnastics, calisthenics, and dance. Jamie quit because of injuries and because, as she explains, "I kind of just fell out of love with it . . . and my mind and attention" were "needed in other places. I'm someone who is all or nothing. I don't believe in half-assing anything . . . I believe in going all in." She believes the skills she learned as a gymnast contribute to what she has been able to accomplish as an activist: "I learned discipline, time management, perseverance, work ethic, and pushing through nervous situations and doing the best that I can under pressure."[2]

Margolin began doing organizing work for the Democratic campaign headquarters in Seattle when she was fourteen, and one of her first tasks was translating documents into Spanish. The climate crisis was always primary on Jamie's political agenda, however, and she participated in many local protests, testified on behalf of various bills, and campaigned for local initiatives designed to address climate issues—but nothing seemed to change. Several events coalesced in the summer of 2017 to compel her into activism at the national level. She was frustrated with the election of Donald Trump and with the fact that she was not seeing the leadership she expected from the Democratic party. She also witnessed several natural disasters that summer—three hurricanes hit Puerto Rico, wildfires burned up and down the West Coast, and smog covered Seattle. Margolin decided she needed to act: "The climate crisis is something that is interconnected with all other issues. If I don't take action on it, it will be too late and then nothing else will matter. I can't pursue my dreams, I can't live out my goals to be happy. The world as we know it is literally coming to an end."[3]

In the summer of 2017, Jamie joined with Nadia Nazar, Madelaine Tew, and Zanagee Artis to form an international nonprofit organization called *Zero Hour*. The name comes from their belief that this is the zero hour for acting on climate change. Margolin explains that "we cannot afford to wait any longer for adults to protect our right to the clean and safe environment, the natural resources we need to not just survive, but flourish. We know that we are the leaders we have been waiting for!"[4] Zero Hour builds coalitions with other movements for social justice to address the roots of oppression that contribute to climate change. The organization also supports "Just Transition," an initiative to move to an environmentally sustainable economy without hurting the workers in the oil and gas industries.[5] This initiative asks industries to reskill employees, to provide fully paid quality healthcare, and to switch to renewable energy and asks local and state governments to invest in zero emissions mass transit, protect the treaty rights and food sovereignty rights of Indigenous people, and divest pensions from companies that support fossil fuels.

The members of Zero Hour are committed to demonstrating the urgency of climate change. As their first major event, they planned a mass action, led by young people, that they hoped would be so big it could not be ignored. What they devised was the first Youth Climate March on July 21, 2018, in Washington, DC and twenty-five other cities around the world. The following July, Zero Hour held another summit in Miami, Florida, where organizers trained over 350 young people in climate-justice activism. This was followed later that month by the delivery of demands to members of the US House and Senate, asking them to take a "No Fossil Fuel Money Pledge."

In addition to starting an organization to address the climate crisis, Jamie also pursues legal action to call attention to and force action on climate change. She was a plaintiff in a lawsuit filed against the state of Washington for denying her generation's constitutional rights to a livable environment. Washington governor Jay Inslee frequently campaigned on a climate-change platform, but Margolin did not believe he had done enough to address the problem: "He hasn't walked the walk. He's in support of a lot of new fossil fuel infrastructure, and that's deadly for my future."[6] The lawsuit was rejected by the courts, so in March 2021 the plaintiffs asked the Washington Supreme Court to hear the case.

Jamie has always considered herself a writer, and writing is another venue through which she pursues her activism: "Ever since I was little, I was always a writer and I was always a creative person. I was always creating stories and worlds of fiction. . . . There are video tapes of me telling stories and making up stories when I was three, even when I was two. It's in my bones. It's who I am."[7] Margolin has authored op-eds for the *New York Times*, *Teen Vogue*, the *Washington Post*, *Time* magazine, and *DAZED*. One of her first pieces, written when she was fourteen, was an op-ed piece published in the *Seattle Times* in support of Hillary Clinton's presidential bid.[8]

That she would write a book while still in high school does not strike Jamie as unusual. In *Youth to Power: Your Voice and How to Use It* (2020), Margolin offers other young activists the book she "desperately wished I had when I was fourteen and just starting my activism journey, with no clue of what I was getting into."[9] She explains that "as a chronically exhausted high school student with too much homework who's running an international movement," she wants to provide others with a "guide to causing good trouble, unlearning everything you've been taught before, disrupting the status quo, making your voice heard, challenging problematic authority, changing the culture, changing laws, and yes, changing the world."[10] Although it may seem to many that Jamie just "tripped into a campaign office, and suddenly . . . was a successful activist," she wants her audiences to understand that this was not the case. She offers specific strategies for the various situations in which activists might find themselves—event planning, lobbying, managing negative press, and using social media, for example—that she wishes she had known about earlier. She also includes short interviews with other activists to provide inspiration and to publicize the diversity of activist causes and strategies.

Following high school, Margolin attended New York University as a film major; for her, film is another vehicle for telling stories. She has always used movies and television as a "form of escapism"—movies and television are her "happy place."[11] Jamie wants to use film—and art generally—to encourage people to become active in addressing the climate emergency and other causes in which they believe because "media shifts the culture and culture shifts policy and people."[12] Art, according to Margolin, "is a universal language, a way of making people see and understand experiences in a profound new light. . . . Art is a way to creatively display facts and messages to appeal to people's humanity and emotions and unlock something inside of them that makes them more receptive to your message."[13] Jamie sees art as "a better way of changing people than attacking them"—something that "never works. Because then they just double down."[14]

Margolin continues to pursue her activism on behalf of the climate crisis through all of her venues—testifying, campaigning, lobbying, writing, and film. Her Twitter bio announces "Future POTUS," which suggests she has plans to add the US presidency to her list of ways to work toward change. She is interested in using many different kinds of change strategies to ensure that climate change is recognized as a problem and that people are motivated to act to address it quickly and effectively.

Definition of Feminism

Jamie's feminism cannot be separated from the other issues that affect people and the planet. According to Margolin, the climate crisis is a matter of human rights and dignity, and "if you don't acknowledge this you're going the wrong way and you won't protect anything."[15] She sees climate change as a "threat multiplier, which means that any issue that is existing in the world, climate change worsens it."[16] The fix, she believes, "isn't simply about slapping a solar panel on the climate crisis" but about tackling the climate crisis through an "intersectional lens."[17] This means dismantling systems of oppression that caused climate change in the first place: colonialism, consumerism, capitalism, racism, and patriarchy. In a Ted Talk, she explains that the climate crisis began not with the industrial revolution, as many believe, but with colonialism.

> With colonialism came the idea that everything on this earth is made for our extraction and that everything is to be bought and sold. . . . When colonizers arrived to the Americas they immediately thought of the land, the water, and all other natural resources in front of them as theirs to claim and extract. Why this entitlement? Because unless someone had explicitly bought the land with a system of currency they valued, it was seen as free pickings. So with colonialism came the idea that nothing—not air not water not trees not animals not land—was sacred or priceless. And this mindset is the core of how we got to climate disaster.[18]

Patriarchy, as a contributor to climate change, is central to what Jamie wants to address with her feminism. Colonialism exploited the earth, and it brought a patriarchal system to Indigenous communities that traditionally were matriarchal. As a result, women were devalued as leaders in their cultures. Yet, women are more affected by the climate crisis than men because they are the primary providers of food and fuel, and they are more vulnerable when natural disasters such as drought and flooding occur. In addition, women are burdened with dealing with the effects of climate change—they "bear the weight of rebuilding and caring for communities after disaster."[19]

Despite and because of the history and impact of patriarchy on women, Margolin wants women to assume leadership of the climate-change revolution. She argues that those "who feel the worst effects of an issue are the experts and must be at the forefront of that issue's solutions."[20] Women must continue to fight to be listened to and be taken seriously; women must claim the power that patriarchy took away. Jamie models this goal with Zero Hour: "I am especially proud of building a movement that is run by women of color. It provides a safe place for girls like me to lead."[21]

Margolin's own experiences with patriarchy show just how entrenched the patriarchal mentality is. As a young woman, she is often underestimated by those in positions of power, especially men. She recounts, for example, having spent the day at a hearing where she listened to fossil-fuel executives explain that there is no proof that fossil fuels damage the environment. When she confronted them afterward, one of the men squeezed her shoulder and said, "'Sweetie, don't worry yourself so much about this environment thing because corporations are actually the ones who do the most for the environment. We got it covered. Just focus on school.'"[22] Similarly, a conservative blogger criticized Jamie's position on climate change and then suggested she "should worry less about the environment and more about getting a boyfriend." Not only did Margolin find this especially funny because she's a lesbian but, she notes, "that's heteronormativity and sexism for you." In the same blog, she was labeled a "dumb teenage girl" who "didn't smile enough," another classic critique directed at women who do not adhere to traditional expectations of femininity.[23] Jamie summarizes: "If I got money every time I was laughed at, interrupted, blatantly told that what I said was 'false,' and just overall mansplained in a professional environment, I think I could pay for college."[24]

Margolin offers a succinct summary of her feminism in the advice she offers women: "Never apologize for your existence, never apologize for your power, or the work you do."[25] She sees women as in the vanguard of the climate revolution and trusts that they have the knowledge, skills, and commitment to tackle not only climate change but the oppressions that created the crisis in the first place.

Change Strategies

Jamie is determined to alert the world to the critical importance of addressing climate change. For her, it is more than a popular cause to which she has chosen to devote her life; it is about the survival of the planet: "It's not just, 'Hey, let's save the turtles.' It's not charity, it's an [act of] survival. I'm protecting my survival and my generation's survival."[26] Margolin employs three change strategies to name the problem so that others begin to see it as something that must be immediately and urgently addressed: (1) continuing to learn, (2) developing personal activist skills, and (3) showing up.

Continuing to Learn

The importance of continuing to learn is Jamie's primary strategy for naming the problem of climate change. To name the problem in ways that motivate people to address it requires that she and other activists keep learning—about climate change and about effective advocacy. She positions herself as still learning, despite her many years of activism, which puts her on equal footing with her audiences. As Margolin notes in *Youth to Power*, "I am in the same boat as you, and I'm not going to order you around and act like

I'm better than you or pretend to know everything. The truth is, I am still learning, just like you. We're in this together."[27]

Jamie encourages her audiences not to put too much pressure on themselves in the learning process. Instead, they need to be open and flexible about what to do and when to do it. There are many approaches that can be effective, she believes, so activists shouldn't worry about figuring out the one path that should be pursued: "Go make some productive noise, make some changes, and learn by jumping in headfirst and doing the work that needs to be done."[28] What's most important is that "as activists, we must keep educating ourselves, listening to other perspectives, and remembering to be aware as much as possible."[29]

Margolin also acknowledges that every activist makes mistakes as they try to call attention to and address problems, and she freely discusses mistakes she has made in the course of her activist journey, such as being too dictatorial, neglecting team dynamics, and continuing to give "responsibility to those who have proved they're not responsible."[30] Her own openness about what she wishes she had done differently makes others more comfortable about making mistakes themselves: "You should accept early on that you're going to make mistakes. As a perfectionist, I don't like the idea of having a 100 percent chance that I am going to mess up over and over again and that I will never fully know it all—but that's the deal in this field. You just have to keep questioning, educating yourself, and doing."[31]

Developing Personal Activist Skills

In addition to the importance of remaining open to and continuing to learn, Jamie stresses that activists need to deliberately develop advocacy skills that bring the problem to the forefront of public consciousness and that work for them personally. This means that activists must discover their own strengths as well as their limitations. She recognizes, for example, that not everyone is comfortable breaking rules or engaging in civil disobedience. Some may not have a "knack for public speaking," while others are not ready "to visit a politician's office and let them know how you feel." For yet others, "working in a group setting is really uncomfortable."[32] Beginning activists should assess their strengths and not be worried if there are actions they are not ready for—and perhaps never will be able to do. Margolin recognizes that there are all kinds of effective ways of "making those in power listen,"[33] including a whole range of strategies that often go unrecognized. Activism, she explains, is often "practiced in many ways that often go unnoticed. It is listening and building relationships. It's writers who focus on issues and perspectives outside the status quo. It's teachers who lift up marginalized voices. . . . Attention-getting strategies are not the only way to create change."[34]

In addition to determining the forms of activism with which they are most comfortable, Jamie also encourages youth activists to become aware of what they will be up against with their activism. Just as they need to know their personal activist preferences, they also need to know the resources the system might use against them: "Beyond knowing what power you do and don't have as a young person, it is also important to know what you will be up against no matter what. . . . Know how the world perceives you (whether their perception is true or not) so you can best arm yourself to overcome their preconceived notions."[35] Young activists, for example, will experience "patronizing and invalidation," "lack of trust" in their abilities, and "systematic silencing."[36] But if they are aware of these attributions and tactics, they can resourcefully compensate for them by knowing "everything there is to know" on a topic, defying "stereotypes and expectations of your immaturity and irresponsibility," and addressing "the elephant in the room"[37] if necessary—calling out those who are rude to or dismissive of young activists. With such strategies, young activists are able to name the problem of climate change in ways that keep it at the forefront of policy makers' and stakeholders' agendas.

Showing Up

Another strategy Margolin uses to name and address the problem of climate change is to show up, to commit, and to persevere. She maintains that every individual can make a difference by choosing to stand up and speak out. She elaborates: "It isn't rare for many people to have the same yearning to be free and the same concerns and dreams of a better world that you have, but they are waiting for someone to be the first person to stand up and speak for it. . . . You just have to stand up and decide, *enough already*, and be the one to break the silence. Then those who have felt that way all along will follow."[38] She claims that "the courage to speak truth to power" is what has "saved people, countries, and movements"[39] in the past, and it can happen again. Furthermore, speaking up is especially important at this "crucial moment in history. The decisions you make, the action you take as a young person in the twenty-first century with a voice and strong convictions will shape the world for thousands of years to come. The action you take now will decide the future of our planet and everything in it."[40] Jamie believes that her generation has influence, and making use of that power to highlight the problem is crucial for the climate change fight: "You as a young person in today's world have something important to say, something special to offer society. . . . Youth have and always will steer our society's culture toward progress. That is our power. That is our job. That is our gift."[41]

Margolin realizes that despite the guidance and reassurance she provides to activists, some might still be reluctant to participate in a social movement. They might feel that they are too young and do not have the skills or knowledge to contribute effectively, or they still might question whether they can make a difference. She asserts that "whoever told you that you don't belong in the political world or that you do not have what it takes to fight for a cause is full of it."[42] She believes all individuals have a role to play: "Wherever you are in your journey is okay—whether you're still a bit nervous about dipping your toe into the tumultuous waters of making an impact, or whether you are confident and ready to go but just need the right guidance to move forward."[43] Jamie shares how she was in that same position not long ago: "I was you. I was an insecure, fourteen-year-old, worried and scared about the state of the world, with no clue how to get started."[44] She admits she was "stumbling along," but more and more opportunities were given to her "because I stuck around and did the hard work."[45]

Margolin wants activists to know that each step they take and each action in which they engage makes a difference in bringing the problem to the forefront of public consciousness, even if those steps seem minor and insignificant. She notes that "one meeting is not going to change everything. But everything adds up.... You never know whether your story, your conversation, your initiative, will be the one to tip the scale and make change happen."[46] What is important is to "keep the pressure on, keep the heat on, and don't ever let them forget you and your power!"[47] She uses the song "Just Keep Swimming" from the movie *Finding Nemo* as a kind of mantra that "has helped me keep fighting,"[48] and she wants others to find their own ways to stay in the fight: "You just have to show up, make it clear you're open to taking on tasks and are ready to learn, and then gradually prove yourself and ask for more, make more connections, learn more ... it snowballs. But no snowballing is going to happen unless you open that door, make yourself available, and just dive in and do."[49]

Jamie's change strategies are designed to help other activists join her in the effort to name and then to begin to address the climate crisis. The issue of climate change is not separate from the other oppressions that characterize society—colonialism, racism, consumerism, capitalism, and patriarchy. Drawing on her own activist experiences, Margolin offers advice to others, and it is advice that remains important to her as well: continuing to learn; developing personal activist skills; and above all, showing up, so there is continual attention directed at and pressure applied to the problem of climate change. Jamie hopes there will come a day when she can do more than imagine a world free of the oppressions and resulting climate crisis; she wants to live in such a world.

> When I close my eyes and imagine the world my kids live in, I imagine a world that has finally healed. In this world, we're healed from our deadly fossil fuel addiction, and healed from our addiction to mass factory farming and industrial animal agriculture. We have gotten to the roots of the climate crisis. The patriarchy, racism, colonialism, and excessive, abusive capitalism that caused the climate crisis will have been addressed.... So, every night, I go to bed with wishful dreams of that beautiful near-future post-climate-change world, and every day I wake up and work to make it happen. You, reading this right now, are one of the people alive today who has the power to shape life on earth forever. So what are you going to do with that?[50]

■ REFLECTIONS

1. Margolin believes that art is critical for changing culture because it is a universal language that makes people more receptive to a message. Choose a work of art or an artist whose work is designed to generate change around an issue other than climate change. Explain how the artwork functions to create change. Does it do more than make people more receptive to change?
2. Margolin recounts examples where her ideas and proposals are dismissed simply because she is a young woman. Have you ever had such experiences because of an identity marker? How have you handled such incidents in the past? What might be effective ways for handling these kinds of situations?
3. Margolin's advice to women includes not apologizing for their existence, their power, or their work. Investigate literature (by feminists or scholars in fields such as psychology or communication) to discover how apologies function. Is a refusal to apologize always a good thing, according to these experts?
4. Margolin says change makers need to know their strengths and limitations as activists. What are the major strengths and limitations that characterize your change efforts?
5. Margolin emphasizes the importance of just showing up. Can you think of a situation in your own life where "just showing up" made a difference?
6. How closely do Margolin's change strategies align with the assumptions outlined in the introduction to part 3? Are there any assumptions that you don't believe pertain to her approach to change?
7. In which feminist wave would you place Margolin and why?

■ NOTES

[1] Jamie Margolin, *Youth to Power: Your Voice and How to Use It* (New York: Hachette, 2020), 224.
[2] Jamie Margolin, "Hey, I'm Jamie Margolin," interview by Wesley Wade, Freshfruit, October 20, 2020, https://www.freshfruitmag.com/hey-im-jamie-margolin/
[3] Margolin, "Hey, I'm Jamie Margolin."
[4] "Who We Are: Our Vision," Zero Hour, n.d., http://thisiszerohour.org/who-we-are/
[5] "Platform Documents: Just Transition," Zero Hour, n.d., http://thisiszerohour.org/files/ZeroHour_JustTransition.pdf/
[6] Ryan Schleeter, "Ten Things You've Always Wanted to Ask a 16-Year-Old Suing the Government Over Climate Change," Greenpeace, January 11, 2018, https://medium.com/greenpeace/10-things-youve-always-wanted-to-ask-a-16-year-old-suing-the-government-over-climate-change-828c983131ca/
[7] Margolin, "Hey, I'm Jamie Margolin."
[8] Jamie Margolin, "Presidential Politics as Seen by a 14-Year-Old," *Seattle Times*, October 28, 2016 (https://www.seattletimes.com/opinion/presidential-politics-as-seen-by-a-14-year-old/). Margolin supported Bernie Sanders in the 2020 primaries and now sees her politics as in line with those of US Representative Alexandria Ocasio-Cortez.
[9] Margolin, *Youth to Power*, xvi.
[10] Margolin, *Youth to Power*, xvii–xviii.
[11] Jamie Margolin, "Ace Interview: Co-Founder of ZeroHour, Jamie Margolin Details What She's Learned about Balancing Mental Health and Activism," interview by Indi Howeth,

Ace: Alliance for Climate Education, February 4, 2021, https://acespace.org/2021/02/04/ace-interview-jamie-margolin/
[12] Margolin, "Hey, I'm Jamie Margolin."
[13] Margolin, *Youth to Power*, 71.
[14] Jane Goodall, "A Wave of Change: Jamie Margolin and Jane Goodall," interview by Jamie Margolin, Atmos, December 10, 2020, https://atmos.earth/jane-goodall-jamie-margolin-climate-interview/
[15] Margolin, "Climate Activist Jamie Margolin. We the Youth are Building an Unstoppable Movement," interview by Camilla Soldati, Lifegate, November 8, 2019, https://www.lifegate.com/jamie-margolin-interview/
[16] Jamie Margolin, "GLAAD 20 Under 20 Honoree," October 28, 2020, https://www.glaad.org/amp/jamie-margolin-election-climate-justice-lgbtq-advocacy/
[17] Alli Maloney, "21 Under 21: Jamie Margolin Knows Climate Justice is the Key to All Justice," *Teen Vogue*, November 5, 2018, https://www.teenvogue.com/story/jamie-margolin-21-under-21-2018/
[18] Jamie Margolin, "Patriarchy, Racism, Colonialism," TEDxYouth@Columbia, Columbia, NY, June 14, 2019, 0:35, https://www.youtube.com/watch?v=amGyIqIBzEk/
[19] Margolin, "Patriarchy, Racism, Colonialism," 7:27.
[20] Maloney, "21 Under 21."
[21] Jamie Saraí Margolin, "Don't Underestimate 17-Year-Old Climate Change Activist Jamie Saraí Margolin—and Don't Call her 'Sweetie,'" Assembly, Malala.org, December 19, 2018, https://assembly.malala.org/stories/jamie-margolin-zero-hour/
[22] Maloney, "21 Under 21."
[23] Jamie Saraí Margolin, "Don't Underestimate."
[24] Maloney, "21 Under 21."
[25] Maloney, "21 Under 21."
[26] Jamie Margolin, "Climate Activist Jamie Margolin."
[27] Margolin, *Youth to Power*, xviii.
[28] Margolin, *Youth to Power*, 224.
[29] Margolin, *Youth to Power*, 153.
[30] Margolin, *Youth to Power*, 213–15.
[31] Margolin, *Youth to Power*, 12.
[32] Margolin, *Youth to Power*, 23.
[33] Margolin, *Youth to Power*, 13.
[34] Margolin, *Youth to Power*, 153.
[35] Margolin, *Youth to Power*, 91.
[36] Margolin, *Youth to Power*, 91.
[37] Margolin, *Youth to Power*, 91.
[38] Margolin, *Youth to Power*, 223.
[39] Margolin, *Youth to Power*, xiii.
[40] Margolin, *Youth to Power*, 222.
[41] Margolin, *Youth to Power*, 222–23.
[42] Margolin, *Youth to Power*, xvi.
[43] Margolin, *Youth to Power*, xvii.
[44] Margolin, *Youth to Power*, xvii.
[45] Margolin, *Youth to Power*, 19–20.
[46] Margolin, *Youth to Power*, 118.
[47] Margolin, *Youth to Power*, 118.
[48] Margolin, "Ace Interview."
[49] Margolin, *Youth to Power*, 20.
[50] Jamie Margolin, "The Day We Save Ourselves From Ourselves," International Congress of Youth Voices, n.d., https://www.internationalcongressofyouthvoices.com/jamie-margolin/

CHAPTER
NINE

Margaret Cho

> *I am the best at what I do, which is the plain and simple truth, undisputed by most people, argued over only by those who have never seen me and/or plainly can't stand to see a woman, especially a foreign one, take that much pride and such a vaingloriously unapologetic stance in the traditional American folk art of stand-up comedy. This is not a realm I was born to nor welcomed into, yet I forced my chinky bound foot in the door, and somehow kept it open by being so fucking good. How dare I? Watch me.*[1]

Although feminists themselves are often treated as a joke and women in general have not been viewed as funny because "to be aggressively funny—is to violate the norms of femininity,"[2] Margaret Cho defiantly uses comedy to unsettle hegemonic ways of thinking and acting. She has been dubbed the "Patron Saint for Outsiders" and proudly declares: "I am a queer, loud, raunchy Asian-American woman with progressive political views and the best dirty jokes coming at you to make you feel real."[3]

Cho was born *Moran Cho* (*Moran* means peony flower in Korean) in 1968 in San Francisco, California. During much of her childhood, her father lived in Seoul, South Korea, where he wrote joke books and authored a newspaper column; he was not allowed to come to the United States until his visa issues were settled. After Margaret's brother was born, their grandparents came from Korea to take care of the children while their parents ran a snack bar in a bowling alley. They then bought a gay/lesbian bookstore called *Paperback Traffic*, where Cho encountered and learned to appreciate the queer community.

Margaret's years in grade and high school were difficult. Between the ages of five and twelve, she was sexually molested by a family friend, and she was bullied mercilessly by her classmates. Expelled from high school at the age of fifteen, she nevertheless participated in a summer-stock theater program for high school students and then was accepted into the San Francisco School of the Arts, where she became involved with Batwing Lubricant, the school's improvisational comedy group. When the improv group performed at the Other Café, a famous comedy club where comedians such as Robin Williams and Paula Poundstone regularly performed, Cho "saw, in that dark and smoky club, the rest of my life. I thought if I could just be allowed to go onstage and make people laugh every night that I wouldn't care if I made money or became famous."[4] She spent the rest of her teenage years doing comedy in the clubs of San Francisco while working as a clerk at the FAO Schwartz toy store, as a salesperson at a lesbian sadomasochism leather boutique, and as a phone-sex operator.

Margaret entered and won a comedy contest for college students (she lied about being in college; she briefly attended San Francisco State University before dropping out). The first prize was the opportunity to serve as the opening act for Jerry Seinfeld on his upcoming comedy tour, which helped her believe she could make a living as a comic. Cho moved to Los Angeles in the early 1990s and began performing on the college comedy circuit, presenting over 300 shows in two years: "I did all those one-nighters and stayed in all those crappy motels and drove a million miles and stuffed the loneliness with food and pot and dreams that maybe this would all lead to something."[5] It did—she won the American Comedy Award for Female Comedian in 1994.

In that same year, Margaret was given her own sitcom called *All-American Girl* on the ABC network. Based on Cho's life growing up in the United States with Korean immigrant parents, it was the first prime-time sitcom to focus on an Asian American family, and she hoped the show "would make it okay for Asians to be on TV."[6] Told to lose weight before the show began filming because of "'the fullness' of her face . . . her Korean-American face,"[7] Margaret lost thirty pounds in two weeks and was hospitalized with kidney failure. Dissatisfaction with the show surfaced almost immediately among ABC executives, and audiences reacted negatively as well. "Deep inside, I knew that the show wasn't good, that I had gotten myself into a big mess," explains Cho. "The jokes weren't so much stereotypical as stale. . . . It was immature and unfunny, and playing an overgrown, oversize teenager was not my forte. I looked stupid, and even worse, I *knew* I looked stupid."[8] The show was cancelled, catapulting Margaret into a spiral of depression, alcoholism, anorexia, and drug addiction.

Cho stayed out of the public eye until 1999, when she decided to deal with the embarrassment of her TV show by launching a comedy tour, *I'm the One That I Want*, and her career took off. She has had numerous sold-out national tours, some of which also have been made into feature films, including *I'm the One That I Want*. Other shows have included *Notorious C.H.O.* (2002), *Revolution* (2003), *Assassin* (2005), *Beautiful* (2008), *Mother!* (2013), and *Fresh Off the Bloat* (2017).

Margaret works in a variety of other mediums in addition to stand-up comedy. She has acted in films such as *Face/Off* and *The Rugrats Movie* and has made her own film, *Bam Bam and Celeste*. She had a starring role in the TV series *Drop Dead Diva* and in the reality sitcom *The Cho Show* and has guest starred on programs such as *30 Rock*, *Dancing with the Stars*, *Sex and the City*, and *Celebrity Family Feud*. Cho has released both music and comedy albums and has directed and appeared in music videos, including ones for Awkwafina, Weird Al Yankovic, and The Cliks. She also has published two books. *I'm the One That I Want* (1999) is an autobiographical book about the difficulties involved in breaking into show business and her struggle with and triumph over body issues and addiction. Margaret's second book, *I Have Chosen to Stay and Fight* (2005), is a collection of essays about contemporary issues, including politics, human rights, race, and feminism. She hosts a weekly podcast, *The Margaret Cho*, and is the cohost of another weekly podcast, *Monsters of Talk*. She founded a clothing line, High Class Cho, with friend and fashion designer Ava Stander. After she took up belly dancing, Cho started Hip Wear, her own line of belly-dancing belts and accessories.

Not afraid to address personal issues in her work, Margaret discusses her struggles with food, body image, and addiction. She has struggled with issues around food since she was a child, when her parents "taught me that eating was this criminal act."[9] When network executives asked her to lose weight to play herself on *All American Girl*, her anorexia burgeoned. After years of dieting, she changed her approach to eating and her disease: "I just pulled myself out of the game."[10] Cho thought, "Fuck it. If I am fat, then I am fat. Fuck it. I am going to eat whatever I want and see what happens."[11] The result was that she began "to get weirdly thinner. I get it now. Because I don't care about food, and it's there when I want it, I don't think about it and crave it. Since I can have everything, nothing is that important.... When I'm hungry, I eat."[12]

Margaret not only struggled with an eating disorder but with addiction as well. She began smoking marijuana at the age of fifteen but soon was experimenting with other drugs, including LSD, speed, and ecstasy, while also taking diet pills, pep pills, Valium, and Xanax. She was drinking heavily as well, starting in the morning to cure her hangover from the night before. When Cho realized she did not want to die, she began to address her addictions, and comedy was one vehicle she used to tackle them: "I couldn't be too high when I performed. I was paranoid enough onstage. Trying to do it high was impossible."[13] After she quit, she observed that "audiences found me funnier, more alive, happy. Sometimes I had drunk because I thought I hated my job. I realized then that I loved my job, and that being fucked up all the time made me hate it because I couldn't do it properly."[14]

Margaret allies herself with gay men, lesbians, and all who identify as queer and goes out of her way to foreground their perspectives in her stand-up routines. She sees queerness as a benefit and an advantage: "I'm just determined to be out in all of my ways. I feel like it's important for me. I don't understand when people aren't out or when they actively don't want to be gay. I think it's so much better to be gay. It's so fun."[15] She credits gay men with sharing important knowledge with her: "I learned everything I know about being a woman from gay men. I learned all about sex from gay men."[16] Cho also proudly claims the label of *fag hag*: "I am fortunate enough to have been a fag hag for most of my life. A fag hag is a woman who prefers the company of gay men."[17]

Despite her close alliance with the queer community, Margaret refuses to put conventional labels on her own sexuality. She practices polyamory, pansexuality, and alternative sexuality and sometimes calls herself *bisexual*. She typically eschews that term, however, explaining: "I think bisexual is wrong as it applies to me because I don't feel that gender is binary. I don't think that we are so easily male or female. I am technically bisexual although I'm also attracted to transgender people so that just makes me greedy."[18] Cho believes there's no need to decide on a label: "It's okay to be attracted to anybody. . . . You don't have to decide, no matter how much you feel the need to. You actually don't have to figure that out at all. Ever."[19]

Definition of Feminism

For Margaret, "feminism is nonnegotiable."[20] As she explains, "Feminism is my life! It's who I am. For me, it's just a logical way to be. It's the way I approach everything."[21] She defines feminism as "a respect for living. But not to be confused with pro-life! It's a matter of respect for life and where life comes from and what life is and to respect women's rights and to respect women's wishes and what women want."[22] One of the reasons Cho believes everyone should be a feminist is because everyone came from a woman: "Do you think you grew out of the ground? That the stork dropped you off? You fell from a tree? No. You came out of a woman. . . . You would not be here if it were not for her. I'm not telling you that you have to do anything for your mom. I'm just saying we need to respect women for the fact that they are where the world begins."[23]

A second reason Margaret claims the label of *feminist* is because she believes the perspectives of women and other marginalized groups should be part of what is considered knowledge and truth in a culture: "Haven't we heard enough from those ancient white guys?," she asks. Cho acknowledges that her profile does not align with those whose ideas are typically revered in the culture: "I am not a man, nor am I white. I am not really old enough or educated enough. What could I possibly have to say that would be of any use to anyone?"[24] She answers her question by explaining that "perhaps the things that set me apart from the commentators we are used to hearing from are the things that make my opinion worthwhile."[25] Margaret believes that incorporating the perspectives of women and other marginalized groups into the culture will produce greater wisdom, but she realizes there is still much work to be done to achieve this goal. She urges women "to appreciate what we have, but we also have to fight for more."[26]

Change Strategies

The problem Cho names in her work is that conventional restrictions prevent individuals from making their own life choices and living their best lives. She uses humor to challenge norms and expectations of all kinds, including the "micropractices of everyday life, practices that make up the normal and normalizing codes of gender and other sites of oppression."[27] By naming issues around societal norms, Margaret's strategies are designed to prompt others to think about those norms and ultimately engage in new ways of acting and thinking: (1) exaggerating stereotypes, (2) valuing the self, and (3) enacting self-determination.

Exaggerating Stereotypes

One strategy Cho uses to highlight expectations or norms that restrict individuals' lives unnecessarily is to exaggerate stereotypes. She takes a stereotype that her audience is likely to hold and stretches or enlarges it. As a result, audiences not only must see and acknowledge the stereotype, but they realize how ridiculous and inaccurate it is. This strategy jolts the audience out of "customary alignments"[28] and opens up fresh ways of seeing outside of the restrictions of the stereotype.

Margaret is particularly attentive to racial stereotypes. She often names or enacts the stereotype, giving audiences a glimpse of what she experiences as a Korean American, for example. She explains that she often receives calls from people who say, "I have this script that you're gonna love. There's this part for an Asian woman—it's really not the lead, but it's such a great part." Cho deletes these calls "because there's no way this part is gonna be anything good."[29] She explains that she never had any desire to play

> a liquor store owner kicking a black person out of my store, . . . an early-rising, loose black cotton pants-wearing elderly woman practicing tai chi in the park, . . . a purveyor of exotic mushrooms and ginseng, . . . a daughter crying with my mom over our constant battle between East and West yet finally coming together over a particularly intense game of mah-jongg. . . . a girl, barely out of grammar school, playing violin for the president in a long, black velvet dress . . . . holding my breath for over three minutes while diving for pearls, . . . saying, "Welcome to Japan, Mr. Bond," . . . going anywhere with a chicken under my arm.[30]

One way in which Margaret enlarges stereotypes is by offering an alternative view that directly contradicts the stereotype. Sometimes, the alternative she provides is not what the audience expects, which functions to make the stereotype painfully obvious. When she was promoting her television show *All-American Girl*, a talk-show host "wanted her to say something in her native tongue. Cho looked into the camera and spoke in clear, West Coast-accented English."[31] Margaret also offers an alternative to stereotypes about how women are supposed to look. She rejects excessively thin women as aspirational models and declares that "the most beautiful women are voluptuous."[32] She elaborates: "I want a big bull dyke. I want a woman who looks like John Goodman. That's fucking hot to me. Don't Sharon Stone me to death."[33]

Valuing the Self

Cho recognizes that marginalized individuals often lack self-esteem because they have internalized or been colonized by the limiting stereotypes assigned to them by the dominant culture. She acknowledges the difficulty of developing self-esteem in this context: "I'm probably somebody who wouldn't necessarily have a lot of self-esteem as I'm considered a minority. And if you are a woman, a person of color, if you are gay, lesbian, bisexual, transgender, if you're a person of size, if you're a person of intelligence, if you're a person of integrity, then *you* are considered a minority in this world. And it's gonna be really hard to find messages of self-love and support anywhere."[34]

When marginalized individuals accept the pictures painted of them by the dominant culture, Margaret believes, they give away their power. She explains that when individuals have low self-esteem, they are hesitant to do all sorts of things that would demonstrate their power: "You will hesitate to go for the job you really want to go for, to ask for a raise, to call yourself an American, to report a rape, to defend yourself when you are discriminated against . . . , to vote, to dream."[35] Cho's commitment to naming and rejecting the limitations society places on her is a source of power for her and a model she wants others to follow: "I don't want to be my own worst enemy anymore. When I tell myself I am fat, that I have to work out, I've taken from myself the energy to go out and do it. I feel hurt, bled of life force, and then I must work with that deficit. I give up before I am through because I feel defeated before I even begin."[36]

According to Margaret, when individuals cure themselves of the self-loathing and self-deprecation that come from accepting the restrictions society places on them, they can begin to generate new self-definitions and to value themselves. "We are perfect as we are," she asserts.[37] Cho is particularly committed to seeing herself as beautiful: "I always thought that people told you that you're beautiful, that this was a title that was bestowed upon you—that it was other people's responsibility to give you this title. And I'm sick of waiting, people! . . . And I think that it's time to take into our own hands this power and to say, 'You know what—I'm beautiful—I just am.'" She describes the impact this choice has had on her life: "It's changed the way that I carry myself, it's changed the way that people respond to me, and it's changed the way that I feel, . . . And it really improves *everything*!" 38

With self-definition comes the realization that "we are powerful enough that we can manifest anything into our lives. To use this power with great care and love is the secret to living a happy life."[39] Margaret sees the application of this power as a revolutionary act: "For us, to have self-esteem is truly an act of revolution, and our revolution is long overdue. I urge you all today . . . to love yourself without reservation and to love each other without restraints. Unless you're into leather. Then by all means, use restraint."[40]

Enacting Self-Determination

Cho advocates for a life unconstrained by the expectations and definitions of the dominant culture—and she personally models such a life. She proclaims that an infinite number of choices are available to all individuals, and all individuals have the right to decide how they want to live their lives. Margaret enacts her commitment to an unrestrained life onstage and in her writings by talking about subjects that are usually considered taboo and sharing how they affect her personally. She doesn't believe "it is possible to get too personal. We all have pain. We all have doubt and sadness and horrible things that have happened that shouldn't have, and when we cover them up and try to pretend that everything is okay, then our stories are forgotten, and our truths become lies."[41]

A frequent topic in Cho's shows is her various sexual practices, which she talks about as if they are normal topics of conversation and not considered taboo. "I've done everything sexual you can do,"[42] she admits. She talks in her shows about having three-way sex, which she doesn't like because it makes her "feel like a competitive eater."[43] She discusses sex toys, explaining that when she is in a new relationship with a woman, "you always get to get new sex toys," and for her, that means getting "the biggest one . . . . I'm like, 'Hey, can I see the one that looks like a pylon?'"[44] Cho also does not shy away from discussing sexual mishaps or difficulties she has experienced. She admits: "I can't come from fucking."[45] She also explains that she cannot find her G spot: "There's a spot in there where you get it just right, and ding, ding, ding. You win a stuffed animal. And I can't find mine. . . . I logged onto Mapquest and everything."[46]

Margaret's discussion of taboo topics goes beyond sex. She discusses her colon hydrotherapy, for example, explaining, "I just had my first colonic. Say what you will, it is the shits."[47] Anal bleaching is another topic she covers in some of her stand-up routines: "Who is bummed out about their anus color? Why is it better to have a white anus? I think it's racist."[48] Cho is heavily tattooed, including tattoos of peonies and portraits of presidents George Washington and Abraham Lincoln, one on each knee. In *Fresh Off the Bloat*, she came close to disrobing at the end of the show, apologizing for her "enormous bush" and turning her back to the audience while pulling down her pants so the audience could see her new tattoos of two women's faces, each facing the crack of her butt. Margaret then demonstrated how shaking her butt makes the faces appear to be talking to one another.[49]

For Cho, the possibilities of an equitable society are limited by the constraints placed on marginalized individuals—limitations that prevent them from fully expressing themselves and making important contributions to society. She challenges these limiting conventions by naming those constraints. Restrictive stereotypes are a major source of such limitations, and Margaret urges all individuals to leave such stereotypes behind and to choose for themselves their own self-definitions and identities. Cho then uses her own experience to demonstrate how an individual can live an unrestrained life, free of conventions, norms, and taboos. She doesn't require that others make the same choices she does, but she holds herself up as a model for those who want to free themselves from societal constraints that denigrate their experiences and desires.

■ REFLECTIONS

1. Watch several comics perform at a local comedy club. To what extent do the various comedians align with Cho's idea that the purpose of comedy is to unsettle hegemonic ways of thinking and acting?
2. Examine Cho's clothing lines. Are there ways in which the design, colors, fabrics, and functions of her clothing embody feminist principles?
3. One of Cho's change strategies is exaggerating stereotypes. Find another contemporary performer who also uses this strategy and compare it to what Cho does. Is one performer more effective than the other in accomplishing change?
4. Are there ways in which exaggerating stereotypes simply reinforces the stereotype rather than prompting change? Cho often mimics her mother in her shows, for example, highlighting all of the unflattering aspects of stereotypes of older Asian women. When does exaggerating stereotypes reinforce the stereotype, and when does it encourage their disruption?
5. Direct discussion of various sexual practices is important to many feminists as part of their change strategies. What do such discussions add to feminist movement? Are there ways in which such discussions might make it difficult for feminists to create change?
6. How closely do Cho's change strategies align with the assumptions outlined in the introduction to part 3? Are there any assumptions that you don't believe pertain to her approach to change?
7. In which feminist wave would you place Cho and why?

■ NOTES

[1] Margaret Cho, *I Have Chosen to Stay and Fight* (New York: Riverhead/Penguin, 2006), 55.
[2] Cynthia Willett, Julie Willett, and Yael D. Sherman, "The Seriously Erotic Politics of Feminist Laughter," *Social Research* 79 (2012): 225.
[3] Margaret Cho, "Interview with Margaret Cho," interview by Martin Wolkner, Wolkner, September 28, 2019, https://wolkner.com/interview-margaret-cho/
[4] Margaret Cho, *I'm the One That I Want* (New York: Ballantine, 2001), 70.
[5] Cho, *I'm the One*, 84.
[6] Cho, *I'm the One*, 104.
[7] Karen Karbo, "In Praise of Difficult Women: Margaret Cho is Wholly, Unapologetically Herself," *National Geographic*, November 23, 2018, https://www.nationalgeographic.com/culture/2018/11/in-praise-of-difficult-women-book-margaret-cho/

8 Cho, *I'm the One*, 112.
9 Cho, "Notorious C.H.O.," YouTube, June 3, 2002, 1:12, https://www.youtube.com/watch?v=2EkMNnNnYFI/
10 Cho, "Notorious C.H.O.," 1:14.
11 Cho, *I'm the One*, 205.
12 Cho, *I Have Chosen*, 132.
13 Cho, *I'm the One*, 70.
14 Cho, *I'm the One*, 19–97.
15 Margaret Cho, "PsyCHO," YouTube, September 25, 2015, 61:13, https://www.youtube.com/watch?v=aReRSKaTwto/
16 Cho, "Notorious C.H.O.," 39:59.
17 Cho, *I'm the One*, 37.
18 Margaret Cho, "Margaret Cho on Power Bottoms and Surviving Bullshit," interview by JD Sampson, Broadly Meets, September 25, 2015, 5:15, https://www.youtube.com/watch?v=aReRSKaTwto/
19 Margaret Cho and Kelsea Stahler, "Margaret Cho: Advice to My 26-Year-Old Self," Refinery29, November 21, 2019, https://www.refinery29.com/en-us/2019/11/8719206/margaret-cho-interview-advice-to-26-year-old-self/
20 Cho, *I Have Chosen*, 93.
21 Margaret Cho, "Conversation with Margaret Cho," interview by Marianne Schnall, Feminist.com, July 13, 2009, https://www.feminist.com/resources/artspeech/interviews/margaretcho.html/
22 Cho, "Conversation with Margaret Cho."
23 Cho, *I Have Chosen*, 93.
24 Cho, *I Have Chosen*, 3.
25 Cho, *I Have Chosen*, 3.
26 Margaret Cho, "Q&A: Margaret Cho on Comedy, Feminism and Identity," interview by Madeline Kim, *Ms.*, July 24, 2017, https://msmagazine.com/2017/07/24/qa-margaret-cho-talks-new-tour-feminism-korean-american-identity/
27 Willett, Willett, and Sherman, "Seriously Erotic Politics," 230.
28 Willett, Willett, and Sherman, "Seriously Erotic Politics," 229.
29 Cho, *I Have Chosen*, 44.
30 Cho, *I Have Chosen*, 44–45.
31 Karbo, "In Praise of Difficult Women."
32 Margaret Cho, "Beautiful," YouTube, November 24, 2009, 9:07, https://www.youtube.com/watch?v=hXRYLb1m4q4/
33 Cho, "Notorious C.H.O.," 1:03.
34 Cho, "Notorious C.H.O.," 1:22.
35 Cho, "Notorious C.H.O.," 1:23.
36 Cho, *I'm the One*, 91.
37 Cho, "Conversation with Margaret Cho."
38 Cho, "Conversation with Margaret Cho."
39 Cho, *I'm the One*, 86.
40 Cho, "Notorious C.H.O.," 1:24.
41 Cho, *I'm the One*, 166.
42 Cho, "Notorious C.H.O.," 57:07.
43 Cho, "Beautiful," 4:56.
44 Cho, "PsyCHO," 53:27.
45 Cho, "Beautiful," 0:58.
46 Cho, "Notorious C.H.O.," 56:29.
47 Cho, "Notorious C.H.O.," 13:39.
48 Cho, "Beautiful," 2:35.
49 Margaret Cho, "Fresh Off the Bloat," YouTube, September 5, 2018, 6:40, https://www.youtube.com/watch?v=E9OjfHzR5mE/

CHAPTER TEN

Camille Paglia

> *I was just a woman born ahead of my time. I was a kind of pioneer.... From my earliest years I had this burning desire to do something for women, to do something so massive for women, to demonstrate that women should be taken seriously.*[1]

Camille Paglia is an outspoken social critic, public intellectual, author, and professor who critiques contemporary feminism. Feminism will not solve society's problems, she believes, until it ceases to be the problem. Paglia was born in 1947 in Endicott, New York. Her father taught high school in Oxford, New York, until 1957, when he moved the family to Syracuse, New York, so he could attend graduate school to become a professor of Romance languages. When Camille was young, her mother worked at home sewing wedding dresses and later became a bank teller.

Paglia recalls her childhood as a nearly constant revolt against gender norms: "I absolutely could not *stand* the way the culture demanded that women be feminine. I did not relate to my sex role *at all*. I have been a totally alienated sexual being since I was a tiny child."[2] She despised the toys and conventions of girlhood and wanted swords instead of dolls so she could play knights instead of princesses. Her Halloween costumes reflected her identification with heroic, adventurous, male roles—a Roman solider, Robin Hood, Napoleon, and Hamlet. The gender labels she has adopted for herself—*lesbian, presexual, transgender,* and *bisexual*—show her revolt against the gender binary: "I would welcome the introduction of 'OTHER' as a gender category in passports and other government documents."[3] Camille calls her alienation from gender norms "the principal source and motivation of my work."[4]

Paglia attended Binghamton University in Binghamton, New York, for her BA degree, graduating in 1968 as class valedictorian. She earned graduate degrees in English from Yale University—an MA in 1971 and a PhD in 1974. In 1972, Camille began teaching at Bennington College in Bennington, Vermont, where she admits to trying to impose an "arrogantly militant Amazon feminism"[5] on her students. In 1979, after several altercations—she literally kicked a student for an offensive skit and got in a fist fight with another—she resigned and accepted a settlement from the college. Paglia then held a series of part-time teaching positions at Yale University, Wesleyan University, and other Connecticut schools while searching for a permanent job and for a publisher for her doctoral dissertation. In 1984, she was hired as a professor of humanities and media studies at the University of the Arts in Philadelphia, Pennsylvania.

The book based on Camille's dissertation, *Sexual Personae: Art and Decadence from Nefertiti to Emily Dickinson*, was rejected by five agents and seven publishers before it was published by Yale University Press in 1990. Described as "every bit as intellectually stimulating as it is exasperating," the book became a best seller and reached number seven on the paperback best seller list, unusual for a scholarly book.[6] Because of the success of *Sexual Personae* and two additional essays published at about the same time—an essay about Madonna in the *New York Times* (1990) and one about date rape in *New York Newsday* (1991)—Paglia became "instantly notorious."[7] Her commitment to thinking rigorously about the problems of contemporary culture combined with a contentious and provocative writing style have kept her in the spotlight, and she continues to write about art, feminism, higher education, and popular culture. Camille's other books include *Sex, Art, and American Culture* (1992); *Vamps and Tramps: New Essays* (1994); *The Birds* (1998); *Break, Blow, Burn: Camille Paglia Reads Forty-Three of the World's Best Poems* (2005); *Glittering Images: A Journey Through Art from Egypt To Star Wars* (2012); *Free Women Free Men: Sex, Gender, Feminism* (2017); and *Provocations: Collected Essays* (2018).

Paglia has also written essays for various newspapers and magazines, including the *New York Times*, the *Wall Street Journal,* the *Washington Post,* the *Hollywood Reporter, The New Republic,* and *The Advocate.* Camille contributed a column to Salon.com from 1995 to 2001 and again from 2007 to 2009; she resumed writing the column in 2016. In 2005, she was voted one of the top 100 public intellectuals by *Foreign Policy/Prospect* magazines, and Super Scholar named her one of the fifty most influential female intellectual scholars. As a metaphor for her life's work, Paglia recalls an incident with an outhouse during a summer at Girl Scout camp when she poured too much quicklime into the latrine. The ensuing explosion "symbolized everything I would do with my life and work. Excess and extravagance and explosiveness. I would be someone who would look into the latrine of culture, . . . and I would drop the bomb into it. I would terrorize everyone [and] create complete disorder."[8]

Definition of Feminism

Camille's feminism began early when, to cope with the "conformist, domestic Fifties,"[9] she escaped into late-night movies, which offered a door into "the first phase of feminism, born from the push for the vote."[10] She was "electrified" by Katharine Hepburn, who portrayed a bold, pioneering, elegant, sophisticated, and sexual woman—quite different from the feminine ideal of the 1950s.[11] When Amelia Earhart's plane was lost over the Pacific Ocean, Earhart became a feminist role model for Paglia as well, and in high school, she wrote a seventy-seven-page term paper about the missing flyer. Given a copy of Simone de Beauvoir's *The Second Sex* for her sixteenth birthday, Camille added de Beauvoir to her list of feminist idols. Hepburn, Earhart, and de Beauvoir served as the gateway into the kind of feminism Paglia advocates—a feminism that is unapologetic, ambitious, plucky, resourceful, and self-reliant. Camille has since added other feminists she admires to her list—Madonna, Barbra Streisand, and Germaine Greer.

In contrast to her feminist role models, Paglia describes most contemporary feminists as "bunglers, whiners, French faddicts . . . and bullying, sanctimonious sermonizers"[12] as well as "bellyachers, anorexics, bulimics, depressives, rape victims, and incest survivors."[13] She claims that feminism "has become a catch-all vegetable drawer where bunches of clingy sob sisters can store their moldy neuroses."[14] She describes her feminism as "equal opportunity feminism"[15] by which she means removal of "all barriers to woman's advancement in the political and professional realms."[16] Camille insists that there should be no special protections for women: "Women must not become wards and supplicants of authority figures. Freedom means rejecting dependency."[17] In line with her libertarian philosophy, Paglia opposes "intrusions of the state into the private realm—as in abortion, sodomy, prostitution, pornography, drug use, or suicide."[18] She believes that all individuals should be free to make their own life choices without the government, laws, or other sources of authority dictating moral standards.

Another label Camille applies to her feminism is "tough-cookie feminism"[19] because "it will be bawdy, streetwise, and on-the-spot confrontational."[20] The *vamp*, a term she uses to refer to prostitutes, seductresses, drag queens, hustlers, and high-glamour movie stars, is Paglia's feminist ideal because the vamp is a "prowler and predator, self-directed and no one's victim."[21] She also employs the word *vamp* in its second meaning—"saving or repairing something old by patching it with a new piece—that is, using ingenuity, cleverness, and commonplace practicality to achieve your aims."[22] Camille wants to improve, customize, update, and recharge feminism by giving it a revamp.

Change Strategies

Paglia's change strategies are directed at what she names as the problem: feminism itself. "I am a feminist who wants to radically reform current feminism, to bring it back to common sense about life,"[23] she asserts. Unlike most other feminists, who fault external structures and systems, Camille believes that how feminists have addressed those systems has had unfortunate consequences for feminist movement. According to Paglia, tackling social issues will be ineffective until feminists resolve the difficulties within feminism, and resolving those difficulties is what her change strategies are designed to do: (1) attending to history, (2) encompassing diversity, and (3) assuming responsibility.

Attending to History

Camille's revamping of feminism begins with a statement of what is wrong with contemporary feminism—its denial of the knowledge that came before. She sees feminists as trapped in the present, unable to see beyond whatever is current in academia at the moment—whether French philosophers, critical theory, deconstruction, or the like. Being unable to see beyond the present fad jeopardizes the possibilities for the future: "If you don't understand the whole path, you can't see where we're going, because you don't see where we've *been*."[24]

To salvage feminism, Paglia argues that academia must return to teaching a basic curriculum. She makes the study of biology a critical starting point because understanding biology involves understanding the relationship between humans and nature. In contrast to contemporary views that see humans as in control of nature because they have invented civilization, Camille disagrees, arguing that "nature is in control" and "indiscriminately exerts its force." She offers as illustration the way nature can indiscriminately exercise its dominance: "Let nature shrug and all is in ruin" whether through "fire, flood, lightning, tornado, hurricane, volcano, earthquake—anywhere at any time."[25] Human civilization is of little use in such situations: "Society is our frail barrier against nature."[26] The study of biology makes clear the illusion of human dominance over nature and suggests the delicate intersection between nature and culture: "It's fantastically intricate. . . . And it requires all of the learning that we can muster"[27] to understand that intersection.

Biology is important to study for yet another reason, according to Paglia: it explains gender as a biological fact, not a social construction. According to contemporary feminism, we are "born blank slates" and become male or female through social conditioning and environmental influences.[28] Camille believes just the opposite: "The cold biological truth is that . . . every single cell of the human body . . . remains coded with one's birth gender for life,"[29] making for established and immutable gender roles. Furthermore, the similarity of gender roles across time and space—polarized norms of masculinity and femininity define virtually every culture—provides additional evidence of a biological basis to gender. Paglia uses her own experience as evidence of the powerful influence of biology on gender: "It might seem that a battle-scarred veteran of the sex wars, born with a personality so ill-suited to the prescribed sex role, would have the most grounds for complaint against society. But the opposite is true: my noisy resistance to primary socialization brought me full circle back to biology. From my militant history comes a conviction of self-knowledge: I can declare that what *is* female in me comes from nature and not from nurture."[30] As long as "the kind of sophisticated discourse that's necessary to talk about sex and gender in history is missing" from the current conversation, Camille believes there will not be any real feminist understanding and advancement.

With biology as a foundation, Paglia believes feminism also should attend to psychology and what it teaches about the nature of human beings. She advocates the study of the works of Sigmund Freud in particular, claiming that to understand anything about sex and/or gender without reading Freud is insulting. In addition to psychology, she also would add the study of archaeology to her core curriculum because it "gives perspective, a vivid sense of the sweep of history, ... satisfies lust for awe and destruction, ... [and] introduces the young to the scientific method."[31] Teaching political science and history from pre-antiquity to the present and examining the world's great religions in the process is also a crucial part of what she sees as necessary to understand the limitations and possibilities of feminist movement. Finally, as a practical consideration, Camille advocates teaching football—what she calls "one of the best educational tools for showing women how to advance in the 'hostile workplace.'" As "a living encyclopedia of military strategy," football is crucial for those "ambitious young women who hope to rise in politics or business."[32] Paglia demands that feminists attend to basic disciplinary knowledge, devised by the important thinkers of the past, in order to productively decide how to proceed in the present.

Camille's insistence on teaching the knowledge of the past doesn't mean she simply accepts those ideas without question: "You read major figures not because everything they saw is the gospel truth but because they expand your imagination."[33] Paglia calls for feminists to engage in "vigorous intellectual inquiry" with an insistence on "free thought and free speech."[34] To this end, she insists that "the writings of conservative opponents of feminism as well as of dissident feminists" be studied; otherwise, "students are getting indoctrination, not education."[35] Camille wants, above all, for feminists to "read widely and think for yourself. We need more dissent and less dogma."[36] She concludes that "the feminist naïveté about life, history, and culture must end.... Maps for the future can be drawn only by those who have deeply studied the past."[37]

Encompassing Diversity

In addition to its denial of past histories and understandings, Paglia faults feminism for claiming to privilege diversity while, in fact, limiting its concerns to a very small group of individuals—white, upper-middle-class career women. Feminism "*claims* to be helping or to be speaking to and speaking *for*" ordinary women,[38] but this alleged diversity, Camille claims, is a myth: "Feminists are always boasting of their 'diversity' and pluralism. This is like white Protestants, in the nineteenth and pre-Sixties twentieth centuries when they controlled American politics, finance, and academe, claiming diversity on the basis of their dozens of denominations. But blacks, Jews, and Italian Catholics, standing on the outside, could clearly see the monolithic homogeneity that the WASP insiders were blissfully, arrogantly unaware of."[39]

Paglia wants feminism to encompass diversity by being "a big tent" open to everyone.[40] To this end, she acknowledges and celebrates several groups that have been dismissed by feminists. The most important of these is mothers. Because Camille grounds her feminism in biology, she recognizes that "there is one place where men can never equal women and where female power is at its height—the realm of procreation." She accuses feminism of having "never dealt honestly with this 'mother power.'"[41] Not only has feminism falsely promised that women could have it all, but feminists attacked those women who chose children over career. In contrast, Paglia acknowledges the difficulties faced by women who try to have both children and career: "Starting a family early has its price for an ambitious young woman, a career hiatus that may be difficult to overcome . . . . On the other hand, the reward of being with one's children in their formative years, instead of farming out that fleeting and irreplaceable experience to daycare centers or nannies, has an inherent emotional and perhaps spiritual value" that feminists have ignored.[42]

In addition to celebrating mothers, Camille wants to include men in her feminism, another group that she believes has been unfairly treated by contemporary feminists. Men are rarely depicted as "devoted friends or loving spouses who sacrifice for women and children"[43] in feminist movement. Instead, male bashing is the norm as feminists rush to blame patriarchy for society's problems. Paglia wants feminists to acknowledge and admire men's contributions to civilization: "Men have every right to claim credit for their vast achievements in conceiving and constructing the entire framework of civilization."[44] She especially valorizes men in traditional working-class trades—"the ones that allow women's studies professors to drive to work (roads), take the elevator to their office (construction), read in the library (electricity), and go to gender-neutral restrooms (plumbing)."[45] She elaborates: "Only a tiny number of women want to enter the trades where most of the nitty-gritty physical work is actually going on. . . . It's men who operate the cranes or set the foundations or wash windows on the 85th floor. It's men who troop out at 2:00 AM during an ice storm to restore power to neighborhoods where falling trees have brought down live wires."[46] The contrast between men's and women's achievements is so considerable that Camille is comfortable asserting that "if civilization had been left in female hands, we'd still be living in grass huts."[47] According to Paglia, feminism can never be successful by weakening or disregarding men; society needs both strong women and strong men.

Assuming Responsibility

Another problem Camille has with contemporary feminism is the refusal of feminists to assume responsibility for their choices and actions. She returns to biology to make this argument, suggesting that the influence of hormones on humans is unavoidable. What she calls "primitive urges" such as aggression and sex[48] are natural and "can be controlled only by the social contract."[49] Rape is thus an extension of this natural aggression, making the world a dangerous place for both sexes: "I believe that every person, male and female, needs to be in a protective mode at all times of alertness to potential danger. The world is full of potential attacks, potential disasters."[50] Paglia thus favors "reasonable sexual harassment guidelines" because "they alert women to the erotic energies they inspire"[51]—energies that put them in danger.

Camille, however, rejects special protections for women as a way to manage rape, assault, and sexual harassment. Paglia does not want to see women returned "to their old status of delicate flowers who must be protected from assault by male lechers."[52] Instead, she applauds the freedoms and risks now available to women and insists they assume the responsibilities that accompany these freedoms: "Go for it, take the risk, take the challenge—if you get raped, if you get beat up in a dark alley in a street, it's okay. That was part of the risk of freedom, that's part of what we've demanded as women."[53]

Camille asks women to assume responsibility for protecting themselves: "A woman's number one line of defense is herself."[54] The woman who is aware and attuned to the risks of the modern world would not leave her purse out in the street unattended, sleep with her doors wide open at night, or dress in scanty and provocative clothing.[55] Instead, a woman "must be prudent and cautious about where she goes and with whom."[56] Paglia refuses to countenance behaviors that are simply foolish: "A girl who lets herself get dead drunk at a fraternity party is a fool. A girl who goes upstairs alone with a brother at a fraternity party is an idiot. Feminists call this 'blaming the victim.' I call it common sense."[57] When a woman makes a mistake, "she must accept the consequences and, through self-criticism, resolve never to make that mistake again."[58] As she puts it: "Pick yourself up, dust yourself off, and go on."[59]

In addition to asserting that women need to take responsibility for their behavior, Camille goes a step further and provides actual examples of how women should handle situations such as sexual harassment: "A male student makes a vulgar remark about your breasts? Don't slink off to whimper and simper with the campus shrinking violets. Deal with it. On the spot. Say, 'Shut up, you jerk! And crawl back to the barnyard where you belong!'"[60] She faults Anita Hill, who charged Clarence Thomas with sexual harassment when he was nominated to the Supreme Court, for not appropriately dismissing his sexual overtures at the time they occurred. If Hill "was thrown for a loop by sexual banter, that's her problem. If by the age of twenty-six, as a graduate of Yale Law School, she could find no convincing way to signal her displeasure and disinterest, that's her deficiency."[61] Paglia similarly faults the Me Too movement for "encouraging uncorroborated accusation . . . dating from ten, twenty, or thirty years ago."[62] She believes any kind of harassment should be dealt with in the moment, and any actual rapes and other assaults should be reported directly to the police.[63]

Camille's feminist strategies—attending to history, encompassing diversity, and assuming responsibility—are directed at naming the problem, which for Paglia, is feminism itself. Paglia believes "feminism is stuck,"[64] and "before it makes prescriptions for society, feminism must put its own house in order."[65] Her efforts are directed to this end, with a goal of producing a feminism that is libertarian, strong, and emancipatory.

■ REFLECTIONS

1. Paglia was in constant revolt against gender norms from the time she was a child, and she sees biology as responsible for what is feminine in her. How much of your gender performance do you attribute to culture and how much to biology?
2. Katharine Hepburn was an early feminist icon for Paglia. Watch a movie that stars Hepburn. What definition of feminism does the Hepburn character embrace, and what are the major change strategies she employs?
3. Paglia is very critical of contemporary feminists. Do you believe her critique is justified? Why or why not?
4. Paglia wants to revamp feminism by improving and updating it. Are there portions of feminism you would like to revamp that are different from the ones she identifies?
5. Paglia's strategy of assuming responsibility runs contrary to many contemporary feminist efforts designed to make men accountable for their behaviors and to protect women from the inappropriate behaviors of men. In situations of sexual harassment or abuse, when should men be held accountable for their actions, and when should women be held accountable for theirs?
6. How closely do Paglia's change strategies align with the assumptions outlined in the introduction to part 3? Are there any assumptions that you don't believe pertain to her approach to change?
7. In which feminist wave would you place Paglia and why?

■ NOTES

[1] Camille Paglia, *Sex, Art, and American Culture* (New York: Vintage, 1992), 256.
[2] Paglia, *Sex, Art, and American Culture*, 255–56.
[3] Camille Paglia, *Free Women: Sex, Gender, Feminism* (New York: Vintage, 2017), 237.

4 Laura Pullman, "Camille Paglia and UArts Fight Back Against the Snowflakes," *Sunday Times*, April 21, 2019, https://www.thetimes.co.uk/article/camille-paglia-and-uarts-fight-back-against-the-snowflakes-rrm0ng5z5/
5 Emily Esfahani Smith, "The Provocations of Camille Paglia," *City Journal* 11 (2019), https://www.city-journal.org/camille-paglia/
6 Terry Teachout, "Siding With the Men," *New York Times*, July 22, 1990, p. 7.
7 Molly Fischer, "Camille Paglia Predicted 2017: What the '90s Provocateur Understands About the Trump Era," The Cut, March 2017, https://www.thecut.com/2017/03/what-camille-paglia-understands-about-the-trump-era.html/
8 Camille Paglia, *Vamps and Tramps: New Essays* (New York: Vintage, 1994), 430.
9 Paglia, *Sex, Art, and American Culture*, 110.
10 Paglia, *Sex, Art, and American Culture*, 111.
11 Paglia, *Free Women*, xi.
12 Paglia, *Free Women*, 60.
13 Paglia, *Free Women*, 90.
14 Paglia, *Free Women*, 90.
15 Paglia, *Vamps and Tramps*, x.
16 Paglia, *Provocations: Collected Essays* (New York: Pantheon, 2018), 199.
17 Paglia, *Vamps and Tramps*, xii.
18 Paglia, *Sex, Art, and American Culture*, vii.
19 Paglia, *Vamps and Tramps*, xii.
20 Paglia, *Sex, Art, and American Culture*, vii.
21 Paglia, *Vamps and Tramps*, x.
22 Paglia, *Vamps and Tramps*, xiii.
23 Paglia, *Sex, Art, and American Culture*, 56.
24 Paglia, *Vamps and Tramps*, 418.
25 Camille Paglia, *Sexual Personae: Art and Decadence from Nefertiti to Emily Dickinson* (New York: Yale University Press, 1990), 1.
26 Paglia, *Sexual Personae*, 3.
27 Paglia, *Sex, Art, and American Culture*, 296.
28 Nicole Narea, "Outspoken Paglia Condemns Traditional Feminism," *Yale News*, September 12, 2012, https://yaledailynews.com/blog/2012/09/12/outspoken-paglia-condemns-traditional-feminism/
29 Paglia, *Provocations*, 197–98.
30 Paglia, *Sex, Art, and American Culture*, 107.
31 Paglia, *Provocations*, 385.
32 Paglia, *Free Women*, 119.
33 Paglia, *Free Women*, 70.
34 Paglia, *Vamps and Tramps*, 120.
35 Paglia, *Free Women*, 181.
36 Paglia, *Free Women*, 275.
37 Paglia, *Sex, Art, and American Culture*, 89–90.
38 Paglia, *Sex, Art, and American Culture*, 292.
39 Paglia, *Sex, Art, and American Culture*, 242–43.
40 Bari Weiss, "Camille Paglia: A Feminist Defense of Masculine Virtues," *Wall Street Journal*, February 9, 2020, https://www.wsj.com/articles/a-feminist-defense-of-masculine-virtuesa-feminist-defense-of-masculine-virtues-1388181961/
41 Margaret Harper McCarthy, "Camille Paglia's Sexual 'Realism,'" *Humanum*, October 11, 2018, https://humanumreview.com/uploads/pdfs/Camille-Paglia%E2%80%99s-Sexual-%E2%80%9CRealism%E2%80%9D-_-Humanum-Review.pdf/
42 Napp Nazworth, "Feminists Ignore Biology, Dissident Feminist Camille Paglia Argues," *The Christian Post*, October 16, 2013, https://www.christianpost.com/news/feminists-ignore-biology-dissident-feminist-camille-paglia-argues.html/
43 Paglia, *Free Women*, 94.

44 Paglia, *Free Women*, xxvi.
45 Weiss, "Camille Paglia."
46 Camille Paglia, "Camille Paglia Discusses Her War on 'Elitist Garbage' and Contemporary Feminism," interview by Mitchell Sunderland, Vice, March 14, 2017, https://www.vice.com/en/article/evgxz7/camille-paglia-discusses-her-war-on-elitist-garbage-and-contemporary-feminism/
47 Paglia, *Sexual Personae*, 38.
48 Paglia, *Sexual Personae*, 3.
49 Paglia, *Sexual Personae*, 23.
50 Weiss, "Camille Paglia."
51 Paglia, *Vamps and Tramps*, 52–53.
52 Paglia, *Sex, Art, and American Culture*, 47.
53 Paglia, *Sex, Art, and American Culture*, 63.
54 Paglia, *Sex, Art, and American Culture*, 53.
55 Paglia, *Sex, Art, and American Culture*, 56.
56 Paglia, *Sex Art, and American Culture*, 53.
57 Paglia, *Sex, Art, and American Culture*, 51.
58 Paglia, *Sex, Art, and American Culture*, 53.
59 Paglia, *Sex, Art, and American Culture*, 63.
60 Paglia, *Free Women*, 56.
61 Paglia, *Sex, Art, and American Culture*, 47–48.
62 Camille Paglia, "Camille Paglia: It's Time for a New Map of the Gender World," interview by Claire Lehmann, *Quillette*, November 10, 2018, https://quillette.com/2018/11/10/camille-paglia-its-time-for-a-new-map-of-the-gender-world/
63 Paglia, *Sex, Art, and American Culture*, 53.
64 Paglia, *Sex, Art, and American Culture*, 293.
65 Paglia, *Sex, Art, and American Culture*, 90.

PART FOUR

ENRICHING A SYSTEM

Societies are composed of an almost infinite number of systems—organized sets of structures, processes, and procedures designed to accomplish certain objectives. Those who want to *enrich the system* start from the premise that a system as it exists is largely functional and basically fair. They see the system, although not perfect, as generally working well and doing what it is supposed to do. Furthermore, they believe that a progressive trajectory characterizes most systems—they evolve and change over time, generally moving in a positive direction. Thus, enriching a system—bringing women and minorities more fully into it—is considered a logical and useful objective.

Enriching a system depends on the following three assumptions: (1) substantial and sustainable change can be achieved by making minor adjustments to a system, (2) all voices in a system deserve to be heard, and (3) a system flourishes when it incorporates diverse perspectives. Shonda Rhimes, Jacinda Ardern, Joana Vasconcelos, and Malala Yousafzai work to enrich systems in order to make those systems more just and equitable.

Assumption 1: Substantial and sustainable change can be achieved by making minor adjustments to a system.

When a system reaches a state of equilibrium, those who are part of that system often come to feel content and secure in it—they experience the system as a comfortable place to be.[1] Individuals who want to enrich a system do not see that system as flawed. Thus, they do not believe that large-scale changes to a system are necessary and instead choose to make various adjustments to it. There is a practical side to this approach: tweaking a system is easier than overhauling it because as a system becomes entrenched, it thickens, hardens, and becomes "real in an ever more massive way."[2] Consequently, the system can no longer be changed easily. The choice to enrich makes sense when a system is large, well established, and has considerable momentum behind it.

James Mahoney and Kathleen Thelen suggest that there are many effective ways to enrich a system.[3] They offer a theory of change based on how rules are altered in organizations, and they identify four ways such changes happen. Displacement is one type of rule change; it involves the replacement of existing rules with new ones. Layering, a second organizational change strategy, occurs when existing rules are layered with amendments, additions, or revisions so that the rules differ substantially from their original framing.[4] Drift, a third category of rule change, happens when the rules of the system remain the same, but changes in the environment substantially alter the meaning and/or impact of those rules. A fourth type of change, conversion, occurs when the rules remain the same but are interpreted in new ways. In choosing to enrich a system, individuals rely on the fact that the various rules that guide a system not only can and do change but also that such changes can prove effective in altering the system.

Title IX, part of the Education Amendments Act of 1972, was designed to enrich the educational system by increasing women's participation in athletics. Specifically, women were to be provided with access to and funding for sports in the same proportion as their representation in an institution as a whole. The University of New Mexico (UNM), for example, eliminated men's soccer in 2018 in part because of financial deficits but largely to move the university toward compliance with Title IX. At the time, 55 percent of students at UNM were female, but only 43 percent were involved in sports.[5] By dropping men's soccer, the gap between men's and women's participation in sports decreased from 4.75 percent to 0.83 percent.[6] Title IX serves as a classic instance of how making relatively minor changes to a system can substantially enrich that system by improving access and equity.

Assumption 2: All voices in a system deserve to be heard.

The need to give voice to those who have not had full access to a system is central to the task of enriching a system. As a metaphor, voice stands for opportunity of access and full engagement within a system, and the end goal is a more equitable, diverse, and inclusive system and society. Change agents who focus on enriching a system seek to make those who have been left out of the system full partners whose views and feelings are taken into account in that system.

Philosopher Jürgen Habermas envisions how the voice metaphor might literally be realized in an ideal speech situation that presumes equality among its participants. According to Habermas, equality emerges from three agreements that participants in a conversation implicitly make with one another: (1) all have the same opportunity to speak because no constraints hinder access to the discussion; (2) all have the right to share fully their attitudes, feelings, intentions, and motives with others; and (3) all are willing to justify their claims and actions—to offer support for what they say and do. When these conditions are met (although rarely realized), Habermas believes that communication is free from domination and hierarchy. Because the principles of equality, access, and full participation in the life of a community are embedded in language, communication is a means of reaching the desirable standard.

Dreamers are one group advocating for voice in the educational, occupational, and political systems of the United States. The name for adults brought to the United States illegally as children comes from the DREAM Act [Development, Relief, and Education for Alien Minors], legislation first introduced in Congress in 2001. Regardless of how long dreamers have lived in the United States and whether they have any connection to their countries of origin, they are limited by the US system in many ways. For instance, more than half of the states require dreamers to pay out-of-state tuition at colleges and universities, many states prohibit them from obtaining drivers' licenses, and dreamers cannot vote. Rather than being a drain on US resources, however, dreamers enrich the system in many ways. Over 90 percent of dreamers are employed, and they start businesses at a higher rate than US citizens of similar ages and skill levels. In any given year, dreamers exercise about $25 billion in spending power and pay more than $5.5 billion in taxes.[7] A path to citizenship would ensure that this population, many of whom cannot remember any home but the United States, be acknowledged and heard as fully participating citizens who make important contributions to US life.

Assumption 3: A system flourishes when it values and incorporates diverse perspectives.

Diversity is essential to those seeking to enrich a system: "The human animal has succeeded precisely because it has been able to diversify, not specialize; to climb *and* swim, hunt *and* nurture, work alone *and* in packs. The same is true of human organizations; they are heathy and they survive when they are diverse and differentiated, capable of many responses; they become brittle and unadaptable and prey to any changing conditions when they are uniform and specialized."[8] Organizations that value diversity are able to produce more insightful and effective responses to the problems and obstacles they encounter. Organizational commitment increases as well when diversity is privileged. Members who see that their views and contributions are taken into account are more willing to participate, to experiment, and to take risks—all of which enhance the organization.[9]

Margaret Wheatley, an organizational scholar interested in the impact of diversity on systems, acknowledges that organizations traditionally have preferred homogeneity over diversity—those in charge are more comfortable when they are surrounded by those who look and think like them. But, she asks, how can an organization "create an accurate picture of the whole if we don't honor the fact that we each see something different because of who we are and where we sit in the system?"[10] When diversity flourishes, the system that emerges is open and inquiring, complicated and creative, and more intelligent as well.[11] According to Wheatley, "an organization rich with many interpretations develops a wiser sense of what is going on and what needs to be done."[12]

The performance of women leaders during the coronavirus pandemic in 2020–2021 suggests how bringing women's perspectives into organizations can enrich and benefit a system. Just as companies with more female executives typically perform better than those with fewer women,[13] countries with female leaders tend to fare better during times of crisis. In the case of COVID-19, women leaders were more willing to reach out to and listen to experts, to act quickly in the country's best interests rather than their own, to experiment with different plans for controlling the spread of the virus, and to be fully transparent about their decisions and the reasons for them. Consequently, female-led countries—New Zealand, Denmark, Finland, Iceland, Norway, and Germany—had only 36 coronavirus-related deaths per million inhabitants, while male-led countries saw an average of 214 such deaths per million.[14]

■ NOTES

[1] Hugh Dalziel Duncan, *Communication and Social Order* (London, UK: Oxford University Press, 1962), 20.

[2] Peter L. Berger and Thomas Luckmann, *The Social Construction of Reality: A Treatise in the Sociology of Knowledge* (New York: Anchor, 1966), 59.

[3] James Mahoney and Kathleen Thelen, "A Theory of Gradual Institutional Change," in *Explaining Institutional Change: Ambiguity, Agency, and Power*, ed. James Mahoney and Kathleen Thelen (New York: Cambridge University Press, 2010), 1–37.

[4] Mahoney and Thelen, "A Theory of Gradual Institutional Change," 17.

[5] Jessica Dyer and Geoff Grammer, "It's Official: Four Lobo Sports are Gone," *Albuquerque Journal*, July 19, 2018, https://www.abqjournal.com/1198470/unm-regents-approve-cutting-four-sports.html/

[6] Angela Catena, Title IX coordinator, University of New Mexico, email message to Karen A. Foss, July 6, 2020.

[7] "Overcoming the Odds: The Contributions of DACA-Eligible Immigrants and TPS Holders to the U.S. Economy," New American Economy, June 3, 2019, https://research.newamericaneconomy.org/report/overcoming-the-odds-the-contributions-of-daca-eligible-immigrants-and-tps-holders-to-the-u-s-economy/

[8] Kirkpatrick Sale, *Human Scale Revisited: A New Look at the Classic Case for a Decentrist Future* (White River Junction, VT: Chelsea Green, 2017), 262.

[9] Margaret L. Wheatley, *Leadership and the New Science: Discovering Order in a Chaotic World*, 3rd ed. (San Francisco, CA: Berrett-Koehler, 2006).

[10] Margaret Wheatley, "Preface: We Can Be Wise Only Together," in *The World Café: Shaping Our Futures Through Conversations That Matter*, by Juanita Brown with David Isaacs (San Francisco, CA: Berrett-Koehler, 2005), x.

[11] Margaret J. Wheatley and Myron Kellner-Rogers, *A Simpler Way* (San Francisco, CA: Berrett-Koehler, 1996), 102.

[12] Wheatley, *Leadership and the New Science*, 67.

[13] Alexandra Kelley, "Companies with More Women in Management Perform Better, According to New Goldman Sachs Study," Changing America, November 11, 2020, https://thehill.com/changing-america/respect/diversity-inclusion/525581-companies-with-more-women-in-management-perform

[14] Nicholas Kristof, "Nations May Be Safer Under Women," *New York Times*, June 14, 2020, sec. SR, p. 9. Germany experienced a surge in COVID-19 cases after prime minister Merkel announced her upcoming retirement: "The political jostling to replace her featured politicians trying to draw contrasts, often with a less cautious approach to COVID-19 than Merkel's." In addition, pandemic fatigue set in (Germans even came up with a word for it—*coronamüde*), and Germans were much less cautious. Merkel's original approach, however, cannot be faulted—it was swift, strong, and based on facts. See German Lopez, "Germany Contained COVID-19. Politics Brought It Back," Vox, April 21, 2021, https://www.vox.com/22352348/germany-covid-19-coronavirus-pandemic

CHAPTER
ELEVEN

Shonda Rhimes

What the hell is up with the "I'm just so lucky" line? I'm not merely lucky. No one who succeeds is merely lucky. . . . Lucky implies I didn't do anything. Lucky implies something was given to me. Lucky implies that I was handed something I did not earn, that I did not work hard for. . . . I am not lucky. You know what I am? I am smart, I am talented, I take advantage of the opportunities that come my way and I work really, really hard. Don't call me lucky. Call me a badasss.[1]

Shonda Lynn Rhimes is a showrunner—creator, writer, and executive producer—for some of the most popular dramas on television. At any given time, she might be responsible for seventy hours of programming a week for an audience of thirty million at a cost of $350 million per season. In addition to telling good stories, Rhimes wants to enrich the world of television by offering realistic portrayals of all the people who inhabit the real world.

Shonda was born in 1970 in Chicago, Illinois, the youngest of six children. Her parents placed a high priority on reading and education, and the family had "Book Sundays," where the family sat around and read. Her father was a college professor who became chief information officer at the University of Southern California. Her mother attended college while raising her children and earned a PhD in educational administration in 1991. That same year, Rhimes graduated from Dartmouth University in Hanover, Vermont, with a major in English and a minor in creative writing. Shonda initially majored in journalism, but she discovered she was more interested in "making stuff up" than in reporting the truth.[2]

Rhimes always knew she wanted to write because "writing was who I was."[3] As young as three or four, she dictated stories into a tape recorder, and her mother typed them up for her.[4] Writing became a way for her to cope as she grew into an awkward girl whom she describes as "highly intelligent, way too chubby, incredibly sensitive, nerdy and painfully shy. I wore Coke-bottle-thick glasses. Two cornrow braids traveled down the sides of my skull in a way that was just not pretty on me. . . . I was often the only black girl in my class. I did not have friends."[5] By the age of eleven, Shonda had created an imaginary place she called *Shondaland* (which later became the name of her production company): "A place to hold my stories, a safe place, a place for my characters to exist. A place for me to exist. Until I could get the hell out of being a teenager and run out into the world and be myself. . . . Until I could find my people in the real world."[6] Rhimes created friends for herself by writing, friends who later came to populate television screens: "They are not just my friends now—they are also everyone else's. Shondaland is open."[7]

After earning an MFA from the University of Southern California film school in 1994, Shonda was hired at Spring Creek Productions, where she read and commented on the scripts that were submitted for possible production. She quit after less than a year to begin writing her own scripts. Her first scripts included *Human Seeking Same, Blossoms and Veils, Crossroads,* and *Introducing Dorothy Dandridge.*[8] By the time Rhimes wrote *Princess Bride 2: Royal Engagement*, she was not only writing regularly but her scripts were also regularly selected for production.

After she adopted her first child, Shonda spent "a lot of evenings with my daughter lying on my chest, catching up with DVDs of a lot of television shows I had never seen before."[9] She realized that television was where good character development was happening because it was not subject to the time constraints of movies, and she told "anybody that would listen, that I was going to take over the world of television."[10] The initial pilot she wrote for television was about four female war correspondents, and it was picked up by Walt Disney Studios. After the terrorist attacks of September 11, 2001, however, the script was perceived as inappropriate, and the network cancelled plans for its production. When Rhimes asked what the studio wanted instead, the answer was another medical show, so she wrote the pilot for *Grey's Anatomy*. The show premiered in 2005, its seventeenth season aired in 2020, and it is the longest prime-time medical drama on television.

Shonda has continued to create dramas that are popular and successful. In 2014, ABC announced what it called *TGIT*, or "Thank God It's Thursday." Her shows—*Grey's Anatomy, How to Get Away with Murder,* and *Scandal*—constituted the entire prime-time lineup of ABC's Thursday-evening programming. In 2017, she left ABC for a multi-year deal with Netflix to produce eight films, including *Dance Dreams: Hot Chocolate Nutcracker, Bridgerton,* and *Inventing Anna.*[11] She describes what she does as a "dream job" that is comparable to "building a nation out of thin air; it is manning the troops, it is painting a canvas, it is hitting every high note, it is running a marathon, it is being Beyoncé, and it is all of those things at the same time."[12]

In 2015, Rhimes wrote a memoir, *Year of Yes: How to Dance It Out, Stand in the Sun and Be Your Own Person*. It recounts a year of deciding to say yes to everything she was invited to do, no matter how uncomfortable she was about doing it. She took up this challenge on Thanksgiving Day in 2012 after a conversation with her oldest sister. Shonda was listing all of the invitations she had received in the previous week, when her sister said, "you never say yes to anything."[13] Rhimes realized that all of those invitations were meaningless if she never accepted them. Consequently, she vowed, beginning on her birthday in January 2013, to say yes to everything for the entire year. This commitment meant saying yes to public speaking, to playing with her children whenever they asked, to losing weight, to engaging in difficult conversations with friends and coworkers, and to not getting married (which she had been planning to do). At the end of the year, she describes herself as an entirely different person: "One hundred twenty-seven pounds thinner. Several toxic people lighter. Closer to my family. A better mother. A better friend. A happier boss. A stronger leader. A more creative writer."[14] The year of yes ultimately became a permanent transformation: "The Year of Yes, I realize, has become a snowball rolling down a hill. Each yes rolls into the next into the next and the snowball is growing and growing and growing. Every yes changes something in me. Every yes is a bit more transformative. Every yes sparks some new phase of evolution."[15]

To her list of accomplishments, Shonda has added the creation of Shondaland.com, a lifestyle website, which she started in 2017. The website is a way of creating community among her followers and inspiring them to embrace their own stories.

> If we can leave you with one lesson, let it be this:
> If you don't like your story, rewrite it.
> If you don't rewrite it, someone else will rewrite it for you.
> Never let that happen.
> Because then you've been silenced.
> We are Shondaland.
> Storytelling is our business.
> Showing you the extraordinary possibilities of your story is why we exist.[16]

In addition, the Shondaland website promotes activism by showcasing change makers who have had an impact on their communities. Rhimes herself is known for supporting causes related to children, AIDS, poverty, and education, with special attention to LGBTQIA+, Black, and women's issues.

Shonda has been honored with awards for both her creative pursuits and her activism. Her artistic awards include a Golden Globe for Outstanding Television Drama, the Norman Lear Achievement Award in Television, and the Writers Guild of America Award for Best New Series. In 2013, President Barack Obama appointed Rhimes to serve as a trustee for the John F. Kennedy Center for the Performing Arts, and she was inducted into the Television Academy Hall of Fame in 2017. In addition, *Time* has twice (2013 and 2021) included her on its list of the 100 most influential people, *Fortune* listed her as one of the 50 most powerful women in 2013, and *Forbes* listed her as one of the 100 most powerful women in 2018. For her work on behalf of diversity, equity, and inclusion, she earned the GLAAD Media Golden Gate Award, the Sherry Lansing Leadership Award, the NAACP Image Award for Outstanding Writing in a Dramatic Series, and the Eleanor Roosevelt Global Women's Rights Award from the Feminist Majority Foundation. Despite all of her accomplishments, Shonda notes, "At the end of the day, I want to be remembered for being a daughter, sister, mother, friend and for writing crazy entertaining characters who talked about stuff that mattered. . . . It's all about the work. I don't focus on things like awards and accolades. I don't spend time thinking about my legacy. My job is to make shows and tell stories."[17]

Definition of Feminism

Rhimes takes feminism for granted; it has always been part of her life: "I think that given the fact that a feminist is a woman who believes that men and women should be treated equally, I think I've probably been a feminist since the day I was born."[18] She explains that her feminism was greatly influenced by her mother: "My mama, she Maya Angelou'd the [expletive] out of me."[19]

For Shonda, feminism is about individuals being able to be what they want, without constraints imposed on them by gender: "The beauty of being a feminist is that you get to be whatever you want, and that's the point."[20] Viola Davis, star of *How to Get Away with Murder*, emphasizes how Rhimes's approach to feminism is evident in all of her television shows: "She doesn't put any limitations on the narrative based on your skin tone, your sex or your age. She doesn't put any limitations on it at all."[21] Neither does Shonda confine her feminism to women. She wants all life options to be open to both women and men: "Lead the life you want to lead. Be whoever you want to be. Have the babies. Be the CEO. Lean out. Lean in. . . . I don't want the girls wishing they could be men for a day. I don't even want men wishing they could be women."[22]

In her television programs and films, Rhimes depicts a feminist world in which women and men can indeed be whatever they want to be. Rather than mirroring the current world in its sexist and racist iterations, "she shows us a world as it ought to be."[23] Her characters aren't superficial caricatures or stereotypes; instead, she presents all kinds of women in a variety of roles—"heroes, the villains, the badasses, the big dogs."[24] Often, she creates a "world where women—often black women—have already broken through the glass ceiling. They are at the absolute top of their game. They've already won."[25] This world, however, is not a feminist utopia in which characters live perfect lives. Instead, it is a world populated with complex, dynamic characters who move through their lives with varying degrees of self-reflexivity, awareness, and understanding and whose actions prompt a range of consequences for themselves and others. In other words, just because women have it all does not mean their lives are easy, and Shonda wants to present women who are strong, capable, interesting, and imperfectly human. Her Shondaland website offers a glimpse at the humanity that characterizes her feminism.

> We embrace our greatness. We embrace our genius.
> We know we are talented. We love that we win.
> A true revolution is never apologizing for being better than other people.
> We also mess up all the time. And we don't care who knows it.
> We know the fall is there so that we can feel the joy of rising.
> We think the most beautiful woman is the one who speaks up.
> Who does not hide. Who won't be silenced.[26]

Change Strategies

Rhimes wants to show the world in all of its normal variety and diversity in order to enrich what the world looks like on television and in film. She creates characters who make their own life choices unconstrained by the expectations imposed by others and who celebrate their power as a way to honor the uniqueness of each human life. Her three major strategies—(1) normalizing diversity, (2) enacting self-determination, and (3) claiming power—are designed to distinguish the shows she creates from the more stereotypic ones that populate the media and to offer audiences an image of what true diversity looks like in the world.

Normalizing Diversity

Shonda's primary change strategy is normalizing diversity. She has difficulty with the word *diversity* because it "suggests something . . . other. As if it is something special. Or rare."[27] She prefers to call what she is doing *ordinary* because "women, people of color, LGBTQ people equal WAY more than 50 percent of the population."[28] The term *diversity*, however, provides an apt description of how she populates the worlds she creates. Her world is filled with "people of all hues, genders, backgrounds, and sexual orientations," which is "perfectly normal in the twenty-first century."[29]

Part of Rhimes's process of normalizing means that she is colorblind when creating and casting characters for her shows. This has been a source of some critique,[30] but in her world, "nobody was particularly black, white, Asian or whatever."[31] She simply takes for granted "that we live in a diverse world,"[32] so she does not write the race of characters into a script but instead waits to see who shows up for auditions. Shonda recounts that during casting for Cristina Yang, one of the female leads on *Grey's Anatomy*, she did not have a picture in mind for that character. But when "Sandra Oh walked in the door . . . . Cristina Yang was born."[33]

Rhimes also avoids explicit discussions of race in her shows because she does not see such discussions as normal. She explains that on many television shows in which there is only one character of color, there is a tendency for that character to serve as a token who spends a great deal of "time talking about the world as 'I'm a black man blah, blah, blah.'" Shonda disagrees with this approach because "that's not how the world works."[34] She notes that "my friends and I don't sit around and discuss race."[35] She elaborates: "I'm a black woman every day, and I'm not confused about that. I'm not worried about that. I don't need to have a discussion with you about how I feel as a black woman, because I don't feel disempowered as a black woman."[36] On *Scandal*, in which Olivia Pope, a Black woman, has an affair with Fitzgerald Grant, the white president of the United States, Rhimes wrote a line in which Olivia says she is feeling "a little Sally Hemings-Thomas Jefferson" about their relationship. Rhimes wrote that line into three separate scripts but took it out each time. She finally included it as a flashback to early in the Pope-Grant relationship when she "knew it would have been on Olivia's mind."[37] Shonda summarizes: "I don't think that we have to have a discussion about race when you're watching a black woman who is having an affair with the white president of the United States. . . . The discussion is right in front of your face."[38]

For Rhimes, normalizing diversity is important because it allows all kinds of people to see themselves reflected back at them from television and movies: "You should get to turn on the TV and see your tribe. And your tribe can be any kind of person, anyone you identify with, anyone who feels like you, who feels like home, who feels like truth."[39] Shonda suggests there is a "fundamental human need for one human being to hear another human being say to them: 'You are not alone. You are seen. I am with you.'"[40] She maintains that "if I am doing my job right, there will be a person here for everyone."[41] In addition to seeing others who are like them on the screen, she believes that all individuals should "turn on the TV and see someone who doesn't look like them and love like them" because that provides an opportunity to "learn from them."[42] Once this kind of learning begins, it also means those who are different will be less likely to be isolated, marginalized, and erased by society.

Enacting Self-Determination

Rhimes adds self-determination to her strategy of normalizing diversity because she believes that what is normal is "living as *you* need to, as you *want* to. As your inner voice tells you to. Happiness comes from being who you actually are instead of who you think you are supposed to be."[43] She believes all individuals need to get "busy becoming" what they can be instead of spending time worrying about what others think about them and tell them to be.[44] She wants each person to be "truly finally always yourself."[45] Her only rule is that there are no rules: "You don't want a baby? Don't have one. I don't want to get married? I won't. You want to live alone? Enjoy it. You want to love someone? Love someone. Don't apologize. Don't explain."[46] Asked to contribute a piece to illuminate the Joan Miró statue in Chicago, *The Sun, The*

Moon, and One Star, Shonda's monologue emphasizes that each person has a right to their uniqueness: "I am different. I am an original. And like everyone else, I am here to take up space in the universe. I do so with pride."[47]

Rhimes uses the metaphor of writing stories to emphasize the importance of living life on one's own terms. "Everyone has a story,"[48] and if individuals feel the need to apologize for or explain that story, they are telling "the wrong story." In such cases, Shonda urges individuals to start over: "Wipe the slate clean. And rewrite it. . . . Be your own narrator."[49] In her television drama *The Catch*, she has the two lead female detectives respond in just this way when a client asks, after her case has been resolved, what she should do next. One detective replies, "you do whatever you want to do," and the other quickly adds, "but on your own terms."[50]

Claiming Power

Rhimes's change efforts also involve women claiming their power by taking credit for their accomplishments as well as acknowledging those who made those accomplishments possible. At an event to honor women in entertainment, she noticed that each of the award winners, herself included, dismissed her achievements by shaking her head in disbelief, looking away, looking embarrassed, or laughing nervously as their accomplishments were named. Shonda's takeaway was that "not a single woman in this room could handle being told, 'You're awesome.' I couldn't handle being told I am awesome. What in the hell is wrong with us?"[51] When she examined her own behavior, she realized that she frequently said "'I'm *just* a writer'" as a "way of making sure people knew that I didn't think that I was doing anything special. My way of not being arrogant or snotty."[52] Whenever she won an award, she "worked to appear a little bit sillier and sweeter and simpler" in the face of her "own greatness."[53]

Rhimes blames women's socialization for their need to diminish their successes and accomplishments—efforts that don't serve women well and in fact diminish their power. She asks: "What is the opposite of a cocky, immodest, brazen women? . . . A meek, chaste, timid woman. Who in the name of Ruth Bader Ginsburg and Queen Bey[oncé] wants to be a meek, chaste, timid woman?"[54] Women should not be afraid to acknowledge their accomplishments because every person has contributions to make: "And I think this is the thing: everyone's got some greatness in them. . . . But in order to really mine it, you have to own it. You have to grab hold of it. You have to believe it."[55] For Shonda, this is *badassery*—knowing, accepting, and celebrating one's own accomplishments and gifts and living life with swagger.[56] Consequently, Rhimes decided to accept "any and all acknowledgments of personal fabulous awesomeness with a clear, calm 'Thank you' and a confident smile and nothing more."[57]

Shonda pairs her strategy of claiming power with an acknowledgment of the contributions and achievements of others. She used to take the focus off of herself by saying, "It's not me, it's them," but now she says, "It's me *and* it's them. It's us."[58] In other words, she shares her power with those around her who contribute to her success. Rhimes's strongest statement of the importance of recognizing and celebrating those who came before occurred when she was honored with the Sherry Lansing leadership award, given annually to a woman trailblazer in Hollywood. When Shonda asked why she was receiving the award, she was told it was because she had broken through "the industry's glass ceiling as a woman and an African-American."[59] In her acceptance speech, Rhimes disagreed with this assessment. She set the stage by arguing that "if I had broken through any glass ceiling, I would know. . . . I would have felt some cuts. I would have some bruises. There'd be shards of glass in my hair. I'd be bleeding. I'd have wounds."[60] She explained that because it was 2014, however, the room was filled with women of all colors who were Hollywood game changers. Fifteen years ago, there would have been many fewer, and thirty years ago, there would have been only two, and, she notes, "I would be serving those two women breakfast."[61] She asked her audience not to privilege her accomplishments but to consider all the women who came before so that when it was finally her turn to break through the ceiling, it was "simply a matter of running on a path created by every other woman's footprints."[62] Shonda ended her speech by thanking the women in the room as well as "all the women who never made it into this room" and "all the women who will hopefully fill a room one hundred times this size when we are all gone."[63]

Rhimes's change strategies—normalizing diversity, enacting self-determination, and claiming power—enable her to create, in television and film, worlds that are enriched by the incredible variety of ways to be human. This is also the world in which she chooses to live and that she wants to leave for her daughters.

> I like how proud they are when they come to my offices and know that they come to Shondaland. There is a land and it is named after their mother. In their world, mothers run companies. In their world, mothers own Thursday nights. In their world, mothers work. And I am a better mother for it. The woman I am because I get to run Shondaland, because I get to write all day, because I get to spend my days making things up, that woman is a better person—and a better mother. Because that woman is happy. That woman is fulfilled. That woman is whole. I wouldn't want them to know the me that didn't get to do this all day long.[64]

■ REFLECTIONS

1. Imagine that you are going to say yes to everything in your life just as Rhimes did. How might your life change? Do you feel inspired to try this approach?
2. Watch several episodes of one of Shonda Rhimes's shows such as *Grey's Anatomy*, *Scandal*, or *Bridgerton*. Where do you see evidence of her color-blind approach to characters, and how does her approach affect the storyline and your perception of the characters?

3. Do you agree or disagree with Rhimes's dislike of the word *diversity*? Can you think of another word that expresses this same concept but better captures the variety of people who inhabit the world?
4. Rhimes explains that her Black characters don't discuss their Blackness for the reason that she doesn't discuss Blackness with her friends and family—she's not confused about being Black, doesn't feel disempowered because she's Black, and doesn't need to have discussions about it. How effective is this as a strategy for enriching a system? Are there reasons why the characters in her TV shows should openly discuss race?
5. Rhimes understands how difficult it is for women to claim their achievements and their power. Have you had similar experiences where you dismissed praise because you didn't want to appear arrogant or selfish? Where did you learn that it is inappropriate for a woman to simply and directly accept praise for her accomplishments? Now that you've read about Rhimes's experience, do you want to approach such situations differently in the future?
6. How closely do Rhimes's change strategies align with the assumptions outlined in the introduction to part 4? Are there any assumptions that you don't believe pertain to her approach to change?
7. In which feminist wave would you place Rhimes and why?

■ Notes

[1] Shonda Rhimes, *Year of Yes: How to Dance It Out, Stand in the Sun and Be Your Own Person* (New York: Simon & Schuster, 2015), 180–81.
[2] Marc Shapiro, *Welcome to Shondaland: An Unauthorized Biography of Shonda Rhimes* (Riverdale, NY: Riverdale Avenue, 2015), 24.
[3] Rhimes, *Year of Yes*, 233.
[4] Rhimes, *Year of Yes*, 232.
[5] Rhimes, *Year of Yes*, 233.
[6] Rhimes, *Year of Yes*, 234.
[7] Rhimes, *Year of Yes*, 239.
[8] Dorothy Dandridge was the first African American woman to be nominated for an academy award for best actress.
[9] Shapiro, *Welcome to Shondaland*, 56.
[10] Shapiro, *Welcome to Shondaland*, 57.
[11] Lacey Rose, "Shonda Rhimes is Ready to 'Own Her S***': The Game-Changing Showrunner on Leaving ABC, 'Culture Shock' at Netflix and Overcoming her Fears," *Hollywood Reporter*, October 21, 2020, https://www.hollywoodreporter.com/features/shonda-rhimes-is-ready-to-own-her-s-the-game-changing-showrunner-on-leaving-abc-culture-shock-at-netflix-and-overcoming-her-fears
[12] Shonda Rhimes, "My Year of Saying Yes to Everything," TED Talk, Vancouver, Canada, February 2016, 4:21, https://www.ted.com/talks/shonda_rhimes_my_year_of_saying_yes_to_everything/
[13] Rhimes, *Year of Yes*, 1.
[14] Rhimes, *Year of Yes*, 296.
[15] Rhimes, *Year of Yes*, 146.
[16] Shonda Rhimes, "About: What We Do," Shondaland, https://www.shondaland.com/about/a12258145/who-we-are/; Rachel Montpelier, "Shonda Rhimes' Lifestyle Website

Shondaland.com has Arrived," *Women in Hollywood*, September 19, 2017, https://womenandhollywood.com/shonda-rhimes-lifestyle-website-shondaland-com-has-arrived-94a2314da080/

17 Shapiro, *Welcome to Shondaland*, 146–47.
18 Shonda Rhimes, "Shonda Rhimes Talks Feminism, 'Grey's Anatomy' and her New Campaign," interview by Ramin Setoodeh, *Variety*, June 28, 2019, https://variety.com/2019/tv/news/shonda-rhimes-showus-portrayals-women-in-media-1203255904/
19 Nardine Saad, "Shonda Rhimes, Jenji Kohan Recognize 'Lucky' Position as Female Showrunners," *Los Angeles Times*, May 19, 2015, https://www.latimes.com/entertainment/tv/showtracker/la-et-st-shonda-rhimes-feminism-jenji-kohan-womens-rights-awards-20150518-story.html#
20 Robbie Myers, "Shonda Rhimes on Power, Feminism, and Police Brutality," *Elle*, September 23, 2015, https://www.elle.com/culture/career-politics/q-and-a/a30186/shonda-rhimes-elle-interview/
21 Shapiro, *Welcome to Shondaland*, 120.
22 Saad, "Shonda Rhimes."
23 Kait Kerrigan, "What Shondaland Has Taught Me about Feminist Narrative," *Medium*, March 20, 2018, https://medium.com/@kait_kerrigan/what-shondaland-has-taught-me-about-feminist-narrative-22ad9189fffa/
24 Rhimes, *Year of Yes*, 139.
25 Kerrigan, "What Shondaland Has Taught Me."
26 Rhimes, "About: What We Do."
27 Rhimes, *Year of Yes*, 234.
28 Rhimes, *Year of Yes*, 235.
29 Rhimes, *Year of Yes*, 139.
30 For discussions of and critiques of colorblind casting, see Micha Frazer-Carroll, "'It's Dangerous Not to See Race': Is Colour-Blind Casting All it's Cracked up to Be," *The Guardian*, August 2020, https://www.theguardian.com/tv-and-radio/2020/aug/11/its-dangerous-not-to-see-race-is-colour-blind-casting-all-its-cracked-up-to-be; Emiel Martens and Débora Povoa, "How to Get Away with Colour: Colour-Blindness and the Myth of a Postracial American in American Television Series," *Alphaville: Journal of Film and Screen Media* 13 (2017), http://www.alphavillejournal.com/Issue13/HTML/ArticleMartensPovoa.html6/; Asia Ewart, "What Colorblind Casting Does for Shows Like Bridgerton in the Long Run," The Beat, March 25, 2021, https://www.premiumbeat.com/blog/colorblind-casting-bridgerton/
31 Shapiro, *Welcome to Shondaland*, 62–63.
32 Shapiro, *Welcome to Shondaland*, 63.
33 Rhimes, *Year of Yes*, 216.
34 Willa Paskin, "Network TV is Broken. So How does Shonda Rhimes Keep Making Hits?," *New York Times Magazine*, May 9, 2013, https://www.nytimes.com/2013/05/12/magazine/shonda-rhimes.html/
35 Shapiro, *Welcome to Shondaland*, 63.
36 Paskin, "Network TV is Broken."
37 Paskin, "Network TV is Broken."
38 Paskin, "Network TV is Broken."
39 Rhimes, *Year of Yes*, 235.
40 Rhimes, *Year of Yes*, 234.
41 Rhimes, *Year of Yes*, 239.
42 Rhimes, *Year of Yes*, 235.
43 Rhimes, *Year of Yes*, 286.
44 Rhimes, *Year of Yes*, 80.
45 Rhimes, *Year of Yes*, 91.
46 Rhimes, *Year of Yes*, 286.
47 Rhimes, *Year of Yes*, 291.

48 "Proust Questionnaire: Shonda Rhimes," *Vanity Fair*, November 2017, https://archive.vanityfair.com/article/2017/11/shonda-rhimes?gclid=Cj0KCQiA4L2BBhCvARIsAO0SBdZidcnrocVwV6b12utoHQPk-s-MZLCi-NDCYp22Tpk1ixXUnsQ6scEaAoYVEALw_wcB/
49 Rhimes, *Year of Yes*, 286.
50 *The Catch*, season 1, episode 8, "The Package," directed by Bill D'Elia, written by Jon Dorsy and Greg Goetz, executive producer Shonda Rhimes, aired May 12, 2016.
51 Rhimes, *Year of Yes*, 177.
52 Rhimes, *Year of Yes*, 198.
53 Rhimes, *Year of Yes*, 199.
54 Rhimes, *Year of Yes*, 182.
55 Rhimes, *Year of Yes*, 196.
56 Rhimes, *Year of Yes*, 195.
57 Rhimes, *Year of Yes*, 179.
58 Rhimes, *Year of Yes*, 180.
59 Rhimes, *Year of Yes*, 168.
60 Rhimes, *Year of Yes*, 169.
61 Rhimes, *Year of Yes*, 171.
62 Rhimes, *Year of Yes*, 173.
63 Rhimes, *Year of Yes*, 173.
64 Rhimes, *Year of Yes*, 87–88.

CHAPTER TWELVE

Jacinda Ardern

> *When you elected us, you didn't just tell us to govern, you asked us to fix existing problems, anticipate emerging ones, and to make sure we weren't caught off guard because we had done neither.... But we also decided we would do things differently. We decided that there was a place in government for concepts like compassion and kindness. That being active and intervening from time to time was a good thing. And that if there was ever a time to be bold and to use our voice on the world stage, it was now. In summary we are a government of change.*[1]

In October 2017, Jacinda Kate Laurell Ardern became the fortieth prime minister of New Zealand—the youngest head of state in the world at the age of thirty-seven and the third female prime minister of her country. As prime minister, her goal is to introduce policies that truly allow the inhabitants of New Zealand to thrive. Ardern was born in 1980 in Hamilton, New Zealand, and was raised in the rural communities of Murupara and Morrinsville, where her father was a police officer and her mother a school-catering assistant. The family was Mormon, but Jacinda left the church in her early twenties, unable to accept its stance against same-sex marriage. She credits her passion for politics to the widespread drug and alcohol dependency, poverty, suicide, and homelessness prevalent in the communities in which she grew up: "My passion for social justice came from what I saw; my love of politics came when I realised that it was the key to changing what I saw."[2]

Ardern's political interests were apparent in high school, where her yearbook reported the results of a class poll with items such as "best looking boy," "best looking girl," "the smartest," and "the funniest." Next to "most likely to become prime minister" was Jacinda's name.[3] Inspired by her grandmother and aunt, both staunch Labour supporters, Ardern had joined the Labour

Party at the age of seventeen. Her political leanings emerged in high school when she founded a chapter of Amnesty International, served on the student council, and was a member of the debate team and school newspaper.

Jacinda attended the University of Waikato in Hamilton, New Zealand, and earned a BA in communication studies in 2001. She spent a semester at Arizona State University and was there on September 11, 2001; the terrorist attacks were an important catalyst for her interest in international politics. After completing college, she worked as a researcher for Phil Goff, a member of the British parliament (MP), and for New Zealand prime minister (PM) Helen Clark. She then spent several years working in the cabinet office of British PM Tony Blair, where she was responsible for improving the ways local authorities interact with small businesses. In 2008, Ardern was elected president of the International Union of Socialist Youth, an umbrella organization of over 150 progressive youth movements from around the world.

In 2008, Jacinda also was selected as the Labour candidate for MP from the Waikato district, an election she lost by 13,000 votes. In New Zealand, however, candidates who run unsuccessfully for a district seat are placed on a list from which forty-nine MPs are chosen in proportion to the number of votes received by their parties. Ardern was one of those selected, and she entered the New Zealand parliament at the age of twenty-eight as its youngest member.

Jacinda was elected deputy leader of the Labour Party in 2017, second in command to Andrew Little. When Little stepped down less than two months before the general election, he convinced Ardern to stand as his replacement. She reportedly said no six times, calling the office of prime minster the "worst job in politics"[4] before finally agreeing to run. Her opponent was Bill English, a member of the National Party and the prime minister. With a campaign slogan of "Let's do this,"[5] Jacinda came to see the campaign and the possibilities it offered to be "nothing but a privilege. . . . I have been incredibly lucky to talk with New Zealanders across the country; lucky to have had a platform to talk about ideas and policies that I knew would change people's lives."[6]

The National Party won the largest number of seats in the election but did not win a majority and was unable to put together a coalition government. This defeat allowed Ardern and the Labour Party, which had not been in power in New Zealand for nine years, to join with New Zealand First and the Green Party to form a coalition government. Her charisma, charm, and optimism—what became known as *Jacindamania*—were credited with the Labour victory, and she was sworn in as prime minister on October 26, 2017. In addition to being the youngest female head of state at the time of her election, Jacinda is one of only a few elected female heads of state to give birth while in office.[7]

Ardern won a second term in a landslide victory in October 2020, earning 50 percent of the vote and sixty-five seats in the 120-member parliament. This margin allowed her to set up a government without having to form coalitions—something no party had been able to do since the current system of government was established in 1996. For her second term, Jacinda put in place a highly diverse cabinet; out of twenty members, eight are women, five are Māori, three are Pacific islanders, and three identify as LGBTQIA+.

Ardern considers herself a progressive social democrat who puts wellbeing at the center of her policies: "That we all do well when we look after our people. This means a country where everyone is earning, learning, caring or volunteering because that's the basis of strong communities. That when your basic needs are met, you have decent health services, a roof over your head and feel safe in your community, that is when you thrive."[8] She created a Living Standards Framework that changed how the government measures and assesses success when developing policies. Rather than paying attention only to economic growth, Jacinda's formula takes into account "what enables us to live fulfilling lives—our material wealth; our capability as individuals, families and communities; the health of our environment; and the strength of our communities."[9]

Among the programs Ardern has implemented during her tenure as prime minister is a Families' Package that includes "best start" payments of $60 per week for a couple's first child, twenty-six weeks of paid parental leave, an energy package to help families with winter heat, and an average increase of $75 per week for 384,000 low- and middle-income families. She also raised the minimum wage in New Zealand and addressed historic inequities in pay for women. Jacinda made the first year of post-secondary education free for New Zealanders, secured passage of a law that treats abortion as a health issue rather than a crime, and established a fund to support organizations working to "improve mental health and wellbeing outcomes" for members of New Zealand's LGBTQIA+ communities.[10]

Ardern has made climate-change legislation a priority, seeking to make New Zealand carbon neutral by 2050. To this end, she introduced plans to plant one billion trees to help stem climate change and to phase out single-use plastic bags. Following the killing of fifty-one worshippers at two mosques in Christchurch on March 15, 2019, she imposed tougher gun laws that ban military-style semiautomatic weapons and assault rifles. Jacinda also has continued efforts to address injustices against the Māori, the Indigenous people of New Zealand—injustices that date back to the 1840 treaty that established the country. Ardern is learning the Māori language and hopes to implement compulsory Māori in the schools so that New Zealand becomes truly bilingual.

Definition of Feminism

"I am a feminist. I remember saying that to a room full of career women once and watching them recoil in horror. A feminist? It was almost as if I had stood up and declared that I considered showering an optional exercise and deodorant to be devil juice. A feminist? Was I trying to be 'retro'? . . . Surely I didn't mean it. But I did mean it, and not only that, I wanted them to join me."[11] Jacinda comes from a family with strong feminist commitments. Her great-great grandmother signed the suffrage petition in 1893 that made New Zealand the first country to give women the vote. That same grandmother was also a long-distance walker and the first woman to walk one hundred miles in twenty-four hours. In high school, Ardern's activities clearly would be called *feminist*. For one class project, she chose to study Marilyn Waring, a New Zealand MP, and she successfully campaigned for girls' right to wear pants rather than skirts to school. At the same time, because she grew up Mormon, she assumed that she would be married and have children by the time she was thirty—career was "never the emphasis."[12] Not surprising, then, Jacinda describes her feminism as coming from her "gut" rather than a textbook.[13]

For Ardern, feminism is "a simple matter of fairness" with equality at its core: "If you believe in equality, you should be a feminist."[14] She elaborates: "If you believe that places like parliament or local government should reflect the people they represent, and that means having equal showing from women, you should be a feminist. If you believe that women deserve to be free from violence, have economic security, and have choices around the roles they take on—be it caregiver, worker or both, then you should be a feminist. If you believe that in New Zealand we have all of that already, then you don't need feminism, you need educating."[15] Although New Zealand has not yet realized its feminist potential, Jacinda sees feminism as very much in line with New Zealand's values: "We are such a fair minded country that when we see something that is unfair, I think it really gets to our core, and some of the issues that we're seeing are just a question of fairness. Is it fair that you experience that deduction in your lifetime earning because you've taken time out to have kids? Is it fair that because of the particular field of work you're in that you can expect to earn less relative to others?"[16] Also important to her view of feminism is that men need to participate: "Men not only can be feminists, they should be feminists, and if . . . they believe in basic principles of equality, then they need to get on board and start rowing as well."[17]

Because feminism is such an inherent part of who she is, Ardern initially had difficulty accepting the way she is held up as a symbol and torchbearer for girls and women in New Zealand and around the world: "We've had three female prime ministers—it's really not a big deal, guys."[18] She usually does not think about the relative rarity of a women as head of government until she travels internationally: "When I go overseas it does become more obvious to me."[19] Once, when she was the only woman in a group of over fifty male leaders, she recalls asking if they would be lining up boy-girl-boy-girl to enter the room: "And they looked at me blankly, not realising I was just making a sarcastic joke with them. Looking around a room like that you do stand out."[20]

Change Strategies

Jacinda's change strategies emerge from and build on her definition of feminism and are designed to enhance and enrich the traditional political system. Feminism is not separate from good governance for her, and she encourages girls and women in particular to choose to participate in their communities so that their perspectives become part of the conversation. Her remarks on International Women's Day in 2018 are typical. Ardern urged young women to "make your voice heard" because unless every citizen is celebrated and empowered, a country cannot "truly prosper."[21] Her strategies consist of (1) normalizing feminism, (2) implementing an ethic of care, and (3) valuing authenticity. Together they enable a government in which feminist values are prioritized.

Normalizing Feminism

Because Jacinda's goal is to incorporate feminist values in government, one of her primary strategies is to normalize feminism as natural, ordinary, and expected. Ardern downplays issues that often would be heralded as feminist causes—such as the fact that she is a female head of state—preferring to treat such issues as routine. When she announced her pregnancy after only a few months in office, she didn't want it to be seen as a feminist or political statement as much as just an ordinary part of life as a woman—a woman who happened to hold a position of high visibility. Disclosing that she had secretly dealt with morning sickness, Jacinda treated that as nothing unusual as well: "It's what ladies do. . . . Lots of people juggle a lot of things in their personal and private lives, and I'm not unusual in that. Plenty of women have multitasked before me, and I want to acknowledge that."[22]

Ardern prioritizes equality in her approach to government and sees her job as working to ensure that no New Zealander is left out: "I know my job is to fight for every New Zealander's rights; every New Zealander's interests; and every New Zealander's quality of life. I take that part of my role very seriously. My job is to have every New Zealander's back, and I will."[23] She doesn't distinguish between New Zealand citizens and those who are migrants or refugees. After the mosque shootings in Christchurch, Jacinda asserted: "Many of those who will have been directly affected by this shooting may be migrants to New Zealand, they may even be refugees here. They have chosen to make New Zealand their home, and it is their home. . . . They are us."[24] Not only does Ardern's vision for a feminist society mean that everyone has equal access to resources, it also means that "everyone should have the opportunity to contribute to their community in a way that is meaningful for them. And if you're not, we're probably all losing out."[25]

Implementing an Ethic of Care

A second strategy that characterizes Jacinda's feminism is grounded in the notion of *kaitiakitanga*, a Māori word meaning care and protection. A *kaitiaki* is a carer, guardian, protector, and conserver, and the term typically is used to refer to guardianship of the environment. Ardern uses it broadly to refer to an ethic of care that encompasses empathy, compassion, responsiveness to and acceptance of others as well as insight into the perspectives, feelings, and needs of others.

Jacinda has made an ethic of care and kindness central to her philosophy of governing, a commitment that became especially clear after the Christchurch shootings. Her response to the shootings was described as "feminine" and contrasted with the bravado and calls for revenge that often characterize the responses of male heads of state in similar situations. Ardern, for instance, wore a head scarf as an expression of solidarity and respect when she met with Muslim victims and mourners. She unabashedly revealed her emotions during meetings with family members, and her government paid all funeral costs for the victims regardless of their immigration status. Although values such as kindness often are considered weak, Jacinda "seems to be finding a language to articulate the idea that compassion is in fact strength."[26]

Ardern's notion of kindness involves not only caring for others but modeling what care looks like: "Our societies must be compassionate and inclusive no matter what religion, race or gender, and we cannot call for others to model this behaviour unless we model it ourselves, in our actions and in our language."[27] After the Christchurch shootings, she called on New Zealanders to assume responsibility for enacting kindness in all areas of their daily lives: "We each hold the power, in our words and in our action, in our daily acts of kindness. Let that be the legacy of the 15th of March."[28] She stressed the importance of "looking outwardly and beyond ourselves"[29] as a "good starting point" for a different kind of world and different kind of politics: "I really rebel against this idea that politics has to be a place full of ego and where you're constantly focused on scoring hits. . . . Yes, we need a robust democracy, but you can be strong and you can be kind."[30] Jacinda's feminism is infused with an ethic of care, which functions to encourage a society in which everyone flourishes and the system is richer as a result.

Valuing Authenticity

Another one of Ardern's change strategies is valuing authenticity. She hopes to create a government and world that are more authentic in their responses to people and issues. Authenticity emerged as one of Jacinda's defining personal characteristics from the time she was young. As one of her high school teachers noted: "There's not a public, private, or political persona. There's just Jacinda."[31] During her tenure as prime minister, Ardern continues to assert a unique, authentic style. Although often asked to compare her government and leadership style to other world leaders—"to compare and find a mould"—she insists that "we will be our own government. And I'm not modelling myself after any political leader."[32]

Jacinda's authenticity is accompanied by a direct approach in terms of speech and actions. She believes that speaking "frankly and openly" about issues is something "we should never shy away from . . . because if we don't speak freely how do we change?"[33] Ardern's response to US President Donald Trump, when he called after the Christchurch shootings to ask what he might do, is typical. She urged him to show "sympathy and love for all Muslim communities."[34] Jacinda wants honesty and transparency to continue to define New Zealand, which entails "speaking up for what we believe in, pitching in when our values are challenged and working tirelessly to draw in partners with shared views."[35] She continues: "I think New Zealand's strength has always been using our voice on the issues that matter and we've been consistent on it. There is power in that."[36]

Ardern's refusal to be anything but who she is became especially clear around her pregnancy and the birth of her daughter. She did not "put on the face of a world-defying-super-mum" and instead willingly shared her vulnerabilities: "Can I be a good politician while also being a good mum? And I believe it's possible, but ask me in three years. . . . I, just at the end of every day, have to feel like I did my best for both." She believes transparency is the best course of action: "Maybe there's some benefit out there in being a bit more open about the struggles we all have in balancing these things in our lives? Maybe I just need to be open and have some faith that it'll be okay."[37] In owning her "humanity . . . messiness . . . and contradictions,"[38] Jacinda has endeared herself to many who appreciate her willingness to share herself and to be precisely who she is as a person and as a head of state.

Ardern's change strategies function to move her country forward in a direction that is authentic, transparent, and empathic. By normalizing feminism, invoking an ethic of care, and valuing authenticity, she shows how government can be enriched with the incorporation of feminist values. She frequently ends her speeches with phrases such as "Let's keep going"[39] and "Let's keep doing this"[40]—variations on her campaign slogan of "Let's do this." For Jacinda, feminism is not a special kind of movement but simply getting "on with things in the Kiwi way"[41] and doing what is necessary to make New Zealand a country where all citizens thrive.

■ REFLECTIONS

1. Ardern treats feminism as a normal and even mundane part of life and wishes others would do the same. To what extent is feminism a matter of fact in your life? What would you need to do to normalize it, as Ardern does?

2. Ardern's efforts to normalize feminism de-emphasize feminism as the source of perspectives and practices designed to create an equitable and just society. As a result, New Zealanders might see the changes she implements as due to things other than feminism, such as traditional New Zea-

land values. Does it matter if feminist values are labeled *feminist*, or is it more important that they are in place? There is a long history of the erasure of women's ideas and contributions. Is normalizing feminism an example of feminism's progress or an example of such erasure?

3. Ardern believes that a value such as care is meaningless unless it is practiced at both governmental and individual levels. What would it look like if care were realized in US politics? Take an issue of concern in the United States and explain how addressing that issue would be different from how it is treated now if care were featured in its solution.

4. Many of the women featured in this book see themselves as role models for girls and women. Ardern chooses not to emphasize this role and wants people to see her leadership as something normal and not exceptional. Other women, however, highlight and loudly publicize their status as role models. Which approach do you believe is most effective in creating change?

5. Compare and contrast the approach to an issue by a US female political leader and a US male political leader. Do you see evidence of different ways of doing politics between the two leaders? Does the female leader enact Ardern's ethic of care? If so, what difference does that seem to make in how she approaches the issue?

6. How closely do Ardern's change strategies align with the assumptions outlined in the introduction to part 4? Are there any assumptions that you don't believe pertain to her approach to change?

7. In which feminist wave would you place Ardern and why?

■ NOTES

[1] Jacinda Ardern, "Our Plan for a Modern and Prosperous New Zealand," Beehive.govt.nz, September 16, 2018, https://www.beehive.govt.nz/speech/our-plan-modern-and-prosperous-new-zealand/

[2] Jacinda Ardern, "Maiden Statements," New Zealand Parliament, *Hansard Reports* 651 (December 16, 2008), https://www.parliament.nz/en/pb/hansard-debates/rhr/document/49HansS_20081216_00001012/ardern-jacinda-maiden-statements/; Amelia Lester, "In Her Prime," *Vogue*, March 1, 2018, https://archive.vogue.com/article/2018/3/1/in-her-prime/

[3] Jessie Stephens, "The Path That Led Jacinda Ardern to Becoming the Most Respected Leader in the World," *MSN News*, March 21, 2019, https://www.msn.com/en-au/news/world/the-path-that-led-jacinda-ardern-to-becoming-the-most-respected-leader-in-the-world/ar-BBV4i5L?li=AA4RE4&%25253Bocid=iehp/

[4] Anna Bracewell-Worrall, "Jacinda Ardern Full Speech: Let's Keep Doing This," *Newshub*, September 23, 2017, https://www.newshub.co.nz/home/election/2017/09/jacinda-ardern-election-will-be-decided-by-mmp.html/

[5] Jacinda Ardern, "Jacinda Ardern's Speech to CTU Conference 2017," *Labour*, October 25, 2017, https://www.labour.org.nz/jacinda_ardern_s_speech_to_ctu_conference_2017/

[6] Bracewell-Worrall, "Jacinda Ardern Full Speech."

[7] Benazir Bhutto, prime minister of Pakistan, gave birth to a daughter in 1990. In contrast to Ardern, she kept her pregnancy a secret, her daughter was delivered by C-section, and she returned to work the next day. See M. Ilyas Khan, "Ardern and Bhutto: Two Different Pregnancies in Power," *BBC News*, June 21, 2019, https://www.bbc.com/news/world-asia-44568537/

8 Jacinda Ardern, "The 100 Day Plan and Beyond: Setting the Direction of Government," Beehive.govt.nz, January 21, 2018, https://www.beehive.govt.nz/speech/100-day-plan-and-beyond-setting-direction-government/
9 Jacinda Ardern, "Prime Minister's Statement at the Opening of Parliament," Beehive.govt.nz, February 12, 2019, https://www.beehive.govt.nz/speech/prime-ministers-statement-opening-parliament/
10 Jacinda Ardern and Grant Robertson, "Government Establishes Rainbow Wellbeing Legacy Fund," Beehive.govt.nz, June 6, 2019, https://www.beehive.govt.nz/release/government-establishes-rainbow-wellbeing-legacy-fund/
11 Jacinda Ardern, "I am a Feminist," Villainesse, May 20, 2015, https://www.villainesse.com/girl-power/jacinda-ardern-i-am-feminist/
12 "Men Can and Should be Feminists—Prime Minister Jacinda Ardern," *Newshub*, September 25, 2019, https://www.newshub.co.nz/home/politics/2018/07/men-can-and-should-be-feminists-prime-minister-jacinda-ardern.html/
13 Ardern, "I am a Feminist."
14 Ardern, "I am a Feminist."
15 Ardern, "I am a Feminist."
16 "'We Need to Say, OK, What Next?' Jacinda Ardern on the Impact of #MeToo," The Spinoff, July 14, 2018, https://thespinoff.co.nz/partner/are-we-there-yet/14-07-2018/we-need-to-say-ok-what-next-jacinda-ardern-on-the-impact-of-metoo/
17 "'We Need to Say, OK, What Next?'"
18 Matt Petronzio, "Jacinda Ardern Wants to Make New Zealand the 'Best Place in the World to Be a Child,'" *Global Citizen*, September 23, 2018, https://www.globalcitizen.org/en/content/jacinda-ardern-social-good-summit-2018/
19 "Men Can and Should be Feminists."
20 "Men Can and Should be Feminists."
21 Jacinda Ardern, "Young Women Urged to Make Their Voices Heard," Beehive.govt.nz, March 9, 2018, https://www.beehive.govt.nz/release/young-women-urged-make-their-voices-heard/
22 Eleanor Ainge Roy, "Jacinda Ardern: New Zealand Prime Minister Announces First Pregnancy," *The Guardian*, January 19, 2018, https://www.theguardian.com/world/2018/jan/18/new-zealand-jacinda-ardern-pregnant/
23 Ardern, "Jacinda Ardern's Speech to CTU Conference 2017."
24 NewstalkZB, "Revealed: What Ardern Wrote in Minutes after Terror Attack," *New Zealand Herald*, April 7, 2019, https://theworldnews.net/nz-news/revealed-what-ardern-wrote-in-the-minutes-after-terror-attack/
25 Ardern, "Our Plan for a Modern and Prosperous New Zealand."
26 Max Rashbrooke, "How Jacinda Ardern is Transforming New Zealand," *Prospect*, March 27, 2019, https://www.prospectmagazine.co.uk/magazine/jacinda-arden-new-zealand-progressive-economy-christchurch-max-rashbrooke/
27 "Christchurch Call: Jacinda Ardern's Speech at Paris Summit," *Stuff*, May 16, 2019, https://www.stuff.co.nz/national/politics/112756909/christchurch-call-jacinda-arderns-speech-at-paris-summit/
28 "Jacinda Ardern's Speech at Christchurch Memorial—Full Transcript," *The Guardian*, March 28, 2019, https://www.theguardian.com/world/2019/mar/29/jacinda-arderns-speech-at-christchurch-memorial-full-transcript/
29 Jacinda Arden, "Kindness and Kaitiakitanga: Jacinda Ardern Addresses the UN," The Spinoff, September 28, 2018, https://thespinoff.co.nz/politics/28-09-2018/kindness-and-kaitiakitanga-jacinda-ardern-addresses-the-un/
30 Chris Bramwell, "Jacinda Ardern on US Breakfast TV Show: Joy of Parenthood 'Far Surpassed Expectations,'" *RNZ*, September 25, 2018, https://www.rnz.co.nz/news/political/367192/jacinda-ardern-on-us-breakfast-tv-show-joy-of-parenthood-far-surpassed-expectations/
31 Liam Fitzpatrick and Casey Quackenbush, "Jacinda Ardern, New Zealand's 37-Year-Old Leader, Rolls Up Her Sleeves," *Time*, November 20, 2017, https://time.com/5028891/jacinda-ardern-worlds-youngest-female-leader-new-zealand/

[32] Toby Manhire, "Jacinda Ardern: 'I'm Not Going to Leave Any Room for Doubt that I Can Do This,'" *The Guardian*, January 31, 2018, https://www.theguardian.com/world/2018/feb/01/jacinda-ardern-interview-new-zealand-pregnancy-sexism/

[33] Jacinda Ardern, "Prime Minister's Waitangi Powhiri Speech," Beehive.govt.nz, February 5, 2018, https://www.beehive.govt.nz/speech/prime-ministers-waitangi-powhiri-speech/

[34] Amelia Lester, "The Roots of Jacinda Ardern's Extraordinary Leadership After Christchurch," *The New Yorker*, March 23, 2019, https://www.newyorker.com/culture/culture-desk/what-jacinda-arderns-leadership-means-to-new-zealand-and-to-the-world/

[35] Ardern, "Our Plan for a Modern and Prosperous New Zealand."

[36] Eleanor Ainge Roy, "Jacinda Ardern: 'Having a Baby Around Changes the Tone a Little Bit,'" *The Guardian*, August 10, 2018, https://www.theguardian.com/world/2018/aug/10/jacinda-ardern-having-a-baby-around-changes-the-tone-a-little-bit/

[37] Jon Michail, "The Authenticity of Jacinda Ardern," *International Policy Digest*, September 10, 2018, https://intpolicydigest.org/2018/09/10/the-authenticity-of-jacinda-ardern/

[38] Michail, "The Authenticity of Jacinda Ardern."

[39] Jacinda Ardern, "The Importance of Family-Friendly Policies Around the World," Beehive.govt.nz, September 24, 2018, https://www.beehive.govt.nz/speech/importance-family-friendly-policies-around-world/

[40] Jacinda Ardern, "Jacinda Ardern's Speech to the 2018 Labour Party Conference," *Labour*, November 4, 2018, https://www.labour.org.nz/jacinda_arderns_2018_conference_speech/

[41] Lester, "The Roots of Jacinda Ardern's Extraordinary Leadership."

CHAPTER THIRTEEN

Joana Vasconcelos

> *The evolution of women in the art world has brought many new things. New techniques, new textures, new sizes, new colours, a new way of seeing the world. This has been very positive, because their participation has made the art world more dynamic and interesting. It was as if the world was only seen in one way, only by men, and never by women.*[1]

Described as "eclectic, magnificent, and pop,"[2] the works of Portuguese artist Joana Vasconcelos enrich the art world by incorporating the voices of women. In the spaces that result, women artists are featured and thrive, providing opportunities for viewers to experiment with new ways of seeing and being. Vasconcelos was born in 1971 in Paris, France, where her parents had fled from their native Portugal because of the authoritarian dictatorship of António de Oliveira Salazar. The family returned to Portugal when Joana was two years old after a military coup restored democracy to Portugal.

Joana's childhood was marked by a passion for karate. She began studying karate when she was nine years old, and her career goal for many years was to become a karate teacher. When a knee injury ended her practice of karate, she turned from the martial to the visual arts, an easy transition because both of her parents were artists (her father was a photographer and her mother a drawing artist and a furniture restorer), so art "was a constant presence and theme" in her home.[3] Between 1989 and 1996, Vasconcelos studied at the Centro de Arte e Comunicacão Visual (Centre for the Arts and Visual Communication) in Lisbon, an independent, multidisciplinary art school. She began studying drawing and jewelry making, but when she discovered that her projects inevitably ended in sculptures, she began to focus on this art form. As an artist, Joana still relies on her karate training and finds the skills she developed useful in her practice of art: "Karate teaches you how to concentrate, how to wait, how to react with knowledge of your opponent rather than just act. You learn to be very demanding of yourself, and very honest."[4]

Vasconcelos's works of art encompass a variety of mediums. Many of her works deal with the accumulation of repeated objects, such as the multiple gold wheel rims and whisky glasses that make up the sculpture *Solitaire*. Other works are made of fabrics, such as *Finisterra*, which consists of huge colorful stuffed forms pressed up against each other and packed into a frame. Another group of works features objects covered with handmade crochet such as *Mesa III*, a wooden table and six chairs, and *Side by Side*, in which two urinals are joined together by crochet. Her *Valkyries* series consists of gigantic and colorful fabric sculptures that reference female deities in Norse mythology who lead the most heroic of the battle dead to the paradise of Valhalla. One such *Valkyrie* is *Mary Poppins*, a gigantic sculpture/chandelier in which pieces of fabric in multiple colors and prints adorn the many arms of the serpent-like creature.

Joana's works of art are created by a team of fifty collaborators in her 10,000-square-foot studio located in a former cereal warehouse in Lisbon's harbor area. Her staff includes architects, engineers, and craftspeople who work at different stations in the studio. Because Vasconcelos works with many excellent technicians, she does not need to be one herself, something she sees as an advantage: "I'm not the specialist, as artists were before me, so in a way that allows me to open my horizons and to pick up different materials and we create something new."[5]

Joana's starting point for her artwork is "an idea in search of material"[6] rather than an idea that emerges from handling raw material. She begins by creating sketches that she gives to the architecture department, where technical drawings for a work are developed. These drawings are then passed along to the production team for the actual crafting of a work. Vasconcelos rarely has to abandon an idea because of the technical constraints inherent in its execution: "The truth is, when I have an idea, I find the right solutions for it. Otherwise, there is no idea. Sometimes we need to take a technology and twist it so that it can make the idea happen; it can take years to develop the right kind of technology. It's a kind of game, with the goal of producing pieces that have never been done before."[7]

Joana became internationally known when she was selected to participate in Italy's Venice Biennale in 2005. The piece she exhibited was *The Bride*, which looked like a gigantic opulent chandelier from afar but actually was made of more than 25,000 tampons. She typically puts together more than twenty exhibitions of her work each year and has exhibited in museums and art spaces such as the Guggenheim Museum in Bilbao, Spain; the Palace of Versailles in France; the Museum of Art in Seoul, South Korea; the Tel Aviv Museum in Israel; the Manchester City Gallery in England; and the National Museum of Women in the Arts in Washington, DC. Vasconcelos's public art pieces appear in the Porte Clignancourt metro station in Paris, France; the Melrose Arch district of Johannesburg, South Africa; and the Jupiter Artland sculpture park in Edinburgh, Scotland. Her work is also shown in unexpected spaces. She decorated a wind turbine on the Douro Sul wind farm in Portugal for the WindArt Project, installed one of her large *Valkyrie* fabric sculptures in Le Bon Marché department store in Paris, and created a tile mural for the façade of Steak 'n Shake in Porto, Portugal.

Joana's works often require considerable funding, and she depends not only on the sale of her works but on corporate support to produce her art. Johnson & Johnson, Dior, Bosch, and Swatch, for example, have sponsored some of her pieces. Vasconcelos also collaborates with companies to create works of art; French furniture brand Roche Bobois, for example, challenged her to reinterpret six iconic pieces from its collection. She has also partnered with Labuta, a Portuguese leather company, to design a limited edition of leather bags and with Sagres beer, illustrating its bottles with images from the ten regions of Portugal.

Definition of Feminism

Joana defines feminism as the effort to make the world "more egalitarian."[8] She does not confine feminism to the effort to gain rights for women alone but sees herself fighting for equal rights for everyone: "I am a feminist, because I fight for human rights, whether for women, children, ethnic minorities, homosexuals, or whatever."[9] Women are the focus of much of her work, however, because she recognizes that "many women are not treated equally today, they don't have the same human rights as men."[10] Women live "in a man's world,"[11] where "they don't earn the same as men, they can't wear what they want, their nature is restricted in many aspects."[12]

Feminism, for Vasconcelos, involves incorporating into the world the insights, perspectives, and contributions of women. She hopes her art encourages viewers "to talk about things that concern women, that reveal their identities." This "means talking about the problems but also about positive experiences."[13] She wants women's lives to be discussed "with openness and truth, without shame or guilt. We have to be honest, and face the problems clearly."[14] Joana acknowledges that her work often makes people uncomfortable because she examines "issues that are very personal and that touch on identity."[15] She features objects such as tampons, cutlery, pots and pans, doilies, high heels, and the Virgin Mary that deal with intimate issues in women's lives.

Vasconcelos credits the feminist movement of the 1960s and 1970s with disrupting established patterns for women and providing them with the opportunity to create new practices. In prior decades, she explains, "the role of women was very established. You would marry and have a family. It was quite simple and now it is very complex. We cannot look back to our mothers and grandmothers to establish a pattern; the pattern was broken. We have to recreate it."[16] Consequently, she believes that the question feminists now must address is: "How will the modern woman make the future?"[17] Joana hopes her art helps women create the future because of the way it reflects "the paradox of our time: private and public; the family woman, the social woman, the timid woman, the sexual woman, the smart woman and the object woman."[18] Vasconcelos is optimistic about women's ability to craft a new future because women "already have a voice, we are already much stronger than the generations before us."[19]

Change Strategies

Joana's change strategies are designed to enrich the art world by highlighting women's perspectives and ways of being. To accomplish this objective, she uses three primary change strategies: (1) recontextualizing, (2) cultivating ambiguity, and (3) celebrating the positive. The world that she hopes will result from these strategies is a festive, optimistic, and playful one.

Recontextualizing

Vasconcelos's strategy of recontextualizing objects is intended to generate new meanings and insights in new contexts. She initially selects objects for her art "for the narrative and emotional weights they carry," but she then "transforms them, converting them into the constituent parts of a new image."[20] As a result, she creates a tension "between their original function and their new contextual reference."[21] This process of recontextualizing is "a way of trying to open from what actually exists into a possible future: not one in which everything is entirely transformed, but one in which the possibilities are multiplying and expanding."[22]

A primary way in which Joana recontextualizes is by placing ordinary, everyday objects—often ones typically used by women—in new contexts. She subverts the traditional functions and meanings of household appliances, medicines, pots and pans, plastic cutlery, hair dryers, mirrors, office chairs, wine bottles, plastic flowers, tampons, and telephones by making new sculptural forms out of them. In *Full Steam Ahead*, for example, she made use of irons not to iron clothes but to create a fountain sculpture. For *Red Independent Heart #3,* Vasconcelos used 1,000 pieces of cheap plastic cutlery bent and bound together using a filigree technique to create an apparently luxurious, bejeweled sculpture of a heart. In *Solitaire,* she created a sculpture of an engagement ring from the wheel rims of cars and crystal whiskey glasses. "I like to create a space for discovery," Joana explains, "a first moment where you capture what is obvious in the piece, where you can consume it in the first instant. But as you come closer, you discover there's more to it and you start to deconstruct it."[23]

A second way in which Vasconcelos engages in recontextualizing is in her application of traditional crafts to new contexts. Crafts traditionally associated with women's domestic spaces, such as knitting, sewing, and crochet, are redeployed "to wrap unusual things or perform new functions,"[24] resulting in "alienation and de-functionalisation."[25] Joana wraps objects in crocheted nets or filigree lace, for example—objects such as a piano (*Piano Dentelle*), a laptop computer and mouse (*Netless '07*), a Darth Vader mask (*Crochet Vader*), and a ceramic bull's head (*McQueen*). In other works, she adds textiles to large architectural structures, which is the case with *Varina*, a crocheted cloth installed on the Dom Luis Bridge in Porto, Portugal. As a result of her textile wrapping, handcrafted items and techniques are transformed into high art, materials typically associated with women are turned into sculptural objects usually associated with men, and the domestic space of women is transformed into a public environment. "Domestic objects," her works proclaim, "can have the same importance as any industrial objects."[26]

Vasconcelos's strategy of recontextualizing is accomplished as well through her use of scale. Her work is consistently outsized and massive in scale so that "the extraordinary and the opulent rise from the commonplace."[27] In some instances, small objects are transformed into large-scale installations, as is the case with *Marilyn*, in which a huge high-heeled shoe is constructed from small pots and lids. In these works, "something seemingly modest" is expanded, "drawing attention to it by making it more hugely itself, while also changing its meaning."[28] In other instances, her works are simply large, as is the case with her *Valkyries*, which can be over 100 feet long. These giant forms are a way of "filling and challenging large spaces, spaces of privilege and power such as Versailles or a Venetian palazzo."[29] Just as with her recontextualizing of ordinary objects and traditional crafts, changes in scale enrich the art world and aesthetic experiences by expanding existing vocabularies and refreshing "their capacities to give pleasure, or playfully to adumbrate or twist them until new possibilities emerge."[30]

Cultivating Ambiguity

Joana's works are also characterized by the strategy of cultivating ambiguity, which encourages viewers to consider multiple possible meanings for them. The works prompt viewers to question "dogmatic positions,"[31] thus allowing for new kinds of spaces and ways of seeing. As she explains, "My works don't close themselves in upon a single discourse or interpretation. They are ambiguous, paradoxical and dichotomous, and I believe the richness and value is in this multiplicity of possible interpretations and readings."[32]

The ambiguity that characterizes Vasconcelos's art derives from several features of the work. Her use of textiles is a primary way by which she cultivates ambiguity. As a medium, textiles combine "various, occasionally contradictory, properties: coarse and soft, smooth and textured, stable and malleable, durable and transient."[33] Textiles themselves serve many functions—to beautify, to cover and conceal, to protect, to envelop, to disgust, and to distance. They can assume the "form of clothing, or as decorative or functional materials such as carpets, curtains, wallpapers, upholstery, bed linens, tablecloths, towels or cleaning rags."[34] Because they carry a variety of connotations, fabrics inherently suggest more possibilities than many other mediums.

Joana's transformation of everyday objects into new items also has the capacity to generate a variety of meanings. The objects that comprise her work—the cooking pots and lids of *Marilyn*, for example—are likely to evoke connotations related to domesticity, women's relegation to the home, drudgery, creativity, and care. But because the pots are made into a high-heeled shoe, additional possible connotations are evoked—Marilyn Monroe and the challenges she faced, the discomfort associated with much of women's clothing, and the glamour and sexiness of women's clothing as well.

Vasconcelos's work *Burka* is another example of how her works can suggest multiple meanings. Several layers of women's dress fabrics—the red polka-dot fabric of the Spanish flamenco dancer, a flowery print, a fabric used in cabaret costumes, Burberry tweed, American Army camouflage fabric, and a sari—are stitched together in a multilayered skirt over which hangs a blue burka. This construction sits atop a wrecking ball, which drops loudly and violently at regular intervals. The piece prompts a variety of readings. Does it depict a woman dying, crushed amid the clothes, destroyed by concealment and erasure? Does it mean that the "loss of identity can offer safety, even power"?[35] Is the work a reference to the assumption of the Virgin Mary, whose own traditional garb shares the garment's blue color? Dramatically different readings of the work are possible, and audiences are not likely to settle on just one meaning.

Joana's work *Top Model* also exemplifies the capacity of her works to generate multiple meanings. In this piece, a female mannequin holds a dog on a leash, with both dressed in a tightly knit, net-like textile casing. Is the textile casing a protective layer that underscores the dismissive posture of the mannequin? Is it a decoration that contradicts the aggressiveness of the dog and the self-confidence of the mannequin? Does it refer, like the leash, to forms of domestication? Is it a mechanism not only of protection but also imprisonment? All of these meanings and many more are possible from the work.

Vasconcelos's cultivation of ambiguity can be seen as well in *The Jewel of the Tagus*, which makes use of the Torre de Belém, an ancient fort and UNESCO world heritage site dating from the sixteenth century that served as a point of embarkation for Portuguese explorers. She draped the fort with orange and yellow buoys, suggesting that the tower was wearing a large, colorful necklace. She thus sought "to domesticate" an austere and dignified monument and to "take care of it, bring it comfort or a little love."[36] Joana neither negated or attacked the tower but let its context and its history be remade. She found in the fort something that could "be, under transformation, used again, seen afresh, both in relation to what it was before and with an eye to what it and we might become."[37]

Celebrating the Positive

Vasconcelos's works create a welcoming, festive, and enjoyable world. With her strategy of celebrating the positive, she is dedicated "to finding what can be used to help make a world which people can enjoy."[38] Her works are confident, optimistic, and playful and exhibit a "jubilant forthrightness"[39] and a "cheerful radiance"[40] as they hint "at something else over the horizon, in which systems of power are slowly transformed by a hundred deflections into systems of pleasure."[41] Her creations have been described as a form of "reenchanted art"—"art for a more *joyeuse* experience" that stands "in contrast to the harsh criticism and cynicism often found in other strands of contemporary art."[42] Her works show "how we can find something in almost everything that is worthy of love and repetition and expansion."[43]

Joana's works celebrate the positive in a number of ways, including through her use of humor. Many of her works provoke a moment of delight when viewers get the joke—when they realize that what seems to be a luxurious heart-shaped sculpture (*Red Independent Heart #3*) is made of disposable plastic cutlery or that a gigantic chandelier (*The Bride*) is made of tampons. Viewers experience a similar kind of delight when they encounter one of her *Valkyries* with its wild colors and shapes and tentacles spreading throughout a normally serious space. Vasconcelos sees humor as an important means of communication: "Humour comes naturally to me but I am perfectly conscious that humour is in fact a serious thing and an excellent means of communication. The questions my work poses seek to broaden people's perceptions of the world and humor is a great instrument for this."[44]

Another characteristic that contributes to Joana's celebratory world is the bright, exuberant color palette she uses in her works, resulting in a vibrant kaleidoscopic world. Even her large-scale *Valkyries*, whose tentacles run through multiple rooms in galleries, appear unthreatening and benevolent because they are soft and cuddly as well as colorful. Her works literally drip with every color of the rainbow, as *Aquarela* does, with hand-painted tiles, felt, and yarns in colors of aqua, olive green, orange, red, burgundy, and purple.

Vasconcelos's optimistic emphasis on the positive does not mean that she ignores oppressive conditions in the world. Her works have a subversive character that suggests "a will to change the society which they reflect, or at least to question it through critical reflection."[45] But she does not dwell on the negative conditions she is critiquing, as illustrated by *Big Booby #3*, an excessively oversized, round pot holder with a crocheted pattern of circles that bulges out from the wall. In its depiction of a woman's breast, the work acknowledges that women's bodies are often objectified, but it also shows what gender "might be without the subordination and the suffering, what it might be as an arena of pleasure."[46] Philosopher Crispin Sartwell explains how Joana's focus on the positive rather than on oppression functions: "There are many reasons to be grim and outraged, or sneering and cynical. These are attitudes that to some extent have dominated the arts for the past several decades, and we often have been instructed, pointedly or subtly, about gender, or poverty, or race, or power, or capitalism." He continues: "I also want moments in which I am grateful to be alive, moments in which I know the world to be beautiful. I want moments of affirmation, perhaps even of some things that are also, looked at from another angle, problems."[47] Vasconcelos's work, he asserts, "registers such moments, expands them, and makes them possible for others."[48]

Through her sculptures, Joana seeks to augment the art world and viewers' experiences of art by incorporating women's interests, values, and perspectives. When she recontextualizes objects and images, often ones common to women's spaces, she transforms them, showing that they can contribute ideas of magnitude and substance to the world. When she allows her works to carry multiple meanings, she opens up possibilities for imagining other kinds of spaces, conditions, and perspectives. The transformed world that results, Vasconcelos suggests, will be enjoyable, optimistic, and delightful. This world of bright colors, incongruity, and laughter is not something to be feared but embraced because it welcomes and affirms the talents, perspectives, and contributions of all.

■ REFLECTIONS

1. Vasconcelos wants to bring women into a man's world, and one of the ways she does this is by bringing artifacts of women's lives into her art. What impact is this practice likely to have on women in her audiences? On men?
2. As a visual artist, Vasconcelos does not rely primarily on words and discourse for creating change, as most of the other women in the book do. How does the fact that she uses images rather than words affect her ability to be effective as a change agent? Are there advantages of images over words in the change process?
3. Vasconcelos credits feminism for disrupting established patterns for women and opening up opportunities for them to develop new and more diverse ways of being in the world. Are there disadvantages to no longer having established patterns and expectations for behavior?
4. One of Vasconcelos's primary strategies is cultivating ambiguity—she encourages viewers to consider multiple possible meanings as a result of seeing her works of art. How effective do you believe cultivating ambiguity is in change efforts? What if viewers do not choose a meaning in line with the desired change?
5. Select one of Vasconcelos's *Valkyries* (https://www.joanavasconcelos.com/obras_en.aspx?s=VALKYRIES) and analyze it to discover what makes it feminist. Do you see in the work her definition of feminism?
6. How closely do Vasconcelos's change strategies align with the assumptions outlined in the introduction to part 4? Are there any assumptions that you don't believe pertain to her approach to change?
7. In which feminist wave would you place Vasconcelos and why?

■ NOTES

[1] Joana Vasconcelos, "Interview with Joana Vasconcelos on Multiculturalism, Tradition, Feminism and Sculpture," interview by Agustín Pérez Rubio, Agustín Pérez Rubio, n.d., 323, https://www.joanavasconcelos.com/multimedia/bibliografia/JV2011_AgustinPerezRubio_EN.pdf/

[2] Joana Vasconcelos, "Joana Vasconcelos: Creating Wonders," interview by Annalisa Chelli, Dyeing House Gallery, January 30, 2017, http://www.dyeinghousegallery.com/en/joana-vasconcelos-exclusive-interview/

[3] Joana Vasconcelos, email message to Sonja K. Foss, May 13, 2020.

[4] Joana Vasconcelos, "Interview: Installation Artist Joana Vasconcelos," interview by Rachel Spence, *Financial Times*, March 6, 2015, https://www.ft.com/content/451c2896-c0c5-11e4-876d-00144feab7de/

[5] Eitan Buganim, "The (Terrifying) New Feminist Art That's Taking Off in Tel Aviv," Haaretz, November 14, 2013, https://www.haaretz.com/israel-news/culture/.premium-a-terrifying-new-feminist-art-1.5290230/

[6] Idalina Conde, "The Artist's Journey," in *I'm Your Mirror: Joana Vasconcelos* (Bilbao, Spain: Guggenheim Bilbao, 2018), 50.

[7] Joana Vasconcelos, "There Must Be an Ambiguity: An Interview with Portuguese Artist Joana Vasconcelos," interview by Agnese Civle, Arterritory, January 23, 2017, https://arterritory.com/en/visual_arts/interviews/18388-there_must_be_an_ambiguity/

[8] Vasconcelos, "Interview with Joana Vasconcelos on Multiculturalism," 324.

[9] Vasconcelos, "Interview with Joana Vasconcelos on Multiculturalism," 324.

[10] Joana Vasconcelos, "An Interview with Joana Vasconcelos," interview by Yitong Wang, Tang Contemporary Art, April 30, 2013, http://www.randian-online.com/np_feature/interview-with-joana-vasconcelos/

[11] Vasconcelos, "An Interview with Joana Vasconcelos."

[12] Joana Vasconcelos, "Talking to Joana Vasconcelos," interview by José Luís Peixoto, in *I'm Your Mirror: Joana Vasconcelos* (Bilbao, Spain: Guggenheim Bilbao, 2018), 112.

[13] Joana Vasconcelos, "Interview with Joana Vasconcelos in Bilbao," interview by Lea Surugue, Euronews, June 29, 2018, https://www.euronews.com/living/2018/06/29/interview-with-joana-vasconcelos-in-bilbao/

[14] Vasconcelos, "Interview with Joana Vasconcelos in Bilbao."

[15] Vasconcelos, "Interview with Joana Vasconcelos on Multiculturalism," 324.

[16] Joana Vasconcelos, "Portuguese Baroque: Interview with Joana Vasconcelos," interview by Alexia Antsakli Vardinoyan, Artflyer, n.d., https://artflyer.net/joana-vasconcelos-interview/

[17] Vasconcelos, "Interview with Joana Vasconcelos on Multiculturalism," 324

[18] Vasconcelos, "Interview with Joana Vasconcelos on Multiculturalism," 324

[19] Vasconcelos, "An Interview with Joana Vasconcelos."

[20] Enrique Juncosa, "I'm Your Mirror," in *I'm Your Mirror: Joana Vasconcelos* (Bilbao, Spain: Guggenheim Bilbao, 2018), 30.

[21] Achim Sommer, "Maximal: Foreword and Introductory Observations," in *Maximal Joana Vasconcelos*, ed. Achim Sommer (Brühl, Germany: Max Ernst Museum Brühl of the LVR, 2019), 10.

[22] Crispin Sartwell, "Beauty and Reconciliation in the Art of Joana Vasconcelos," in *Joana Vasconcelos: Material World*, comp. Joana Vasconcelos (London, UK: Thames & Hudson, 2015), 314.

[23] "Joana Vasconcelos: Time Machine," Manchester Art Gallery, n.d., http://www.manchestergalleriestimemachine.org/

[24] Sartwell, "Beauty and Reconciliation," 316.

[25] Frederike Vosskamp, "Material Change: Material and Transformation in the Works of Joana Vasconcelos," in *Maximal Joana Vasconcelos*, ed. Achim Sommer (Brühl, Germany: Max Ernst Museum Brühl of the LVR, 2019), 184.

[26] Vasconcelos, "An Interview with Joana Vasconcelos."

27. Conde, "The Artist's Journey," 56.
28. Sartwell, "Beauty and Reconciliation," 310.
29. Sartwell, "Beauty and Reconciliation," 310.
30. Sartwell, "Beauty and Reconciliation," 310.
31. Enrique Juncosa, "The Soft Machine," in *Joana Vasconcelos: Material World*, comp. Joana Vasconcelos (London, UK: Thames & Hudson, 2015), 305.
32. Joana Vasconcelos, "Joana Vasconcelos Explains Contemporary Kitsch," interview by Rajesh Punj, Culture Trip, June 26, 2017, https://theculturetrip.com/europe/portugal/articles/interview-with-joana-vasconcelos-interventions-in-kitsch/
33. Vosskamp, "Material Change," 177.
34. Vosskamp, "Material Change," 175.
35. Margaret Carrigan, "How Joana Vasconcelos's Feminist Work is Redefining Art History," *Galerie*, July 23, 2018, https://www.galeriemagazine.com/joana-vasconcelos-guggenheim-bilbao/
36. Sartwell, "Beauty and Reconciliation," 315.
37. Sartwell, "Beauty and Reconciliation," 314.
38. Sartwell, "Beauty and Reconciliation," 313.
39. Juncosa, "The Soft Machine," 299.
40. Sommer, "Maximal," 15.
41. Sartwell, "Beauty and Reconciliation," 313.
42. Conde, "The Artist's Journey," 48.
43. Sartwell, "Beauty and Reconciliation," 316.
44. Vasconcelos, "Joana Vasconcelos Explains Contemporary Kitsch."
45. Juncosa, "I'm Your Mirror," 28.
46. Sartwell, "Beauty and Reconciliation," 315.
47. Sartwell, "Beauty and Reconciliation," 308.
48. Sartwell, "Beauty and Reconciliation," 308.

CHAPTER
FOURTEEN

Malala Yousafzai

My world has changed so much. On the shelves of our rented living room are awards from around the world—America, India, France, Spain, Italy and Austria, and many other places. . . . I am grateful for them, but they only remind me how much work still needs to be done to achieve the goal of education for every boy and girl. I don't want to be thought of as the "girl who was shot by the Taliban" but the "girl who fought for education." This is the cause to which I want to devote my life.[1]

A Pakistani activist who gained sudden fame when she was shot by the Taliban, Malala Yousafzai has made education—and especially education for girls—her life's mission. Yousafzai was born in 1997 in Mingora in the Swat district of Pakistan. Her father welcomed her as he would a son and encouraged friends and relatives to throw dried fruits, sweets, and coins into her cradle, a practice typically reserved for boys. A strong advocate for education, he believed that "nothing was more important than knowledge" and that education "should be available for all, rich and poor, boys and girls."[2] He started the Khushal School in Mingora, and his daughter grew up with it as her playground.

When Malala was ten years old, the Taliban, led by Maulana Fazlullah, came to the Swat Valley. Fazlullah set up his own radio station, broadcasting for two hours every morning and evening and offering increasingly conservative interpretations of the Quran. He declared television, music, and dancing sinful; suggested it was decadent for women to go shopping at the local bazaar; and closed beauty and barber shops. Because education teaches people to think for themselves, the Taliban was against educating children and argued especially against the education of girls. By the end of 2008, 400 schools in Pakistan had been destroyed, and on January 15, 2009, all girls' schools were ordered closed.

Yousafzai's father spoke out frequently against the Taliban: "'My only ambition . . . is to educate my children and my nation as much as I am able. But when half of your leaders tell lies and the other half is negotiating with the Taliban, there is nowhere to go. One has to speak out.'"[3] He carried in his pocket Martin Niemöller's poem, written during the Nazi era in Germany, that ends with the line, "Then they came for me, and there was no one left to speak for me."[4] In 2009, the BBC decided to ask a schoolgirl in Swat to blog about her life as a way to illustrate the Taliban's growing influence. Because of his reputation for speaking out, the BBC reporter asked Malala's father for the names of girls who might be willing to write such a diary, but all those he recommended backed out, afraid of Taliban retribution. His daughter then volunteered, and under the pseudonym *Gul Makai* (the name of the female protagonist in a well-known folk tale), she wrote a daily diary from January to March 2009.

The Yousafzai family was forced to leave Swat for several months in 2009 because of fighting between the Taliban and the Pakistani army. When the prime minister announced that the Taliban had been defeated, the family returned home and rebuilt the Khushal School, which reopened on August 1, 2009. In 2010, Adam Ellick, a correspondent for the *New York Times*, made a documentary film called *Class Dismissed* about the impact of the Taliban's actions on Yousafzai's school and family. The documentary increased Malala's public profile, and Desmond Tutu nominated her for the International Children's Peace Prize, sponsored by the KidsRights Foundation, the following year. She was also awarded Pakistan's first National Peace Prize in December 2011—a prize given to a child under the age of eighteen who contributes to peace and education in the country.

Yousafzai's visibility was met with various threats from the Taliban, and her father suggested they "go into hibernation," an idea she adamantly opposed. As she reminded her father, "You were the one who said if we believe in something greater than our lives, then our voices will only multiply even if we are dead."[5] Despite the potential risks, her family did not forbid Malala from continuing her activism, believing that while the Taliban might kill her father, they would not kill a child. On October 9, 2012, however, while she was riding home from school, a gunman stopped the bus and asked which girl was Malala. None of the girls responded, but they all looked in her direction, and the gunman fired three shots at her. Because Yousafzai slumped over after the first shot, the remaining bullets grazed two other girls—Shazia Ramzan and Kainat Riaz.

Malala was airlifted to a military hospital in Peshawar, where the bullet, which had entered near her left eye and lodged in her shoulder, was removed.[6] Doctors also removed a piece of her skull to relieve pressure on her brain. Because of conflicting reports about Yousafzai's condition, Javid Kayani and Fiona Reynolds—two British doctors in Pakistan to advise the government about setting up a liver-transplant program—were asked to examine her. They found that her condition was compromised by less than optimal aftercare, so she was airlifted to the Armed Forces Institute of Cardiology in the city of Rawalpindi, which had the best intensive care in Pakistan. In the meantime, Reynolds had Googled Malala and learned that this was no ordinary case: "If anything had happened to her it would have been blamed on the white woman. . . . If she'd died I would have killed Pakistan's Mother Teresa."[7]

Yousafzai's condition stabilized, and because Pakistan does not have the rehabilitation facilities she needed to learn to talk and walk again, she was flown to Queen Elizabeth Hospital in Birmingham, England, which specializes in treating British soldiers injured in Afghanistan and Iraq. She had a series of surgeries to repair the facial nerve that had been severed by the bullet and that kept her from being able to smile, to replace the piece of missing skull, and to insert a cochlear implant to restore hearing in her damaged left eardrum.

The Taliban claimed responsibility for the shooting of Malala, declaring her to be an infidel who was promoting Western culture. The mastermind of the shooting was Maulana Fazlullah, whose radio broadcasts had first announced the Taliban's presence in the Swat Valley and who had become emir of the Pakistani Taliban. Never arrested for his role in the shooting, he was killed in a US drone strike on June 14, 2018. The actual shooter was alleged to have been Ataullah Khan, who also was never arrested and is believed to be hiding in Afghanistan.

The international reaction to the attack on Yousafzai was outrage, and she received bouquets of flowers, boxes of chocolates, teddy bears, and over 8,000 cards and letters. The children of Benazir Bhutto, one of her heroes, sent Malala two shawls that had belonged to their late mother. The day after the attack, Madonna dedicated her song "Human Nature" to Yousafzai at a concert in Los Angeles. In addition, Angelina Jolie donated $50,000 toward girls' education in Pakistan, and former first lady Laura Bush wrote an op-ed piece in the *Washington Post* comparing Malala to Anne Frank.[8] Yousafzai's own attitude toward her assailants is one of forgiveness: "My only regret was that I hadn't had a chance to speak to them before they shot me. Now they'd never hear what I had to say."[9]

In Malala's home country, reactions to the shooting were mixed. Many hailed her as a peace icon, and protests over the assassination attempt were held in several cities. Over two million people signed a Right to Education petition delivered to the president of Pakistan, and a few months later, the government passed a bill guaranteeing free and compulsory education for Pakistani children. Many Pakistanis, however, remain ambivalent about Yousafzai. They see her as a puppet of the West who supports Western agendas over Pakistani ones. Those opposed to gender equality, either for religious or secular reasons, see her as undermining the proper place of women in Pakistan.

In part because of continuing threats against her, Malala and her family have remained in Birmingham, where her father was given a diplomatic post at the Pakistani consulate. Yousafzai chose to pursue her education in England as well. In 2017, she was admitted to Lady Margaret Hall at Oxford University, where she studied philosophy, politics, and economics; she completed her degree in 2020. Malala did not return to Pakistan until March 2018, when she made a surprise visit to her home country.

Yousafzai's activism has continued if not intensified since the attack on her life. On her sixteenth birthday, she spoke at the United Nations—her first speech following the shooting—and the occasion was dubbed *Malala Day*. Over 500 youth and education advocates from around the world were in attendance. In 2013, she established the Malala Fund to advocate for and invest in free, safe, quality secondary education for girls around the world, and her first grant of $45,000 went to educate forty girls in Pakistan. In addition, she has funded education projects in Afghanistan, Brazil, India, Nigeria, and Syria. Since the attack, Malala also has written several books. Her memoir, *I Am Malala: The Girl Who Stood Up for Education and Was Shot by the Taliban*, was published in 2013, and a children's edition of the book was published in 2014 under the title *I Am Malala: How One Girl Stood Up for Education and Changed the World*. She also authored a picture book, *Malala's Magic Pencil*, published in 2017, and *We Are Displaced: True Stories of Refugee Lives*, published in 2019.

Yousafzai has been honored by numerous awards and recognitions. She was the corecipient (with Kailash Satyarthi, a children's rights activist from India) of the 2014 Nobel Peace Prize—the youngest Nobel laureate at the time. Malala also has been awarded the Anne Frank Award for Moral Courage; the Mother Teresa Award for Social Justice; and the Sitara-e-Shujaat, Pakistan's second highest civil award for bravery. She was named one of the twenty-five most influential teens by *Time* magazine and was also awarded the Ellis Island International Medal of Honor and the Gleitsman Award from the Center for the Public Leadership at Harvard Kennedy School. She was the subject of a 2015 documentary, *He Named Me Malala*, which was nominated for six Emmys, winning in the category of individual achievement in animation.

Definition of Feminism

Yousafzai has her father to thank for her feminism because her father was determined to raise his sons and daughters as equals. He and his wife deliberately "chose to build an egalitarian family, respecting each other as equal partners,"[10] and they raised their daughter Malala the same way they raised their sons. Although her father was unfamiliar with the term *feminism*, it was his guiding philosophy: "I didn't hear the word feminist until I was 45, after the attack on Malala led us to move to the city of Birmingham in the U.K. But it was feminism I had been trying to spread in my family, and in my community, for years."[11] According to her father, feminism is simply wanting "girls everywhere to live in a world that treats them with love and meets them with open arms. I wanted then and still want the end of patriarchy, of a man-made system of ideas that thrives on fear, that dresses up suppression and hatred as the tenets of religion, and that at its heart fails to understand the beauty to be had for us all in living in a truly equal society."[12] He calls patriarchy "sheer stupidity,"[13] and he proudly asserts that "in my part of the world most people are known by their sons. I am one of the few lucky fathers known by his daughter."[14]

Just as her father did not have the label *feminism* to describe his approach until the family moved to the UK, Yousafzai was initially unfamiliar with the term as well. When first asked about being a feminist, she was reluctant to claim the label because she had heard it meant "women being superior to men." When she "realized feminism is just another word for 'equality,'" she embraced the term and sees it as closely linked to the causes she espouses: "We cannot succeed when half of us are held back. We call upon our sisters around the world to be brave, to embrace the strength within themselves and realize their full potential."[15]

Malala recognizes that, in the past, women needed to rely on men to speak up for them, but now, she believes, women can and need to stand up for themselves: "There was a time when women social activists asked men to stand up for their rights. But, this time, we will do it by ourselves. I am not telling men to step away from speaking for women's rights. Rather I am focusing on women to be independent to fight for themselves."[16] Although she sees women as primarily responsible for efforts to achieve equality, men do have a role to play: "What can men do? What can boys do? . . . Women don't need any extra training or any other extra skills. All they need is no one standing in their way in allowing them to achieve their dreams—no one stopping them. . . . My father says, 'Don't ask what I did for my daughter, ask me what I did not do. I did not clip her wings.'"[17] Both women and men play important roles in Yousafzai's vision of feminism.

Change Strategies

Malala seeks to contribute to a world in which no one is denied access to the educational systems and resources that are important to the well-being of every human being. Yousafzai's strategies—(1) holding others accountable, (2) modeling agency, and (3) empowering others—are consistent with her goal of ending restrictions on girls' education and furthering human rights. She makes that goal realizable by insisting that others do their part, just as she herself is doing.

Holding Others Accountable

Malala sees education as the vehicle that will result in equality and advancement for a society because, if allowed access to education, girls will be able to fulfill their potential and contribute fully to their communities. In advocating for twelve years of free compulsory education for children as a basic right, Yousafzai isn't afraid to confront members of the Taliban and hold them responsible for their inaccurate and harmful views on education. To the Taliban's claim that education is a form of Westernization, she counters by saying that "education is education. . . . Education is neither Eastern nor Western, it is human."[18] Malala argues that the Taliban distorts Islam, and she calls out its members for their misreading of the Quran: "In the Quran it is written, God wants us to have knowledge. He wants us to know why the sky is blue and about oceans and stars."[19] She makes education a basic right and "part of this movement for equality."[20]

Yousafzai also avails herself of opportunities to speak with world leaders as a way to hold them accountable for their actions and policies. In her speech at the United Nations, she called on all world leaders, governments, and nations to act to address policies that harm girls and women, inhibit educational opportunities, and further terrorism. She asked governments to work to create policies that affirm the dignity and rights of women, strive for peace and prosperity, and make education available to every child. Education and human rights are not her only concerns, however. She also confronts leaders' policies on terrorism, poverty, hunger, AIDS, fair trade, disaster relief, human trafficking, and the environment. Not afraid to confront particular policies when she has the chance, Malala questioned President Barack Obama, for example, about his use of drone strikes in Pakistan. Holding others accountable is a first step toward shifting the way systems currently operate and making them more fair and equitable.

Modeling Agency

Yousafzai also believes that each individual needs to contribute to making the world a better place, and she herself models the agency she asks of others. She strongly believes that every individual can make a difference, and even the smallest act is helpful: "Even if I send one child to school I will feel like I have done a great thing."[21] For Malala, even a small action that enriches the system is significant and worthwhile.

Yousafzai's father was a strong role model who spoke out against the Taliban when most others were unwilling to do so. Like her father, Malala also was willing to speak out on behalf of girls' education, even when her family knew of the dangers involved. Her willingness to model the kind of activism needed made her a Taliban target, and the assassination attempt encouraged her to be even more outspoken: "They thought that the bullets would silence us. But they failed."[22] Yousafzai shares the story of the assassination attempt and of not being able to safely return to her home country to point out that despite considerable obstacles, an individual still can find ways to make a difference in the world.

In modeling agency, however, Malala is careful not to let her story become a focus in and of itself. She often downplays the shooting because she doesn't want people to get so caught up in the trauma of the event that they are unable to move beyond it to action. She consistently shifts conversations about her to the larger issues involved. For example, when asked if she still fears for her safety, she broadened the question to address safety issues across the globe.

> No, I don't worry about my safety. The truth is, I think about the safety of people all around the world, especially poor people in the Middle East because they are in a very bad situation. And there are not just thousands, there are millions and millions of people who are homeless, who are forced to leave their countries, who are suffering because of war. I get very worried about them and think that we should make a stand for their safety and for peace. We should all work together for this. It is very important that we all think about bigger solutions to these problems.[23]

Yousafzai does not want others to see her as so special that they cannot see themselves as similarly able to act. A frequent refrain in her speeches is that she is no different from the many activists around the world who are equally committed to the causes in which they believe. In the introduction to her speech at the United Nations, she admonished: "Do remember one thing. Malala day is not my day. Today is the day of every women, every boy, and every girl who have raised their voice for their rights."[24] Malala sees herself as but one of many individuals who are making the world more equitable and just, and she similarly wants every individual to find ways to contribute.

Empowering Others

At the same time that Yousafzai downplays her story in order to show that everyone has within them the same agentic capabilities she does, she understands that her celebrity status has given her a valuable platform for empowering others. Malala takes advantage of this platform "so that those without a voice can be heard."[25] When speaking at the United Nations, for example, she looked out and imagined an audience of millions: "I did not write the speech only with the UN delegates in mind; I wrote it for every person around the world who could make a difference. I wanted to reach all people living in poverty, those children forced to work and those who suffer from terrorism or lack of education. . . . I hoped to reach every child who could take courage from my words and stand up for his or her rights."[26]

Yousafzai's efforts to empower others to speak out and act was acknowledged by pianist Kate Whitely, who was commissioned by BBC Radio to compose a piece for broadcast on International Women's Day 2017. Whitely called the piece "Speak Out," and it incorporates words from Malala's speech to the United Nations. Yousafzai feels responsible for using the platform she has been given to the benefit of as many people as possible, and the interest the world has taken in her has increased her sense of responsibility: "What I did in the past for girls' education was just the beginning. And now I need to do more and more."[27]

Malala wants to use her platform to encourage and accomplish the changes necessary to ensure that all children have access to education.

Diverting attention from herself, her strategies of holding others accountable, modeling agency, and empowering others enable her to call on others to do their part to ensure that all have access to education. Everyone is responsible, and everyone can do something: "So let us wage a global struggle against illiteracy, poverty and terrorism and let us pick up our books and pens. They are our most powerful weapons. One child, one teacher, one pen and one book can change the world. Education is the only solution. Education first."[28]

■ REFLECTIONS

1. Yousafzai believes that men can make a major contribution to feminism by not stopping women or "clipping their wings." Are there more specific activities men can do to help achieve equality for women? Have you seen evidence that such activities by men can make a real difference in generating change?
2. Yousafzai insists that she is no different from other activists, and she often downplays her own personal story. Is this a useful strategy for furthering the cause of education, or should she take advantage of the special position she holds because of the shooting?
3. Watch Yousafzai's speech at the United Nations (https://www.un.org/youthenvoy/video/malala-yousafzai-addresses-united-nations-youth-assembly/) and look for evidence of her three main change strategies. Do you find evidence of other strategies she appears to use that are not included in this chapter about her?
4. One of Yousafzai's primary change strategies is modeling agency. Enacting agency is difficult for many women who do not believe they have the appropriate expertise, education, resources, or personality to be able to generate change. Can modeling agency both encourage and discourage others from stepping up as change agents? What can those who model agency do to encourage those who might be hesitating to engage in change efforts?
5. Yousafzai seeks both to empower others and to hold them accountable. In what ways do these strategies work together effectively to enhance each other? Are there ways in which they work against each other?
6. How closely do Yousafzai's change strategies align with the assumptions outlined in the introduction to part 4? Are there any assumptions that you don't believe pertain to her approach to change?
7. In which feminist wave would you place Yousafzai and why?

■ NOTES

[1] Malala Yousafzai with Christina Lamb, *I Am Malala* (New York: Back Bay/Little, Brown, 2013), 309.
[2] Yousafzai with Lamb, *I Am Malala*, 41.
[3] Yousafzai with Lamb, *I Am Malala*, 216.
[4] Yousafzai with Lamb, *I Am Malala*, 140.

5 Yousafzai with Lamb, *I Am Malala*, 224–25.
6 Yousafzai with Lamb, *I Am Malala*, 250.
7 Yousafzai with Lamb, *I Am Malala*, 263.
8 Laura Bush, "A Girl's Courage Challenges us to Act," *Washington Post*, October 10, 2012, https://www.washingtonpost.com/opinions/laura-bush-malala-yousafzais-courage-challenges-us-to-act/2012/10/10/9cd423ea-1316-11e2-ba83-a7a396e6b2a7_story.html/
9 "Malala Yousafzai Turns 19 Today and Look at All She Has Done," *Time*, July 12, 2016, https://time.com/4402630/malala-yousafzai-accomplishments/
10 Ziauddin Yousafzai, "What Being Malala's Father Taught Me About Feminism," *Time*, June 14, 2019, https://time.com/5605625/malala-yousafzai-father/
11 Yousafzai, "What Being Malala's Father Taught Me."
12 Ziauddin Yousafzai with Louise Carpenter, *Let Her Fly: A Father's Journey* (New York: Little, Brown, 2018), 16–17.
13 Yousafzai, "What Being Malala's Father Taught Me."
14 Yousafzai with Lamb, *I Am Malala*, 306.
15 "Full Text of Malala Yousafzai's Speech at the United Nations," Opportunity Desk, July 16, 2013, https://opportunitydesk.org/2013/07/16/full-text-of-malala-yousafzais-speech-at-the-united-nations/
16 "Full Text of Malala Yousafzai's Speech at the United Nations."
17 Malala Yousafzai, "Malala Yousafzai on Her Critics, Western Feminism and the Role of Men in Her Movement," interview by Dakshana Bascaramurty, *The Globe and Mail,* April 12, 2018, https://www.theglobeandmail.com/canada/article-malala-yousafzai-on-her-critics-western-feminism-and-the-role-of-men/
18 Yousafzai with Lamb, *I Am Malala*, 162.
19 Yousafzai with Lamb, *I Am Malala*, 311–12.
20 Alexandra Gibbs, "How Nobel Peace Prize Laureate Malala Yousafzai Embraced Feminism," *CNBC,* January 31, 2018, https://www.cnbc.com/2018/01/31/malala-yousafzai-on-feminism-and-raising-awareness-about-female-rights.html/
21 "Reading Group Guide: *I Am Malala,*" in Malala Yousafzai with Christina Lamb, *I Am Malala* (New York: Back Bay Books/Little, Brown, 2013), 14.
22 "Full Text of Malala Yousafzai's Speech at the United Nations."
23 "Reading Group Guide," 10.
24 "Full Text of Malala Yousafzai's Speech at the United Nations."
25 "Full Text of Malala Yousafzai's Speech at the United Nations."
26 Yousafzai with Lamb, *I Am Malala*, 309–10.
27 "Reading Group Guide," 8.
28 "Full Text of Malala Yousafzai's Speech at the United Nations."

PART
FIVE

CHANGING A SYSTEM

Those who seek to *change a system* see that system as so dysfunctional and defective that minor adjustments are inadequate for addressing its deficiencies.[1] Instead, major changes to the system are seen as necessary in order to achieve the kinds of modifications these change agents desire. They reject efforts to salvage or improve an existing system and instead call for substantial changes to it.

Carrie Goldberg, Nadia Bolz-Weber, Serena Williams, and Amanda Gorman exemplify feminists who advocate major systemic changes to achieve their goals of creating more equitable, just, and inclusive systems. Their strategies are grounded in three assumptions: (1) substantial and sustainable change requires major transformation of an existing system, (2) resistance may function to preserve and strengthen a system rather than dismantle it, and (3) working for change within a system involves the risk of cooptation by that system. Aware that large-scale changes of the kind they advocate will not be accomplished without difficulty, these feminists nonetheless persist in their efforts to achieve substantial systemic change.

Assumption 1: Substantial and sustainable change requires major transformation of an existing system.

Because those who seek to change systems believe that minor changes are insufficient for addressing the substantial problems they see with those systems, they seek large-scale changes. Rather than addressing superficial symptoms of a problem, they tackle the conditions that "hold the problem in place,"[2] seeking to alter expectations, attitudes, policies, rules, and laws. This approach has the capacity to be genuinely transformative—to significantly impact the forms of domination that characterize many systems—but the process is usually a gradual one.

Social movement theorists have delineated the process by which systemic social change occurs. According to Judith Horton, the system first needs "shaking up"[3] in order to create a sense of urgency, energy, and commitment to the cause that will engage "'hearts and minds and attitudes.'"[4] Once a desire for change has been created, leaders and influencers must create a "receptive context for triggering conditions that will bring a movement to life."[5] They must articulate their values and vision for the new social order and align that vision with personal interests in order to attract and mobilize members. Systemic change requires a compelling narrative about the need for change and an equally compelling vision of what can be to foster and sustain a committed membership.

Efforts by universities to address gender inequities in computer programming demonstrate how systemic change occurs. Computer science as a major has attracted far more men than women, and universities have begun to recognize "the serious consequences" of the "under-representation of women among the creators of information technology, . . . not only for those women whose potential goes unrealized, but also for a society increasingly shaped by that technology."[6] Carnegie Mellon University was one university that recognized the need for substantial programmatic change if it were to succeed in increasing gender diversity in its computing courses. Among its many efforts, the college de-emphasized, in its admission criteria, experiences that women are less likely to have growing up, accommodated incoming students' different levels of programming experience, and created a supportive peer community for women in the major. Consequently, women's representation in computing rose 33 percent over a period of four years.[7] The university's success demonstrates how embarking on deliberate and systematic change efforts can be productive and effective at changing a system.

Assumption 2: Resistance may function to preserve and strengthen a system rather than to dismantle it.

When substantial change to a system is desired, a typical response is to hammer away at what is wrong with the system and to fight, attack, and oppose it until it changes. This kind of resistance is often assumed to be the only way to substantially change a system. Many activists are beginning to realize, however, that railing against something—criticizing, opposing, protesting—focuses attention on what is not wanted rather than on what is. Consequently, the efforts designed to achieve change may backfire, perpetuating rather than changing the system. This is not to say that these kinds of protests are of no value. They can remind protesters of their capabilities, strength, courage, and power and can bring like-minded collaborators together in a common cause. These benefits, however, do not negate the fact that resistance may actually reinforce rather than change a system.

Feminist activist Sonia Johnson actively protested against the patriarchy for decades without considering the extent to which such activity "deceives us into thinking that we are getting somewhere, achieving something."[8] Johnson realized she was "living constantly in reaction.... When we identify ourselves in *opposition* to something we become its unwilling accomplices. By bestowing the energy of our belief upon it, by acquiescing to it, we reinforce it as reality. The very difficult truth is that what we resist persists."[9] To show how resistance functions, she offers the illustration of patriarchy as a fortress on a hill "with its pennants flying, its great bulwarks, its massive gate."[10] To try to topple patriarchy, some women pole-vault over the walls, shouting, "If we can just get in there, we can change everything!"[11] Other women run at the gate of the fortress with "a huge battering ram in their arms," and they have done so "with unsurpassed cunning, craft, and passion for at least 5,000 years."[12] All of these attacks, however, simply spur men to "incredible heights of creativity. They have invented bionic metals to reinforce the gate and walls wherever the ram reveals a weak spot, gradually making the fortress impregnable, impenetrable.... The assault, by forcing them to strengthen, refine, and embellish the original edifice, serves to entrench patriarchy further with every Whoom."[13] Johnson insists that "we must face and accept that these methods have come to the end of their usefulness even as a way of attracting notice, to say nothing of changing things—if indeed they ever fundamentally changed anything."[14]

The limits of resistance as a strategy are evident in the invention of the impossible burger. Raising cattle for hamburgers has been recognized as a serious environmental threat, and many vegetarian and vegan alternatives have been created as replacements, including black bean, tofu, and chickpea burgers. Stanford biochemistry professor Patrick Brown, however, wanted to create a vegetarian burger that tasted and sizzled like meat when cooked.[15] He succeeded in his task, creating what he called an *impossible burger* from a blend of soy and potato proteins. The burger has the same amount of protein as a burger, a meat-like taste, and even the sizzle expected with a meat burger when cooked, and it requires 95 percent less land and 74 percent less water to produce. Brown organized an academic conference to share his research and raise awareness about the role of animal agriculture in a sustainable global food system, but it had minimal impact: "Virtually no one cared."[16] Rather than continue to try to persuade meat eaters that beef burgers are not sustainable, Brown realized he had to do something different. He realized that "people who make and sell beef burgers don't preach at their customers; they give them the product they want."[17] Thus, he chose not to continue to fight against meat eaters but instead to produce a burger that meat eaters would eat.

Assumption 3: Working for change within a system involves the risk of cooptation by that system.

Major systemic change carries with it the potential cooptation of those seeking such change. Cooptation is a process by which something is taken over or appropriated for a different purpose; it occurs when the goals or interests of an outsider group, such as a social movement, are assimilated by an established group or system. On the surface, the integration of a group's agenda into an organization seems positive; it suggests that the organization's vision aligns with and is committed to the same goals as the social movement. In fact, however, those goals often are "robbed of their radical edge and their transformative potential"[18] when they become part of the larger system. The organization essentially pays lip service to change but does little to actuate changes within the organization.

Feminist scholars Sally Miller Gearhart and Kathy Ferguson have theorized the potential for cooptation when feminists attempt to change a system from within. Gearhart acknowledges that there are many reasons feminists might choose to work in an organization and try to change it. These can range from the opportunity to learn and use skills that the organization will pay for and to work with the other women in that organization. Nevertheless, the risk of cooptation remains: "If we are really making noises that cannot be ignored, and if the [institution] really senses that we are dangerous, . . . we are separated out and awarded a crumb of power, for which we are expected to be undyingly grateful. . . . Whatever the crumb, our energy is now successfully channeled. We are adorned with garlands of red tape; we can be carefully watched."[19] Kathy Ferguson echoes Gearhart's warning. After internalizing a system's rules, values, and norms for most of their working lives, feminists who reach the top ranks in an organization often are unable to change it because the system affects "the way one thinks, feels, responds to others, and conceives of and presents oneself. . . . It is hard to be a 'closet radical' when an inspection of the closets is part of the organization's daily routine."[20]

Hester Eisenstein's study of femocrats in Australia illustrates how cooptation can occur within a system.[21] Hired to help implement Equal Employment Opportunity legislation, these feminist bureaucrats were immersed in all aspects of the organization, and they became comfortable with its structures of power. A major part of their job, for example, was to solicit and grade affirmative action plans. When a plan was approved, the letter of approval was passed around at meetings to show how committed a particular department was to diversity. This action, however, frequently stood in for the actual implementation of those plans. In other words, the *devising* of a diversity policy replaced *doing* something to truly make the organization more diverse. As Sara Ahmed notes, "You end up doing the document rather than doing the doing."[22] Despite their recognized role in the system, femocrats ultimately were dependent on those in power for their success, and their goals were secondary to and frequently sacrificed to the priorities and needs of the larger system. They were coopted by the system despite their knowledge of it.

■ NOTES

1. Matt Ripley, "Systemic Change: Walking the Talk?" The Lab, n.d., https://www.ilo.org/wcmsp5/groups/public/---ed_emp/documents/publication/wcms_718091.pdf
2. John Kania, Mark Kramer, and Peter Senge, "The Water of Systems Change," FSG, June 2018, https://www.fsg.org/blog/new-article-water-systems-change#:~:text=The%20
3. Judith A. Holton, "Social Movements Thinking for Managing Change in Large-Scale Systems," *Journal of Organizational Change Management* 33 (2020): 705.
4. Holton, "Social Movements Thinking," 703.
5. Holton, "Social Movements Thinking," 710.
6. Allan Fisher and Jane Margolis, "Women in Computer Sciences: Closing the Gender Gap in Higher Education," Carnegie Mellon Project on Gender and Computer Science," n.d., https://www.cs.cmu.edu/afs/cs/project/gendergap/www/index.html/
7. Fisher and Margolis, "Women in Computer Sciences."
8. Sonia Johnson, *Going Out of Our Minds: The Metaphysics of Liberation* (Freedom, CA: Crossing, 1987), 26.
9. Johnson, *Going Out of Our Minds*, 26–27.
10. Sonia Johnson, *Wildfire: Igniting the She/Volution* (Albuquerque, NM: Wildfire, 1969), 16.
11. Johnson, *Wildfire*, 17.
12. Johnson, *Wildfire*, 16.
13. Johnson, *Wildfire*, 17.
14. Johnson, *Going Out of Our Minds*, 26.
15. Burt Helm, "A Lot of Companies Want to Save the World. Impossible Foods Just Might Do It with Its Plant-Based Meats," Inc., n.d., https://www.inc.com/magazine/202002/burt-helm/impossible-foods-pat-brown-plant-based-burger-vegan-fake-meat-protein-beef.html
16. Martin Dempsey and Ori Brafman, *Radical Inclusion: What the Post-9/11 World Should Have Taught Us About Leadership* (Arlington, VA: Missionday, 2018), 126.
17. Dempsey and Brafman, *Radical Inclusion*, 126.
18. Angelika Striedinger, "How Organizational Research Can Avoid the Pitfalls of a Co-optation Perspective: Analyzing Gender Equality Work in Austrian Universities with Organizational Institutionalism," *International Feminist Journal of Politics* 19 (2017): 201.
19. Sally Gearhart, "The Miracle of Lesbianism," in *Loving Women/Loving Men: Gay Liberation and the Church*, ed. Sally Gearhart and William R. Johnson (San Francisco, CA: Glide, 1974), 145.
20. Kathy E. Ferguson, *The Feminist Case Against Bureaucracy* (Philadelphia, PA: Temple University Press, 1984), 193.
21. Hester Eisenstein, "Femocrats, Official Feminism, and the Uses of Power: A Case Study of EEO Implementation in New South Wales, Australia," *Yale Journal of Law and Feminism* 2 (1989): 51–73.
22. Sara Ahmed, *Living a Feminist Life* (Durham, NC: Duke University Press, 2017), 104.

CHAPTER FIFTEEN

Carrie Goldberg

> It's a new day. We are going to take over and make things right....
> We will erect statues that depict us and write statutes that protect
> us. We will win elections, change the face of Congress, and move
> into the White House. Our heels are clicking down the warpath. To
> all psychos, stalkers, trolls, and pervs, your time is up. We may have
> been victimized once, but we're not victims. We are an army of war-
> riors and we won't back down.[1]

Carrie Goldberg is an attorney specializing in sexual privacy violation, revenge porn, cyberstalking, sexual extortion, and sexual assault. She fights to change the legal system that makes "every one of us" just "a moment away from crossing paths with somebody hellbent on our destruction."[2] She wants to be the advocate she wishes she had had when she herself was confronted with internet stalking and harassment.

Goldberg was born in 1977 in Aberdeen, Washington, the second of four children. The family owned and operated a furniture store, and her father also worked to reopen a shuttered paper mill, restoring jobs to the community. Before staying home to raise her children, Carrie's mother wrote obituaries for the local paper and later worked in public relations at a local community college. Goldberg attended Vassar College in Poughkeepsie, New York, where she inspired a song, "Carrie Goldberg," written and performed by the punk-pop band The Steinways. She graduated from Vassar in 1999 with a BA in English.

Following graduation, Carrie moved to New York City, where she was hired as a case manager at Selfhelp, an organization that provides home care and community services to Holocaust survivors. In this position, Goldberg came "to terms with the cruelty of life." As she explains, "I grappled daily with the harsh reality that lives are not valued equally.... The perspective I gained on human suffering, and the rage I banked during those years informs everything I do for my clients today."³ In 2003, Carrie began taking evening classes at Brooklyn Law School, hoping "that maybe with a law degree I could do the same type of work I was doing with my clients at Selfhelp—advocating for survivors of genocide—but on a larger scale."⁴

When she graduated with her law degree in 2007, Goldberg accepted a position at Housing Conservation Coordinators, a nonprofit agency that works with low-income individuals facing eviction. She calls this job "the best thing that could have happened to me" because of the litigation skills and work ethic she acquired.⁵ Between 2009 and 2014, she served as lead lawyer for the Guardianship Project, one of several programs at the Vera Institute of Justice, whose mission is addressing inequities in the criminal justice system.

Carrie's personal experiences with sexual assault were central to her eventual decision to open her own law firm. In high school, Goldberg once dropped a friend off at a motel party that was hosted by a man on whom her friend had a crush. Her friend was sexually assaulted by the man and his friends, but "back then," Carrie recalls, "'it didn't occur to her or me to tell the police or even to call it rape. . . . But, as I think about it now, that was a pivotal moment for me.'"⁶ Goldberg also experienced sexual harassment when she returned home from Vassar for the summer and worked in her father's mill. She was routinely groped by some of her male coworkers and eventually went on a hunger strike as a way of coping: "By the end of the summer, my diet consisted primarily of Baskin-Robbins Rainbow Sherbet and these little white pills we called 'mini-thins' that truckers used to stay awake."⁷ She took a semester's leave from Vassar to address her eating disorder.

Carrie's two most traumatic episodes with sexual assault occurred when she joined the dating site OkCupid. In the first instance, a doctor she met online took her out for drinks. At some point in the evening, he spiked her drink. Her memories of what followed consist of "a series of hazy snapshots."⁸ The man sutured something onto her buttocks (she later discovered it was a swastika), photographed his work, and raped her. Later, on the same dating site, Goldberg met a man who seemed ideal—attentive, smart, creative, and romantic. After dating for a few months, however, he became possessive and obsessive—checking up on her constantly and sending threatening texts if she did not respond immediately. When Carrie ended the relationship, the threats accelerated, and he went to great lengths to discredit her. He filed a false police report claiming she had assaulted him, an accusation for which Goldberg spent a night in jail. He also told her friends and family that she was a drug addict, had a sexually transmitted disease, and slept with judges to secure favorable outcomes for her legal cases. When he threatened to post intimate pictures of her online, she begged a judge to prevent him from doing so but was told, "Ms. Goldberg, I know you are a lawyer but I recommend you get a lawyer because you've got a First Amendment problem."⁹ Appalled that sending nude pictures could be considered free speech, Carrie continued trying to address the problem on her own. By the end of 2013, she had spent about $30,000 in legal fees to clear her name, had filed a restraining order but still felt unsafe, and was afraid she might never be free of harassment by her former boyfriend.

In December 2013, Goldberg was invited to join a friend for a vacation in Ireland. One evening during that trip, she found herself standing on a cliff in a storm. Overwhelmed by the doctor's rape and the psycho's stalking, she wanted to jump. Instead, she made a pact with herself: If she couldn't turn her life around in a year, she would come back to Ireland and kill herself. At the same time that she contemplated suicide, Carrie also experienced an epiphany—no matter how alone she felt, she couldn't possibly be the only one suffering from this kind of trauma.

> There had to be other people out there who had suffered the same kind of attack. It occurred to me that they were probably searching for the same kind of support I had longed for in my darkest days: a skilled fighter who could navigate both the law and the changing digital landscape; someone who understood the threat of privacy violations and knew what to do when a psycho was spinning out of control. In that moment, drenched in the pouring rain, I decided I was going to advocate for victims the way I wish somebody had fought for me. I would become the lawyer I'd needed when I was most desperate.[10]

Goldberg returned home, gave notice at the Vera Institute, and two weeks later, on January 24, 2014, opened her own law firm.

In her law practice, Carrie handles issues ranging from revenge porn, stalking, harassment, extortion, sextortion, and anti-abortion harassment to crises that affect public figures—"defamation, harassment, and privacy issues unique to those in the spotlight."[11] In addition to fighting for people "under attack,"[12] her firm fights "against the abusers—whether person, school or company—who think they can get away with it."[13] Goldberg and her associates use various actions to accomplish these ends, including lawsuits, orders of protection, Title IX proceedings, class-action suits, online-content removal, and de-anonymizing offenders.

Carrie's many legal successes include 30,000 revenge porn videos and pictures removed from the internet, 164 harassing email and social media profiles de-anonymized, 90 orders of protection secured, and 18 school sexual violation cases opened.[14] Over the years, Goldberg came to realize that those who target her clients are "boring and predictable," with "patterns and similarities in their behaviors that are hard to miss once you know what to look for."[15] She and her staff developed a shorthand to describe the abusers they encounter most often: "psychos, who obsessively stalk, threaten, and intimidate their prey; assholes, who exploit or mistreat victims out of willful ignorance or arrogance or for their own financial gain; trolls, who terrorize victims under the cloak of internet anonymity; and pervs, who get off on overpowering victims into sex against their will."[16] These abusers became the focus of her book, *Nobody's Victim*, published in 2019, in which Carrie weaves together her personal narrative, accounts of the various cases she has handled, and suggestions for victim protection in the age of the internet.

One of Goldberg's most well-known cases was *Herrick v. Grindr*, in which she sued the gay-male dating site Grindr on behalf of Matthew Herrick. Herrick's former boyfriend posed as him on the website and invited over 1,200 men to his door for violent sex. Carrie took the suit all the way to the US Supreme Court, arguing that Grindr's product was defective because it had not built in safety precautions. The Supreme Court refused to hear the case, arguing that the actions constituted free speech protection under Section 230 of the Communications Decency Act, which states, "No provider or user of an interactive computer service shall be treated as the publisher or speaker of any information provided by another information content provider."[17] In others words, those who host or republish speech online are not legally responsible for what others say and do via the internet. In October 2020, however, Justice Clarence Thomas advised the Supreme Court to take up a case about Section 230 and cited *Herrick v. Grindr* as evidence that this section "was being interpreted so broadly that courts were granting immunity even on claims of design defects."[18] Until review of a relevant case by the Supreme Court, Goldberg will continue to work to change Section 230, believing it makes technology companies largely untouchable.

Using Title IX, Carrie also has filed several suits against the Department of Education in New York City for failing to protect young women who were sexually assaulted at school; one such suit resulted in a $950,000 settlement for the victim. In these cases, Goldberg discovered that rather than aiding the victims, the schools further traumatized them by allowing the pictures taken of their assaults to remain in circulation. Furthermore, the girls were suspended while awaiting safety transfers to other schools, while the boys who were the perpetrators of the assaults went unpunished. In addition to Title IX cases, she has taken on some high-profile celebrity cases. She represented five victims of Harvey Weinstein in the sexual assault case against the movie producer, and she was hired by US Representative Katie Hill of California after nude photos of her, leaked in a sex scandal, forced her resignation.

As a lawyer, Carrie has developed a signature appearance and style—glamorous, bold, and often outrageous. She is known for her five-inch stiletto heels and impeccably manicured nails, usually painted in lively colors. She drives a GTO, starts most days by boxing at the gym, and runs marathons. When asked what she most appreciates about being her own boss, Goldberg replied: "Wearing what I want, swearing when I want, and controlling the thermostat. Just kidding. Sort of. My biggest joy is getting buckets of money for my clients from the pervert abuser or the institutions that enabled the abuse."[19]

In addition to practicing law, Carrie is active in organizations that work to end online privacy violations and harassment. She is a board member and volunteer attorney at the Cyber Civil Rights Initiative and a founding member of the New York City Cyber Sexual Exploitation Task Force. She is also a founding advisory board member of the Tyler Clementi Foundation, named for the Rutgers University student who committed suicide after his roommate videotaped him having sex with a man. She was the recipient of the Privacy Champion Award from the Electronic Privacy Information Center and was featured in *Netizens*, a 2018 documentary film about three women whose lives were upended by online harassment.

Definition of Feminism

Goldberg's definition of feminism centers on the issues central to her life's work. Her definition begins by addressing the range of rights that comprise, for her, the core of feminism: "First, believing women and men should have equal rights, privileges, and opportunities. That includes bodily autonomy—the right to be left alone, to take up space, to not be touched, to have sex your way, and to end bad relationships without retaliation."[20] Rights are nothing, however, if they cannot be implemented, so her definition of feminism also includes "the action it takes to obtain that equality." That action "can be big and public like protesting, suing, lawmaking. And it can be quiet and private like teaching, parenting, mentoring, donating, and being kind."[21] Carrie is committed to working to guarantee rights by using whatever means she has available for doing so.

Change Strategies

As a lawyer, Goldberg's change strategies are designed to provide justice, compensation, and relief for her clients. Her strategies—(1) learning a system, (2) deploying the resources of a system, and (3) transforming trauma—contribute in various ways to tackling a legal system that has not caught up to the potentially damaging outcomes of interaction on the internet.

Learning a System

To pursue every possible course of action for her clients, Carrie believes in the importance of learning whatever system she is targeting. She advises: "Study the organization or structure that gives your nemeses power. Figure out how the systems work and what it takes to dismantle them. . . . If your enemies have the law on their side, find legal loopholes and charge through them. Be creative and relentless."[22] By thoroughly researching the systems involved in a case, Goldberg can decide which tactics to use when and can devise appropriate solutions for her clients. Finding solutions is the most satisfying aspect of her job: "I actually have solutions and I know what to do and the people that are coming to me are like drowning in a tsunami and don't know there's a rescue boat. . . . There's such joy in just knowing what to do when someone is experiencing something awful. We're fixers here."[23]

Deploying the Resources of a System

Carrie supplements her knowledge of a system by using it to her full advantage. Her strategies in a legal case range from working within a system to working to change a system to working around a system—and she sometimes employs all of these strategies in a single case. When working within the system, Goldberg typically files both a criminal complaint and a civil suit—the latter allows her to demand monetary damages. She acknowledges that many clients don't want to pursue monetary settlements, but it is a legitimate alternative, especially if a criminal case has little likelihood of success.

> A lot of people think it's crude to put a price on suffering. And, of course, it doesn't undo the harm. But in this world we live in, money buys power. A client, even if she doesn't want the money, can donate to an organization that fights for the things that she values, or she can donate it to a political candidate. . . . There are a lot of different kinds of work we do where the object is not money—cases where we're just trying to get a restraining order for our clients, or we're trying to get that motherfucker arrested, or we're trying to get that content off the internet. But on the other hand, when it does come to having offenders who can pay, I'm adamant that wealth distribution needs to happen. That includes schools, religious institutions, online platforms, social media companies. If they can prevent it, or if they're monetizing, in any way, the injuries my client has sustained, then I want them to pay for it.[24]

Sometimes Carrie seeks to change a system, which is what she hoped to achieve by taking *Herrick v. Grindr* to the Supreme Court. She wanted to shift how Section 230 of the Communications Decency Act is interpreted and to make technology firms accountable for what happens to those who use their websites. At other times, Goldberg believes that "the best strategy is to fuck the system and work around it."[25] This was her strategy with a man who threatened to post nude videos of a college student unless she agreed to have sex with him. She located the perpetrator's Facebook page, where a photograph showed him and his wife posing in front of a house in Louisiana. She enlarged the picture so she could see the address and then sent a cease-and-desist letter to the house, detailing the laws he was guilty of breaking and the penalties he would face if he were convicted of those crimes.

Carrie also takes advantage of her appearance to disarm her opponents, another tactic by which she makes full use of the resources available to her. Her signature style emerged when she worked at Housing Conservation Coordinators and began to dress to stand out from the other attorneys.[26] She continues the practice, calling her style a super power "because then you can catch people by surprise."[27] Not only does her dress make her memorable, but it throws people off balance. Her office functions similarly. Decorated with pastel velvet furniture and navy and gold wallpaper, it often leads other attorneys to underestimate her. Her letterhead, which Goldberg describes as "pretty" with "gold foil," is also meant to disarm those she targets. Despite her feminine style, if someone receives a demand letter from her firm, she explains, "it's going to be a really bad day for them."[28]

Transforming Trauma

Transforming trauma is another one of Carrie's strategies, which she describes as moving from victim to warrior. In channeling the rage and outrage of her clients and converting it to action, she helps her clients feel in control again: "You are not crazy. The situation is. . . . Take back the control!"[29] She wants her clients to know that no matter how traumatic an experience is, "you can turn that shit into gold. You can learn from it and be fueled by it. Trauma is a burden, but it can also be a gift."[30]

Watching her clients move from victim to warrior is one of the most satisfying aspects of Goldberg's work. When her clients first come to her office, they are often so exhausted, beaten down, and fearful that they can hardly look at her. But once they begin to fight, they are "just as ruthless and angry as the motherfuckers" trying to take them down.[31] For Carrie, "the only thing more satisfying than watching these a$$holes topple like a row of dominoes is knowing they were felled by the very people they'd tried to destroy: women who refused to be quiet and would not back down."[32] She relishes the transformation that occurs as her clients emerge from trauma and become very different kinds of people: "I have seen the alchemy that occurs when a woman decides that enough is enough and sets out on a journey to make the madness stop. By coming to us, she acknowledges that she matters—that she is worthy of support, camaraderie and a life free from fear, and that she is willing to fight for that. Standing beside her is an honor."[33]

Converting trauma into agency does more than benefit clients' self-confidence and ability to act. It can inspire those who have experienced similar trauma but never thought action was possible or would do any good. Goldberg notes that "there are millions of women who work in the service sector or retail jobs, in factories, on farms, and at hotels who don't have the financial freedom to speak out against their bosses."[34] But as more women speak up, more and more women from all walks of life will be galvanized to act. Furthermore, she believes that openly discussing the trauma puts harassers on notice: "We survivors, activists, and allies are just getting started untangling the harm wrought by eons of abuse, secrecy, shaming, and oppression. And we are already making a difference. All around us powerful men are running scared."[35] Carrie encourages women to "find your fellow warriors—the advocates, survivors, and students working at think tanks or nonprofits, as legal scholars or in schools—and arm yourselves with bullhorns, pussy hats, placards, and petitions."[36] By joining with others and making complaints public, women can move from traumatized victims to strong warriors, can inspire others to act, and can help create an environment in which sexual harassment and assault are no longer tolerated.

Goldberg's strategies are designed to change the legal system, right injustice, and transform her clients' lives—objectives she pursues by learning and making full use of a system's resources. As a result, she is confident she can help transform her clients' trauma so that they come to feel "strong, safe and whole."[37] Through her work, she has transformed her own life as well, and this is the kind of change she seeks for her clients.

I don't think I would be who I am without the worst experiences that I've had. I was a different person entirely before. I was somebody who was content with a middle management job, and wasn't a leader in my field.... There were so many decisions that it's like I became a new person, forced to trust myself. I stopped being afraid of the things that I had been afraid of my whole life—dumb things like worms, or phobias about speaking in public, or starting a business. I wasn't afraid to fail. Because it couldn't have been worse than living in physical fear.[38]

■ REFLECTIONS

1. Goldberg uses her signature over-the-top feminine style to disarm opponents. Is there anything about you that leads others to make assumptions about you that are not necessarily accurate? Is there a way in which misleading opponents in this way can be detrimental to a cause? What do you see as its advantages?
2. Goldberg has an unusual definition of feminism that includes the right to be left alone, to take up space, to not be touched, to have sex your way, and to end bad relationships without retaliation. Do you see all of these as feminist issues, or are they simply basic rights of individuals in relationships?
3. One of Goldberg's primary strategies is to learn the system in which she is operating. Have you had an experience where you spent time and energy researching a system and discovered resources available to you in that system that you could use to change it? Explain the results of your efforts.
4. Goldberg likes to use all the resources of a system to ensure that she does everything possible for her clients. You have encountered a wide variety of change strategies in the book. Are there some strategies others use that Goldberg also could use to help her clients?
5. There is considerable discussion in the United States today of individual and cultural trauma stemming from negative life experiences. Goldberg transforms trauma by encouraging those who experience it to get in the fight. Are there ways in which this means of dealing with trauma can backfire? Are there other ways of dealing with trauma that might be as or more effective?
6. How closely do Goldberg's change strategies align with the assumptions outlined in the introduction to part 5? Are there any assumptions that you don't believe pertain to her approach to change?
7. In which feminist wave would you place Goldberg and why?

■ NOTES

[1] Carrie Goldberg with Jeannine Amber, *Nobody's Victim: Fighting Psychos, Stalkers, Pervs and Trolls* (New York: Plume, 2019), 219.
[2] "Introduction," Herrick v. Grindr, Santa Clara Law Digital Commons, April 10, 2019, https://digitalcommons.law.scu.edu/historical/1923/
[3] Goldberg with Amber, *Nobody's Victim*, 100.

4. Goldberg with Amber, *Nobody's Victim*, 105.
5. Goldberg with Amber, *Nobody's Victim*, 109.
6. Margaret Talbot, "The Attorney Fighting Revenge Porn," *The New Yorker*, December 5, 2016, https://www.newyorker.com/magazine/2016/12/05/the-attorney-fighting-revenge-porn/
7. Jessica Testa, "Revenge Porn Lawyer Carrie Goldberg Has Taken on Psychos, Stalkers, and Trolls. Now She Confronts Her Own Worst Demons," *Elle*, July 17, 2019, https://www.elle.com/culture/books/a28401678/carrie-goldberg-nobodys-victim-interview/
8. Goldberg with Amber, *Nobody's Victim*, 213.
9. Jennifer Bain and Laura Italiano, "This Badass Lawyer Fights for Victims of 'Revenge Porn,'" *New York Post*, December 8, 2016, https://nypost.com/2016/12/08/this-badass-lawyer-fights-for-victims-of-revenge-porn/
10. Goldberg with Amber, *Nobody's Victim*, 4.
11. "Practice Areas," C. A. Goldberg, cagoldberglaw.com
12. "Practice Areas," C. A. Goldberg, cagoldberglaw.com
13. "Who We Are," C. A. Goldberg, cagoldberglaw.com
14. "Our Stats Speak Volumes," C. A. Goldberg, cagoldberglaw.com
15. Goldberg with Amber, *Nobody's Victim*, 5.
16. Goldberg with Amber, *Nobody's Victim*, 6.
17. Casey Newton, "Everything You Need to Know About Section 230," The Verge, May 28, 2020, https://www.theverge.com/21273768/section-230-explained-internet-speech-law-definition-guide-free-moderation/
18. Carrie Goldberg, "Winning Through Losing," American Bar Association, December 18, 2020, https://www.americanbar.org/groups/diversity/women/publications/perspectives/2021/december/winning-through-losing/
19. A Champion for Internet Victims," *Daily World*, September 14, 2019, https://www.thedailyworld.com/news/a-champion-for-internet-victims/
20. Carrie Goldberg, email message to Karen A. Foss, November 6, 2020.
21. Carrie Goldberg, email message to Karen A. Foss, November 6, 2020.
22. Goldberg with Amber, *Nobody's Victim*, 218–19.
23. Bain and Italiano, "This Badass Lawyer Fights for Victims of 'Revenge Porn.'"
24. Carrie Goldberg, "This Lawyer is Bringing the Internet's Worst Men to Heel," interview by Madison Pauly, *Mother Jones*, August 30, 2019, https://www.motherjones.com/politics/2019/08/carrie-goldberg-lawyer-interview/
25. Goldberg with Amber, *Nobody's Victim*, 210.
26. Testa, "Revenge Porn Lawyer."
27. Callie Beusman, "The Lawyer Taking on 'Pervs, Psychos, and Trolls,'" The Cut, June 11, 2019, https://www.thecut.com/2019/06/how-carrie-goldberg-revenge-porn-lawyer-dresses-for-work.html/
28. Beusman, "The Lawyer Taking on 'Pervs, Psychos, and Trolls.'"
29. Melinda Garvey, "Carrie Goldberg: She's Our Online Heroine," On the Dot Woman, https://onthedotwoman.com/woman/carrie-goldberg/
30. Goldberg, "This Lawyer is Bringing the Internet's Worst Men to Heel."
31. Goldberg with Amber, *Nobody's Victim*, 210.
32. Goldberg with Amber, *Nobody's Victim*, 136.
33. Carrie Goldberg, "The Ms. Q&A: Why Carrie Goldberg Takes Trolls to Court," interview by Carrie N. Baker, *Ms.*, April 29, 2019, https://msmagazine.com/2019/04/29/the-ms-qa-carrie-goldberg-is-nobodys-victim/
34. Goldberg with Amber, *Nobody's Victim*, 209.
35. Goldberg with Amber, *Nobody's Victim*, 218.
36. Goldberg with Amber, *Nobody's Victim*, 218.
37. "A Champion for Internet Victims."
38. Goldberg, "This Lawyer is Bringing the Internet's Worst Men to Heel."

CHAPTER
SIXTEEN

Nadia Bolz-Weber

> *I am not the only one who sees the underside and God at the same time. There are lots of us, and we are at home in the biblical stories of antiheroes and people who don't get it; beloved prostitutes and rough fishermen. How different from that cast of characters could a manic-depressive alcoholic comic be? It was here in the midst of my own community of underside dwellers that I couldn't help but begin to see the Gospel, the life-changing reality that God is not far off, but here among the brokenness of our lives.*[1]

A pastor, writer, speaker, public theologian, and "spiritual disrupter,"[2] Nadia Bolz-Weber broadens the Christian community to include "underside dwellers"[3] who not only are excluded from but also are likely to feel uncomfortable in traditional churches. She was born in 1969 in Colorado Springs, Colorado, and was raised in the Church of Christ, a fundamentalist denomination of Christianity that prohibited drinking, smoking, swearing, dancing, and sex outside of marriage. The girl who would grow up to become a six-foot-one heavily tattooed CrossFit athlete, amateur body builder, and yoga practitioner was told in Christian charm class that the subordination of women was God's will, and women could not serve as pastors or lay leaders in the church. Instead, her focus should be on her femininity, which meant being demure, humble, modest, subservient, chaste, and pretty.

Bolz-Weber left fundamentalist Christianity at the age of sixteen, rebelling by becoming sexually promiscuous, an alcoholic, and a drug addict; she also got a tattoo—an uncommon act for a teenaged girl in 1986. During Nadia's rebellion against the church, she explored various other religions, including Quakerism, Unitarianism, and the Wiccan religion, but she felt she "was more of a spectator"[4] than a participant in them. She still craved a traditional Christian community but one that was more open than the Church of Christ.

Bolz-Weber began her road to sobriety in 1991 by attending Alcoholics Anonymous. In the early stages of her journey, she supported herself by working as a stand-up comic, which functioned as a form of therapy for her: "I was broken and trying to become fixed and only a few months sober. I couldn't afford therapy, so being paid to be caustic and cynical on stage seemed the next best thing." She stopped working as a comic as she became healthier and discovered that she "just wasn't that funny anymore. Less miserable = less funny."[5] Nadia sees her work as a comic as good practice for becoming a pastor: "I actually have no idea how people manage to be preachers without being stand-up comics first. . . . Comics see the reality from the underside. . . . They come to the truth from a different angle than most people, but people can still recognize that it's the truth. And I think a good preacher does the same thing."[6]

Bolz-Weber returned to traditional Christianity when, after four years of sobriety, she met the man who would become her husband. A seminary student who later became a Lutheran minister, he invited her to attend a service at a Lutheran church, and she fell in love with its liturgy. She joined the Evangelical Lutheran Church in America, a progressive denomination that ordains women, "because the Lutheran church is the only place that has given me language for what I have experienced to be true in my life."[7] Nadia returned to school (she had dropped out of Pepperdine University much earlier after attending for only a semester), graduating from the University of Colorado Boulder in 2005 with a degree in religious studies.

When fellow stand-up comic Keith "PJ" Moore died by suicide in 2004, Bolz-Weber conducted his funeral at the Comedy Works nightclub in Denver. She realized that the mourners would not have been comfortable in a conventional church, but they still needed a pastor. She felt called to serve in that role, so she enrolled in the Iliff School of Theology in Denver to become a minister, graduating in 2018. While still in seminary, Nadia founded the House for All Sinners and Saints (HFASS, pronounced *half-ass*) in Denver, part of a loosely defined movement called the *emerging church*, in which participants reimagine Christianity.[8] The congregation began with 8 participants and grew to a membership of 600.

Bolz-Weber's church was designed to be a place where outcasts like herself—recovering addicts and alcoholics, cynics, queers, freaks, the foul mouthed, and the tattooed—would be welcomed: "Few of us at House for All Sinners and Saints feel comfortable in traditional, mainstream churches," she explains.[9] People are drawn to her congregation by "the fact that they feel like they can comfortably be themselves."[10] She describes her church members using a metaphor of a pasta strainer: "If you took one of those colanders, like those pasta strainers with the round holes in the bottom, and you put all the Christians in Denver in this, or even the people who were even vaguely interested in Christianity in the big colander, the ones that are too oddly shaped to fit through the holes, the ones that are left in the bottoms afterwards, that's House for All Sinners and Saints. They're too oddly shaped to go through the holes."[11]

House for All Sinners and Saints is characterized by a number of unconventional practices. At its Sunday evening services, the congregation sits in the round so they can see each other, and Nadia sits among them. Congregants decide when they walk in if they want to perform one of the tasks in the liturgy—offering the greeting or the prayer of the day, saying the benediction, or serving communion. Nobody has to deem them worthy of or good at these tasks, so the entire liturgy is conducted by the people in attendance that day. Bolz-Weber describes the practice as "anti-excellence, pro-participation.... We don't do anything really well, but we do it together."[12] Parishioners in the church sing hymns a cappella rather than relying on a choir, organist, or band, and the Easter service concludes with a huge dance party that features a chocolate fountain in the baptismal font. Nadia describes her church as "a group of folks figuring out how to be liturgical, Christo-centric, social-justice oriented, queer inclusive, incarnational, contemplative, irreverent, ancient-future church with a progressive but deeply rooted theological imagination."[13]

In 2018, Bolz-Weber left the leadership of her church to focus full time on her writing and speaking as a public theologian. She reached a point, she said, where "the church still loves me, but I don't think the church still needs me."[14] She also wanted to increase her contact with secular audiences because she believes "there's a hunger for the basic message of the gospel. Most people aren't going to show up to church on Sunday morning... but it doesn't mean that the message of the gospel can't still be freeing to them."[15]

Nadia has written four books as a way to reach a broader audience. Her first book, *Salvation on the Small Screen? 24 Hours of Christian Television* (2008), was written when she was in seminary, and Episcopal Publishing House asked her to watch twenty-four consecutive hours of bad Christian television and write about it. The books that followed explain her approach to Christianity: *Pastrix: The Cranky, Beautiful Faith of a Sinner and Saint* (2013); *Accidental Saints: Finding God in All the Wrong People* (2015); and *Shameless: A Sexual Reformation* (2019).

Definition of Feminism

Bolz-Weber defines feminism as "an orientation toward life that centers on the well-being, voices, success, sorrow, struggle, beauty, and brilliance of women." She doesn't exclude men from feminism, but she chooses to focus on women in her definition because "when women thrive, everyone thrives."[16] Nadia rejects the idea that God is literally gendered male or that everyone who performs a gender other than masculinity is not valued: "I needed to bask in the female face of God for a good long while outside the church before I ever could return to it whole and be able to see the divine feminine in my own tradition.... There was some undoing to be done inside of myself after a childhood of being told that God is male and I am not."[17]

Bolz-Weber finds inspiration for her feminism in the actions of women in the Bible, pointing to examples such as the mother and sister of Moses, who conspired to save Moses from Pharaoh's genocide of Hebrew babies. Risking everything, the two women orchestrated his adoption by a princess and maneuvered to become his nanny and wet nurse. She sees this story as an illustration of the strength of women: "We are totally a threat. God has sprinkled midwives and Pharaoh's daughters and other holy people all over the place whose job is to birth life from death."[18]

Nadia also finds feminist power in the story of Mary Magdalene. Due to a conflation of two different characters in the Bible, Mary Magdalene is often mistakenly framed as a prostitute. After Jesus cast seven demons out of her, Mary Magdalene bankrolled Jesus's ministry, witnessed his execution by crucifixion while the male disciples fled, and was chosen as the first one to whom Jesus appeared after rising from the dead. Bolz-Weber particularly appreciates Mary Magdalene because "she didn't hightail it out when things got hot. She showed up."[19] She elaborates: "Mary Magdalene didn't necessarily know what to say or what to do or even what to think when she encountered the risen Jesus. But none of that was nearly as important as the fact that she was present and attentive to him."[20] The tattoos that cover Nadia's arms are a testament to her appreciation for Mary; her forearms are covered in tattoos of Mary Magdalene and the other women who stayed with Jesus during the crucifixion.

Bolz-Weber holds Mary, the mother of Jesus, in similar regard as a feminist model. She rejects the two common interpretations of Mary—as "the docile picture of purity and virginity" or as "a sort of first-century teenage female Che Guevara" who wants to overthrow the social order.[21] She retells Mary's story from a different perspective: "Here we have a girl, likely between thirteen and fifteen years of age. She's a peasant and she's engaged to a pretty religious guy. An angelic figure visits her saying that she's found favor with God and is going to conceive a son by the Holy Spirit and that this child will be holy and will sit on David's throne—none of which seems terribly likely to be true, given her socioeconomic status."[22] Nadia continues: "Maybe the really outrageous act of faith on Mary's part was trusting that she had found favor with God. . . . Mary is what it looks like to believe that we already are who God says we are."[23]

Change Strategies

Those who want to change systems are often located outside the system or are at lower levels of the system's hierarchy. Bolz-Weber represents someone who is trying to generate change within a system in which she is squarely and happily located and in which she has some power. She is not trying to change the doctrine of the Lutheran Church, nor is she trying to convert people who are not Christians to Christianity. Rather, the system that Nadia wants to change is exclusionary church culture. Her change strategies are directed at those who embrace Christianity but have decided that the church is not for them—not because they disagree with its doctrine but because they do not feel welcomed by other members of the church community. She thus provides insight into change strategies that can be used by those who have the capacity to influence a system from within.

Those who have positioned themselves outside of the Christian community do so because they have experienced "horrible things that were said and done to them in Christian settings"[24] by the "doctrine police" who wanted "to get the unsavory folks away from their table."[25] Nadia acknowledges that Christians sometimes "seem to value parameters over people" and deny people participation in a Christian community because they fall outside of particular parameters or categories that are deemed appropriate.[26] Those who are divorced, have had an abortion, are gender nonbinary, or have tattoos are among those who have been singled out for exclusion in many Christian communities. To address the sometimes unwelcoming nature of Christianity, Bolz-Weber employs three primary strategies: (1) normalizing outsiders, (2) nostalgizing the system, and (3) updating the system. The result is a system that is more relevant and welcoming to the "spiritual refugees"[27] she seeks to serve.

Normalizing Outsiders

Nadia transposes insiders and outsiders, centering and featuring those who typically have been excluded or marginalized by Christian communities. Bolz-Weber uses the green crop circles of eastern Colorado as a metaphor for this exclusion. The plots in which the crops are planted are square, but the plants grow in circles within the squares because the farmers use a center-pivot irrigation system that waters crops in a circular pattern; consequently, the water never reaches the plants in the corners. This practice applies to the spiritual refugees from Christian communities as well: "Many of us were taught that if you do not fit inside the circle of the church's behavioral codes, God is not pleased with us, so we whittled ourselves down to a shape that could fit those teachings, or we denied those parts of ourselves entirely."[28] Nadia sees her church and her efforts to create a welcoming church community as designed "for those planted in the corners."[29]

A primary way in which Bolz-Weber normalizes outsiders is by accepting—and even flaunting—the broken parts of them that typically are cause for exclusion from church communities. Nadia calls the members of her congregation "Jesus-y misfits"[30] and welcomes the whole person, faults and all: No one can avoid sin, which she defines as the normal "state of human brokenness in which what we say and do causes these sometimes tiny and sometimes monstrous fractures in our earth, in ourselves, in those we love, and sometimes even in our own bodies."[31] Being broken does not mean that individuals have to experience major trauma, as she explains: "I think that we've sort of glamorized certain types of brokenness. You know, there's like the big ones: mental illness, addiction. And in a way, it can be very tempting to allow those people who are so obviously broken to just carry all of the brokenness for us."[32] In contrast, Bolz-Weber explains that all people are burdened by the ugly things they have done—"that time we spanked our child too hard, the times we have to erase our browser history, the time we lied about ourselves to get a job, the times we flirt online with people who aren't our spouses."[33] She turns to scripture to demonstrate how brokenness is precisely the point of Christianity, speculating that God might say, "I love the world too much to let your sin define you and be the final word. I am a God who makes all things new."[34]

Nadia sees Jesus as a model for embracing all individuals in their brokenness. As she explains, "Jesus could have hung out in the high-end religious scene of his day, but instead he scoffed at all that, choosing instead to laugh at the powerful, befriend whores, kiss sinners, and eat with all the wrong people. He spent his time with people for whom life was not easy."[35] She interprets his actions to mean that "when a party is thrown we should invite the lame, the poor, the crippled, and the blind." In other words, "the uncool parts of us are exactly what Jesus invites to sit and eat around his table."[36] As one of her parishioners explains, "I'm a sex worker and I don't know how to change that, but I can come here and receive bread and wine and I can hold onto the love of God without being deemed worthy of it by anyone but God."[37]

In fact, Bolz-Weber finds that broken, imperfect people are the ones from whom she has learned the most or who have changed her in significant ways. She thus elevates those who once were excluded, just as Jesus did: "Never once did Jesus scan the room for the best example of holy living and send that person out to tell others about him," she notes. "He always sent stumblers and sinners."[38] Nadia asserts that she continually needs "the stranger, the foreigner, the 'other' to show" her the faith[39] and acknowledges that "a huge part of my spiritual life has been the lessons I've learned by being around people who I wouldn't choose out of a catalog."[40]

Nostalgizing the System

Bolz-Weber's approach to creating a welcoming community for all is deeply rooted in tradition, and she frequently reminds spiritual refugees of what they value about participating in a Christian community. One way she does this is by highlighting aspects of a Christian community these outsiders are likely to remember fondly and positively. As she says of her experience growing up in the Church of Christ, "There were beautiful things, there were good things, there were things worth saving, there were good things about me that it gave me."[41] In her church services, for example, she features traditional hymns, prayers, and liturgy—the "ancient pattern of worship shared mainly in the Catholic, Lutheran, Orthodox, and Episcopal churches."[42] When she preaches, she bases her sermons on the scripture reading for each week assigned by the Lutheran lectionary and wears a clerical collar, seeing it as representing both "the church's catholicity and the Lutheran tradition."[43]

Nadia also hopes to awaken the memories of spiritual refugees by telling stories they are sure to know and by reminding them of their important meanings. She believes in and often preaches about the miracles found in the Bible—Noah's ark, the virgin birth, and Jesus's resurrection from the dead, for example. As she explains, "Now I know it's crazy, but I think that Jesus resurrected from the dead. . . . It's dear to me and it's foundational to all of my work."[44] The Bible and Christianity, she explains, are about issues such as death and resurrection with which spiritual outsiders are likely to be concerned: "It's about how God continues to reach into the graves we dig for ourselves and pull us out, giving us new life, in ways both dramatic and small."[45]

Bolz-Weber also encourages spiritual refugees to recognize the key role that a Christian community plays in their lives. She suggests that God's grace—the love and acceptance of God—is operationalized in the interactions among members of the community and that participants can only really know God's grace when they bestow that on others: "We cannot create for ourselves God's word of grace. We must tell it to each other."[46] Nadia hopes, then, not only to generate a longing among spiritual refugees for the traditions they remember fondly but also to remind them that they are a vital part of the community marked by these traditions.

Updating the System

To create identification between spiritual refugees and the Church community, Bolz-Weber updates the system by implementing activities and events that connect her congregants to contemporary places and ideas. Her church, for example, holds an annual blessing of bikes and sponsors Beer & Hymns evenings every few months in local bars, where people gather and sing old hymns. After the liturgy on Good Friday, parishioners bring a large crucifix to a spot where brutal violence has taken place and pray, sing, and lay down tulips that were handed out during the liturgy. The church holds naming rites for trans parishioners to honor and celebrate their transitions from old to new names, and Nadia holds office hours in a coffee shop, where people from the church gather and talk.

In other instances, Bolz-Weber and her parishioners modify or adjust traditions to make them more relevant to contemporary Christians, "tweaking them in ways that are super meaningful or funny or relevant for us."[47] In one church service, parishioners created their own stations of the cross—a traditional form of prayer in which observers walk around a room, meditating on fourteen images of Jesus from when he was condemned until he was laid in the tomb. They chose to cut out news photos of the earthquake that had just occurred in Haiti to replace the traditional images of Jesus's suffering and death. For the second station, for example, when Jesus carries his cross, they found and posted a photograph of a man wearing a medical mask who was helping to carry a pine box.

At other times, Nadia reconceptualizes or reframes church doctrine to make it fit contemporary lives. Sometimes she does this by relating contemporary ideas to scripture or doctrine, as she does when she applies the Bechdel test to the books in the Bible. The Bechdel test, devised by Alison Bechdel, requires that at some point in a film or piece of literature two female characters have a conversation with each other about something other than a man.[48] (Only six books in the Bible pass the test—Exodus, Ruth, Samuel, Kings, Mark, and Luke.) In other instances, she explicitly discusses and recalibrates subjects such as sex that typically are linked to shame and prohibition in Christian churches. Bolz-Weber calls out the sexual shame that is prominent in conventional religious messaging, for instance, and instead honors "sexual pleasure as something that can connect us more deeply to ourselves and others and God."[49]

Nadia reconceptualizes the doctrine of the church as well by redefining and rethinking biblical texts. Her approach is not to reject or change a biblical story but to look at it from the perspective of a character who is typically not the main character—and often one with whom spiritual refugees are more likely to identify. She retells the story of Adam and Eve, for example, noting that although the story is conventionally thought to be about disobedience, another moral to be taken from it is that Adam and Eve listened to a voice other than God's, something that occurs often in contemporary society. These voices tell stories that are so familiar that people think they are the truth—stories about, for example, how someone's body is not beautiful and worthy of being loved, that God cannot forgive, or that what someone has done (good or bad) is actually who someone is. Bolz-Weber concludes: "So if that snake starts talking blasphemy, don't listen."[50] She redefines the story of Christmas as "a story of alienation and political tyranny, homelessness, working class people, pagans, and angels."[51] Nadia also rewrites the Beatitudes, blessings Jesus gave in his Sermon on the Mount. While Jesus is portrayed in the Bible as blessing those who are poor in spirit, who mourn, who are meek, and who are pure of heart, she imagines Jesus now offering blessings to those whom no one notices, such as the mothers of the miscarried, the closeted, the unemployed, and the ones without lobbyists.[52]

Bolz-Weber is not challenging the theological or doctrinal system of which she is a part—the Lutheran Church. She is "absolutely grounded in the heart of Lutheran theology" and bristles at the notion that she is a "rogue Lutheran."[53] Instead, she challenges the system that would keep some people out of a Christian community because they are seen as too broken or inappropriate to participate. Rather than marginalizing them or excluding them altogether, she joyfully welcomes broken individuals into a Christian community by placing them in the center rather than in the margins. Nadia also revels in the nostalgia they are likely to remember from earlier participation in that community and updates those traditions to make them even more relevant to spiritual refugees. The strategies she deploys embody her guiding philosophy: "Scripture and theology and liturgy are too potent to be left in the hands of those who would only use them to justify their dominance over another group of people. And that's how it's been typically used: weaponized against people so that one group can maintain dominance over another group, and it's horseshit. I am too defiant to leave all those things and those words in the hands of people who only twist them to do that."[54]

■ Reflections

1. Bolz-Weber left fundamentalist Christianity and became the pastor she herself wanted as an outsider. If you were raised in a church, did you experience any similar feelings? If so, how did you resolve them? If you have not had experiences with a religious setting, is there another setting in your life in which you felt like an outsider? What strategies did you devise to deal with it, or did someone within the system make you feel welcome?
2. Bolz-Weber rejects an image of God as male. Do you have an image of God that is gendered in any way? Do you believe gender is a critical element of an image of God?
3. Read the references to Mary Magdalene in the Bible. Does Bolz-Weber's interpretation of Mary's role in Jesus's life change how you understand these passages?
4. Bolz-Weber offers an example of someone in power within a system who seeks to change it from within. Do the change strategies she employs differ in significant ways from those used by the women in the book who do not have much power within systems but who are trying to change those systems? What seem to be the major differences between the strategies Bolz-Weber uses and those used by these other women?
5. When she employs the strategy of updating the system, Bolz-Weber often looks at Biblical stories from the perspective of lesser characters. Can you think of other examples where telling a story from the perspective of someone who is not typically featured makes a big difference in how the story is perceived and understood? How does featuring the perspective of a lesser character facilitate change in a system?
6. How closely do Bolz-Weber's change strategies align with the assumptions outlined in the introduction to part 5? Are there any assumptions that you don't believe pertain to her approach to change?
7. In which feminist wave would you place Bolz-Weber and why?

■ Notes

[1] Nadia Bolz-Weber, *Pastrix: The Cranky, Beautiful Faith of a Sinner and Saint* (New York: Jericho, 2013), 9.
[2] Nadia Bolz-Weber, "Screw It, I'll Go First: Nadia Bolz-Weber," interview by Kerri Kelly, CTZN, May 2, 2019, https://www.ctznwell.org/ctznpodcast/nadia-bolz-weber/
[3] Bolz-Weber, *Pastrix*, 9.
[4] Bolz-Weber, *Pastrix*, 29.

[5] Bolz-Weber, *Pastrix*, 5.
[6] Nadia Bolz-Weber, "Nadia Bolz-Weber: Seeing the Underside and Seeing God: Tattoos, Tradition, and Grace," interview by Krista Tippett, *On Being,* American Public Media, September 5, 2013, https://onbeing.org/programs/nadia-bolz-weber-seeing-the-underside-and-seeing-god-tattoos-tradition-and-grace/
[7] Bolz-Weber, *Pastrix*, 49.
[8] Bolz-Weber, "Nadia Bolz-Weber: Seeing the Underside and Seeing God."
[9] Bolz-Weber, *Pastrix*, 182.
[10] Bolz-Weber, *Pastrix*, 54.
[11] Nadia Bolz-Weber, "Nadia Bolz-Weber: The Insight of Outsiders," interview by Kate Bowler, Everything Happens, n.d., https://katebowler.com/podcasts/nadia-bolz-weber-the-insight-of-outsiders-s1e1/
[12] Bolz-Weber, "Nadia Bolz-Weber: Seeing the Underside and Seeing God."
[13] Electa Draper, "Pastor Turns Heads by Blending Tradition and Irreverence," *Denver Post*, April 22, 2022, https://www.denverpost.com/2011/04/22/pastor-turns-heads-by-blending-tradition-and-irreverence/
[14] Carina Julig, "Headed for a Larger Stage, Nadia Bolz-Weber Leaves Her 'House' in Order," Religious News Service, August 5, 2018, https://religionnews.com/2018/08/05/headed-for-a-larger-stage-nadia-bolz-weber-leaves-her-house-in-order-2/
[15] Julig, "Headed for a Larger Stage."
[16] Nadia Bolz-Weber, email message to Sonja K. Foss, October 9, 2020.
[17] Bolz-Weber, *Pastrix*, 16.
[18] Bolz-Weber, *Shameless: A Sexual Reformation* (New York: Convergent Press, 2019), 93.
[19] Bolz-Weber, "Nadia Bolz-Weber: Seeing the Underside and Seeing God."
[20] Bolz-Weber, *Pastrix*, 198.
[21] Nadia Bolz-Weber, *Accidental Saints: Finding God in All the Wrong People* (New York: Convergent, 2015), 67.
[22] Bolz-Weber, *Accidental Saints*, 68.
[23] Bolz-Weber, *Accidental Saints*, 69–70.
[24] Bolz-Weber, *Shameless*, 82.
[25] Bolz-Weber, *Pastrix*, 109.
[26] Nadia Bolz-Weber, "The Parameters We Prefer Jesus to Work Under," *Sojourners*, August 27, 2013, https://sojo.net/articles/parameters-we-prefer-jesus-work-under/
[27] Bolz-Weber, "Screw It, I'll Go First."
[28] Bolz-Weber, *Shameless*, 4.
[29] Bolz-Weber, *Shameless*, 6.
[30] Bolz-Weber, *Accidental Saints*, 53.
[31] Bolz-Weber, *Accidental Saints*, 130–31.
[32] Bolz-Weber, "Nadia Bolz-Weber: Seeing the Underside and Seeing God."
[33] Bolz-Weber, *Accidental Saints*, 16.
[34] Bolz-Weber, *Pastrix*, 50.
[35] Bolz-Weber, *Accidental Saints*, 110.
[36] Bolz-Weber, *Accidental Saints*, 125.
[37] Bolz-Weber, *Pastrix*, 193.
[38] Bolz-Weber, *Accidental Saints*, 30.
[39] Bolz-Weber, *Pastrix*, 94.
[40] Bolz-Weber, "Screw It, I'll Go First."
[41] Bolz-Weber, "Screw It, I'll Go First."
[42] Bolz-Weber, *Pastrix*, 47.
[43] Bolz-Weber, *Accidental Saints*, 61.
[44] Nadia Bolz-Weber, "Contemplating Faith and Forgiveness with Pastor and Author Nadia Bolz-Weber," interview by Erik Weihenmayer, Jeff Evans, and Dave Shurna, No Barriers, March 27, 2019, https://podtail.com/about/faq/
[45] Bolz-Weber, *Pastrix*, xviii.

46 Bolz-Weber, *Accidental Saints*, 165.
47 Bolz-Weber, "Nadia Bolz-Weber: Seeing the Underside and Seeing God."
48 Bolz-Weber, *Shameless*, 89.
49 Bolz-Weber, *Shameless*, 146.
50 Nadia Bolz-Weber, "Adam, Eve and that Damned Snake," *Sojourners*, June 11, 2012, https://sojo.net/articles/adam-eve-and-damned-snake/
51 Nadia Bolz-Weber, "A Thrill of Hope: Nadia Bolz-Weber Uncovers the Unlikely Miracles of Christmas," interview by Jen Hatmaker, For the Love, December 24, 2019, https://jenhatmaker.com/podcast/series-23/a-thrill-of-hope-nadia-bolz-weber-uncovers-the-unlikely-miracles-of-christmas/
52 Bolz-Weber, "A Thrill of Hope."
53 Draper, "Pastor Turns Heads."
54 Nadia Bolz-Weber, "Episode 45: Grace for F*ck Ups with Nadia Bolz-Weber," interview by Erin Wickersham, She Recovers, May 26, 2020, https://www.stitcher.com/podcast/she-recovers-podcast/e/69947562/

CHAPTER SEVENTEEN

Serena Williams

In this society, women are not taught or expected to be that future leader or future CEO. The narrative has to change. And maybe it doesn't get better in time for me, but someone in my position can show women and people of colour that we have a voice, because Lord knows I use mine. I love sticking up for people and supporting women. Being the voice that millions of people don't have.[1]

Serena Jameka Williams, a championship tennis player, is the only athlete to have won singles titles in four different decades. She works to enrich both the sport of tennis and the larger society by her performances on the court and her actions and philanthropy off the court. Williams was born in 1981 in Saginaw, Michigan, the youngest of five daughters. When Serena was a baby, her family moved to Compton, California, a suburb of Los Angeles, where her father owned a security firm, and her mother was a nurse.

Because of the prize money that comes with being a tennis champion, Williams's father saw tennis as his daughters' tickets out of Compton, and he learned the game by reading books and watching videos. He then taught the game to his wife, and the two of them taught their daughters. When Venus and Serena, the two youngest, excelled, he pushed them harder: "We went from playing just a couple hours a day four or five times a week, to three or four hours a day every day of the week."[2] At the age of eight, Williams entered a tournament in which her sister Venus was playing. Her father thought Serena was too young to compete, but she sent in the registration form without her parents' knowledge. On the day of the tournament, Williams brought her racket with her, as she always did when she watched Venus play. She managed to play her first game before her father figured out what she had done. Serena came in second behind Venus and went on to win forty-six of the forty-nine tournaments she entered on the pre-teen circuit.

Williams's father moved the family to Palm Beach Gardens, Florida, in 1991, so Venus and Serena could attend the Rick Macci Tennis Academy. Both girls were home schooled so they could concentrate on tennis. After graduation from high school, they attended classes in fashion design at the Art Institute in Ft. Lauderdale, Florida. This coursework provided the basis for their later interest in designing clothing, jewelry, and luggage.

Williams turned professional in 1995 at the age of fourteen. She didn't win the qualifying round in her first pro tournament, which surprised her and taught her not to take anything for granted: "Playing in all those little-kid events out in California, I'd always expected to win—and I usually did. . . . Here, though, I could no longer expect to win. I'd have to earn it, fight for it."[3] She didn't play professionally again until 1997, when she competed in the Indian Wells Masters in Indian Wells, California. At this tournament, Serena defeated Mary Pierce, ranked seventh in the world, and Monica Seles, ranked fourth in the world, before losing to Lindsay Davenport in the semifinals.

By 2002, Williams was consistently winning tournaments. She defeated the top three players in the world at the NASDAQ-100 Open in Miami, Florida, and she also defeated her sister in the three tournaments in which they played each other. At the end of the year, she was named the top woman tennis player in the world. Serena left tournament play in 2017 to give birth to a daughter. Despite an emergency C-section, a pulmonary embolism, blood clots, and a popped C-section wound, Williams returned to tournament play ten months later. Ranked number one when she left, she was ranked 453rd when she returned because tennis rules stated that a player who left because of injury lost her seeding. An outpouring of support for Serena, however, made tennis officials change the rules. They gave Williams the twenty-fifth seed and agreed to take maternity into consideration in the future when seeding players. As of 2021, Serena had won twenty-three grand slam tournament titles,[4] four Olympic gold medals, and $92.7 million in prize money, and she was ranked number one in the world on nine different occasions.

In addition to her tennis career, Williams has taken on a variety of other avocational and entrepreneurial projects. She has acted in various television shows, including *Law & Order* and *Street Time*, and admits that if she hadn't chosen tennis as a career, she would have pursued acting. In 2004, she launched a clothing line called *Aneres* (Serena spelled backward) as well as a Nike apparel line, and she launched a second clothing line—*S by Serena*— in 2019. She also has developed a line of jewelry that features necklaces and bracelets that spell out words such as *sexy, loved, great, winner, inspire, mama,* and *queen*. In addition, Serena has designed two luggage collections for Away that draw on what she has learned about packing as a result of her travels on the tennis circuit.

Williams has engaged in considerable philanthropy as well. She started the Serena Williams Foundation in 2008 in memory of her oldest sister who was murdered in gang crossfire five years earlier; the foundation is designed to assist young people affected by violent crime. Serena also served as an ambassador with the Allstate Foundation Purple Purse to help survivors of domestic violence. In 2011, she was appointed a UNICEF Goodwill Ambassador, a program designed to promote the rights of women and children around the world. After Williams visited Africa in 2006 and 2008, she funded the construction of a school in Senegal and later partnered with Build African Schools to help build schools throughout Africa and Jamaica. She consistently invests in women-owned companies, especially those owned by women of color.

Serena has been repeatedly honored for her contributions on and off the tennis court. These honors include the Image Award (with Venus) from the National Association for the Advancement of Colored People (NAACP) and the Laureus World Sportsman of the Year Award—both in 2003. She was named Best Female Athlete of the Year in 2003 and 2013 and ESPY Best Female Tennis Player of the Year in 2003, 2004, 2009, 2010, 2011, 2013, 2014, 2015, and 2017. In 2018, Williams was given the People's Choice Award for Favorite Game Changer.

Definition of Feminism

Serena's embrace of feminism is straightforward: "I definitely am a feminist. I like to stick up for women and women's rights."[5] Williams defines feminism as the effort to achieve equality and uses a game metaphor to emphasize her commitment to this principle: "Equality isn't a game. But achieving it will be our greatest victory."[6] She works to promote feminism on and off the tennis court, believing it can contribute to a system that is richer and more equitable because diverse voices are recognized and included in it.

Equal pay has been an especially important issue for both Serena and Venus. Venus criticized Wimbledon for the disparity between women's and men's prize money, and that gap was eliminated in 2007. Serena has been particularly vocal about pay disparities for women of color, who are subjected to both gender and racial discrimination. In an essay published on Black Women's Equal Pay Day in 2017, she noted that "for every dollar a man is paid, a black woman makes just 63 cents and black women earn 17 per cent less than white women." Williams adds: "The cycles of poverty, discrimination, and sexism are much, much harder to break than the record for Grand Slam titles. For every black woman that rises through the ranks to a position of power, there are too many others who are still struggling." She acknowledges: "I am in the rare position to be financially successful beyond my imagination. I had talent, I worked like crazy and I was lucky enough to break through. But today isn't about me. It's about the other 24 million black women in America. If I never picked up a tennis racket, I would be one of them; that is never lost on me."[7]

Inclusion is also part of Serena's approach to feminism. She wants to "get rid of the word exclusive, and bring in the word inclusive."[8] Her commitment to inclusion derives in part from the criticism she has endured for not meeting traditional expectations for women. In the voice-over for a Nike ad, she explains: "I've never been the right kind of woman. Oversized and overconfident. Too mean if I don't smile. Too black for my tennis whites. Too motivated for motherhood. But I am proving, time and time again, there's no wrong way to be a woman."[9] Williams believes every woman should have the opportunity to choose for herself the kind of life she wants to live, unencumbered by others' expectations and prejudices. In this kind of inclusive feminism, whatever each woman brings to the table is accepted and appreciated: "We shouldn't be made to feel like we have to act a certain way because we are women and we shouldn't be made to feel like we need to fit into the same box. We are all different and we should celebrate those differences."[10]

Serena credits several women with fostering her commitment to feminism. In the tennis world, she points to Billie Jean King and Chris Evert as "women who go above and beyond."[11] Her sister Venus has been a constant presence in her life, protecting her when she was young and encouraging her despite often competing against her on the tennis court. She also names her mother as a powerful influence: "If it wasn't for my mom, I wouldn't be here. I wouldn't be Serena Williams. If I could just do half of what she did for me, for my daughter, it would be beyond anything I could ever dream of."[12] She also considers her daughter an important part of her feminism: "I think sometimes women limit themselves. . . . I'm so glad I had a daughter. I want to teach her that there are no limits."[13]

Change Strategies

Williams seeks to transform the system of tennis and, by extension, society at large by modeling how to confront and move beyond a system's limitations. She employs three strategies that suggest the changes she wants to see in the systems of which she is a part: (1) making boundaries visible, (2) transforming limitations, and (3) modeling agency.

Making Boundaries Visible

One of Serena's primary strategies is to make the boundaries of the existing system visible, and she does this primarily by pointing out stereotypes so they can be considered, discussed, and addressed. In terms of tennis, this strategy most often takes the form of pushing against the traditional image of tennis and who should be playing the game. Invented near the end of the Victorian era, tennis was designed and managed by upper-class white men; thus, tennis traditionally has been "staunchly white in its sensibilities and participants."[14] Femininity was carefully policed for both white and Black players, and the stamina and endurance of women players were questioned. Men played best out of five matches, for example, while women played (and still do) best out of three matches.

Chapter Seventeen ☰ Serena Williams

Tennis still carries many vestiges of its white, elitist origins, and Williams contradicts those expectations in many ways. She is Black, not white, and she grew up playing on city courts in rough neighborhoods, rather than in staid, upper class country clubs. Furthermore, she is athletic, strong, and confident—qualities that contrast with lingering expectations from the Victorian era that women are the weaker sex. Because she is not the typical tennis player, she has been subjected to greater scrutiny and criticism than white players. Her powerful body and style of play led the president of the Russian Tennis Federation to call both Serena and her sister Venus "scary" and to refer to them as the "Williams brothers."[15] In addition, Williams is drug tested more frequently than other competitors, and her celebratory dance after one tournament win was labeled a *crip walk* reminiscent of gang culture. Her very presence in the game of tennis violates expectations for the game, so no matter what she does, she is pushing its boundaries.

Serena consciously pushes boundaries with her tennis outfits, many of which she designs herself. A favorite is what she calls "biker-tennis chic"—a black tank top and pleated denim skirt. A biker look is far from the demure, ultra-feminine, and pastel look reminiscent of the lawn dresses in which women originally played.[16] Williams once wore a snakeskin print tennis dress, which called up historical associations of Blacks with Africa as a wild, dark, uncivilized, jungle continent and perhaps was a deliberate response to the many times she has been called a *gorilla*.[17] She has several times worn a catsuit, a one-piece, form-fitting garment, usually in black but sometimes in pink. At the 2021 Australian Open, she wore a black, pink, and red catsuit with one full-length leg and one short leg in a nod to Florence Griffith Joyner (Flo-Jo), a track star known for her one-legged outfits. When Serena wore a catsuit to the French Open in 2018, however, she was told that it was inappropriate for play at that tournament and that she could not wear it again. She responded by wearing its exact opposite at her next tournament—a tutu befitting a ballerina. At the French Open in 2019, she wore an outfit that consisted of a sports bra, a skort (a pair of shorts made to resemble a skirt), and a jacket covered in words describing women in both English and French—*queen/reine, goddess/déesse, champion/championne,* and *mother/mere*.

Williams's outfits at Wimbledon, however, have been the ones that have most pushed the acceptable boundaries for tennis wear. At Wimbledon, players are required to wear white, a dress code left over from the Victorian era when sweat stains, which show more on colored clothing, were considered unsightly. The term *tennis whites* continues to reference the origins of tennis and is held up as a way of respecting the traditions and gentility of the game. Serena, however, has pushed against these rules in several ways. Once she wore a purple headband, purple sweatbands, and purple shorts, all accessories that were exempt from the all-white rule at Wimbledon. After 1995, however, Wimbledon changed the regulation from "predominantly white" to "almost entirely white" and closed the loophole that had exempted her purple accessories.[18] Williams has since played in a specially made white trench coat, a white blazer layered over her tennis dress, and white dresses with see-through panels and cut-outs. With each of these outfits, she follows the rules at the same time that she calls attention to them, continually asking those who see her to think about what the rules say about tennis and its players.

In her life off the court, Serena also calls attention to inequities and injustices—limitations imposed by those who establish and maintain society's norms. She continually points out pay discrepancies for male and female tennis champions. Although she has won twenty-three grand slams to Roger Federer's twenty, for example, her career winnings are about $30 million less than his. She points out discrepancies in language as well that suggest differential treatment for women and men. When a male tennis champion is introduced, he is referred to as "the best tennis player in the world." In contrast, "female tennis players are always introduced with their gender distinction, stating bluntly they are not world champions, just champions of their gender."[19] Williams rejects this differential labeling. Her dream growing up was to be the best tennis player in the world—not the best *female* tennis player in the world.

Transforming Limitations

At the same time that Serena calls attention to stereotypes, constraints, and discriminatory practices that operate in tennis and in society at large, she builds on those limitations to advance new emancipatory possibilities: "What others marked as flaws or disadvantages about myself—my race, my gender—I embraced as fuel for my success."[20] On and off the court, she consistently reframes what might be seen as less-than-opportune events and conditions and turns them into positives: "Find some takeaway moment in the fizzle and carry *that* with you instead."[21] An example is evident in Williams's account of how she and her four sisters shared a room with two sets of bunk beds. As the fifth and youngest child, Serena had to bunk with a different sister each night. Although many might consider this situation unacceptable and look back on it as evidence of disadvantage, she casts the experience as just the opposite: "Each night, I'd crawl into bed with a different sister, and as a result we each had a special bond. Instead of feeling like I didn't quite belong anywhere, I felt like I belonged everywhere."[22]

Williams's emotional displays on the court are often seen as unfortunate episodes that hurt her image and the game of tennis because such displays violate the gentility of the sport. Her emotional outburst at the finals of the US Open in 2018, when she was playing Naomi Osaka, is often held up as a prime example. Serena argued with the umpire over calls she deemed unfair and ultimately broke her racquet in frustration, and the penalties she received cost her the title (a point was taken away from her score and she was fined a total of $17,000 for receiving coaching, breaking her racquet, and verbal abuse). Despite losing, Williams turned the event around during the trophy ceremony when the crowd began to boo Osaka. In response, she put her arm around Osaka and told the crowd: "Let's make this the best moment we can, and we'll get through it. Let's give everyone the credit where credit's due. Let's not boo anymore. We're gonna get through this, and let's be positive. So congratulations, Naomi!"[23] She rose above the controversy and turned her own loss into something positive for her opponent.

Another instance in which Serena transformed limitations occurred on her first visit to Africa in 2006. After visiting the slave castles on the coast of Ghana, from which slaves were sent to the Americas, she recognized how this experience could either be cause for despair or a source for transformation.

> Someone else might have been depressed by what I'd just seen, and it certainly was depressing, but I chose to find the power in it, to be lifted by it. After all, if we weren't strong, I wouldn't be here. My ancestors would have never made it to the United States. . . . My entire mind-set changed as a result of that trip. . . . The very next time I held a racquet in my hands I thought, *There's nothing that can break me. On the court. Off the court. Anywhere.*[24]

Williams grew up expecting that a positive attitude could and would affect outcomes, whether in tennis or life. Her mother's mantra was, "'whatever you become, . . . you become in your head first.'"[25] Serena writes notes and affirmations to herself in a journal that she looks at between tennis matches, and these showcase her positive attitude. One such entry reads, "Good thoughts are powerful. Negative thoughts are weak. Decide what U want to be, have, do and think the thoughts of it. Your vision will become your life. Hold on to the thoughts of what U want. Make it absolutely clear in your mind. U become what U think about most. U attract what you think about most. Think. Do. Be."[26] Another entry continues the same theme: "Be positive. Have only positivity going through your body. Be the best. Being the best starts by acting like U R the best. Believing U R the best. Becoming the best. Believe. Become."[27]

Modeling Agency

Williams does not simply push the boundaries of a system and transform its limitations but also demonstrates the agency required to change that system. This was not something she thought about at the beginning of her career: "I never thought, 'I want to open up doors for black athletes,' and then to female athletes. I ended up on this path and people started looking up to me."[28] Serena acknowledges that she sometimes feels the weight of the expectations: "When I'm playing a final of a Grand Slam, that's when I feel a lot of expectations and that's when I'm like, 'Serena, would you rather be having your 22 titles, or would you rather have, like, two or three and people not have these expectations?'"[29]

Once Williams recognized that she does have a platform from which to speak and to model agency, she has embraced that stance: "We want to stand up for what we feel is right, and we want to empower people to stand up for what they feel is right as well."[30] She frequently acknowledges that "women are not supported enough or are discouraged from choosing their path," and she uses the "highs and lows" of her own experiences to "inspire all young women out there to push for greatness and follow their dreams with steadfast resilience."[31] She does not claim that serving as an inspiration is easy, but she continues to "embrace who I am and what I am"[32] in the hopes that she can encourage other women to take control of their own lives and recognize their agency. Serena's line of Nike tennis shoes, released in 2015, has the phrase "You are strong, powerful and beautiful!" written on the soles of the shoes.[33] This is the image she holds up to women to encourage them to stand up for themselves, to have confidence in themselves, and not to pay attention to those who would dismiss or discount them.

Williams also recognizes the role of hard work in her success, and she expects it from others as well. For her, hard work is what is necessary to achieve one's goals: "You may never be as talented as the absolute best in the field or pursuit you choose," but with hard work, you "will definitely achieve much more than your self-imposed limits allowed you to think was ever possible."[34] This attitude applies both on and off the tennis court. If Serena plays poorly in a match, she practices for hours the next day, often hitting 2500 serves, backhands, or whatever stroke was causing her difficulty.

Whether in tennis or other arenas, Williams's presence and actions call out the often-hidden and taken-for-granted rules of the systems in place and the stereotypes that are part of those systems. At other times, she deliberately cultivates these stereotypes to make sure that they are acknowledged and addressed. In addition to pointing out limitations, Serena also finds the positive in those limitations, and this attitude grounds her personal sense of agency. She understands that her success allows her a platform, which she uses to encourage others to claim their own agency in whatever way they can in their own lives. Confident about who she is on and off the tennis court, she models what she wishes for others: "I like who I am, I like how I look, and I love representing the beautiful dark women out there. . . . I wouldn't want it any other way. . . . I've never been like anybody else in my life, and I'm not going to start now."[35]

■ REFLECTIONS

1. Williams consistently sees the glass as half full rather than half empty. What does that attitude enable her to do that would not be possible otherwise? Is this strategy more likely to generate change than if she took a more pessimistic stance? Can you think of situations in your own life when you did something similar?
2. One of Williams's primary strategies is making boundaries visible, and she consciously pushes boundaries with her tennis outfits. Look at several of Williams's outfits (https://www.vogue.co.uk/fashion/gallery/serena-williams-tennis-outfits) that are not discussed in the book. How do these

make boundaries visible and reflect her strategies designed to change the system of tennis?

3. Making boundaries visible may illuminate boundaries that are unnecessary, silly, or dysfunctional, but the strategy also can reinforce boundaries by encouraging people to embrace tradition and what is familiar. Does Williams's strategy of making boundaries visible always function positively? Are there ways in which this may lead to an affirmation of boundaries rather than a rejection of them?

4. Williams makes use of affirmations frequently, whether on the soles of the shoes she promotes or in the entries in her journal. What do psychologists and communication scholars say is the effect or impact of self-affirmation? How does it work to change the individual who is making the affirmations?

5. Williams's contributions both on and off the tennis court have been especially striking because of the contrast between the elitism and gentility of tennis and Williams's background. Can you think of something similar in your life where there was a strong contrast between your talent or behavior and the expectations around that activity? How did that affect your perceptions of and performance in that activity?

6. How closely do Williams's change strategies align with the assumptions outlined in the introduction to part 5? Are there any assumptions that you don't believe pertain to her approach to change?

7. In which feminist wave would you place Williams and why?

■ NOTES

[1] Hayley Maitland, "'Tennis is a Small Play in the Whole Scheme of Things': Serena Williams is Just Getting Started," *Vogue*, October 5, 2020, https://www.vogue.co.uk/arts-and-lifestyle/article/serena-williams-interview/

[2] Serena Williams with Daniel Paisner, *On the Line* (New York: Grand Central, 2009), 17.

[3] Williams with Paisner, *On the Line*, 115.

[4] The term *grand slam* is used to refer to the four major tennis events—the Australian Open, the French Open, Wimbledon, and the US Open. Technically, however, the term describes winning all four of those tournaments in a single calendar year. *Career grand slam* refers to a player who wins each of the four major championships in the course of her or his career.

[5] Liz Connor, "Serena Williams on Feminism and Motherhood: There are Barriers I Hope to Break for my Child," *Evening Standard*, August 7, 2017, https://www.standard.co.uk/lifestyle/london-life/serena-williams-on-feminism-and-motherhood-there-are-barriers-i-hope-to-break-a3605476.html/

[6] Cindy Boren, "Serena Williams Will Deliver Message about Women's Power during the Super Bowl," *Washington Post*, January 26, 2019, https://www.washingtonpost.com/sports/2019/01/16/serena-williams-will-deliver-message-about-womens-power-during-super-bowl/

[7] Francesca Gillett, "'I've Had Racist Remarks On and Off the Tennis Court': Serena Williams Makes Passionate Pleas for Equal Pay for Black Women," *Evening Standard*, August 1, 2017, https://www.standard.co.uk/news/world/i-ve-had-racist-remarks-on-and-off-the-tennis-court-serena-williams-makes-passionate-plea-for-equal-pay-for-black-women-a3600896.html/

[8] Vikki Jones, "Serena Williams Talks Tennis Career, Fashion, Business, and Investing," *VMH Magazine*, October 1, 2019, 22.

[9] Boren, "Serena Williams Will Deliver Message."

10. Manuel Zierer, "Nike and Serena Williams Support Equal Rights for Women," Keller Sports, https://www.keller-sports.com/guide/nike-and-serena-williams-support-equal-rights-for-women/
11. Paulina Cachero, "Serena Williams: 5 Fierce Feminists who 'Encourage Me to Do Better,'" Yahoo!Life, July 13, 2018, https://www.yahoo.com/lifestyle/serena-williams-5-fierce-feminists-054800895.html/
12. Cachero, "Serena Williams."
13. Cachero, "Serena Williams."
14. For instance, not until 1950 did the first Black woman tennis champion, Althea Gibson, compete in the US national championship, and she did not compete at Wimbledon until 1957. See David Whelan, "Does Tennis Have a Race Problem?," Vice, June 18, 2015, https://www.vice.com/en/article/pg5njm/does-tennis-have-a-race-problem/
15. "Serena: Comments 'In a Way Bullying,'" ESPN, October 18, 2014, https://www.espn.com/tennis/story/_/id/11726918/serena-williams-responds-russian-tennis-federation-official-comments-supports-suspension/
16. Vinciane Ngomsi, "13 of Serena Williams' Most Memorable Tennis Outfits of All Time," Insider, July 3, 2019, https://www.insider.com/serena-williams-best-outfits-2018-8/
17. Robert C. Smith, *Now You See It, Now You Don't* (Albany, NY: State University of New York Press, 1995), 20; Halie LeSavage, "Serena Williams' Best Tennis Outfits of All Time," *Glamour*, August 22, 2019, https://www.glamour.com/gallery/serena-williams-best-tennis-outfits-of-all-time/
18. Tom Perrotta, "Why You Won't See Any Colorful Characters at Wimbledon," *Wall Street Journal*, July 9, 2015, https://www.wsj.com/articles/why-you-wont-see-any-colorful-characters-at-wimbledon-1436394555/
19. Frances Bridges, "Serena Williams Writes Open Letter About Gender Equality, Empowerment and Resilience," *Forbes*, December 7, 2016, https://www.forbes.com/sites/francesbridges/2016/12/07/serena-williams-writes-open-letter-about-gender-equality-empowerment-and-resilience/?sh=227b39b4307a/
20. Bridges, "Serena Williams Writes Open Letter."
21. Williams with Paisner, *On the Line*, 22–23.
22. Williams with Paisner, *On the Line*, 31.
23. Emily Zauzmer, "Serena Williams Comforts Tearful Naomi Osaka in Viral U.S. Open Moment: 'Let's Not Boo Anymore,'" Yahoo!News, https://www.yahoo.com/news/serena-williams-comforts-tearful-naomi-145843689.html
24. Williams with Paisner, *On the Line*, 184–85.
25. Williams with Paisner, *On the Line*, 20.
26. Williams with Paisner, *On the Line*, 28.
27. Williams with Paisner, *On the Line*, 231.
28. Serena Williams and Common, "Behind the Scenes of Undefeated In-depth: Serena with Common," interview by Brent Lewis, The Undefeated, December 19, 2016, https://theundefeated.com/galleries/behind-the-scenes-of-undefeated-in-depth-serena-with-common/?view=list/
29. Williams and Common, "Behind the Scenes."
30. Jones, "Serena Williams Talks Tennis Career."
31. "Serena Williams' Letter to the Dreamers," Net-A-Porter, December 1, 2017, https://www.net-a-porter.com/en-us/porter/article-588f25bb0cc300bd/incredible-women/incredible-women/serena-williams-letter/
32. Williams and Common, "Behind the Scenes."
33. Zierer, "Nike and Serena Williams."
34. Jeff Haden, "Serena Williams Says These 10 Words are the Most Important Thing She Wants to Teach her Daughter," Inc., January 17, 2018, https://www.inc.com/jeff-haden/serena-williams-says-these-10-words-are-most-important-thing-she-wants-to-teach-her-daughter.html/
35. Maitland, "'Tennis is a Small Play in the Whole Scheme of Things.'"

CHAPTER EIGHTEEN

Amanda Gorman

> *I would say anyone who finds themselves suddenly visible and suddenly famous, think about the big picture. Especially for girls of color, we're treated as lightning or gold in the pan—we're not treated as things that are going to last. You really have to crown yourself with the belief that what I'm about and what I'm here for is way beyond this moment. I'm learning that I am not lightning that strikes once. I am the hurricane that comes every single year, and you can expect to see me again soon.[1]*

Performance poet Amanda Gorman, who found herself "suddenly visible" when she read a poem at the inauguration of President Joe Biden, uses her poetry to create change in unjust and inequitable systems. She and her twin sister were born in 1998 in Los Angeles, California. Raised by a single mother who taught middle-school English, the girls and their older brother were encouraged to read and write. Watching television was discouraged—to watch something, they had to make an argument to their mother that "the show had good politics."[2] After the television broke for the third time, their mother decided not to fix it, observing that her children were "livelier, more creative, when they found ways to entertain themselves."[3]

Gorman's interest in poetry began in the third grade, when her class read the novel *Dandelion Wine* by Ray Bradbury. The book introduced her to the idea of metaphor: "I was like, 'Oh, my goodness. Bradbury just related candy to something completely different.' . . . It was like magic."[4] Her mother's reaction when Amanda told her she wanted to be a writer was "Dear God." She imagined that she would become a "solitary creature" who made very little money and would be "living in her basement [and] eating Cheetos."[5] Her mother became very supportive of this career goal, however, when she saw how serious Gorman was about her writing.

Amanda's poetic aspirations were difficult to achieve because of a speech impediment that affected both her and her sister—they were born early and experienced some developmental delays. Not until the age of twenty was Gorman able to say the *r* sound properly, which meant that she couldn't say words like *poetry* or even her last name. She used to try to eliminate words with *r*'s from her poems and was reluctant to read her poems out loud if they contained this letter, but then she made a decision: "I had a moment of realization where I thought if I choose not to speak out of fear, then there's no one that my silence is standing for. And so I came to realize that I cannot stand standing to the side, standing silent. I must find the strength to speak up."[6]

To overcome her impediment, Amanda started including words in her poems that forced her to practice the *r* sound. She also used flashcards to practice words that contained the letter; listened to orators she admired such as Barack Obama and Martin Luther King Jr.; and practiced the song "Aaron Burr, Sir" from the musical *Hamilton* because it has so many *r*'s in it. Although she saw her speech impediment as a weakness for many years, she came to see it as something positive: "Now I really look at it as a strength because going through that process, it made me a writer, for one, because I had to find a form in which I could communicate other than through my mouth, and two, when I was brave enough to try to take those words from the page onto the stage, I brought with me this understanding of the complexity of sound, pronunciation, emphasis."[7]

Gorman began to be recognized as a poet at the age of sixteen. She started a nonprofit organization, One Pen, One Page, designed to increase literacy by providing reading and writing supplies to under-resourced and underserved students. In that same year, she was selected to serve as the National Youth Poet Laureate of Los Angeles, which led to her being named Youth Poet Laureate of the West. Amanda then applied to be the first US Youth Poet Laureate and was selected for the honor in 2017. During her one-year term in this position, she visited libraries and schools across the country, showing "people that poetry can be anywhere in any space and in any capacity."[8]

Gorman attended Harvard University, where she majored in sociology and graduated *cum laude* in 2020. While in college, she won an OZY Genius Award of $10,000, an award given to students from ten different colleges to help them pursue innovative visions and ideas. She also was selected as one of *Glamour*'s College Women of the Year and was featured in *The Root* magazine's annual "Young Futurist" list of the twenty-five best and brightest young African Americans.

In September 2017, Amanda performed her poem, "In This Place (An American Lyric)" at the Library of Congress to commemorate the inauguration of Tracy K. Smith as poet laureate of the United States. Joe Biden's wife Jill was in the audience, and when her husband, newly elected as president, was looking for a poet to perform at his inauguration, she recommended Gorman. Every time Amanda had written a poem prior to the inauguration, she tried to make it good enough to read at an inauguration, never thinking that she would actually be performing a poem at one: "Every single time I wrote a public poem, before I began writing it, I would tell myself, 'Write a poem that is worthy of a presidential inauguration.' I wanted to hold myself to a high standard."[9] Gorman was halfway done writing her poem for the inauguration, "The Hill We Climb," when a group of rioters stormed the Capitol, and she decided that she needed to address that event in her poem.

> So for me, it was trying to say, we've had this reminder of the ways in which democracy is both fragile and also enduring and how necessary it is to defend it. And I think a lot of times in cultures, we think of the ways in which we can cleanse ourselves with water. I think of the ways that we can cleanse ourselves with words. Meaning that this poem was an opportunity to kind of resanctify, repurify, and reclaim not just the capitol building but American democracy and what it stands for.[10]

Although Amanda had expected to rehearse her poem every day in the week leading up to the inauguration, she was still working on the poem during that week, so she wasn't able to practice performing the poem until the night before. As she explains, "Most of my preparation was stepping into the emotionality of the poem, getting my body and my psyche ready for that moment."[11] She "felt prepared both emotionally and fashionably"[12] for her performance because she wore a ring and earrings given to her by Oprah Winfrey, and the yellow coat she wore acknowledged Jill Biden, who had complimented the yellow outfit Gorman was wearing when Biden first saw her perform. As she does before she performs any of her poems in public, she recited a mantra to herself before taking the stage: "I am the daughter of Black writers. We're descended from freedom fighters who broke their chains and changed the world. They call me."[13]

Amanda's performance of "The Hill We Climb" brought her national attention, and her world turned upside down.

> When I was writing the poem, I knew it was a historic moment, I knew it was an important moment, which is why I wanted to do just service, but I wasn't really paying attention to the ways in which my own personal life might change. So I went, I did my inaugural poem, I walked off and just kind of expected everything to be the same. And then I remember trying to open my Instagram just to, you know, look at other people's posts, and all of my apps have just crashed because all the followers that were just, you know, flocking to my channel. So it's been amazing.[14]

Her poems immediately became popular. Her first book of poetry, *The One for Whom Food Is Not Enough*, had been published prior to the inauguration. Gorman's inauguration poem, "The Hill We Climb," became available in book form shortly after the inauguration, followed by a children's book, *Change Sings: A Children's Anthem*, and *The Hill We Climb and Other Poems*. Amanda is dealing with her newfound fame by "handling it day by day. I'm learning that 'No' is a complete sentence. And I am reminding myself that this isn't a competition. It's me following the trajectory of the life I was meant to lead."[15]

Gorman plans to run for president of the United States in 2036, a plan she often articulates publicly: "What's so funny is that people act like I'm joking. I'm like, I'm dead serious. Why wouldn't I be?"[16] Consequently, Amanda and her sister are very deliberate about their images on social media: "You have to be really conscious about the image that you're putting out into the world—not necessarily that you have to be inauthentic, but you are part of a generation where every single thing you do is going to be documented. So I remember countless times hanging with friends and them taking a selfie and me just not being in it or me removing myself from the situation because I was like, 'Guys, I'm running for president in thirty years!'"[17] Both Gorman's poetry and political ambitions derive from her passion for social change and social justice: "I think that passion comes from my heritage. It comes from a place where I must write. I must speak up because there's been too many people who've been kept from that opportunity."[18]

Definition of Feminism

For Amanda, feminism "is all about breaking our chains collectively."[19] The chains, for her, are chains of oppression and repression. Because she categorizes herself as an intersectional feminist, she seeks to change systems marked both by sexism and racism. She explains that feminism is "about synthesizing our dismantling of both racism and sexism so all genders are rewarded equally in our economy."[20] The result, she envisions, will be "liberty and equality" for all individuals.[21]

Breaking the chains of oppression allows room for new models and ways of doing and being that are not possible under current systems and their rules. In this way, Gorman sees feminists as disrupters growing, as she says in her poem "Incredible," "into an irrefutable, indisputable, beautiful mind, this era's sign / of paradigm shifters."[22] She gives as an example how women leaders use language and develop leadership styles that are different from men: "I tend to notice women leaders more so using a rhetoric of hope, compassion, and fairness. That type of language not only restructures how we think about women leaders, and all the gifts they bring to the table, but also leadership in general, which should be unafraid of empathy and generosity."[23]

The changes Amanda envisions can only be accomplished collectively, with women working together. Feminist change is achieved when women join forces in a tide of "brave-her-y."[24] She asserts, "I close my eyes and I am with this army of young women standing in a line and I imagine us walking forward together. That's what excites me—not the idea that I am in front of them with the mic or a voice for everybody, but rather that I have the great honor of linking arms with other women of this time."[25] The unity among women Gorman envisions, however, must have a specific purpose: "To me, unity without a sense of justice, equality and fairness is just toxic mob mentality. Unity that actually moves us toward the future means that we accept our differences—

we embrace them and we lean into that diversity. It's not linking arms without questioning what we're linking arms for. It's unity with purpose."[26]

Making change collectively also involves empowering other women. "Our lives are most powerful when they lift up girls and women," [27] Amanda observes. At the 2019 Vital Voices Global Leadership Awards highlighting the power of women to transform and inspire, Gorman stated: "Today everyone's eyes are on us as we rise in this hour, it is our fine duty to find the beauty in rooting for other women so they too know that we are not victims we are victors."[28] She sees empowerment as bringing visibility to the most vulnerable and freedom to those who don't have a choice. Individual power is important, she believes, but it multiplies when it is joined with empowered others: "To their own power, every single woman is entitled," Gorman asserts, "but it's how our power empowers others that makes women's voices so vital."[29]

Change Strategies

Amanda seeks to change the sexist and racist systems that pervade US culture in order to make those systems more fair and just. As she explains, "Our goal has never been revenge—just restoration, not domination; just dignity, not fear; just freedom, just justice." She is not deterred by obstacles that might stand in the way of the changes she envisions: "Whether we prevail is determined not by all the challenges that are present but by all the change that is possible."[30] Gorman holds this stance in part because she sees all women as potential change agents: "Close your eyes. Visualize that all of us in this room and outside of these walls or in these halls—all of us change makers."[31] She employs three primary strategies to change the current racist and sexist systems: (1) expanding the platform for change, (2) enacting change, and (3) conjuring hope from negativity.

Expanding Platforms for Change

A primary strategy Amanda uses to change systems of sexism and racism is to expand the venues in which change can occur. When change is seen as potentially happening anywhere, more people have the opportunity to discover the need for change and to become change agents. Poetry is one such place. In contrast to traditional conceptions of poetry as a "dead art form for . . . old white men who just seem like they were born to be old,"[32] Gorman sees poetry as a vehicle or catalyst for change because "it's inherently rebellious in its nature"[33] and is often at the "heartbeat of movements for change."[34] Poetry functions as a major change mechanism because it is "democratic"[35] in that "anyone can enjoy poetry, and it's this openness, this accessibility, of poetry that makes it the language of the people."[36] Poetry is also a catalyst for change because poets "help bring vision to change before it comes" and "craft language for our dreams that are still unnamed."[37] In other words, by articulating "the future we stand for,"[38] poets write "a new world into being."[39] Furthermore, poetry is about asking "charged and challenging questions" and thus "is always at the pulse of the most dangerous and the most daring questions that the nation or a world might face."[40] Amanda also believes that poetry generates change because it connects "the beliefs of the private individual with the cause of change of the public, the population, the polity, the political movement."[41]

Because of Gorman's view of poetry as a vehicle of change, she is irritated when she gets a call from someone who asks her to write a poem about a particular subject but then requests that it not be political. Her response is that such a request "sounds like I have to draw a square but not make it a rectangle or like build a car and not make it a vehicle. It doesn't make much sense because all art is political. The decision to create, the artistic choice to have a voice, the choice to be heard is the most political act of all."[42]

Not only does Amanda see poetry as a venue for change but she also brings poetry into places where it is usually not expected to be. She has delivered poems, for example, on MTV, at the top of the Empire State Building, in front of the Boston Pops orchestra, and at Beautycon and Bach festivals. Gorman also performed a poem at Super Bowl LV to honor three frontline workers chosen as the game's honorary captains. She explains her rationale for introducing poetry into such venues: "And so these are the moments I strive for in my lifetime, which is to bring poetry into the spaces that we least expect it so that we can fully . . . grapple with the ways in which it can heal and . . . resurrect us."[43]

Amanda reinforces her belief that poetry is everywhere when she points out all of the places where poetry resides: "Maybe later you're going to be at a protest and someone's gonna have a poster that says, 'They buried us, but they didn't know we were seeds.' That's poetry. You might be in your US history class, and your teacher may play a video of Martin Luther King Jr. saying we will be able to hew out of this mountain of despair a stone of hope. That's poetry. Or maybe even here in New York City, you're going to go visit the Statue of Liberty, where there's a sonnet that declares, as Americans, 'give us your tired, your poor, your huddled masses yearning to [breathe] free.'"[44] In her poem "In This Place," Gorman names multiple physical spaces where poetry resides, ranging from Copley Square in Boston "where protest chants / tear through the air" to Lake Michigan in Milwaukee and Chicago to Florida to East Texas streets like a nexus of rivers with "cows afloat like mottled buoys."[45] She also recognizes that the internet is now a space where poetry happens: "What's really exciting, especially now with technology and the digital age, is there's a lot of access and exposure that instantly happens when you have spoken word poets who can get millions of views online. You have poets posting their work on Instagram, and that becomes shareable and accessible. So poetry is no longer just siphoned to an exclusive realm, but it really can be by anyone, for anyone."[46]

Enacting Change

Amanda does not want women to think that they have to wait for a particular time or occasion or until circumstances improve in order to begin to act, model, and experience the change they are seeking. Enacting change for her begins in the current moment. "We need no invitation to make change in our cities or communities, in our nations," she explains.[47] Neither do women need the blessing of anyone to proceed: "We don't need permission to make it our mission to make change."[48] She continues: "You will be told that this is not a problem, not your problem, you will be told that now is not the time for change to begin, told that we cannot win."[49] But, she explains, "there is no rehearsal; the time is now, now, now" to enact change.[50] Because of her belief that the first step is to take a step, Gorman does not believe in aspiration: "I don't believe in an aspiring anything. I don't believe in an aspiring writer, an aspiring director. . . . If you want to go do it, go out there and do it. If you want to lead your community, if you want to be a scientist, that's something you can desire to do, but it's also something that you can get started on right now. Don't hesitate, don't wait. . . . 'Don't aspire, achieve!'"[51]

Amanda believes that women must actually become the change they want to see—they must embody and enact it to create change in a system. Change agents must bring "great ideas" out "of the best of ourselves,"[52] which they then must put into practice in the world: "We don't just make change. We become it."[53] Gorman admonishes women to "focus on your purpose and how you, especially as yourself, can break through a barrier,"[54] and she uses a metaphor of a storm to elaborate: "We're not the sand that absorbs the water of the sea. You see, we are the storm—the very form of change that the world has been waiting for."[55] She concluded the poem she performed at the Biden inauguration with this same idea. In that poem, she talked about stepping unafraid into the new dawn, where there is always light "if only we're brave enough to see it / If only we're brave enough to be it.[56]

When women enact the change they envision, they provide new routes and paths for themselves and others to follow. The changes they enact generate opportunities and resources that facilitate change in systems. These do not have to be identified and planned in advance because the act of making a change creates in a system the route for producing it. As Amanda explains, "The way forward isn't a road we take. The road forward is a road that women make."[57] In one of her poems, she uses metaphors to make the same point: "We *can* make mountains as we run . . . we *can* shape the sea as we sail."[58]

Conjuring Hope from Negativity

When Gorman writes a poem, she is less interested in its format or in the specific words it contains than in "an end point, which is a feeling, how do I feel when I read this poem? How do the people around me feel when I share with them?"[59] Hope is the feeling she most often tries to evoke in both herself and others through her poetry. She explains that "it's really easy to write a poem that makes people feel really bad about themselves and the country and the people and the culture and the race," but she believes that poets should "observe that darkness, to listen to it, but also to lead people out of the shade."[60] She gives as an example her poem "The Miracle of Morning," which was triggered because of the news she was hearing at the time: "I was really looking around at the news that I and my family and my community was taking in, and I felt like my world and my country was in a very dark place. And so I decided to try to write this poem as a type of reminder of all the things that we have to be grateful and hopeful for."[61]

Amanda sees hope or optimism as a powerful force for change because it allows people to analyze and reflect on what caused current negative conditions and to use them to imagine future systems that are different. She sees negative conditions and feelings as something that can be transformed into positives. She urges people not to ignore pain but to give it purpose and use it: "For it's our grief that gives us our gratitude, / Shows us how to find hope if we ever lose it."[62] Gorman explains that "optimism shouldn't be seen as opposed to pessimism, but in conversation with it. Your optimism will never be as powerful as it is in that exact moment when you want to give it up. The way we can all be hopeful is to not negate the feelings of fear or doubt, but to ask: What led to this darkness? And what can lead us out of the shadows?"[63] Hope, for Amanda, is not "an end state" but "a struggle, as a journey, as something that you have to continuously fight for"[64]—continuously transforming the darkness into optimism.

Gorman acknowledges that hope is a dangerous emotion for change agents to feel because it allows them to imagine new systems and to have the courage to create them, often in defiance of those who are entrenched in and supported by current systems. Because hope allows individuals to imagine something different and to commit to not repeating the negative conditions they currently are experiencing, anyone who is optimistic automatically becomes a powerful change agent: "you can't stop a dreamer / or knock down a dream."[65]

Amanda's efforts to change oppressive systems assume the form of three primary strategies. She envisions the change process as taking place in unexpected places, and she sees poetry as a dynamic and powerful tool for change. Generating change in these spaces does not require that women have special talents or resources—they simply must enact the desired change without waiting for others to give their approval. As they enact the desired changes, women take the negative and repressive conditions of the old system and transform them into a sense of optimism, which then helps them move forward to envision how systems might be transformed to embody justice and equality. Employing these strategies, women become a threat to the system, a position Gorman herself embraces: "I am a threat: a threat to injustice, to inequality, to ignorance. Anyone who speaks the truth and walks with hope is an obvious and fatal danger to the powers that be. A threat and proud."[66]

■ REFLECTIONS

1. At least two women in this book—Amanda Gorman and Jamie Margolin—would like to become president of the United States. Why might the presidency appeal to young women such as Gorman and Margolin? Does the presidency somehow seem more accessible than it did earlier?
2. Gorman had to overcome a speech impediment, which she did with considerable practice. Is there something in your life that you worked to overcome and managed to do so successfully?
3. Read Gorman's poem, "The Hill We Climb" (https://news.harvard.edu/gazette/story/2021/01/amanda-gormans-inauguration-poem-the-hill-we-climb/), which she read at the inauguration of Joe Biden. In what ways does it embody Gorman's definition of feminism and the strategies she uses to generate change?
4. Gorman's version of feminism requires collective action, with women working together in what she calls "brave-her-y." Do you believe feminism requires collective action, or can it be practiced just as effectively by individuals?
5. Both Gorman and President Barack Obama focus on hope as a force for change. Compare and contrast their two approaches to the use of hope as a rhetorical resource. Which approach do you believe offers a more effective route to change?
6. How closely do Gorman's change strategies align with the assumptions outlined in the introduction to part 5? Are there any assumptions that you don't believe pertain to her approach to change?
7. In which feminist wave would you place Gorman and why?

■ NOTES

[1] Amanda Gorman, "'Unity with Purpose,'" interview by Michelle Obama, *Time*, February 15–22, 2021, 80.
[2] Doreen St. Félix, "The Rise and Rise of Amanda Gorman," *Vogue*, May 2021, https://www.vogue.com/article/amanda-gorman-cover-may-2021/
[3] St. Félix, "The Rise and Rise of Amanda Gorman."
[4] Amanda Gorman, "Amanda Gorman: Meet the First African-American Youth Poet Laureate," interview by Jenna Bush Hager, *Today*, February 9, 2018, 1:44, https://www.youtube.com/watch?v=OuOMApb1qBs/
[5] Amanda Gorman, "Amanda Gorman Talks Poetry, Running for President, and Social Change," interview by Paige Lorentzen, The Paige Show, August 19, 2019, 1:24, https://www.youtube.com/watch?v=ZMQqRnO984Y/
[6] Amanda Gorman, "Using Your Voice is a Political Choice," TEDEd Student Talks, New York, NY, January 20, 2021, 1:38, https://www.youtube.com/watch?v=zaZBgqfEa1E/
[7] Gorman, "'Unity with Purpose,'" 78.
[8] Gorman, "Amanda Gorman Talks Poetry," 3:19.
[9] Amanda Gorman, "Amanda Gorman on Poetry, Beauty and Sudden Fame," YouTube, *Time*, February 4, 2021, 0:19, https://www.youtube.com/watch?v=qloAWjTQiCM/
[10] Amanda Gorman, "Amanda Gorman: 'The Hill We Climb' and Activism Through Poetry," interview by Trevor Noah, YouTube, *The Daily Show with Trevor Noah*, January 27, 2021, 1:58, https://www.youtube.com/watch?v=IRGO5g1rqTw/

11. Gorman, "'Unity with Purpose,'" 76.
12. "Inaugural Poet Goes Viral After Making History at Inauguration," interview by Robin Roberts, YouTube, *Good Morning America*, January 21, 2021, 7:44, https://www.youtube.com/watch?v=aHo3MqnBmZM/
13. Amanda Gorman, "My Mantra," YouTube, Together Live Events, April 29, 2020, 0:14, https://www.youtube.com/watch?v=zFqTHAaVz2A/
14. Gorman, "Amanda Gorman: 'The Hill We Climb' and Activism Through Poetry," 0:49.
15. Gorman, "'Unity with Purpose,'" 80.
16. Amanda Gorman, "Presidential Dreams: Inaugural Poet Amanda Gorman on Her Life as the First Youth Poet Laureate," interview by Jared Bowen, YouTube, GBH, January 21, 2021, 12:47, https://www.youtube.com/watch?v=WppDqkXUyok/
17. Gorman, "Amanda Gorman on Poetry, Beauty and Sudden Fame," 1:37.
18. Gorman, "Amanda Gorman: Meet the First African-American Youth Poet Laureate," 1:10.
19. Amanda Gorman, "The Power of Words to Empower Women: Five Questions to Poet Amanda Gorman," interview by Jean-Christian Agid, Thirty Seven East, September 9, 2020, https://thirtyseveneast.com/2020/09/09/the-power-of-words-to-empower-women/
20. Amanda Gorman, "Today is #BlackWomensEqualPayDay," Instagram, August 22, 2019, https://www.instagram.com/p/B1fCpcwlfiK/
21. Amanda Gorman, "Lift Every Voice," YouTube, Los Angeles Public Library, February 7, 2021, 8:34, https://www.youtube.com/watch?v=min6Q60dWKI/
22. Amanda Gorman, "Incredible," Facebook, Porter, April 30, 2019, https://www.facebook.com/watch/?v=843717849340526/
23. Gorman, "The Power of Words to Empower Women."
24. Gorman, "Incredible."
25. Amanda Gorman, "I close my eyes and I am with this army of young women standing in a line and I imagine us walking forward together," Instagram, August 11, 2019, https://www.instagram.com/p/B1ByjY8FpJq/?utm_source=ig_embed&utm_campaign=loading/
26. Gorman, "'Unity with Purpose,'" 78.
27. Amanda Gorman, "This is everything ♥ raising her fist to my portrait painted by @gaylekabaker for @vitalvoices!," Instagram, March 9, 2020, https://www.instagram.com/p/B9hkc6CFuBZ/
28. "Vital Voices Delivers Calls to Actions for Aspiring Women Leaders on International Women's Day," Vital Voices Global Partnership, March 8, 2021, https://www.prnewswire.com/news-releases/vital-voices-delivers-calls-to-action-for-aspiring-women-leaders-on-international-womens-day-301242394.html
29. Amanda Gorman, "Next," Facebook, Now This, October 19, 2020, 1:37, https://www.facebook.com/NowThisNews/videos/3515998431799865/
30. Amanda Gorman, "Amanda Gorman Reads Her Poem 'Fury and Faith,'" YouTube, Bach Virtuosi Festival, August 16, 2020, 1:08, https://www.youtube.com/watch?v=n9Tco9MiLVc/
31. Amanda Gorman, "24 Hours of Reality: 'Earthrise' by Amanda Gorman," YouTube, December 4, 2018, 3:14, https://www.youtube.com/watch?v=xwOvBv8RLmo/
32. Gorman, "Using Your Voice," 0:27.
33. Gorman, "Amanda Gorman: 'The Hill We Climb' and Activism Through Poetry," 5:58.
34. Gorman, "'Unity with Purpose,'" 76.
35. Gorman, "The Power of Words to Empower Women."
36. Gorman, "Using Your Voice," 2:30.
37. Amanda Gorman, "Happy World Poetry Day!," Instagram, March 22, 2021, https://www.instagram.com/p/CMtLgf0FZjn/?hl=en/
38. Gorman, "'Unity with Purpose,'" 78.
39. Gorman, "Happy World Poetry Day!"
40. Gorman, "Using Your Voice," 5:19.
41. Gorman, "Using Your Voice," 4:19.
42. Gorman, "Using Your Voice," 2:59.
43. Gorman, "Amanda Gorman: 'The Hill We Climb' and Activism Through Poetry," 4:45.
44. Gorman, "Using Your Voice," 4:39.

45 Amanda Gorman, "In This Place (An American Lyric)," Poets.org, n.d., https://poets.org/poem/place-american-lyric/
46 Cortney Clift, "Amanda Gorman is Speaking Out," Brit + Co, January 21, 2021, https://www.brit.co/amanda-gorman-future-women-of-america/
47 Amanda Gorman, "National Youth Poet Laureate Amanda Gorman Performs at the Forbes Women's Summit," YouTube, January 21, 2021, 0:46, https://www.youtube.com/watch?v=ZojzZ-BivEQ/
48 "Sherrie Silver and Amanda Gorman's Spectacular Dance/Poetry Performance," YouTube, April 10, 2019, 0:26, https://www.youtube.com/watch?v=2eJfmvAHUsk/
49 Gorman, "Amanda Gorman Reads Her Poem 'Fury and Faith,'" 0:08.
50 Gorman, "24 Hours of Reality," 2:18.
51 Clift, "Amanda Gorman is Speaking Out."
52 Amanda S. C. Gorman, "Making Mountains as We Run: Amanda Gorman '20: Harvard Inauguration of Lawrence S. Bacow," YouTube, October 5, 2018, 2:11, https://www.youtube.com/watch?v=jdAHu4ozQKc/
53 Sherrie Silver and Amanda Gorman's Spectacular Dance/Poetry Performance," 3:38.
54 Gorman, "Amanda Gorman: Meet the First African-American Youth Poet Laureate," 4:27.
55 Gorman, "National Youth Poet Laureate," 1:23.
56 Amanda Gorman, "Read: Transcript of Amanda Gorman's Inaugural Poem," The Hill, January 20, 2021, https://thehill.com/homenews/news/535052-read-transcript-of-amanda-gormans-inaugural-poem/
57 Gorman, "National Youth Poet Laureate," 1:39.
58 Gorman, "Making Mountains as We Run," 3:59.
59 Gorman, "Presidential Dreams," 2:58.
60 Gorman, "Amanda Gorman on Poetry, Beauty and Sudden Fame," 0:40.
61 Gorman, "Presidential Dreams," 0:17.
62 Amanda Gorman, "The Miracle of Morning," Purse for Change, June 3, 2020, 1:28, https://www.youtube.com/watch?v=IgowcHu-Jfk/
63 Gorman, "'Unity with Purpose,'" 80.
64 Gorman, "Presidential Dreams," 1:16.
65 Gorman, "In This Place."
66 "Amanda Gorman Says She Was Racially Profiled by Security Guard While Walking Home in L.A.," PBS, March 6, 2021, https://www.pbs.org/newshour/nation/amanda-gorman-says-she-was-racially-profiled-near-her-home/

PART
SIX

CREATING AN ALTERNATIVE SYSTEM

Some believe that systems of domination are themselves the problem—and fixing them is impossible. In such cases, change agents see the only option as *creating an alternative system*. Bell hooks argues that the world's problems—"systematic dehumanization, worldwide famine, ecological devastation, industrial contamination, and the possibility of nuclear destruction"[1]—are traceable to interlocking systems of domination that she terms the "white-supremacist capitalist patriarchal society."[2] She sees no hope for the creation of a "just, more humane world"[3] as long as these forms of oppression "remain intact."[4]

In their efforts to create a new system, Sara Ahmed, Leslie Kanes Weisman, Jennifer Armbrust, and Alexandria Ocasio-Cortez strategize from the following assumptions: (1) substantial and sustainable change can be achieved only by creating an entirely new system, (2) limitless possibilities are available for the invention of a new system, and (3) acting in ways consistent with a desired system can bring that system into being.

Assumption 1: Substantial and sustainable change can be achieved only by creating an entirely new system.

When ideologies of domination and oppression are so entrenched and pervasive in systems, some believe they are not worth fixing. Sonia Johnson's description of her alienation from the dominant patriarchal system suggests how utterly foreign a system can seem to members of marginalized groups: "I look out upon the world men have made—their legislatures, courts, churches, schools, art, architecture, their politics, their economics—and I don't see anything I would have done as they have done it. *Not one single thing.* Their system does not reflect me at all, neither my mode of being in the world nor my world view; rather, it is inimical to all I love, all I desire, all I *am.* . . . It is not my home."[5] At the same time that a system can feel foreign in every respect, it also can feel natural because everyone is socialized into it and more often than not takes it for granted. When a system is so pervasive and entrenched, it cannot easily serve as the basis for large-scale transformation.

William Rees, a professor of human ecology, suggests that efforts to reform a system are often ineffective precisely because the system is taken for granted. That system privileges a particular perspective—a perspective each person learns simply by "living, growing up, and being educated in a particular sociocultural milieu."[6] Most people are unaware of how the prevailing paradigm affects virtually everything they do, and thus they do not consider that "there may be more viable alternatives."[7] That the world was flat, for example, functioned as a worldview that was taken for granted for centuries, and only a complete paradigm shift enabled this belief to be overturned.[8] To disrupt existing assumptions and ways of doing things requires revolutionary change—not just a minor modification of what is. As Black feminist Audre Lorde aptly explains, "The master's tools will never dismantle the master's house. They may allow us to temporarily beat him at his own game, but they will never enable us to bring about genuine change."[9]

One effort to invent a new system was triggered by the death of George Floyd in May 2020 in Minneapolis, Minnesota. Arrested on suspicion of paying for cigarettes with a counterfeit bill, Floyd was handcuffed and his neck was pinned to the ground under the knee of Derek Chauvin for more than nine minutes. In response to Floyd's death, members of the Minneapolis city council vowed to dismantle the city's police department because they believed it could not be reformed. City councilor Jeremiah Ellison made this clear when he announced: "We are going to dismantle the Minneapolis Police Department. And when we're done, we're not simply gonna glue it back together. We are going to dramatically rethink how we approach public safety and emergency response."[10] The council was not specific about what a new public safety system for the city would look like, but proposals included shifting money spent on policing to mental health services, education, and housing as well as developing response teams composed of police officers, social workers, and mental health professionals.[11] Members of the city council believed that dismantling the police department was necessary because the excessive use of force by police officers against citizens and systemic racism in the department could not be eliminated in any other way.

Assumption 2: Limitless possibilities are available for the invention of a new system.

Systems are always under construction, so change agents always have the option of creating new systems. In other words, because all systems are invented, they can be invented again. As feminist writer Gloria Anzaldúa suggests: "The life you thought inevitable, unalterable, and fixed in some foundational reality is smoke, a mental construction, fabrication. So, you reason, if it's all made up, you can compose it anew and differently."[12] Because there is no end to the ways ideas and the symbols used to describe ideas can be configured and reconfigured, change agents, at any moment, can "choose a different word, a different metaphor, and a different story, each of which makes available another set of resources and options" and thus another system.[13]

The theory of social construction provides support for the idea that an entirely new system can in fact be created because every system starts the same way—as a linguistic construction.[14] Theoretically, an infinite number of new systems can be invented because language provides an infinite number of ways to think about and frame something. In reality, however, humans create systems of meaning that end up limiting the range of possibilities available for conceptualizing and talking about the things in that world. The options are constrained by the worldviews inherent in a given linguistic system.

The invention of Uber shows how a new system can be created no matter how entrenched an old one might be. Calling a cab is a system known the world over. An individual in need of a ride either arranges for a cab in advance or waits on the street for one to come by. Once the destination is reached, the driver announces the fare, and the customer pays with cash or a credit card and exits the cab. This procedure is so familiar, established, and ubiquitous that it is difficult to imagine another system that might replace it. But on a winter evening in Paris in 2008, Travis Kalanick and Garrett Camp—friends attending a tech conference—did just that. Unable to find a cab, they started talking about how nice it would be if they could call a cab using an app on their phones. The idea lay dormant until 2009, when they started a company called *UberCab* (later changed to *Uber*).[15] They developed an app to order a ride by phone, with the ride automatically charged to a credit card on file. Not only does the ride come quickly, but there is no fussing over payment before leaving the car. Kalanick and Camp imagined an alternative to taxi cabs that transformed the transportation industry.

Assumption 3: Acting in ways consistent with a desired system can bring that system into being.

Often overlooked in efforts to bring a new system into being is the possibility of enacting the desired new system—to actually live as if it were already in place. Sonia Johnson's "live the way you want the world to be"[16] and Gandhi's "be the change you want to see in the world"[17] both reference enactment as a strategy. With enactment, individuals behave as if the system has already been transformed; they live in the present as though the system they want is already realized: "We *do now* what we want to be doing in the future, we *be* now, *feel now* how we thought we would be and feel only in some future time."[18] According to this assumption, the way to get to a future world in which women are not afraid, for example, is for women to be unafraid now; to create a peaceful world requires that individuals be peaceful now.

Bell hooks is one of many feminists who have theorized the strategy of enactment. She describes it as the "lived practice of interaction"—the process of making one's life "a living example of one's politics."[19] When feminists begin to live differently in the world, they communicate their commitments to others and demonstrate that a new and different kind of system is possible. Feminists who decide to engage in enactment, for example, might stop participating in dominating practices and interact in ways that embody the values they wish to foster—values such as self-determination, nondomination, cooperation, respect, and fairness.[20]

East Central Ministries (ECM), a community development organization in the international district in Albuquerque, New Mexico, exemplifies the strategy of enactment.[21] Against the backdrop of this under-resourced section of town (which used to be called the *war zone*), ECM chooses to enact development efforts that value rather than dismiss community members. In contrast to how under-resourced individuals are often viewed in development efforts—as suspect and in need of help if not disciplining and policing—ECM assumes that each member of the community is trustworthy. The doors to the office are left open even when it is unstaffed, no space is off bounds to anyone, and keys to the car are given to any volunteer to make deliveries or bank deposits. ECM enacts the kind of community it desires and thus brings it into being—a system in which its members are seen as valued, contributing, and trusted members of the community.

■ NOTES

[1] bell hooks, *Talking Back: Thinking Feminist, Thinking Black,* 2nd ed. (New York: Routledge, 2015), 19.
[2] hooks, *Talking Back,* 20.
[3] bell hooks, *Outlaw Culture: Resisting Representations* (New York: Routledge, 1994), 6.
[4] hooks, *Talking Back,* 22.
[5] Sonia Johnson, *Wildfire: Igniting the She/Volution* (Albuquerque, NM: Wildfire, 1969), 87.
[6] William E. Rees, "Achieving Sustainability: Reform or Transformation?," *Journal of Planning Literature* 9 (May 1995): 344.
[7] Rees, "Achieving Sustainability," 344.
[8] Thomas S. Kuhn, *The Structure of Scientific Revolutions,* 50th anniversary ed. (Chicago, IL: University of Chicago Press, 2012).
[9] Audre Lorde, "The Master's Tools Will Never Dismantle the Master's House," in *Sister Outsider: Essays and Speeches,* by Audre Lorde (Berkeley, CA: Crossing, 2007), 104.
[10] Oliver Milman, "Minneapolis Pledges to Dismantle Its Police Department—How Will It Work?," *The Guardian,* June 8, 2020, https://www.theguardian.com/us-news/2020/jun/08/minneapolis-city-council-police-department-dismantle/
[11] Dionne Searcey, "What Would Efforts to Defund or Disband Police Departments Really Mean?," *New York Times,* June 8, 2020, https://www.nytimes.com/2020/06/08/us/what-does-defund-police-mean.html?action=click&module=RelatedLinks&pgtype=Article/
[12] Gloria Anzaldúa, "Now Let Us Shift . . . the Path of Conocimiento . . . Inner Work, Public Acts," in *This Bridge We Call Home: Radical Visions for Transformation,* ed. Gloria Anzaldúa and Analouise Keating (New York: Routledge, 2002), 558.
[13] Sonja K. Foss and Karen A. Foss, "Constricted and Constructed Potentiality: An Inquiry Into Paradigms of Change," *Western Journal of Communication* 75 (2011): 213.
[14] Peter L. Berger and Thomas Luckmann, *The Social Construction of Reality: A Treatise in the Sociology of Knowledge* (New York: Doubleday, 1966).

[15] Dan Blystone, "The Story of Uber," Investopedia, June 25, 2019, https://www.investopedia.com/articles/personal-finance/111015/story-uber.asp/
[16] Johnson, *Wildfire*, 251.
[17] Mahatma Gandhi, *Mahatma Gandhi: Inspiring Thoughts*, comp. by M. Johri (Delhi, India: Rajpal, 2009), 98.
[18] Johnson, *Wildfire*, 39.
[19] bell hooks, *Teaching to Transgress: Education as the Practice of Freedom* (New York: Routledge, 1994), 48.
[20] hooks, *Teaching to Transgress*, 108–09.
[21] Sarah De Los Santos Upton, "Practicing Invitational Rhetoric: East Central Ministries' Approach to Community Development," in *Inviting Understanding: A Portrait of Invitational Rhetoric*, ed. Sonja K. Foss and Cindy L. Griffin (Lanham, MD: Rowman & Littlefield, 2020), 207.

CHAPTER
NINETEEN

Sara Ahmed

What do you hear when you hear the word feminism? It is a word that fills me with hope, with energy. It brings to mind loud acts of refusal and rebellion as well as the quiet ways we might have of not holding on to things that diminish us. It brings to mind women who have stood up, spoken back, risked lives, homes, relationships in the struggle for more bearable worlds.[1]

Feminist scholar and activist Sara Ahmed is interested in how feminists become feminists and willingly "get into trouble"[2] in order to create an alternative feminist world. Ahmed was born in 1969 in Salford, England, one of three daughters of a Pakistani father and an English mother. Her parents met when her father pursued postgraduate medical training in England. The family emigrated to Adelaide, Australia, in 1974, when her father secured a position as a physician there.

Sara remembers not being able to "positively address"[3] how she was different growing up. She was "very aware of not being white, not being like 'the others.'"[4] Ahmed recalls an incident when, walking with her father, she encountered friends from school and tried "to walk as far away as possible" from him in the hopes of passing for white.[5] Objects in the family home literally contrasted the whiteness of her English heritage with the color of her Pakistani one—Christmas cards from England brought images of white snow, "memories of cold white days,"[6] and relatives with white faces, while the items that arrived in the mail from Pakistan were colorful, whether spices or photos of weddings with women wearing bright red dresses. Although Sara has said that "I do not feel like a real or proper white or black person,"[7] she now identifies as Black, in part because Black feminists in British universities created a community in which she feels "more at home" and because of the influence of Black US feminists such as Audre Lorde and bell hooks.[8] Her identification as a Black feminist is "self-consciously political and affirmative," although, as she explains, it is "not without its hesitations and uncertainties."[9]

Ahmed earned her BA in English, philosophy, and history from the University of Adelaide in 1989 and a BA in English with honours (similar to a master's degree) from the same university in 1990. She completed her doctorate at the Centre for Critical and Cultural Theory at Cardiff University in Cardiff, England, in 1995. Sara's first academic appointment was at Lancaster University in Lancaster, England, where she served as lecturer (1994–2001), senior lecturer (2001–2002), and reader in women's studies (2002–2003). Between 1998 and 2003, she also served as acting director, codirector, and director of women's studies at Lancaster University. In 2005, Ahmed moved to Goldsmiths College at the University of London to assume a position as professor of race and cultural studies, where she directed the Centre for Feminist Research from 2013 to 2016. At the end of 2016, she resigned her position at Goldsmiths College to protest the institution's handling of sexual harassment, and she is now an independent scholar, writer, and speaker.

A prolific writer, Sara's single-authored books include *Differences that Matter* (1998), *Strange Encounters* (2000), *The Cultural Politics of Emotion* (2004), *Queer Phenomenology* (2006), *The Promise of Happiness* (2010), *On Being Included* (2012), *Willful Subjects* (2014), *Living a Feminist Life* (2017), *What's the Use? On the Uses of Use* (2019), and *Complaint!* (2021). She is the coeditor of *Transformations: Thinking Through Feminism* (2000) with Jane Kilby, Celia Lury, Maureen McNeil, and Beverley Skeggs; *Thinking Through the Skin* (2001) with Jackie Stacey; and *Uprootings/Regroundings: Questions of Home and Migration* (2003) with Claudia Castañeda, Anne-Marie Fortier, and Mimi Shelier.

Interested in the "ways in which words and objects are put together as world-making devices,"[10] Ahmed typically engages with an object, emotion, or representation—the home, happiness, or the idea of a stranger, for example—to understand how race and gender come into being and function to both uphold and challenge existing systems. She wants to demonstrate how these concepts can deliberately be accessed to create a different world. In 2013, she started a blog, feministkilljoys.com, as a vehicle for exploring feminist worldmaking. Sara chose the term *feminist killjoy* because the killjoy's function—pointing out moments of sexism, racism, and other instances of injustice—is, she explains, "what I do. It is how I think. It is my philosophy and my politics."[11]

Definition of Feminism

Ahmed's definition of feminism centers on a recognition of the evolving nature of the term. For her, *feminism* is not a singular category with "identifiable boundaries and a consistent set of ideas." Rather, feminism has "mobilised different women in different times and places, . . . who are not necessarily seeking the same thing, nor even necessarily responding to the same situation."[12] A definition that captures the many iterations of feminism for Sara is "a history of causing disturbance."[13] Feminism seeks to disturb the world as it is—to encourage individuals to learn "to see the world as something that does not have to be."[14] Nascent feminists move from their starting point—taking the world for granted—to profound disbelief that the world is the way it is. Feminism "calls into question the way in which the world is organized" and seeks to "engender new ways and forms of living"[15] that involve "more egalitarian distributions of power and resources."[16]

Gender is at the core of Ahmed's feminist politics. Gender is the process by which bodies become "identified and materialized as sexed";[17] it is "a bodily orientation, a way in which bodies get directed by their actions over time."[18] Feminism is about debating "*better* ways of understanding how gender relations operate, and how those relations can be challenged more effectively,"[19] which requires feminists to examine critically the ways the world is as a first step in transforming it into something new. This feminist critical gaze is not simply directed externally at the larger world but at feminism itself. Nothing can be taken for granted—not gender, not how the world is, not even feminism as a political movement. Sara insists that feminists continually need to ask why feminism takes the forms it does and whether those forms are moving feminism forward and accomplishing its aims.[20]

Ahmed identifies as lesbian, an identity realized in a "dramatic redirection" in the middle of her life: "I left the 'world' of heterosexuality" even though it "also meant leaving the well-trodden paths."[21] Sara sees lesbian feminists as ideal feminists because they constitute a threat even in their most ordinary, everyday actions. She calls lesbianism "willful carpentry"[22] because lesbian feminists make room for new rooms that do not yet exist. Ahmed considers transfeminism the current equivalent of lesbian feminism in its capacity to disrupt both the world that is and feminism itself: "I would suggest that it is transfeminism today that most recalls the militant spirit of lesbian feminism" by "showing not only how the sex-gender system is coercive, how it restricts what and who can be, but how creativity comes from how we survive a system that we cannot dismantle by the force of our will alone."[23]

Change Strategies

To introduce her change strategies, Sara asks, "What kind of world are we building?" Her strategies are directed at creating a feminist world, which she envisions as a do-it-yourself project, a "form of self-assembly."[24] Because she sees feminism as a DIY endeavor, Ahmed offers a progression of strategies designed to prepare budding feminists for what to expect as they begin to build a feminist world. Her strategies proceed through three stages of feminist consciousness: (1) recognizing a problem, (2) becoming a problem, and (3) enacting willfulness.

Recognizing a Problem

Sara's initial strategy on the path to a feminist life involves recognizing that there is a problem with how the world is. This recognition is a first step toward feminist consciousness and toward creating a system in which feminists can thrive. A common starting point for feminist transformation is discomfort with the existing gendered system: "You sense that something is wrong or you have a feeling of being wronged. You sense an injustice. You might not have used that word for it; you might not have the words for it; you might not be able to put your finger on it."[25] Ahmed identifies three indicators—sweaty concepts, misalignment, and happiness—that provide individuals with clues about their lack of fit with the world as presently organized.

A sweaty concept emerges from a body that is not at home in the world. It is a concept that comes from strain or from an experience that is "trying."[26] According to Sara, that the world doesn't make sense is a sweaty concept that requires ongoing effort on the part of an incipient feminist to determine exactly what is troubling and why. It involves trying to describe something "that is difficult, that resists being fully comprehended in the present."[27] The point, however, is to "stay with the difficulty, to keep exploring and exposing this difficulty"[28] in the hopes of eventually coming to terms with why the world is causing discomfort.

Pondering sweaty concepts leads to a recognition of misalignment. Individuals in the process of becoming feminists and creating feminist systems realize they are misaligned with the world because they do not go along or fall in line with the way the world is structured. Instead of going along with things and fulfilling the investments others have made in them—by following a particular career path, marrying, or having children, for example[29]—emerging feminists choose misalignment. They decide not to comply "with the order of things."[30] They refuse to go along with the way things are supposed to be and instead choose their own sources of and routes to happiness.

Happiness, another of Ahmed's clues about the true nature of the world, provides budding feminists with contrast between what should make them happy and what actually does. She explains that the world insists on directing individuals "toward those things that would or should" make them happy,[31] and Sara remembers her childhood as "full of the attempt to use happiness to stop us talking about difficult things."[32] But emerging feminists realize they will not be "made happy by the right things."[33] They choose instead to reject the typical paths to happiness and to take their chances by making their own choices—choosing to be happy as a lesbian, remaining childfree, or not attending college, for example. Happiness, then, is a rejection of prescriptive expectations imposed from the outside in favor of making choices that work for one's own life. Rebelling against the "shoulds" of happiness lets a feminist know she is heading down the right path.

Becoming a Problem

When emerging feminists fail to align themselves with the world as it is and instead choose their own means of happiness, they become a problem by causing problems for others. Becoming a problem, another one of Ahmed's change strategies, occurs when newly aware feminists cause tension by saying or doing things that put others on edge. They disrupt the flow of everyday life by calling attention to the inequities of the world, thereby creating unhappiness for others. They then become responsible for that unhappiness because were it not for them speaking up, the system would continue to function just fine: "To become feminist is to cause a problem for oneself by making oneself one's own cause."[34]

Sara identifies numerous nonverbal, verbal, and institutional maneuvers that are used to show feminists that they—and not the problems they point out—are the problem. Eye rolling and nodding are two of the nonverbal behaviors used to stifle feminist activity. When feminists make statements that call attention to a sexist/racist remark or to an injustice of some kind, those around them roll their eyes as if to say "oh, here she goes."[35] When those around a feminist nod, it is another nonverbal indicator that a feminist is becoming a problem. The act of nodding gives feminists the feeling that they are being heard and are getting somewhere with a complaint, but the sympathetic nod is given on the condition that feminists not take their complaints any further. In the end, "to be left with a sense you are getting somewhere is how you end up not getting anywhere. . . . Over time, nods wear out."[36]

The nonverbal devices Ahmed identifies often are accompanied by a verbal tool that she calls *overing*, which occurs when a feminist is asked to "get over" or "'get beyond'" some injustice having to do with gender or race "as if the categories themselves are the blockage points."[37] Again, feminists themselves become the problem because "what stops it from being over is that [they] are not over it."[38] All of these tactics preserve the illusion that without feminists continually pointing out the injustices of the world, all would be well.

Sara also names various institutional maneuvers that make feminist themselves the problem. Among the most prominent are various forms of strategic inefficiency, which function to silence complaints.[39] Intentional slowness is a common form of strategic inefficiency. When a complaint takes months to be addressed, followed by more months of requests for additional information and additional meetings, the intent is to tire the complainant out—to ensure that an accusation is not pursued further. Bumbling along is another form of strategic inefficiency. It occurs when those in charge of hearing a complaint act incompetently—failing to take notes of the meeting or losing the notes—so there is no record of the complaint, and the complaint cannot go forward. Institutional venting is another strategy designed to contain a complaint. With this strategy, the complaint is allowed to be expressed, perhaps in a conversation with administrators or in a public hearing of some kind. Designed to give the appearance of taking a complaint seriously, venting is, in fact, a "technique of preventing something more explosive from happening." Once feminists have been allowed to vent and "have got complaint out of *their* system, the complaint is out of *the* system."[40]

Diversity work itself can become an institutional action that inhibits the achievement of diversity goals. Writing good documents about diversity replaces action, and the organization is "judged as good *because of the document.*" A good diversity document produces a good feeling about diversity that suggests an organization is "doing enough, or doing well enough, or even that there is nothing left to do."[41] The document "does" race, gender, diversity, or equality for the organization and thus produces the appearance that the problem has been solved when, in fact, nothing has been done at all.

According to Ahmed, all of these nonverbal, verbal, and institutional responses to feminist observations and complaints divert attention from a perceived injustice, preserve the status quo, and make feminists who speak up the problem: "Oh the frustration of being found frustrating! Oh the difficulty of being assumed to be difficult! You might even begin to *sound like* what they hear you as *being like*: you talk louder and faster as you can tell you are not getting through."[42] Sara believes that feminists need to be aware of the range and number of tactics that can be used against them in order to be prepared for and able to counter these strategies.

Becoming a problem ends with a snap. A snap signals the end of one era and the beginning of another because, by means of a snap, everything falls into place. Things that had been obscured or were confusing begin to make sense. Feminists are no longer willing to endure the "situation that should not be patiently endured."[43] Ahmed describes the strategy of snapping as "the basis of a feminist revolt, a revolt against what women are asked to put up with; a revolt that breaks things, that breaks things up."[44] Feminist history can be considered "a history of snappy women" because it is the history of women infected "with a desire to speak in ways other than how [they] have been commanded to speak."[45] Feminist snap is about acquiring the "tendencies" necessary to break damaging ties and "invest in new possibilities" for individuals and systems.[46]

Enacting Willfulness

For the feminist who has snapped, willfulness becomes a primary strategy. Sara defines *willfulness* as audacity—a standing against or an embodied vitality. It is the "very potential to deviate from well-trodden paths, to wander, to err, to stray."[47] Feminists are often called *willful*, so in one sense, this strategy simply means living up to the judgments that have already been applied to them. But feminists also can be willful when they are actually being just the opposite—when they are unwilling to go along with sexist/racist culture, refusing to "adjust to an unjust world."[48] Thus, feminists are willful both when they refuse to go along with a dominant system and when they choose to go their own ways.

The feminist killjoy is the trope Ahmed chooses to symbolize the feminist in action as she navigates the strategic stages of feminist evolution and arrives to live willfully in a world of her own creation.[49] The killjoy figure is apt because "to become feminist is to kill other people's joy; to get in the way of other people's investments."[50] Killjoys enact the misalignment that creates feminist awakening and are willing to cause unhappiness in order to imagine and create new pathways and possibilities. There is no single way to be a feminist killjoy. Instead, each killjoy enacts feminist politics in her own way, and this feminist praxis is captured in Sara's killjoy personal survival kit, which consists of the reading list, tools, and names of individuals that comprise her personal killjoy community.[51]

The set of strategies that results in the emergence of the feminist killjoy comprehensively addresses the evolution of the feminist from the first sweaty concepts that signal something is troublesome to becoming a problem to choosing to live a willful feminist life. In offering a blueprint or steps for how to enact a feminist world, Ahmed recognizes that the evolution is not necessarily easy, but it is a process that is worthwhile and life changing: "Someone says something you consider problematic. At first you try not to say anything. But they keep saying something. So maybe you respond, carefully, perhaps. You say why you think what they have said is problematic. You might be speaking quietly, but you are beginning to feel wound up, . . . The feminist killjoy appears here: when she speaks, she seems wound up. I appear here. This is my history: wound up."[52]

■ REFLECTIONS

1. Ahmed is interested in how feminists become feminists—the journey that involves finding the world somehow problematic and negotiating that to a feminist outcome. If you are a feminist, describe your feminist journey. If not, interview someone who is. Does the journey follow the pathway Ahmed outlines?

2. Ahmed does not consider herself to be either Black or white (but she has chosen to identify as Black), just as Padma Lakshmi does not see herself as fully American or fully Indian. Are there advantages and/or disadvantages to holding a liminal position between two or more identity categories?

3. Ahmed chose to leave her academic position to protest the institution's handling of sexual harassment. How effective is it to protest in this way? Do you know of other instances when individuals resigned from institutions as a way to generate change? What was the result?

4. Ahmed's definition of feminism is "a history of causing disturbance." What do you most want feminism to disturb or disrupt?

5. Have you encountered instances when an institution or system supposedly implemented changes but then somehow subverted those changes so they couldn't really take effect? Describe what happened. Were actual changes ever implemented?

6. How closely do Ahmed's change strategies align with the assumptions outlined in the introduction to part 6? Are there any assumptions that you don't believe pertain to her approach to change?
7. In which feminist wave would you place Ahmed and why?

■ Notes

[1] Sara Ahmed, *Living a Feminist Life* (Durham, NC: Duke University Press, 2017), 1.
[2] Sara Ahmed, "Being in Trouble: In the Company of Judith Butler," *Lambda Nordica* 2 (2015): 185.
[3] Sara Ahmed, "'It's a Sun-Tan, Isn't It?': Autobiography as an Identifactory Practice," in *Black British Feminism: A Reader* (London, UK: Routledge, 1997), 155.
[4] Ahmed, "'It's a Sun-Tan,'" 154.
[5] Ahmed, "'It's a Sun-Tan,'" 155.
[6] Sara Ahmed, *Queer Phenomenology: Orientations, Objects, Others* (Durham, NC: Duke University Press, 2006), 147.
[7] Sara Ahmed, "'She'll Wake Up One of These Days and Find She's Turned into a Nigger': Passing through Hybridity," *Theory, Culture & Society* 16 (1999): 96.
[8] Sara Ahmed, "Feminist Politics: An Interview with Sara Ahmed," interview by Salla Tuori and Salla Peltonen, *NORA—Nordic Journal of Women's Studies* 15 (2007): 259.
[9] Ahmed, "'It's a Sun-Tan,'" 165.
[10] Ahmed, "Feminist Politics," 260.
[11] Sara Ahmed, "About," Feministkilljoys, n.d., https://feministkilljoys.com/2018/12/20/
[12] Sara Ahmed, Jane Kilby, Celia Lury, Maureen McNeil, and Beverly Skeggs, "Introduction: Thinking Through Feminism," in *Transformations: Thinking Through Feminism*, ed. Sara Ahmed, Jane Kilby, Celia Lury, Maureen McNeil, and Beverly Skeggs (London, UK: Routledge, 2000), 11.
[13] Sara Ahmed, "Creating Disturbance: Feminism, Happiness and Affective Differences," in *Working with Affect in Feminist Readings: Disturbing Differences*, ed. Marianne Liljeström and Susanna Paasonen (London, UK: Routledge, 2010), 39.
[14] Sara Ahmed, *The Cultural Politics of Emotion*, 2nd ed. (London, UK: Routledge, 2015), 180.
[15] Sara Ahmed, "This Other and Other Others," *Economy and Society* 31 (2002): 558–59.
[16] Sara Ahmed, "Beyond Humanism and Postmodernism: Theorizing a Feminist Practice," *Hypatia* 11 (1996): 79.
[17] Sara Ahmed, "Deconstruction and Law's Other: Towards a Feminist Theory of Embodied Legal Rights," *Social and Legal Studies* 4 (1995): 58.
[18] Ahmed, *Queer Phenomenology*, 60.
[19] Sara Ahmed, *Differences that Matter: Feminist Theory and Postmodernism* (Cambridge, UK: Cambridge University Press, 1998), 18.
[20] Sara Ahmed, "Feminist Futures," in *A Concise Companion to Feminist Theory*, ed. Mary Eagleton (Malden, MA: Blackwell, 2003), 250.
[21] Ahmed, *Queer Phenomenology*, 19. One of the paths that Ahmed left behind was her relationship with her father, who ended contact with Ahmed after she came out as lesbian. See Sara Ahmed, "Mixed Orientations," *Subjectivity* 7 (2014): 106.
[22] Ahmed, *Living a Feminist Life*, 232.
[23] Ahmed, *Living a Feminist Life*, 227.
[24] Ahmed, *Living a Feminist Life*, 27.
[25] Ahmed, *Living a Feminist Life*, 22.
[26] Ahmed, *Living a Feminist Life*, 13.
[27] Ahmed, *Living a Feminist Life*, 12.
[28] Ahmed, *Living a Feminist Life*, 13.
[29] Ahmed, *Queer Phenomenology*, 15.
[30] Ahmed, *Living a Feminist Life*, 56.

[31] Ahmed, *Living a Feminist Life*, 49.
[32] Sara Ahmed, "Affect/Emotion: Orientation Matters: A Conversation Between Sigrid Schmitz and Sara Ahmed," interview by Sigrid Schmitz, *Budrich Journals* 2 (2014): 102.
[33] Ahmed, *Living a Feminist Life*, 53.
[34] Ahmed, *Living a Feminist Life*, 74.
[35] Ahmed, *Living a Feminist Life*, 99.
[36] Sara Ahmed, "Nodding as a Non-Performative," Feministkilljoys, April 29, 2019, https://feministkilljoys.com/2019/04/29/nodding-as-a-non-performative/
[37] Sara Ahmed, *On Being Included: Racism and Diversity in Institutional Life* (Durham, NC: Duke University Press, 2012), 180.
[38] Ahmed, *Living a Feminist Life*, 155.
[39] Sara Ahmed, "Strategic Inefficiency," Feministkilljoys, December 20, 2018, https://feministkilljoys.com/2018/12/20/strategic-inefficiency/
[40] Sara Ahmed, "Nodding as a Non-Performative."
[41] Sara Ahmed, "Equality Credentials," Feministkilljoys, June 10, 2016, https://feministkilljoys.com/2016/06/
[42] Sara Ahmed, *Willful Subjects* (Durham, NC: Duke University Press, 2014), 154.
[43] Ahmed, *Living a Feminist Life*, 211.
[44] Ahmed, *Living a Feminist Life*, 210. For an example of Ahmed's notion of snap used as the basis for a feminist analysis, see Matthew Salzano, "Lemons or Lemonade? Beyoncé, Killjoy Style, and Neoliberalism," *Women's Studies in Communication* 43 (2020): 45–66.
[45] Ahmed, *Living a Feminist Life*, 191.
[46] Ahmed, *Living a Feminist Life*, 162.
[47] Sara Ahmed, "Willful Parts: Problem Characters or the Problem of Character," *New Literary History* 42 (2011): 249.
[48] Ahmed, *Living a Feminist Life*, 84.
[49] Sara Ahmed, *The Promise of Happiness* (Durham, NC: Duke University Press, 2010), 50–88.
[50] Ahmed, *Living a Feminist Life*, 65.
[51] Ahmed's feminist survival kit and feminist manifesto are described at the end of *Living a Feminist Life*, 235–68.
[52] Ahmed, *Living a Feminist Life*, 37.

CHAPTER TWENTY

Leslie Kanes Weisman

> *My feminist and activist consciousness may have begun with my involvement in social change movements, but over the years that consciousness has been transformed into a way of being and behaving in the world; into a set of ethics and values that permeate everything I do, every interaction I have with every person, whether it's a student or a colleague or someone who's bagging groceries at the grocery store.... One "wears" a feminist/activist perspective almost like a pair of glasses, like corrective lenses through which one sees and understands the world.*[1]

Leslie Kanes Weisman, a feminist architect, educator, and activist, has dedicated herself to "defining and solving the social problems that plague society through socially responsible architectural education and community activism."[2] She wants to demonstrate that transforming the practice of architecture can lead to the creation of alternative systems in the form of more livable and sustainable environments. Weisman was born in 1945 in Detroit, Michigan; her father was an attorney and her mother a housewife.

Her parents encouraged Leslie and her younger sister to be concerned about the racial divide between Blacks and whites in Detroit: "I became exposed to social justice issues at a very early age.... I was very fortunate to have progressive parents who not only encouraged me to look at the horrible consequences of racism but took pride in my participation in anti-racism demonstrations.... And because my family is Jewish, my childhood awareness of anti-Semitism probably fostered an ability to empathize with other victims of discrimination."[3] In the late 1960s, Weisman discovered "another 'ism'"—the women's movement—which "raised my consciousness about the pervasive sexism that defined and limited women's lives and aspirations."[4]

Leslie attended Michigan State University in Lansing, Michigan, as a pre-veterinary medicine major. When she realized her interests lay elsewhere, she transferred to Wayne State University in Detroit, Michigan, earning a BFA with a major in interior architecture in 1967 and an MA in urban studies in 1973. In 1968, Weisman took a part-time teaching position in the School of Architecture at the University of Detroit, an all-male, Jesuit university; the secretary was the only other woman in the entire building. The position became tenure track in her second year, and Leslie held the position until 1975, when she became an associate professor and founding member of a new school of architecture at the Newark College of Engineering (later renamed the *New Jersey Institute of Technology*).[5] She moved up through the academic ranks to become a full professor and an associate dean at the New Jersey Institute. Although she did not intend to have primarily an academic career, Weisman found she loved teaching, so she did not pursue an architecture practice "other than through pro-bono services" that she and her students provided through her service-learning courses: "I quickly found out that for me, finding ways to use design thinking and processes to foster the unique creative potential in each of my students was as important, or perhaps even more important, than teaching 'architecture.'"[6]

Leslie's career has been devoted to revealing how architecture is "a social system that has historically functioned to contain, control, or exclude women,"[7] and she has written two books that explore this theme. *Discrimination by Design: A Feminist Critique of the Man-Made Environment*, published in 1992, was selected as one of the best academic books of 1993. It is an analysis of how feminism challenges and changes "the forms and values encoded in the man-made . . . environment, thereby fostering the transformation of the sexist and racist conditions that define our lives."[8] Weisman also coedited (with Diana Agrest and Patricia Conway) *The Sex of Architecture*, published in 1996. In this book, women architects, historians, and urban planners examine "some long-suspect 'truths': that man builds and woman inhabits; that man is outside and woman is inside; that man is public and woman is private; that nature, in both its kindest and its cruelest aspects, is female and culture, the ultimate triumph over nature, is male."[9] This volume was recognized with an American Institute of Architects award for excellence in design theory in 1997. Leslie also has published over fifty articles, book chapters, book reviews, and scholarly papers and has lectured at universities throughout North America, South America, Great Britain, Europe, and Australia. She has received numerous awards for public service and teaching excellence, including the National Creative Achievement Award from the Association of Collegiate Schools of Architecture for her work in multiculturalism and service learning.

Weisman has pursued various projects in the course of her academic career that have allowed her to continue her activism within the field of architecture. In 1974, she was invited to a conference for women architects and educators organized by feminist graduate students in architecture at Washington University in St. Louis, Missouri. After one of the conference programs, Leslie and several other women went out for drinks, and they "just couldn't stop talking!"[10] Because the women appreciated being able to talk about their shared experiences as women in architecture, Weisman suggested that "what we really need is a School of our own, an environment in which we can freely explore how the teaching and practice of architecture can be transformed to embody the political values that we hold as feminists."[11]

With six others from the conference, Leslie cofounded the Women's School of Planning and Architecture (WSPA) in 1975.[12] The WSPA was a two-week intellectual summer camp for women in architecture. Limited to fifty women each summer, the school was held in different geographic locations to encourage participation by architects from various parts of the country: St. Joseph's College in Biddeford, Maine (1975); Stephenson College in Santa Cruz, California (1976); Roger Williams College in Bristol, Rhode Island (1978); and Regis College in Denver, Colorado (1979).[13] Two primary questions were at the heart of the sessions: how to transform traditional architectural education and practice to make it welcoming to women and how women experience buildings and places differently from men.[14] Sessions were organized around six core courses that overlapped with at least one other core course so participants had some exposure to the entire curriculum.

Recognizing that "there was a different dynamic among women when men were present," the WSPA was a course of study for women only, designed to offer both "recreation" and "re-creation'" in an environment "in which women could truly be themselves without gender roles playing a part."[15] The "temporary separatism" the camp provided was designed to enhance "personal empowerment and professional confidence in the 'real world'" to which the women returned after each session.[16] Traditional boundaries between student and teacher were replaced with a mutual learning environment in which the "experiences and expertise" of every participant were valued.[17] The WSPA spawned several spin-offs, including a women's development corporation, women in architecture courses at many institutions, and many all-female architecture firms.

In 1987, Weisman and Katrin Adam, another cofounder of the Women's School of Planning and Architecture, created a second women's program in Cincinnati, Ohio, Sheltering Ourselves: A Women's Learning Exchange (SOWLE). An international educational forum on housing and development, SOWLE offered a series of learning exchanges that dealt with topics of interest to women as homeowners, such as home maintenance and repair, as well as topics of interest to community members concerned about housing and urban environments. SOWLE, which continued into the 1990s, brought together women of all races, ages, economic levels, and educational backgrounds, including residents of public housing, neighborhood organizers, architects, planners, builders, and academics. Both the WSPA and SOWLE were products of their time—accessible and empowering spaces in which women could gain confidence for working in venues traditionally dominated by men.

Leslie became active in the disability rights movement and universal design when she discovered that her own campus, the New Jersey Institute of

Technology, was not compliant with Section 504 of the 1973 Rehabilitation Act. Under this act, programs that receive federal funds cannot exclude qualified students solely on the basis of their disabilities. Not only were many campuses not compliant, but for Weisman, the solutions they devised in order to become so, such as "ugly add-ons like ramps," were "stigmatizing and segregating."[18] In contrast, the principles of universal design provide people of differing levels of ability with accommodations that are invisible when properly applied. For example, rather than two entrances to a building—a ramp and a set of stairs—a landscape plan can be designed that has a slight change in grade leading to a zero-threshold entrance that everyone can use. Leslie continues to explore how the concepts of universal design can provide equal access, comfort, and functionality to campuses, buildings, houses, and entire cities.[19]

In 2002, Weisman decided to become more involved in issues facing Southold Town, a town on the east end of Long Island where, beginning in 1976, she rented a house for six months each year. In 1985, she bought and renovated a house in Southold Town and began commuting there more frequently from her home in New York City. When Leslie was appointed to both the Southold Hamlet Stakeholders Committee and the Housing Advisory Commission, she took early retirement from the New Jersey Institute of Technology. Since her retirement in 2004, she has accepted several short-term teaching appointments at various institutions, including the University of Ulster in Belfast, Northern Ireland; the University of Illinois at Urbana-Champaign; the Massachusetts Institute of Technology; and Brooklyn College, but her primary commitment is working with housing and zoning issues in Southold Town: "'I simply decided that it was time to apply my energy and professional expertise elsewhere. For me this work is another rewarding vehicle for socially and environmentally responsible activism.'"[20]

Weisman was appointed to the Zoning Board of Appeals of Southold Town in 2005, becoming vice chair in 2008 and chair in 2010. Historically, the secretary/board assistant ran the zoning board, and when the secretary who had served in the position for forty years left, the department did not know how to function. Leslie agreed to assume leadership of the board, taking over "all of the responsibilities I believed a department head, rather than a secretary, should be doing. . . . Because I was previously both an academic administrator and professor, I figured I would be able to figure out how to set up running this department properly."[21] Her work with the zoning board was recognized in 2010 when she was named Public Servant of 2010 by the *Suffolk Times*.

Definition of Feminism

Growing up seeing racism, anti-Semitism, and sexism as examples of oppressive "isms," Weisman's definition of feminism focuses on oppression:

"Sexism seemed like just another manifestation of the same patriarchal system in which those in power, typically affluent white males, marginalize and segregate those who are not. I never believed that any one group—be it women, African Americans, those with low incomes, or gay people—had a monopoly on being the victims of oppression."[22] Leslie's solution to oppression is equity: Feminism is "simply about striving to create a world in which human differences" are "respected and valued" and where all individuals are "treated with human decency and dignity."[23] She prefers the term *equity* to *equality* because equality "suggests sameness. We don't all need the same things, and our needs change throughout our lives. Equity means that people have what they need when they need it."[24]

Weisman's feminism is designed to create a different world from the one that exists under patriarchy: "I don't think feminism is about women getting an equal piece of a poisonous pie. I want another recipe."[25] The new system she envisions will be realized when patriarchy itself is abolished: "The ultimate goal of feminism must not be the integration of women and minorities into 'mainstream' society, but rather the abolition of patriarchy itself. By its very definition, a patriarchal society depends upon the unequal distribution of social resources and social power among many fragmented groups. Patriarchy pits one oppressed group against another in a hierarchy of oppression."[26]

Leslie envisions a feminist future that is "sane, human, ecological." The new frontiers of this future "are psychological and social, not technical and economic," and "the development of people, not the development of things, will be important."[27] The intimate connection between architecture and feminism provides the catalyst for transformation: "If we are to design a society in which all people matter, more architects and planners need to become feminists and more feminists need to concern themselves with the design of our physical surroundings."[28]

Change Strategies

By gaining an understanding of the nature and consequences of "patritecture,"[29] Weisman believes feminists can imagine other possibilities for their environments and, in the process, move from being victims to agents. Her three strategies—(1) critiquing the system, (2) fantasizing, and (3) exercising agency—work together to facilitate the creation of a new environment designed by women with women in mind.

Critiquing the System

Leslie's first step in the creation of an alternative future is an analysis of what currently exists: "We must begin by evaluating our *man-made* environment from a feminist perspective."[30] Weisman considers public architecture "but a reflection of a comprehensive system of institutionalized racism, sexism, and classism,"[31] and the process of critique involves understanding the "origins and expressions of sexism" manifest in spaces and buildings oppressive to women.[32] Weisman elaborates, "One of the most oppressive aspects of today's actual built environment is that it is a totally male fantasy, a projection of their monumental egos in concrete . . . , each building shouting for individual recognition."[33] A critique of the current system will explore "why the acts of building and controlling space have been a male prerogative; how our physical surroundings reflect and create reality; and how we can begin to challenge and change the forms and values" that define the man-made environment.[34]

Leslie engages in a critique of the current environment in her book *Discrimination by Design*, in which she explores topics such as the gendered uses of space, the privileging of the masculine in public architecture, and the significance of the home as a domestic space for women. These and similar analyses are critical in order to break free from established conventions about how homes, buildings, and cities should look: "We will first have to recognize how conceptually disadvantaged we all are by the immutable social and architectural preconceptions we have about our housing and our households. Then we will have to find ways to free ourselves of the inhibitions they cause."[35]

Fantasizing

Weisman's strategy of fantasizing offers the solution for how to break free from preconceptions about space and buildings. Usually contrasted with reason, logic, and practicality, fantasizing often is seen as immature, childlike, unproductive, and impractical, and being able "to fantasize, be playful and reflective are trained out of us as we grow up."[36] Leslie, however, sees fantasizing as "a way of dealing *with* reality and problem solving, not an escape from it. It is a productive and useful method for creating change."[37] Fantasizing is critical if women are to overturn the world that has been created by men and begin to imagine different and more appropriate environments for themselves. Fantasizing works by enabling primary creativity, which stems from the unconscious and generates new ideas and insights. By contrast, "secondary creativity is based upon what already exists."[38] Only an emphasis on primary creativity can accomplish "a completely fresh vision rather than a mere re-ordering of the 'givens' of the past and present."[39]

Weisman offers an example of how powerful fantasizing can be in making architectural spaces more suitable for women. She cotaught, with Noel Phyllis Birkby, a class at the Women's School of Planning and Architecture in which they asked women to engage in environmental fantasizing by drawing their ideal living environments. The images the women created were dramatically different from existing conceptions of buildings and cities. One woman imagined a series of "wombs," for example—pods that contained the services women want to have nearby—such as quick health food, self-help schools, a library, printing press, legal self-help, and even a pod for strategizing for how to overturn patriarchy. Another woman fantasized about a "great goddess percolation system" that enables women to "perk" to anywhere in the country in seven minutes or less. The percolation system has another benefit as well—women can have ice cream and/or cake and coffee while waiting on the goddess platform for the percolation process to begin.[40] Leslie believes women "need to see our own imagery in the visible, external world," and projecting images by means of fantasy is a way to "begin to experience and create the woman-identified environment."[41]

Exercising Agency

Exercising agency is a third strategy Weisman employs as a necessary step in creating an alternative feminist world. Without the deliberate exercise of agency, the strategies of critique and fantasizing will be wasted. Leslie understands that many women are still reluctant to offer input about what they want and need and to take action on their own behalf because their perspectives have been devalued and dismissed for so long. She believes that women must "act consciously and politically,"[42] demanding access to and helping to create architectural settings that "support the essential needs of all women."[43] Women's organizations, feminist architects, and legislators will be important to the creation of these new spaces for women, but each woman must step up as well: "Each woman must become her own architect, that is, she must become aware of her ability to exercise environmental judgment and make decisions about the nature of the spaces in which she lives and works."[44] For Weisman, the appropriation and use of space is a political act, and women must become comfortable engaging politically in this way.

Leslie cites as an example of feminist agency in architecture the takeover by women of an abandoned building in New York City on New Year's Eve in 1971. Although the takeover lasted for only twelve days—the women were arrested and the building was eventually torn down to make a parking lot for the adjacent police station—it was a space where women could, albeit briefly, take control of their own lives. They restored electricity, heating, and plumbing to the building and used it to offer a variety of services to women, including day care and a clothing and book exchange. Most important, however, the takeover empowered the women to "survive, grow, be ourselves."[45] When women take charge of their choices and begin to exercise their agency in their own environments, Weisman believes, the sense of control they experience extends to all areas of their lives.

Leslie's life work is providing women with the tools necessary to understand, reimagine, and create alternative environments that better serve their needs than do male-designed ones. Critiquing the system gives women an understanding of how ill-equipped the present system is to address their interests and desires, and fantasizing provides the tools to imagine something different. Exercising agency gives women an awareness that they have a right to their perspectives and the right to make them visible in the world. Weisman summarizes what will be required to create the alternative world she imagines: "To achieve a feminist future in which all people and all life matters, we will have to move beyond the politics of exclusion, intolerance, and competing special interests; we will have to recognize the interdependence among all of humanity, the natural world, and the products of human design; and we will have to learn to think and act out of that recognition."[46]

■ REFLECTIONS

1. Weisman argues that the buildings we live in are best described as an outcome of patritecture rather than architecture because of the influence of patriarchy on the built environment. What evidence do you see in the construction of the building you are in now that supports her assertion?
2. Are you familiar with any building that does not appear, as Weisman says, "to contain, control, or exclude women"? Describe one of these buildings to show how it is different from the buildings typical of patritecture.
3. According to Weisman, women will not be able to contribute fully to building a different world unless they can begin to imagine that world. What would a house look like in the ideal world? You may find that drawing the house rather than describing it in words is a better way to present your vision.
4. Exercising agency is important to many of the women in this book, including Leslie Kanes Weisman and Padma Lakshmi. They also want others to enact agency. How can the concept of agency be taught so that those who are not yet aware of their agency can access it?
5. Weisman helped found two schools that provided women with spaces in which to learn apart from men, and both were products of a time when very few women were working in the field of architecture. Is there still a place for separatist environments today when women are integrated into virtually every academic discipline and career field?
6. How closely do Weisman's change strategies align with the assumptions outlined in the introduction to part 6? Are there any assumptions that you don't believe pertain to her approach to change?
7. In which feminist wave would you place Weisman and why?

■ NOTES

[1] Leslie Kanes Weisman, "Educator, Activist, Politician," interview by Cristina Cerulli and Florian Kossak, *Field* 3 (2009): 14–15.
[2] "Leslie Kanes Weisman: Biographical Introduction," email message to Karen A. Foss, June 4, 2020.
[3] Weisman, "Educator," 8.
[4] Weisman, "Educator," 8–9.
[5] Weisman, "Educator," 13, 18.

6. Weisman, "Educator," 13.
7. Diana Agrest, Patricia Conway, and Leslie Kanes Weisman, "Introduction," in *The Sex of Architecture*, ed. Diana Agrest, Patricia Conway, and Leslie Kanes Weisman (New York: Harry N. Abrams, 1996), 11.
8. Leslie Kanes Weisman, *Discrimination by Design: A Feminist Critique of the Man-Made Environment* (Urbana: University of Illinois Press, 1992), 2.
9. Agrest, Conway, and Weisman, "Introduction," 11.
10. Weisman, "Educator," 9.
11. Weisman, "Educator," 9.
12. The other cofounders of the Women's School of Planning and Architecture were Katrin Adam, Ellen Perry Berkeley, Noel Phyllis Birkby, Bobbie Sue Hood, Marie I. Kennedy, and Joan Forrester Sprague.
13. In 1977, several original coordinators stepped down, and the program could not be reorganized in time to make a session happen. A session planned for Hood College in Fredrick, Maryland, in 1980 was cancelled when registration targets were not met. A final weekend symposium was held in Washington, DC, in 1981. See "Historical Note," Women's School of Planning and Architecture Records, Five College Archives & Manuscript Collections, https://archive.is/20140517231247/http://asteria.fivecolleges.edu/monarch/findaids/sophiasmith/mnsss77_bioghist.html/; Leslie Kanes Weisman, email message to Karen A. Foss, June 7, 2020.
14. Weisman, "Educator," 8.
15. Weisman, "Educator," 11–12.
16. Weisman, "Educator," 12.
17. Weisman, "Educator," 10.
18. Weisman, "Educator," 15.
19. Leslie Kanes Weisman, "Creating the Universally Designed City: Prospects for the New Century," in *Universal Design Handbook*, ed. Wolfgang F. E. Preiser and Elaine Ostroff (New York: McGraw Hill, 2001), 69.3–69.18.
20. "The Environmental is Political: Universal Design and Social Sustainability with Leslie Kanes Weisman," *Universal Design Newsletter*, April 2012, https://archive.is/20140517231259/http://www.universaldesign.com/2013-08-16-19-05-11/public-and-commercial/531-the-environmental-is-political-universal-design-and-social-sustainability-with-leslie-kanes-weisman.html/
21. Leslie Weisman, email message to Karen A. Foss, June 7, 2020.
22. Weisman, "Educator," 9.
23. Weisman, "Educator," 9.
24. Weisman, "Educator," 16.
25. Weisman, "Educator," 16.
26. Weisman, *Discrimination by Design*, 63.
27. Weisman, *Discrimination by Design*, 160–61.
28. Weisman, *Discrimination by Design*, 179.
29. Phyllis Birkby and Leslie Weisman, "Patritecture and Feminist Fantasies," *Liberation* 19 (1976): 47.
30. Noel Phyllis Birkby and Leslie Kanes Weisman, "A Woman Built Environment: Constructive Fantasies," *Quest* 2 (1975): 8.
31. Weisman, *Discrimination by Design*, 63–64.
32. Birkby and Weisman, "A Woman Built Environment," 8.
33. Birkby and Weisman, "A Woman Built Environment," 15.
34. Weisman, *Discrimination by Design*, 2.
35. Weisman, *Discrimination by Design*, 156.
36. Birkby and Weisman, "A Woman Built Environment," 15.
37. Birkby and Weisman, "A Woman Built Environment," 15.
38. Birkby and Weisman, "A Woman Built Environment," 15–16.
39. Birkby and Weisman, "A Woman Built Environment," 16.
40. Birkby and Weisman, "A Woman Built Environment," 10–11.

[41] Birkby and Weisman, "A Woman Built Environment," 18.
[42] Leslie Kanes Weisman, "Prologue—Women's Environmental Rights: A Manifesto," in *Gender Space Architecture: An Interdisciplinary Introduction*, ed. Jane Rendell, Barbara Penner, and Iain Border (New York: Routledge, 2000), 4.
[43] Weisman, "Prologue," 4.
[44] Weisman, "Prologue," 4.
[45] Weisman, "Prologue," 3.
[46] Leslie Kanes Weisman, "Diversity by Design," in *The Sex of Architecture*, ed. Diana Agrest, Patricia Conway, and Leslie Kanes Weisman (New York: Harry N. Abrams, 1996), 275.

CHAPTER
TWENTY-ONE

Jennifer Armbrust

> *We build feminist businesses because we cannot stop dreaming and imagining the world we want to live in. We build feminist businesses because we are compelled to create the world we know is possible.*[1]

Jennifer Armbrust is an artist and consultant who uses the "collisions and collusions of art, business, gender, embodiment and economics"[2] to create alternative feminist businesses and business practices. Born in 1977 in Olympia, Washington, Armbrust describes her upbringing as "white, middle-class, Lutheran, active, social, creative, outdoors-y and family-centric with an emphasis on education."[3] When she was thirteen years old, she heard a cassette tape of Jane's Addiction, an alternative rock band, which influenced her to want "to embody rebellion."[4] One of the ways she rebelled was to reject idealized femininity by shopping in the men's sections of clothing stores.

Jennifer earned a BA in critical theory from Evergreen State College in Olympia, Washington, in 2000. Her study of feminist theory, critical race theory, Marxist philosophy, poststructuralist theory, postmodern theory, and postcolonial theory allowed her to investigate power—"what it is, how it flows, and strategies for redistributing it."[5] She continued her studies in small business administration at Portland Community College and in interactive design at the Pacific Northwest College of Art in Portland, Oregon.

Although she did not have any background in art history or gallery administration, Armbrust founded a fine art gallery called *Motel* in Portland in 2002. During the five years that she directed the gallery, she featured the work of over one hundred emerging artists from around the world in over fifty exhibitions. In 2004, Jennifer cofounded *PORT*, a visual art blog with daily art news, interviews, and reviews that provided critical and cultural content for the creative communities of Portland. When she closed the gallery, she moved to New York City, which she found depressing and depleting. She returned to Portland after a year, and to heal herself from the experience, she studied at Lotus Lantern Healing Arts for seven years, learning tools and techniques for using energy to heal.

Armbrust continued to work in the arts following her return to Portland. She ran a small design firm, Motel Projects, between 2005 and 2010, providing branding, print, and interactive design for arts-related businesses. That experience led her to begin to articulate some questions that graphic designers should ask themselves about their work—questions that foreshadowed her interest in incorporating feminist values into business practices. Among the questions she posed were: "Are you using tropes of dominance or violence to create the illusion of authority?" "Is there a way in which your work might be creating or contributing to other problems?" "Who benefits from your creative work?" "Who profits?" "These products you are selling, what are they made of—the raw materials?" "Do you think about how long these things will last?" "And where they will go when we're done with them?" "What are you working for?" "What would it look like to thrive financially, while living and working with integrity?" "Can you create the world you want to live in?"[6]

Jennifer first articulated her vision for a feminine economy in 2015, when she was asked to give a talk about revolution. She found herself in "an exciting moment of integration. My persistent passions, my ideological fascinations, and my love of feminist theory collided with my business acumen and seven years of healing arts training."[7] Her talk led her to found Sister, a company through which she consults with businesses on tools for the feminine economy. As part of Sister, she developed and runs Feminist Business School, an online school to help "students understand what feminism is and how to find their own passion and purpose within its ideals."[8] The school addresses questions such as: "What's our internal relationship with money and power? What is empathy in business? How do you build business structures that honor intuition and make room for rest?"[9] Armbrust's book, *Proposals for the Feminine Economy*, published in 2018, provides an overview of her feminist philosophy as applied to business. At the heart of her philosophy is the idea that "business can be a site of feminist practice if we embody our values, create new economies, and experiment with redistributions of power and resources."[10]

Jennifer now works as a consultant to provide "an entrepreneurial framework for people who are critical of capitalism, and who are creative, visionary and independent. I don't aspire to be an economist. I make my work for people who want to thrive without compromising their creative integrity and political beliefs. These tend to be women and artists. They're wondering: Where can I go and what can I do with all my passion and purpose?"[11]

Definition of Feminism

Feminism as the term generally is conceptualized, Armbrust explains, vaguely means something about women's empowerment. She would like feminism to be acknowledged as something more concrete than this: "'Feminism' is a thing. It's a movement. It has a history. There's scholarship around it. There is feminist art. There's feminist theory."[12] She also rejects feminism as a trendy commodity: "It is not a brand or a style or a trend. It's not about t-shirts."[13] Instead, for Jennifer, feminism has a socio-political agenda—it is about "radical social transformation."[14] She elaborates: "It's a multi-generational movement committed to consciousness, empowerment, empathy, and importantly, to actively dismantling myriad systemic, institutionalized, normalized, interpersonal, and internalized oppressions."[15]

Armbrust is interested in feminism as a site to explore how power moves: "How is power distributed—globally, nationally, culturally, socially? How could it be redistributed?"[16] She is not interested in women's lack of access to certain forms of power and how women can get more power, prestige, money, and validation within existing systems and structures: "This narrative assumes (and therefore reinforces) that money equals merit, that the world is a pyramid and it's better to be on the top than the bottom, that the problem of equality is just a numbers game and that having more slots filled by women will mark some sort of cultural shift."[17]

In contrast, Jennifer's version of feminism includes using feminine principles and values to create new systems. This focus was prompted by her friend Lisa Radon's use of the word *feminine-ism*. Armbrust calls feminine-ism the "fourth wave of feminism"[18] and explains that it was the concept she had been looking for: "Not a celebration of all things girly or a sexualization of womanhood. But rather, a valuation of feminine *characteristics*"[19] such as interdependence, collaboration, generosity, embodiment, sustainability, honesty, gratitude, resourcefulness, a connection with nature, empathy, receptivity, nurturing, and introspection.[20]

Although women traditionally have been the carriers of the feminine, feminism does not exclude men: "Eastern thought has long understood 'masculine' and 'feminine' as principles that extend beyond 'man' and 'woman.'"[21] All humans embody masculine and feminine qualities and, in a healthy and balanced world, they would manifest both "fluidly and in unique balance, regardless of their sex organs."[22] Such embodiment of the feminine, Jennifer believes, would empower everyone because all individuals then would have the "agency, dignity, voice and the self-esteem to make wise choices in their highest good."[23]

Change Strategies

Armbrust's framework for creating new business systems relies on three strategies that celebrate and cultivate feminine qualities in individuals and in the structures in which they live and work: (1) critiquing the system, (2) enacting self-determination, and (3) learning through improvising. These three strategies must be engaged, she believes, in coalition with other feminists: "The very principles of feminine and feminist ideas say *together*.... We do this together because we know that together is more important and more powerful than what one person can do alone."[24] Jennifer is "interested in working in collaboration and coalition with other people who want a different way to see if we can find new practices that will lead us to new models."[25]

Critiquing the System

Armbrust rejects the current system of capitalism as anathema to feminist principles. She defines capitalism as "both an economic system (defined by private ownership of the means of production and their operation for profit) and a worldview, an ideology"[26] that operate according to toxic and unhealthy masculine values. These masculine values include growth, individualism, competition, speed and efficiency, a lack of accountability, hierarchy, the domination of people and nature, and perpetual consumption.[27] They produce a number of negative consequences, including systemic racism and sexism, individuals who are gluttonous and narcissistic, the subjugation of human needs to productivity, extreme wealth disparity, and floods and wildfires exacerbated by climate change.[28]

Jennifer critiques capitalism by showing how different an economic system would be if it embodied feminine values. She sees these values "as a collection of qualities deserving of reverence"[29] that can be used to create new kinds of systems. She realizes that her task is not an easy one because systems built on masculine traits feel like the natural order, so "most Americans have no idea what it actually feels like to be in a feminine workplace or in an environment that really, deeply honors feminine values and feminine principles."[30] Armbrust believes that integrating such values into systems and structures, however, will transform individuals' relationships "to money, to work, to the earth, to our bodies, and to each other."[31]

Jennifer's critique of capitalism requires that individuals unlearn the system of capitalism by engaging in self-work. As she explains, creating new systems and structures requires "a certain amount of deep work" and "vigorous self-reflection"[32] because only when individuals embrace new values and ways of being can they conceptualize something different from what is. This self-work involves both developing a critical consciousness and acting in new ways on the basis of that transformed consciousness.

The development of a critical consciousness begins by examining society and culture, institutions and government, communities, relationships, and businesses, asking questions about sexism and exploitation, racism, classism, elitism, and accessibility. Individuals must find the places where they are complicit with or are "actively perpetuating (often unknowingly) sexism and other forms of oppression."[33] They must take responsibility for unearned privileges and heal internalized oppressions. Armbrust sees men as often having to do more self-reflective work than women to "unlearn their patriarchal and masculine thinking ... because they are the ones who have benefited from it." They must understand what male privilege is and acknowledge it, and they must understand what masculine principles are "and how those have been tied to success, to monetary value." There also "has to be a concerted effort by men to reclaim and allow for their own feminine qualities and to see the value of those in others and to begin to embed those qualities in their business models."[34]

Self-work also involves enacting or practicing a new set of behaviors and practices as a result of the new consciousness. Individuals must show up "every day with humility, heart, intrepid creativity, criticality, courage, self-love, and a passion for growth."[35] In order to enact this self-work, individuals also need to "take a step out of ego, a step out of the hero model or the charismatic leader" and be "in a constant state of learning and listening."[36]

Enacting Self-Determination

Jennifer's long-term goal with her work—and one she knows she shares with many others—is to survive and thrive in systems with "personal and creative integrity intact."[37] To accomplish this objective, individuals must choose themselves and take full responsibility for their lives and happiness.[38] The result will be new kinds of systems built on different sets of values. By choosing themselves, Armbrust means that individuals make their own choices based on their own inner authority. She believes that most people are who other people want them to be—they are "created by society, others' expectations, and inherited beliefs,"[39] with "society (religion, politics, media)" telling them every day that they need "outside validation, permission or expertise to find" the truth. Jennifer counters: "This is a lie."[40] The person who conforms to others' expectations must die if individuals are going to live on their own terms.[41] She wants individuals to recognize where they have given their power away and to "reclaim it from those who have taken it."[42] Then they can begin to script their own lives.[43]

Because individuals must make their own choices according to what they perceive as right for them, Armbrust doesn't lay out explicit criteria or principles for individuals to use for making life choices. Instead, she suggests that "our biography, our soul, provides us all the answers we seek. Our challenge is to learn how to ask the question and then receive the answer."[44] Such a commitment requires both large and small steps to cultivate an inner authority. A large step, for example, is to "build structures and practices in alignment with your values and deeply-held beliefs."[45] Smaller steps include becoming attuned to needs and to honor them as they arise: "Let inner wisdom be your guide. Go where you are called. Eat when you are hungry. Rest when you are tired."[46] Individuals also can move toward the things that bring them nourishment and joy.

> Truly find where your pleasures lie, where your passions lie, not what you're told will make you happy. Not the car, the house, the two-and-a-half kids or whatever. But what happens when you let go of the life you

were told you would, should, or could have—other people's scripts for you? What happens when you let that go and start to follow your pleasure, your passions? . . . That initially sounds really selfish. But once you begin that project, you start to hear your own inner voice. You start to hear your colleagues connect with why they are here on earth. That's really when your life begins.[47]

Another way Jennifer suggests for cultivating inner authority is to nourish and pay attention to the body. She encourages the creation of structures "that support and nourish your body and all the other bodies you know."[48] She notes that because businesses are given a great deal of authority, they become entities that "we all then bend our bodies, our days, our lives around."[49] She challenges this practice and encourages individuals to question what it means to have a body in such structures: "Your body does not want to work 60 hours a week. It does not want to sit all day. . . . Your body might want to go to the beach. Your body craves nourishing food and rest and movement. Your body delights in pleasure and play."[50] Armbrust wants to honor the body and sees a healthy, nurtured body as providing support for making other kinds of personal choices. Drinking water, going to bed on time, exercising, prioritizing health and wellness, and eating the best-quality food available are examples of how attending to the body provides a foundation for enacting self-determination and for creating systems that nurture and sustain individuals.

Learning Through Improvising

"Do not wait until you know how to act. Anything you don't know, you will learn in the process."[51] This precept is the foundation for Jennifer's strategy of improvising or experimenting. If a new world is going to be created, there must be a great deal "of agency and freedom to create new models and to make new rules."[52] Improvisation or experimentation is one way in which individuals "will find a way out of the dysfunction of where we are now and into something new."[53] This strategy derives in part from when Armbrust started and managed an art gallery with no expertise in arts administration—she saw it as "a practice in improvisation, innovation, and determination."[54]

Jennifer encourages others to "consider everything an experiment"[55] and details the kinds of practices that go into the experimenting and improvising required to create alternative systems: "Ask questions. Ask more questions. Explore! Give yourself permission to not know and to make mistakes. Find freedom in uncertainty. Be receptive and responsive instead of predictive and protective."[56] Other improvisational practices she advocates include showing up and making space for ideas to arrive, using rules and limitations as creative constraints, and taking risks.[57] Armbrust acknowledges that as individuals begin to incorporate feminine values into businesses and other systems, they "will unquestionably make mistakes, have blind spots, and grapple with constraints." But they will learn and grow and find new ways as long as they take accountability for themselves and practice forgiveness.[58] By trying out new ideas and experimenting with new practices, they will find new routes—they will "make the road by walking."[59]

Jennifer's change strategies are designed to create an alternative world, particularly a new business world. She does not believe that the current system of capitalism, the context for business in the United States, can be repaired or remedied because it is a system built on toxic masculine values. When individuals critique the capitalist system and engage in self-work to unlearn its oppressive values, a new feminine economy can emerge. Change agents then are able to enact self-determination, trusting themselves as their own inner authorities to guide their lives and their businesses. Once individuals go off script to create new models, they learn to construct a new system through improvising and experimenting. These feminist businesses, Armbrust believes, will produce massive changes that will be "deeply disruptive" to the capitalist model: "As entrepreneurs, we have the opportunity to agitate the current social, political, and economic order by experimenting with new business models that honor our values, our humanity, and the earth. As we bring feminine and feminist principles into our business practices, we give birth to a new economic paradigm."[60]

■ REFLECTIONS

1. Compare and contrast Armbrust's view of a system that would replace capitalism with Alexandria Ocasio-Cortez's proposed system (chapter 22). Are there significant differences between them? Do you prefer one over the other?

2. Armbrust uses the term *feminine-ism* to indicate that she wants business to incorporate feminine values such as collaboration, generosity, gratitude, receptivity, and introspection. Do you believe, as she does, that there are differences between masculine and feminine values?

3. Armbrust wants individuals to make their own choices based on their inner authority rather than on the expectations of others. How realistic is this? Is it really possible to act on your inner authority? What if your inner authority is in conflict with people who are close to you or systems you value?

4. Armbrust suggests that we need to pay more attention to the body in business and other systems. Select a system of which you are a part and analyze it for how it treats bodies. Who has the authority in that system—the body or the system?

5. Armbrust's strategy of improvising is not unlike Weisman's fantasizing (chapter 20). Both of these function to help feminists move beyond what is to something new. Is it ever possible to devise an entirely new system, or does every system rely to some degree on what existed in the past?

6. How closely do Armbrust's change strategies align with the assumptions outlined in the introduction to part 6? Are there any assumptions that you don't believe pertain to her approach to change?
7. Armbrust places her "feminine-ism" in the fourth wave. Do you agree that the fourth wave is where she and her ideas belong?

■ NOTES

[1] Jennifer Armbrust, "Bringing Feminist Principles into Business Practices," Sister, n.d., https://sister.is/a-feminist-business
[2] Jennifer Armbrust, "About," Linkedin, n.d., https://www.linkedin.com/in/jennifer-armbrust-9494ab184/
[3] Jennifer Armbrust, "Women in Clothes," interview by Sheila Heti, Heidi Julauits, Leanne Shapton, and Mary Mann, Women in Clothes, n.d., https://www.womeninclothes.com/view/by-author/entry/9/
[4] Armbrust, "Women in Clothes."
[5] Jennifer Armbrust, *Proposals for the Feminine Economy* (Topanga, CA: The Fourth Wave, 2018), 21.
[6] Jennifer Armbrust, "50 Questions for Every Graphic Designer," Design Portland, n.d., https://ddsignportland.org/stories/2016/50-questions-for-every-graphic-designer/
[7] Armbrust, *Proposals for the Feminine Economy*, 21.
[8] Jennifer Armbrust, "What Do You Learn in a Feminist Business School?," interview by Stephanie Newman, *Forbes*, September 28, 2017, https://www.forbes.com/sites/stephanienewman/2017/09/28/what-do-you-learn-in-a-feminist-business-school/?sh=2fd3cbd96733/
[9] Armbrust, "What Do You Learn in a Feminist Business School?"
[10] Armbrust, "About."
[11] Armbrust, "What Do You Learn in a Feminist Business School?"
[12] Jennifer Armbrust, "Could a More Feminine Economy Save the World?," interview by Rachel Zurer, SOCAPGlobal, January 26, 2018, https://socapglobal.com/2018/01/feminine-economy-save-world/
[13] Armbrust, *Proposals for the Feminine Economy*, 46.
[14] Armbrust, "Could a More Feminine Economy Save the World?"
[15] Armbrust, *Proposals for the Feminine Economy*, 46.
[16] Jennifer Armbrust, "Jennifer Armbrust on The Feminist Future: Tiny Interview 7," interview by staff of Carville Annex Press, September 30, 2014, http://www.carvilleannexpress.com/blog/2014/9/30/jennifer-armbrust-on-the-feminist-future/
[17] Armbrust, "Jennifer Armbrust on The Feminist Future."
[18] Armbrust, *Proposals for the Feminine Economy*, 25.
[19] Armbrust, *Proposals for the Feminine Economy*, 23.
[20] Armbrust, *Proposals for the Feminine Economy*, 37, 23.
[21] Armbrust, "Jennifer Armbrust on The Feminist Future."
[22] Armbrust, *Proposals for the Feminine Economy*, 24.
[23] Armbrust, "Jennifer Armbrust on The Feminist Future."
[24] Tara McMullin, "What Works for Jennifer Armbrust: Building a Business with Feminist Values," What Works, May 15, 2018, https://medium.com/help-yourself/what-works-for-jennifer-armbrust-building-a-business-with-feminist-values-b9c9f7e73018/
[25] Armbrust, "Could a More Feminine Economy Save the World?"
[26] Armbrust, *Proposals for the Feminine Economy*, 33.
[27] Armbrust, *Proposals for the Feminine Economy*, 35.
[28] McMullin, "What Works for Jennifer Armbrust," 3; Armbrust, "Could a More Feminine Economy Save the World?"; Armbrust, *Proposals for the Feminine Economy*, 71, 40.

29 Armbrust, "Jennifer Armbrust on The Feminist Future."
30 Armbrust, "Could a More Feminine Economy Save the World?"
31 Armbrust, *Proposals for the Feminine Economy*, 81.
32 Armbrust, "Could a More Feminine Economy Save the World?"
33 Armbrust, *Proposals for the Feminine Economy*, 48.
34 Armbrust, "Could a More Feminine Economy Save the World?"
35 Armbrust, *Proposals for the Feminine Economy*, 49.
36 Armbrust, "Could a More Feminine Economy Save the World?"
37 Armbrust, "Could a More Feminine Economy Save the World?"
38 Armbrust, "What Do You Learn in a Feminist Business School?"
39 Armbrust, *Proposals for the Feminine Economy*, 67.
40 Armbrust, "Jennifer Armbrust on The Feminist Future," 5.
41 Armbrust, *Proposals for the Feminine Economy*, 67.
42 Armbrust, *Proposals for the Feminine Economy*, 67.
43 Armbrust, "What Do You Learn in a Feminist Business School?"
44 Armbrust, "Jennifer Armbrust on The Feminist Future."
45 Armbrust, *Proposals for the Feminine Economy*, 64.
46 Jennifer Armbrust, "Principles for Prototyping a Feminist Business: A Framework for the Practical Application of the Tenets of the Feminine Economy," Sister, n.d., https://sister.is/12-principles/
47 Armbrust, "Could a More Feminine Economy Save the World?"
48 Armbrust, *Proposals for the Feminine Economy*, 57.
49 Armbrust, "Could a More Feminine Economy Save the World?"
50 Armbrust, *Proposals for the Feminine Economy*, 57.
51 Armbrust, *Proposals for the Feminine Economy*, 68.
52 Armbrust, "Could a More Feminine Economy Save the World?"
53 Armbrust, *Proposals for the Feminine Economy*, 42.
54 Armbrust, *Proposals for the Feminine Economy*, 11.
55 Armbrust, *Proposals for the Feminine Economy*, 68.
56 Armbrust, *Proposals for the Feminine Economy*, 68.
57 Armbrust, *Proposals for the Feminine Economy*, 12.
58 Armbrust, *Proposals for the Feminine Economy*, 88.
59 Armbrust, *Proposals for the Feminine Economy*, 89.
60 Armbrust, *Proposals for the Feminine Economy*, 79.

CHAPTER
TWENTY-TWO

Alexandria Ocasio-Cortez

For me, it's about asking, "Am I serving the people around me? Am I doing my best to make their lives better?" And it doesn't mean that I have to be perfect every single time, it doesn't mean that I don't make mistakes; but I think what it means is, "Have I made an active and conscious effort to make people's lives better in my little pocket of the world?"[1]

Activist Alexandria Ocasio-Cortez, elected to Congress at the age of twenty-eight, works to create alternative US economic and political systems that will make the lives of Americans better. She was born in 1989 into a Catholic family in the Bronx, the most populous and poorest borough of New City. Her father, from a Puerto Rican family in the Bronx, owned a firm that offered home remodeling services, including renovation, building inspection, and landscaping. Her mother, who was born in Puerto Rico, worked as a secretary and a house cleaner. The family moved to Yorktown Heights in Westchester County when Ocasio-Cortez was young so that she and her brother could attend better schools than were available in the Bronx.

Alexandria attended Boston University, graduating in 2011. As a first-year student, she moved into pre-med housing intending to major in science. After studying abroad in Niger, West Africa, where she worked in a maternity clinic helping midwives deliver babies in under-resourced and often unsanitary conditions, she decided that attending medical school was not the right option for her. She realized she could help more people by approaching health-care issues from a broader societal perspective, so she chose to major in economics and international relations. She was active in politics in college, serving as an intern in the areas of foreign affairs and immigration for US Senator Edward Kennedy and leading Boston University's Alianza Latina. On most Friday afternoons, she participated in Coffee and Conversations, campus discussions in which students debated current issues and politics.

After graduation, Ocasio-Cortez returned to the Bronx, where she held a number of positions largely related to community education. She served as an educational strategist for the consulting firm GAGEis, which connects students with careers. Working with the Sunshine Bronx Business Incubator, she developed training materials for entrepreneurs hoping to launch new businesses in the borough. She started a publishing company, Brook Avenue Press, to provide books for children that portray the Bronx in a positive light. Alexandria also worked with the National Hispanic Institute, serving as the educational director for the Northeast Collegiate World Series, a program that helps high school students succeed in college.

When Donald Trump was elected president in 2016, Ocasio-Cortez experienced a "political awakening" that prompted her to become more politically active. She and some friends traveled across the country, participating in various demonstrations for environmental justice. Among other sites, they visited Flint, Michigan, where lead had leached into residential water pipes, and the Standing Rock Indian Reservation on the border of North and South Dakota, where members of the tribe were fighting the proposed Dakota Access Pipeline. Visiting the two sites helped her "connect a lot of different dots" among corporate money, political power, environmental and health threats, marginalized populations, and government inaction.[2]

On the drive back to the Bronx, Alexandria received a phone call from Brand New Congress, a political action group formed to recruit progressive candidates to run for office. Her brother had nominated her, which is how the group learned about her. She had doubts, however, about the feasibility of running for Congress: "I felt like the only way to effectively run for office is if you had access to a lot of wealth, high social influence, a lot of high dynastic power, and I knew that I didn't have any of those things."[3] She agreed to run when she saw that her political liabilities could be seen as potential strengths: "In order for us to change course, and change the future, it's going to take people who haven't typically been seen or thought of as a typical candidate."[4]

Ocasio-Cortez ran for US representative from New York's Fourteenth Congressional District in 2017. Her opponent in the Democratic primary was ten-term incumbent Joseph Crowley, who had not faced competition in a Democratic primary for fourteen years. She conducted her campaign while waiting tables and tending bar at Flats Fix Taco y Tequila Bar in Manhattan. She kept her campaign materials and a change of clothes behind the counter in the bar: "I would work my shift for that day. I would get out. I would change my clothes. I would go to community events. I would go to people's living rooms and say, 'Hey, we need to change our politics in America.'"[5]

Alexandria ran an unconventional campaign out of necessity. Because she faced a major financial disadvantage, she decided she had to take a different approach from most campaigns: "You can't really beat big money with more money. You have to beat them with a totally different game."[6] Instead of sending out glossy mailers or purchasing airtime for television ads, she and her staff tried to forge a personal connection with as many residents of the Fourteenth District as possible, a goal facilitated by the fact that she had campaign workers who were able to speak with voters in English, Spanish, Albanian, Arabic, Bengali, and Mandarin. They targeted people who had not voted before and who were likely to support her progressive platform—young people, immigrants, and working-class families. Ocasio-Cortez's staff identified 76,000 individuals who met these criteria and contacted each person three ways—in person, by telephone, and by email. Because of the unusual approach she took to campaigning, Crowley and his staff paid very little attention to Alexandria: "And it was such a joke, I think, to the establishment and it was so small potatoes that nobody paid attention and nobody thought of us as a threat."[7]

On June 26, 2018, Ocasio-Cortez won the Democratic primary election, receiving 57.13 percent of the vote to Crowley's 42.5 percent. Because her district is overwhelmingly Democratic, she was expected to and did win the general election for the seat in November, defeating Republican opponent Anthony Pappas 78 percent to 14 percent. In her victory speech on November 6, 2018, Alexandria declared, "We have made history on multiple levels. We have elected the first campaign and the first member of Congress from this district to not accept any corporate lobbyist funds, in a generation. In addition, . . . we have elected the first person of color to ever represent the people of New York's 14th Congressional District. And lastly, it is a privilege and an honor to say that we have also elected the youngest woman in American history to serve in Congress."[8]

The 116th Congress convened on January 3, 2019, and Ocasio-Cortez wore a white pants suit for her swearing-in. She wore white, she explained, because it was the color the suffragists often wore in their protests and to honor Shirley Chisholm, the first black woman elected to Congress in 1968, who also wore white to her swearing-in ceremony. Her bright red lipstick was in honor of Supreme Court Justice Sonia Sotomayor, who, like Ocasio-Cortez, is a Latina from the Bronx; Sotomayor wore bright red nail polish for her confirmation hearing.[9]

Alexandria entered Congress with no seniority but with a large social media presence. "She is a digital native of a generation raised on social media," explained social media consultant Peter Friedman, "and a master of its language, forms, and emotional energy."[10] She uses Instagram Live to explain her positions on important issues by speaking directly to the camera in an intimate, personal setting. For example, she streamed one episode from her kitchen, answering questions from viewers as she listened to music and made macaroni and cheese. In other episodes, Alexandria has chatted about her policy goals while assembling IKEA furniture in her living room and while planting seeds in a community garden. Ocasio-Cortez is so skilled in her use of social media that she was asked to teach other members of Congress how to be social media-savvy politicians. Her advice included: "Don't post a meme if you don't know what a meme is," and "Don't talk like the Founding Fathers on Twitter."[11]

Alexandria supports a number of progressive issues. She is an advocate for a single-payer health-care system, tuition-free public college and trade school, a federal job guarantee, guaranteed family leave, the cancellation of student debt, abolition of US Immigration and Customs Enforcement, a two-state solution for Israel and Palestine, and a $15 minimum wage. She also favors the enactment of gun-control policies, the development of an energy policy based on renewables, termination of the privatization of prisons, and the granting of further civil rights to Puerto Ricans.

Some Democrats believe that Ocasio-Cortez's policy proposals are too radical and that she is moving too fast. But she's impatient for what she believes is a good reason: "By the time legislation actually gets through, it is five years from now. So everything we introduce needs to have 2025 or our kids in mind."[12] As she explains, "We are capable of so much [more] than what we're doing right now. We are capable of everything in the world. . . . The position should be not, 'Let's not do it because we haven't figured out all the details yet.' How about the goal is, 'Let's figure out all the details because we've decided we're going to the moon and we're going to get there before the end of the decade, and then we're going to do it.'"[13]

Definition of Feminism

"Feminism is about women choosing the destiny that they want for themselves," explains Alexandria.[14] She believes that women's rights are human rights, and she wants to create a society in which women—women of color, Indigenous women, immigrant women, poor women, working women, disabled women, Muslim women, lesbian, queer and trans women—"are free and able to care for and nurture their families in safe and healthy environments, free from structural impediments."[15]

In contrast to second wave feminism that privileged educated, middle-class women and their advancement in the corporate world, Ocasio-Cortez takes a different approach to feminism. Because working-class women and women of color are often the hardest hit by structural inequalities, she believes that a feminism aimed at liberating all women must be "anti-capitalist" and designed "to transform the very structures that oppress women in poverty and women of color."[16]

Alexandria supports a number of policies designed to produce the systemic nationwide changes she believes will allow all women to thrive. She wants equal pay for equal work and believes that the United States "should be creating workforce opportunities for caregivers and parents, as well as additional support for them at home as workers caring for their families." She supports legislation that provides basic workplace protections, "including benefits like paid family leave, access to affordable childcare, sick days, health care, fair pay, vacation time, and healthy work environments." Ocasio-Cortez is against "any federal, state, or local rollbacks, cuts, or restrictions on the ability of women to access quality reproductive healthcare services, birth control, or medically accurate sex education. This includes open access to safe, legal, affordable abortion; birth control; and family-planning services." She also wants to expand existing programs such as Social Security, Medicaid, and the Family and Medical Leave Act "to cover doula and midwife services, diapers and other basic childcare costs, menstrual hygiene products, and other services."[17]

Change Strategies

Alexandria wants to replace capitalism—the system that governs virtually all areas of life in the United States—with democratic socialism. She sees capitalism as responsible for many of the issues facing the United States and wants to encourage her fellow congressional representatives and the American public to consider a different way. To replace the system of capitalism, she engages in three primary strategies: (1) critiquing the system, (2) making complexity accessible, and (3) enacting change.

Critiquing the System

Ocasio-Cortez's strategies are designed to abolish and replace the system of capitalism in the United States. Her major problem with capitalism is that "it's an ideology of capital . . . and it means that we seek and prioritize profit and the accumulation of money above all else, and we seek it at any human and environmental cost."[18] Capitalism is fundamentally undemocratic, she believes, because free-market forces tend to benefit a small number of wealthy business owners instead of serving the public good. Alexandria believes that there are sectors where the profit motive should be removed and that, at the very least, a public option should always be available. She uses the US public school system as an example: "Imagine if we had to pay tuition for our kids to go to school from kindergarten all the way through twelfth grade. It would be untenable, unfeasible, and we would have to rely on businesses that are always trying to profiteer," she said. "But we as a society have decided that it is important and that it is vital enough that we provide a public option for elementary education in the United States."[19]

Ocasio-Cortez sees many of the problems that capitalism has created as interconnected: "We're looking at all of these issues, Medicare for all, a living wage, tuition free public colleges and universities, and there's this false idea that we need to put them all in a line and say do this or do that. Do you care about health care or do you care about the economy or jobs? And then I started to realize that these are not different problems. These are all part of the same problem."[20] She offers the food industry as an example of how issues are intertwined because of the effects of capitalism: "The food industry is the nexus of almost all of the major forces in our politics today. It's super closely linked with climate change and ethics. It's the nexus of minimum wage fights, of immigration law, of criminal justice reform, of health care debates, of education. You'd be hard-pressed to find a political issue that doesn't have food implications."[21] Similarly, Alexandria links climate change to many other issues, all having roots in the capitalist system: "For so long, people have thought of climate-change legislation as saving polar bears, but they don't think of the pipes in Flint. They don't think of the air in the Bronx. They don't think of coal miners getting cancer in West Virginia."[22]

Because Ocasio-Cortez sees the capitalist system as the cause of many problems, she focuses her efforts on replacing it with a system of democratic socialism. In contrast to capitalism, democratic socialism "means putting democracy and society first, instead of capital first."[23] Alexandria is explicit that by *socialism* she means "worker power," not "government ownership." She explains, "Socialism does not mean government owns everything. I disagree with that notion as well because I think it is undemocratic. . . . But I do think that having more democracy in our economy, aka worker power, worker accountability, is a very positive thing."[24]

Ocasio-Cortez points out that the kind of democratic socialism she embraces has been implemented successfully elsewhere. She points, for example, to countries that provide free health care to their citizens: "We're talking about single-payer health care that has already been successful in many different models, from Finland to Canada to the UK."[25] Alexandria also conceptualizes some of the bold reforms enacted in the United States earlier as democratic socialist programs, including Franklin Roosevelt's New Deal and Lyndon Johnson's Great Society.[26] She also notes that a federal job-guarantee program—a democratic socialist goal—already exists in the form of the US military.

Ocasio-Cortez argues that there are myriad ways to fund her proposals for a new democratic socialist system: "You can pay for it by saving costs on expenditures that we're already doing. We can do it by saving money on military spending. We can pay for it by raising taxes on the very rich. We can pay for it with a transaction tax,"[27] a tax on buying or selling a stock or bond. She also believes her proposed programs can be paid for with deficit spending. Alexandria subscribes to an unconventional economic concept called *modern monetary theory* (MMT), which rejects the basic notion that the federal government must operate with a balanced budget, requiring new expenditures to be covered by tax increases or spending cuts. Instead, proponents of MMT argue that deficit spending is an important tool that enables the federal government to make large-scale investments that pay off over time.[28]

Making Complexity Accessible

Ocasio-Cortez educates individuals about how the system of government works and the issues facing it by making complex issues accessible, understandable, and compelling. She hopes that by making problems with the current system visible and understandable, citizens will be more likely to consider an alternative system. One example of where Alexandria made a complicated process clear occurred during her first congressional hearing as a member of the Financial Services Committee. Questioning a panel of ethics experts from campaign finance watchdog groups, she used a fictional scenario to highlight how federal regulations that govern political spending operate. She positioned herself as a "bad guy" who is trying to "get away with as many bad things as possible, ideally to enrich myself and advance my interests."[29] She then asked questions about the kinds of practices that would be allowed under those regulations such as collecting campaign donations from wealthy corporations and using the money to make hush payments to prevent unsavory information from becoming public. By constructing this scenario, Ocasio-Cortez demonstrated the illegality of many actions currently allowable under campaign finance rules, and "a subject that seemed esoteric and unrelatable was all of a sudden clear."[30]

Alexandria also has the ability to break complex issues down into a key idea or experience, often through the use of metaphors. She compares an issue or a policy to something people experience in their daily lives and to which they can relate. For example, when she was asked what an America with defunded police looks like, she responded, "It looks like a suburb." She elaborated: "Affluent white communities already live in a world where [they] choose to fund youth, health, housing etc. more than they fund police. When a teenager or preteen does something harmful in a suburb (I say teen bc this is often where lifelong carceral cycles begin for Black and Brown communities), white communities bend over backwards to find alternatives to incarceration for their loved ones to 'protect their future,' like community service or rehab or restorative measures. Why don't we treat Black and Brown people the same way?"[31]

Another example of Ocasio-Cortez's ability to break down issues to their component parts and explain them in accessible language occurred when Georgia's governor signed a bill banning most abortions after the detection of an embryo's heart beat—typically around six weeks into a pregnancy. She tweeted, "'6 weeks pregnant' = two weeks late on your period. . . . It's relatively common for a woman to have a late period + not be pregnant."[32] She thus pointed out that many women might not even know they are pregnant six weeks after their last period, but by then, it would be too late to have an abortion. In a tweet in response to debates over restrooms for trans individuals, she said, "Going by track record, I'd feel safer in a bathroom w/ a trans woman than a powerful male executive any day of the week."[33] She thus translates complex, controversial issues into pithy, accessible statements to which ordinary individuals can easily relate, helping them understand the nature of the current system and the issues it involves.

Enacting Change

Alexandria not only talks about how the existing system needs to be changed, but she enacts the differences she wants to see in it. She does not seek approval or ask permission to engage in these acts; she simply goes ahead and does them. "Stop trying to navigate systems of power, and start building your own power," she advocates. "Stop trying to navigate those systems because they weren't built for you. We need to build our own systems."[34] She explains her philosophy concerning breaking the rules of the system: "They'll tell you you're too loud—that you need to wait your turn; and ask the right people for permission. Do it anyway."[35]

Part of Ocasio-Cortez's readiness to enact different ways of doing things is the result of her lack of knowledge about how things are supposed to be done in Congress.

> When you come in, no one kind of tells you exactly how to do everything, every little thing. And so we just structure everything in order to prioritize social, racial and economic justice from how we staff to how we prioritize a particular policy. And we don't know that we're even doing things differently. You know, we'll go to another member and say this is how we're doing [things] and they're like what? And we are like, oh, is this strange? . . . We don't know any different, but it's to our advantage because we can structure our approach differently.[36]

She is able to do things differently in large part because of who she hires as her staff. Many of her staff members are progressive activists, not careerist congressional staffers. Traditional staffers "conceive of the world as it is, and work within that frame," but Alexandria's staffers are willing "to think outside the box and make mistakes. . . . They didn't come up in this system. So they don't know how it works. And as a result, they don't feel constrained by it."[37]

One example of Ocasio-Cortez's enactment of a different practice is how she pays her staff. When she discovered that the common practice among representatives is to hire unpaid interns and to pay staffers such low wages that they often have to take second and third jobs to make ends meet, she introduced a new pay system in her office. She pays her interns $15 an hour plus benefits, and she flattened the pay scale for her regular staff members, paying all of them a minimum of $52,000 per year, which enables them to afford the high rents in Washington, DC. Although chiefs of staff typically make about $150,000 per year, Alexandria capped all staff salaries at a maximum of $80,000 per year in order to fit all of her staff members into her office budget: "It is unjust for Congress to budget a living wage for ourselves, yet rely on unpaid interns and underpaid overworked staff," she tweeted.[38]

Ocasio-Cortez displayed a similar commitment to doing things differently when representatives Ted Yoho (R-FL) and Roger Williams (R-TX) accosted her on the steps of the Capitol, and Yoho called her "disgusting" and a "fucking bitch."[39] When called sexist and offensive names, most women do not speak up, but Alexandria took to the House floor and, in a widely televised speech, condemned male privilege, systemic sexist behavior and culture, and violent language against women. "My mother got to see Mr. Yoho's disrespect on the floor of this House towards me on television," she noted. "And I am here because I have to show my parents that I am their daughter and that they did not raise me to accept abuse from men."[40]

Ocasio-Cortez's appearance is also a way in which she enacts difference. In Congress, women are expected to dress and present themselves in conventional and conservative ways—usually by wearing skirted suits in black, beige, blue, or red; conservative jewelry; and low-key makeup. In contrast, Alexandria often wears brightly colored outfits that draw attention because, as one witness noted, "a hot-pink pantsuit intends to announce itself."[41] She frequently wears large gold or silver hoop earrings, a reference to her Latina heritage. Her signature bright red lipstick—what one follower calls "'blood of those who dare oppose me' roja"[42]—is another example of doing things differently. As she asserts, "There are so many subconscious forces that make us try to act like somebody else. When you're a woman of color, there are just so many things about you" that are "nonconforming."[43]

Because she is willing to break the rules of the system in order to create a new one does not mean that Ocasio-Cortez is disrespectful of her colleagues or that she doesn't do the work that is required of a congressional representative. A longtime House Democratic aid observed, "Members who come in with big names tend to go in one of two directions. They can try to trade on that name and make issues all about themselves. Or they can put their head down and work." Alexandria, he notes, falls into the latter category: "She's not out there saying, 'Hey, look at me, look at me, look at me.'"[44] She is respectful to members and constructive in internal party debates and, as Alexandria herself explains, "I do want my priority, especially as a freshman, to be listening and learning, paying a lot of attention to dynamics, navigating, building relationships."[45]

Ocasio-Cortez has set for herself a daunting task—replacing the capitalist system of the United States with a democratic socialist one. She believes this is the only way to solve the many interconnected issues that the country is facing—issues in which capital is privileged over people and their needs. As a representative in Congress, she is taking three steps to push the system to change. She begins by critiquing the system, explaining that the problems facing the United States cannot easily be solved within such a system and, in fact, are often caused by it. Alexandria also uses a variety of mechanisms to explain how the system works, making processes, proposals, and concepts that are complicated and often hidden from public view understandable and relatable. Ocasio-Cortez's third strategy for creating an alternative system is to begin to make changes to help people see that the current system does not have to be the way it is. Not afraid to act boldly and courageously to expose and challenge the rules of the system, Alexandria has been described as bringing "a different color palette and an eagerness to the usual . . . stale air" in Congress. "She does not belong. At the same time, it feels like she's taken over the place."[46]

■ REFLECTIONS

1. Ocasio-Cortez has taken advantage of not knowing a system in order to begin to create an alternative system. What are the advantages and disadvantages of approaching change in this way? Have you ever had the opportunity to create change in a system in part because you were not aware of the intricacies of how it functioned?
2. Assess Ocasio-Cortez's notion that capitalism as a system prioritizes profit and the accumulation of money above all else and thus does not serve the public good. Do you agree or disagree?
3. Ocasio-Cortez encourages change agents to begin to enact the changes they want to see without seeking approval or asking permission. This is a strategy that, although it certainly can be effective, can create enemies and obstacles. Have you ever used such a strategy? Explain what you did and what happened as a result.
4. Ocasio-Cortez deliberately chooses to stand out visually in the system (the US Congress) in which she works. How effective is nonconforming as a change strategy? What are its advantages and disadvantages?
5. Ocasio-Cortez works hard to explain the current system and its problematic aspects clearly. How important is it for people to learn in detail about the problems of the current system before they try to create an alternative one? Does such understanding keep change agents tied to the old system, or does it facilitate their creation of a new system?
6. How closely do Ocasio-Cortez's change strategies align with the assumptions outlined in the introduction to part 6? Are there any assumptions that you don't believe pertain to her approach to change?
7. In which feminist wave would you place Ocasio-Cortez and why?

■ NOTES

[1] Alexandria Ocasio-Cortez, "A No-Nonsense Conversation Between Alexandria Ocasio-Cortez and Kerry Washington," interview by Kerry Washington, *Interview*, September 5, 2018, https://www.interviewmagazine.com/culture/a-no-nonsense-conversation-between-alexandria-ocasio-cortez-and-kerry-washington/

[2] Charlotte Alter, "'Change is Closer Than We Think': Inside Alexandria Ocasio-Cortez's Unlikely Rise," *Time*, March 21, 2019, https://time.com/longform/alexandria-ocasio-cortez-profile/

[3] Alexandria Ocasio-Cortez, "The 28-Year-Old at the Center of One of This Year's Most Exciting Primaries," interview by Gabriella Paiella, The Cut, June 25, 2018, https://www.thecut.com/2018/06/alexandria-ocasio-cortez-interview.html/

[4] Alexandria Ocasio-Cortez, "'We Have to Apply Pressure': Alexandria Ocasio-Cortez Is Done with the Democratic Status Quo," interview by Ecleen Luzmila Caraballo, Jezebel, June 26, 2018, https://theslot.jezebel.com/?startTime=1530044100513/

[5] Alexandria Ocasio-Cortez, "An Interview with Alexandria Ocasio-Cortez, the Young Democratic Socialist Who Just Shocked the Establishment," interview by Jeremy Scahill, The Intercept, June 27, 2018, https://theintercept.com/2018/06/27/an-interview-with-alexandria-ocasio-cortez-the-young-democratic-socialist-who-just-shocked-the-establishment/

6. John Ferguson, "US Democrat Alexandria Ocasio-Cortez on Course to Light Up White House," *Daily Record*, March 3, 2019, https://www.dailyrecord.co.uk/news/politics/talented-democrat-alexandria-ocasio-cortez-14080017/
7. Ocasio-Cortez, "An Interview with Alexandria Ocasio-Cortez."
8. Alexandria Ocasio-Cortez, "General Election Victory Speech," Archives of Women's Political Communication, Carrie Chapman Catt Center for Women and Politics, Iowa State University, November 6, 2018, https://awpc.cattcenter.iastate.edu/2019/03/11/general-election-victory-speech-nov-6-2018/
9. Roberta Gorin-Paracka, "Rep. Alexandria Ocasio-Cortez Explains Why She Wore Red Lipstick and Gold Hoop Earrings to Swearing-In Ceremony," *Teen Vogue*, January 5, 2019, https://www.teenvogue.com/story/alexandria-ocasio-cortez-red-lipstick-gold-hoop-earrings-swearing-in-ceremony/
10. Peter Friedman, "The 2018 Social Media Political Wars: How Alexandria Ocasio-Cortez Used Social Media to Beat Joe Crowley," LiveWorld, July 6, 2018, https://www.liveworld.com/2018-social-media-political-wars-how-ocasio-cortez-used-social-media-beat-joe-crowley/
11. Lynda Lopez, *AOC: The Fearless Rise and Powerful Resonance of Alexandria Ocasio-Cortez* (New York: St. Martin's Press, 2020), 130.
12. Alter, "'Change Is Closer Than We Think.'"
13. Alexandria Ocasio-Cortez, "Alexandria Ocasio-Cortez and the New Left," interview by Briahna Gray, The Intercept, March 9, 2019, https://theintercept.com/2019/03/09/alexandria-ocasio-cortez-aoc-sxsw/
14. Alexandria Ocasio-Cortez, "Feminism is about women choosing the destiny that they want for themselves," Instagram, July 11, 2018, https://www.instagram.com/p/BlHFPNflhB3/
15. "Women's Rights," Alexandria Ocasio-Cortez Official Campaign Website, https://www.ocasiocortez.com/issues#womens-rights/
16. Mohammed Rawwas, "A Feminism for the 99 Percent," *The Northern Iowan*, October 21, 2019, https://issuu.com/northern-iowan/docs/10-21-19/
17. "Women's Rights," Official Campaign Website.
18. Alexandria Ocasio-Cortez, "Alexandria Ocasio-Cortez and the New Left."
19. Lopez, *AOC*, 153.
20. Alexandria Ocasio-Cortez, "Town Hall with Alexandria Ocasio-Cortez, interview by Chris Hayes, MSNBC, March 29, 2019, https://www.msnbc.com/transcripts/all-in/2019-03-29-msna1214456/
21. Hilary Cadigan, "Alexandria Ocasio-Cortez Learned Her Most Important Lessons from Restaurants," *Bon Appétit*, November 7, 2018, https://www.bonappetit.com/story/alexandria-ocasio-cortez-lessons-from-restaurants/
22. Alexandria Ocasio-Cortez, "Alexandria Ocasio-Cortez Wants the Country to Think Big," interview by Alex Morris, *Rolling Stone*, February 21, 2019, https://www.rollingstone.com/politics/politics-features/alexandria-ocasio-cortez-congress-interview-797214/
23. Alexandria Ocasio-Cortez, "Alexandria Ocasio-Cortez and the New Left."
24. Lopez, *AOC*, 150.
25. Nisha Stickles and Barbara Corbellini Duarte, "Exclusive: Alexandria Ocasio-Cortez Explains What Democratic Socialism Means to Her," Business Insider, March 4, 2019, https://www.businessinsider.com/alexandria-ocasio-cortez-explains-what-democratic-socialism-means-2019-3/
26. Laurie Collier Hillstrom, *Alexandria Ocasio-Cortez: A Biography* (Santa Barbara, CA: ABC-CLIO, 2020), 153.
27. Eliza Relman, "The Truth About Alexandria Ocasio-Cortez: The Inside Story of How, in Just One Year, Sandy the Bartender Became a Lawmaker Who Triggers Both Parties," Yahoo!Finance, January 6, 2019, https://au.finance.yahoo.com/news/truth-alexandria-ocasio-cortez-inside-111600396.html/
28. Dylan Matthews, "Modern Monetary Theory, Explained," Vox, April 16, 2019, https://www.vox.com/future-perfect/2019/4/16/18251646/modern-monetary-theory-new-moment-explained/

29 Caroline Fredrickson, *The AOC Way: The Secrets of Alexandria Ocasio-Cortez's Success* (New York: Skyhorse, 2020), 21.
30 Fredrickson, *The AOC Way*, vi.
31 Emily Dixon, "Alexandria Ocasio-Cortez Was Asked About Defunding the Police and Her Answer Went Viral," Yahoo!News, June 12, 2020, https://news.yahoo.com/aoc-asked-defunding-police-her-130800430.html/
32 Alexandria Ocasio-Cortez, "6 weeks pregnant = 2 weeks late on your period," Twitter, 10:28 p.m., May 7, 2019, https://twitter.com/aoc/status/1125980728976715776?lang=en/
33 Alexandria Ocasio-Cortez, "Lastly, we wouldn't need to talk about bathrooms at all if we acted like adults, washed our hands + minded our own business instead of trying to clock others," Twitter, January 20, 2019, 3:55 p.m., https://twitter.com/AOC/status/1087121559444172803/
34 Ocasio-Cortez, "Alexandria Ocasio-Cortez and the New Left."
35 Alexandria Ocasio-Cortez, "They'll tell you you're too loud - that you need to wait your turn; and ask the right people for permission," Twitter, 7:04 p.m., March 9, 2018, https://twitter.com/aoc/status/972292022362165249/
36 Ocasio-Cortez, "Town Hall."
37 Jeff Stein, "'Here's the System; It Sucks': Meet the Staffers Hired by Ocasio-Cortez to Upend Washington," *Washington Post*, February 14, 2019, https://www.washingtonpost.com/us-policy/2019/02/14/heres-system-it-sucks-meet-hill-staffers-ocasio-cortez-has-tapped-upend-washington/
38 Eliza Relman, "'This is a Disgrace': Alexandria Ocasio-Cortez Slams Her Future Colleagues in Congress for Employing Unpaid Interns and Failing to Pay Staffers a 'Living Wage,'" Business Insider, December 4, 2018, https://www.businessinsider.in/this-is-a-disgrace-alexandria-ocasio-cortez-slams-her-future-colleagues-in-congress-for-employing-unpaid-interns-and-failing-to-pay-staffers-a-living-wage/articleshow/66941422.cms/
39 Mike Lillis, "Ocasio-Cortez Accosted by GOP Lawmaker Over Remarks: 'That Kind of Confrontation Hasn't Ever Happened to Me,'" The Hill, July 21, 2020, https://thehill.com/homenews/house/508259-ocasio-cortez-accosted-by-gop-lawmaker-over-remarks-that-kind-of/
40 "Rep. Alexandria Ocasio-Cortez (AOC) House Floor Speech Transcript on Yoho Remarks July 23," Rev, July 23, 2020, https://www.rev.com/blog/transcripts/rep-alexandria-ocasio-cortez-floor-speech-about-yoho-remarks-july-23/
41 Ocasio-Cortez, "Alexandria Ocasio-Cortez Wants the Country to Think Big."
42 Cheryl Wischhover, "Alexandria Ocasio-Cortez's Red Lipstick is a Symbol of Change," Racked, June 27, 2018, https://www.racked.com/2018/6/27/17511304/alexandria-ocasio-cortez-red-lipstick/
43 Ocasio-Cortez, "Alexandria Ocasio-Cortez and the New Left."
44 Russell Berman, "'If We Pass Medicare for All, I'm Going to be Silent as a Lamb,'" *The Atlantic*, November 19, 2018, https://www.theatlantic.com/politics/archive/2018/11/alexandria-ocasio-cortez-makes-her-washington-debut/576085/
45 Berman, "'If We Pass Medicare for All.'"
46 Bridget Read, "36 Hours with Alexandria Ocasio-Cortez," *Vogue*, June 26, 2019, https://www.vogue.com/article/36-hours-with-alexandria-ocasio-cortez-primary-anniversary/

Questions for Reflection

1. What were your main takeaways from the book?
2. Did the book introduce you to ideas that are new to you about feminism? Did it change your perspective on feminism in any way?
3. Share a favorite passage from the book. Why did it stand out for you?
4. When did you first learn about feminism and how? How did this first experience affect your view of feminism?
5. The authors don't insist that you align with feminism in order to appreciate and make use of the change strategies described in this book. What was your reaction when you read this statement?
6. Are you a feminist? Why or why not?
7. If you are a feminist, with which wave do you identify and why?
8. Select your favorite definition of feminism offered by one of the women. Why do you like that definition?
9. Is there a definition of feminism offered by one of the women with which you don't agree? What is problematic about this definition for you?
10. Many of the definitions of feminism offered by the women in the book feature equality for women with men. Given the problems with this definition identified in chapter 1, why do you believe this definition persists? Does the persistence of this definition hurt or help the progress of feminist movement?
11. You have now read about many feminists who employ a variety of change strategies. Use them to assess the current state of feminist movement. What do these change strategies suggest about where feminism is now?
12. Two of the women—Sara Ahmed and Camille Paglia—are scholars who theorize about feminism. In contrast, the other women focus on applying

feminist principles in their various professions. Which approach is more likely to have a positive impact on feminist movement?

13. Many of the women were reluctant initially to claim the label of *feminist* because of negative stereotypes associated with feminism. Are there ways in which these women encourage, lessen, or transform these stereotypes?

14. One of the characteristics of third wave feminism is that problems are framed in exclusively personal terms rather than as political issues that should be addressed collectively. As noted in chapter 2, these feminists turn the slogan of "the personal is political" on its head. Identify several women in the book whose approaches to feminism focus on the personal and others who focus on the political. Which approach do you believe is most effective in generating change?

15. What questions do you have about feminism after reading this book?

16. Speculate on what a fifth wave of feminism might look like. Can you imagine what its triggering event(s) might be, the places where it is most likely to happen, and the key ideas that will animate it?

17. Did the book introduce you to ideas that are new to you about ways to generate change?

18. What questions do you have about how change happens after reading this book?

19. What change strategies have you used most often in your life? After reading the book, did you discover other change strategies you'd like to try?

20. The authors structure their blueprint for change around five major objectives for change: proclaiming identity, naming a problem, enriching a system, changing a system, and creating an alternative system. Do these adequately describe how change happens? If not, what other objectives would you include?

21. The book features the change strategies used by women who are well known in their fields. Does the fact that they have achieved some degree of fame make it easier for them to use the change strategies they do, or are they confined to a restricted range of strategies because they are in the public spotlight?

22. Scholars in numerous fields—psychology, sociology, and communication, for example—theorize the processes by which people change. Choose a theory of change from one of these disciplines. Assess whether the strategies used by the four women who share the same change objective—proclaiming identity, naming a problem, enriching a system, changing a system, or creating an alternative system—align with that theory.

23. Are some of the strategies used by the women in the book likely to be more effective than others in generating change?